Book Markets for Children's Writers

2021

IFW INSTITUTE FOR WRITERS
FOUNDED 1989

Acknowledgments

The editors of this directory appreciate the generous contributions of our instructors and students, and the cooperation of the publishers who made clear their policies and practices.

Marni McNiff, Editor in Chief

Sarah Goldie, Editor

Katie Davis, Cover Illustrator

Cover art from *I Hate To Go To Bed!* (Harcourt Brace, Inc. 1999) by Katie Davis.

About the Illustrator:

Katie Davis is a children's book author/illustrator whose work includes ten picture books, a middle grade and a young adult novel. Her book, Kindergarten Rocks! was given to every preschool child in the state of Georgia. In addition, Katie has published several reference books for writers, and is the producer of two literary podcasts, Brain Burps About Books and Writing for Children. Katie also creates digital courses and resource products for writers, including How to Create Your Author Platform, Video Idiot Boot Camp, and Launch Your Book Blueprint, and is a co-founder of Picture Book Summit, a world-class online conference for picture book authors, now in its fifth year.

Katie has led workshops for prisoners at Bedford Hills Correctional (a maximum-security prison), elementary school children across the US and Europe, and conference attendees and students at UCONN, Yale, and Stony Brook University. She currently runs the 52-year-old Institute of Children's Literature, as well as its sister school, the Institute for Writers, where, to date, over 470,027 people have participated in college-level writing courses for both children and adults.

International Standard Book Number ISBN: 978-1-944743-21-5
203-792-8600. www.instituteforwriters.com
email: learn@instituteforwriters.com

Printed and bound in Canada

Table of Contents

Articles

Publisher Listings

Contest Listings

Agent Listings

Podcast Listings

Indexes

Submissions

Standing on Your Platform: Write and Publish in a Changing Marketplace

New This Year

Like many industries, publishing entered new territory in 2020 as the world dealt with the COVID-19 pandemic. With children unable to attend schools in most areas, students transitioned to a "distance learning" model. Publishers seized this opportunity to reach young audiences by finding creative ways to engage young readers. Publishers worked with educators to facilitate virtual author visits, bringing authors and artists into the homes of kids and their families through appearances on bookstore websites, social media, and in digital classrooms.

Books that celebrate diversity as well as titles on anti-racism and activism took center stage in 2020. Titles for early readers through young adult helped celebrate diversity and the acceptance of all people.

The YA fantasy market also continued to expand with previously underrepresented characters taking the spotlight in new worlds. Publishers are looking for more diverse voices, plots, and topics for their YA fantasy.

Whether you are an aspiring writer or an established author, *Book Markets for Children's Writers* will give you all the information and resources you need to improve your skills, break into the children's market, and stay on top of the trends and changes for 2021.

Some 2020 news of the year:

- Penguin Young Readers Group launched Rise, a new imprint featuring titles that empower children to feel smart and capable.

- Quill Tree Books, the new imprint from HarperCollins, is looking to work with authors who have a strong point of view.

- Blue Dot Press hopes to empower the next generation of global citizens with empathy, resilience, creativity, and the shared value of nature and its stewardship.

The Writing & Publishing Process

You have the inspiration already or you wouldn't be using this book. You may know the subject or genre that most interests you and what you want to research. You may have identified the audience that most appeals to you (kindergartners? teens?) and have a plot or a plan for structuring a book. You may even know your writing career goals (hobbyist? professional? part-time? full-time?) and be ready to put together queries and energetically sell your work. However, you may not know how to put the whole together, or you may be looking for advice on one or two aspects of the whole. You most certainly will need to know the markets and how they change from month to month, year to year.

Understanding the markets and pulling the whole together is what *Book Markets for Children's Writers* is all about. It has all the information you need to improve your resources and knowledge. In this 2021 edition:

- Listings are organized into sections for practical use. Sections include trade publishers that publish books for children and young adults, classroom and educational publishers, parenting, regional, and religious publishers, contests, and agents.

- Listings reflect the online presence of publishers, from their guidelines to products to specializations in new media.

- Cross-references among parent companies, divisions, and imprints will help you navigate the marketplace, know who is related to whom, and better target your submissions.

- An extensive agents section will help you impress agents as well as editors.

All these features will help you build your *platform*, the buzz word that refers to how you present yourself as a writer via the writing itself, networking, websites, social media, and more. You are, or want to be, a writer, and more specifically, a published writer for children. How do you pursue that goal while simultaneously refining your craft, carving a career, and earning a living? How do you create a voice and a visible identity—your platform as a writer?

Book Markets for Children's Writers 2021 is here to help you become an author who knows your reader, knows where you want to go with your writing, and knows how to sell your work to the markets best suited for your books and your aspirations.

Inspired

Writing may have always been your aspiration. Perhaps you have been told you have a gift for language or storytelling. You may want to write to please your children, family, or just yourself. *Book Markets for Children's Writers 2021* is for those who want to go beyond the dream and carve a writing career. It is all about finding places to sell the book that you put your heart and soul into.

Whatever your aspiration, it will inform and help you accomplish: the idea generation, research, interaction with editors and agents and audience, even your technology and tax decisions.

Idea Generation

Along with the desire to write comes an attraction to certain subjects and genres. Most experienced writers will start by writing about what they know. Choose subjects that are familiar and of interest to you. You will get ideas from what you have experienced, from

what you see in daily life, from the news, from listening to children and adults.

When you are in the inspiration stage, ask yourself:

- What do I want to write about? Will it interest editors? Do I have a passion for the subject that will inspire others?

- Am I ready to write this? Have I honed my writing skills with practice, classes, workshops, writers' groups?

- Do I know my audience? What is its age range? Interests? Skills? Will these readers be interested in my idea, topic, or story?

- Is the idea substantial enough? Is it worth researching further, developing more deeply?

To explore an idea you already have in mind, or find one that makes you enthusiastic and ready to jump into researching and writing, try some of the idea-generation strategies on page 8.

Researched

Inspiration and research create a positive creative spiral that, once sparked, will continue to drive and motivate you throughout your writing process. If you are already feeling inspired, use your research to really ground your ideas in a tangible way, using the details you uncover to create or describe your world in a way that lifts it off the page and into your reader's imagination. On the other hand, if you are lacking inspiration, you can use the research process to unearth ideas and get your creative juices flowing. Research is an important, ongoing journey that embraces a subject, audience, books, and markets.

Subject Research

Topical research is core to nonfiction but can be as important in creating authentic fiction. Accuracy and an appropriate level of information are essential in children's literature today. Editors will not stand for anything less.

Idea Generation Strategies

Ideas for subjects on which to write or stories to develop come in many ways, perhaps as many ways as there are writers. But ideas may generally be grouped into those born of experience, brainstorming, research, or even editor assignments. Here are ways to help you add to your potential idea pile.

- **Do brainstorming exercises.** Brainstorming is an important creative tool. Today, a variety of resources beyond the tried-and-true pencil and paper can help you brainstorm. But first, here are a few ways to loosen up your creativity:

  - Try writing prompts:

    Hatch's Plot Bank (www.angelfire.com/nc/tcrpress/plots1.html); Creative Writing Prompts (creativewritingprompts. com); Build Creative Writing (http://www.build-creative-writing-ideas.com/writing-prompts-online.html); or Think Written (www.thinkwritten.com).

  - Image Association: Similar to word association, this process uses a visual image to trigger ideas in context.

  - Word banks Creating a word bank helps solve the problem of finding the right words to use in your project. For instance, if you were writing about the water cycle, your word bank might include: evaporation, condensation, precipitation, vapor, steam, and liquid.

  - Mind-mapping: Put your key word or phrase in the center of your page and write whatever else comes to mind down on the page next to it. You can then make connections from your key word to your mapped words to expand your ideas.

- **Scour the media.** Daily newspapers, magazines, and specialized and aggregate websites all have stories that range from serious and fascinating to bizarre and funny. Clip or bookmark stories with potential interest for research. You can also use services such as Google Alerts (www.google.com/alerts) to have online news and articles on specific topics emailed to you.

- **Cultivate creative habits.** Meditate, listen to music, knit, paint, take a walk, journal, free-write, go to an Internet cafe (not unlike a certain English billionaire children's author who sat in a coffee shop writing about a wizard). Focus on developing a series of questions, and then let the answers unfold or lead you in other directions.

- **Review the curriculum guidelines for your state and other states.** School subjects can help you develop ideas for classroom books, and generate possibilities for trade titles, too.

- **Read, read, read!** It may sound strange, but the more quality children's books you read, the more ideas you're likely to generate for your own stories.

Living in an age when any museum, university, organization, or expert can be found and often accessed freely with a few clicks of a mouse, research is easier and infinitely more wide-ranging than a generation ago. The quantity of thin, inaccurate information online is also great. Be very cautious about the quality of your sources in this technological age, when anyone can write virtually anything he or she wants on a website without verification. Research Rule number one: *Know the value of your sources.*

Primary sources: Firsthand information in the form of original documents (letters, diaries, statistics, maps, legal papers, and so on), photographs, artwork, film, audio recordings, witness testimonies, journals, and even objects like clothing or crafts. They are the most highly valued resources regarding objectivity and accuracy because they date to the time, place, event, or person being investigated. That could involve a historical period, a contemporary event, or even a scientific experiment.

Secondary sources: Information that is one or more steps removed from the topic's point of origin. Secondary sources include scholarly studies, biographies, databases, encyclopedias, commentaries, textbooks, newspapers, magazines, or other media that contain secondary accounts. These sources analyze and interpret. They can be very accurate and objective, or they can be highly subjective. It is up to the writer to judge and use these sources appropriately.

Interviews with experts: A writer's personal research with an individual. Experts are often professionals in a field—scientists, historians, businesspeople—but they can also be the local kid, an ordinary person who had an interesting experience, or anyone who is knowledgeable and has firsthand information about a given subject. Thus, experts can be either primary or secondary sources.

Fiction: Don't think fiction doesn't need research because it is "made up." True, some picture books, chapter books, and novels taken largely from personal and observed experience may not need extensive research, but details must be right. The most obvious genre calling out for research is historical fiction, but even in contemporary novels characters, places, and environments all need to be right, too. Otherwise, readers will not have what Samuel Taylor Coleridge called the "willing suspension of disbelief."

Consider how character traits and setting might be researched. Perhaps the hero of your tale has traveled back in time from the hectic bustle of modern day London to the Victorian period of English history. Consider what you may need to know about the time setting to create a believable atmosphere. What would the characters of that time be wearing? What would they eat, and how would their daily routine look? Research aspects that apply to all the senses, such as what your protagonist would see, hear, and smell.

Fact-Checking: At the end of the writing process, you will need to factcheck your own research, so keeping good records of what you learn along the way is vital.

For every fact you include, whether in nonfiction or fiction, try to have three reliable sources to support it, if possible. For interviews, record them when you can as backup. When you get to the revision stage for your writing, fact-checking should confirm your accuracy. Publishers require such accuracy of writers; some publishers—by no means all—do additional fact-checking on their own.

The last thing you want to do is undermine your authority in nonfiction or believability in fiction. Who hasn't had a book or movie ruined by some wrong tidbit that misrepresented the truth of an event or shattered the necessary suspension of disbelief?

Audience Research

You may have been drawn to write for a particular age group even before you honed in on a subject area or genre of interest. Picture books for preschoolers or kindergartners might appeal to you, or perhaps writing for beginning readers excites you. Middle graders in love with reading—or reluctant to read—may be the audience for you. YA writing has never before appealed to quite so many readers, from teens themselves to adults, and it continues to evolve. Whichever age group is your desired audience, study it, know it well, and remember the variations within it.

Learn by reading the literature already published and acknowledged as strong. Talk to teachers, coaches, mentors, and librarians. Look at curricula to see what is being taught in school. Keep up with age-related websites, and check professional resources, such as those for the American Library Association (ALA). Learn about vocabulary and reading levels. Is it an age that wants its books in chapters? Does rhythm have little or great value at this age?

For a sense of the developmental stages among young people, see the sidebar on page 39, Authentic Kids.

Competitive Title Research

Publishers often want competition or market research as part of nonfiction book proposals. Some may also want to know something about the competition for fiction. Imagine if just a few years ago you were writing a novel about wizards or vampires.

Internet Research Sources

The Internet has made the number and range of research sources limitless; here is a sampling that reveals how broad they are.

- *Archives*
  - Internet Archive: www.archive.org. Includes audio, moving images, live music, and texts.
  - United States National Archives: www.archives.gov/research. States and localities also may have collections.
  - Bibliotheque Nationale de France: http://gallica.bnf.fr. A very wide-ranging collection (access is available in English as well as French), including books, manuscripts, maps, periodicals, images, sound recordings, and more.
  - Look for other national archives around the world, including: United Kingdom, nationalarchives.gov.uk; Russia, russianarchives.com; Australia, https://www.naa.gov.au; and so on.

- *Experts*
  - ThoughtCo: www.thoughtco.com. Education resource divided into categories.
  - ProfNet: https://profnet.prnewswire.com/ProfNetHome.aspx. Journalism site that helps find professionals and experts to interview or help develop leads.

- *Gateway Sites*
  - Bible Gateway: http://biblegateway.com. A searchable religious gateway in over 150 versions.
  - The WWW Virtual Library: www.vlib.org.
  - Library Spot: www.libraryspot.com. A virtual library.
  - NoodleTools: www.noodletools.com. Data on many topics, and guidance in using statistics and graphs.
  - National History Education Clearhinghouse: www.teachinghistory.org. History gateway.
  - Refdesk.com: http://refdesk.com. An Internet fact-checker.

- *Government Sites*
  - Federal Resources for Educational Excellence: https://www2.ed.gov/free/index.html. Covers the arts, health, history, language, math, science.
  - Library of Congress: www.loc.gov. The largest library in the world. Many collections and avenues of research available.
  - NASA: www.nasa.gov.
  - National Institutes of Health: http://nih.gov.
  - National Science Foundation: http://nsf.gov.
  - Smithsonian: www.si.edu.
  - United States Geological Survey: www.usgs.gov.
  - USA.gov: www.usa.gov. Focuses on governmental issues, including the economy, consumer protection, environment, health, public safety, transportation, and culture.
  - CIA World Fact Book: https://www.cia.gov/library/publications/the-world-factbook/index.

Internet Research Sources

- *Media*
  - NewsLibrary: http://nl.newsbank.com. Links to thousands of U.S. newspapers.
  - NewspaperARCHIVE: www.newspaperarchive.com. Claims to be the world's largest historical newspaper archive. It focuses on people and history. Subscription-based, $49.95/6 months.

- *Museums*
  - Museums: www.umich.edu/~motherha/museums.html. A list of museums, large and small, around the world, with links. Ranges from the Museum of Decorative Arts in Prague, London's Tate Gallery, and the Vatican Collections to Taipai's Museum of World Religions and the Institute of Egyptian Art and Archaeology in Memphis, TN.
  - Museum Stuff: www.museumstuff.com. Guide to international museums, from air and space to the arts and the history of pharmacy.

- *Professional Organizations*
  - American Library Association: http://www.ala.org/rusa/sections/history/resources/primarysources. A helpful introduction to primary sources, how to use them, and where to find them.

- *University Collections*
  - Princeton: www.princeton.edu/~refdesk/primary2.html.
  - Tulane University Howard-Tilton Memorial Library: http://library.tulane.edu/libraries.
  - University of Chicago: www.lib.uchicago.edu/e/spcl/arch.html.
  - Voice of the Shuttle: http://vos.ucsb.edu. A gateway database for scholarly resources, maintained by the University of California, Santa Barbara.
  - Yale: https://primarysources.yale.edu. A directory of primary sources from Yale's libraries.

- *Select Specialized Sources*
  - Artcyclopedia: www.artcyclopedia.com. Information on artists, art sites, and related links.
  - BioMedCentral: www.biomedcentral.com. An "open access publisher" with articles from medical journals.
  - History Sourcebooks: www.fordham.edu/Halsall/index.asp. From ancient to medieval to modern, from East Asian to African to Islamic to Women's studies, sources for historical resources, from Fordham University.
  - Sportscience: www.sportsci.org. Research about all areas of sports, from performance to training and health.

- *Search Engines and Other Useful Sites*
  - Scholar.google.com: Google Scholar performs broad searches for scholarly literature, including articles, theses, court documents, books, abstracts, and professional societies.
  - Academic.research.microsoft.com: Semantic search provides highly relevant academic content from 120 million publications.
  - Http://www.blogsearchengine.org: Search engine for blogs.
  - WebCrawler.com: Search engine for news, images, and videos.

What you would have to report today and what you would have found in a pre-Potter or pre-Twilight universe would have been very different.

When you include information about competitive titles into your submission to an editor or agent, it signals that you are a professional, and are serious about not just your writing but about creating a platform for yourself—knowing the markets and doing something to distinguish yourself in them.

On page 14 is a form to help you list and analyze competitive titles. You should also note in the listings in *Book Markets for Children's Writers 2021* exactly which publishers want competition or market reports, and the details of how they want them structured, if available. Note the other items that are expected in the submission package. For example:

- Flux accepts queries with a 1–2 paragraph plot synopsis, author bio, and list of 3–5 comparative titles.

- Rise accepts hard copy submissions only. It looks for complete manuscripts for picture book submissions. Query with synopsis, 10 manuscript pages, and publishing credits for longer works.

- Graphia accepts complete manuscripts for fiction submissions. Query with synopsis and sample chapters for nonfiction.

- Sky Pony Publishing accepts queries or complete manuscripts. Include author bio, publishing credits, and qualifications.

- Splashdown Books accepts proposals through their website only. Include a brief bio, summary, and a 500 word sample from the manuscript.

For educational publishers producing classroom and library books, competition reports can be particularly important. Some have extensive series of books focusing on curriculum areas and related subjects. Among the classroom publishers that request competition reports are Creative Teaching Press, History Compass, Edupress, Nelson Education, and Chelsea House.

Age Targeting Resources

- *American Academy of Pediatrics:* www.healthychildren.org. Provides extensive information about child development and other child-related issues.
- *American Academy of Child & Adolescent Psychiatry:* www.aacap.org. Look for child development resources and a page of helpful links.
- *American Library Association:* www.ala.org. The ALA website includes many resources about children and reading. The Young Adult Library Services Association (YALSA) section is particularly active.
- *Bright Futures:* www.brightfutures.org. A national health promotion initiative.
- *Childcare.gov:* www.childcare.gov. A U.S. government resource site for parents, educators, and policymakers.
- *International Reading Association:* www.reading.org. A nonprofit organization focused on literacy.
- *Child & Family WebGuide:* https://ase.tufts.edu/cfw/. Child development topics.
- *Guysread.com:* www.guysread.com. A site promoting reading among boys, who generally read less than girls, from author Jon Scieszka.
- *ReadKiddoRead*: www.readkiddoread.com. A literacy site sponsored by author James Patterson.
- *Search Institute:* www.search-institute.org. A nonprofit research and service organization for children and families. See the What Kids Need to Succeed section.
- *Zero to Three:* www.zerotothree.org. A national nonprofit focused on early learning.

So how do you do this competitive title research? Using *Book Markets for Children's Writers 2021*, begin by noting which of the listings sections cover subjects and forms of interest to you: trade, classroom, religious, regional, etc. Even easier, start with the Category Index, beginning on page 349, to find publishers whose books are similar to yours. Then look at their catalogues or websites for relevant titles.

- You can get considerable information on sites like Amazon and search engines like Google. Do subject and age searches on Amazon to help compile a list of titles. Pay attention to reviews and sales rankings, and to other titles the sites automatically suggest. This process may help you shift your angle of approach as you research and compose the book. Again, check publisher websites in case more information is available about the competitive titles you have identified.

- When you find the titles that are competitive to yours, use the library to read and review as many of them as possible. Or, buy the books you want to own at a bookstore, or download them to your electronic reader. A brief description and some reviews on Amazon won't give you the full flavor and necessary details to know your competition well.

What are you looking for as you do the research and put a report together?

- Ask yourself, what titles look similar to the concept I have in mind, or the book I have outlined or written?

- Who published the title, and how many other titles of this kind or category are included on the publisher's list? When were they published?

- Is it an overcrowded list, or is this publisher likely to be open to another title on a similar subject? Are the books old enough that a newer treatment might be welcome?

- How are the books similar to or different from mine? What is the slant, and can I adapt mine if needed? How is my slant better? Similarly, what's the target age and book structure?

Then do an analysis of what you have discovered, for yourself first, but also to help convince an editor or agent. Is a new book needed on the topic? Why is one or another publisher the right one for you to approach? How can this book be marketed in the framework of the publisher's other titles? Why are you the one to write and help sell it, and *how* will you help sell it? (Remember, being able to market your book is a big part of your platform.)

Market Research

With all your idea generation and research, you have also been gathering market research along the way—that is, determining the best publishers for your particular book.

One of the advantages of *Book Markets for Children's Writers 2021* is that it can help you target your research more efficiently and accurately from your very first steps. Are you interested in writing nonfiction that will be read in classrooms or taken off the shelf in libraries?

Alternatively, in writing historical fiction that will complement the state curriculum, look in the Classroom/Educational Publishing section. Don't limit yourself—the Category Index will help you find related genres, categories, and publishers across all the sections—but you can take better aim by using the new structure of this market directory.

Gather a list of potential publishers and look at each of them more closely. How do you evaluate publishers most likely to be interested in your book? Ask and analyze:

- Has the company published other books related to this subject, this audience, this format?

- Does your book fit and bring something fresh to the list?

- How big is the company? How many new titles does it publish annually? Does it have a strong backlist?

- Are the company's books literary, commercial, mass-market, educational? Can you see your work fitting into that

Competitive Title Research Form

My Book: real-life stories of a service dog and girl with autism, ages 8–10

Title	Author	Publisher	Pub. Date	Description
Helping Dogs	Hoffman	Gareth Stevens	January 2011	library market series, grades 2-3
Assistance Dogs	Tagliaferro	Bearport	January 2007	hi-lo, library market, grades 3-4
Service Dogs	Schuh	Capstone/Pebble	August 2010	school/library market, grades K-1

type? If you think your fiction is meant to be a literary hardcover, don't send it to a mass-market paperback publisher.

- Is it a company that specializes in a genre or niche (for example, multicultural authors or a strong line of fantasy)? Remember, the one complaint editors make over and over again is that so many writers submit books of a type the company has never published—YA novels sent to a picture book publisher, or nonfiction texts submitted to a dedicated fiction imprint.

- Do you want the wide-ranging and large-scale support of a big publishing house, or the more personalized support of a small press?

- If you're a new author, does the company (or agent) appear to be open to new voices? In *Book Markets for Children's Writers 2021*, pay attention to the description of interests, the freelance potential, and the categories of interest in particular.

- Find other titles the company has published (as you would do for the competition report), and read some. Representative titles of this kind are annually updated in *Book Markets for Children's Writers 2021*.

When you feel confident you have identified a half-dozen or so good markets for your fiction or nonfiction, make use of your research in your query, cover letter, proposal, or whatever materials the publisher requests. Convince the editor, as you would a potential employer in another industry, that you have the work that is best suited to the company.

Be sure you have the quality of goods to sell! Stay aware of changes in the industry through trade publications such as *Publisher's Weekly*. Find blogs and websites by publishing industry insiders. Join the Institute of Children's Literature's Writers' Block or the Society of Children's Book Writers and Illustrators (SCBWI) and stay aware of its publications and conferences. Follow news on editors, agents, and other writers. Moreover, make others aware of you through networking, a website, and more. Stand on your platform.

Devised

You have been inspired, you have researched, but you still have to do it—write the book, find your voice, and fit the doing of it into your life. The devising of the book can be broken down into two components: (1) the characteristics of writing that need to be developed—voice, style, and structure, and (2) the practicality of accomplishing the writing task—goal-setting, time management, and organization. The first must evolve out of the book you want to write. However, here are tips for the latter.

Goal Setting

Whatever the projected length or complexity of your book, to become a writer with a successful career you will need to set goals for completing your projects, as well as for approaching editors, revising accepted manuscripts, and so on. Setting goals for your career itself is also important.

- How much do you want to write in a week, a month, six months, a year?

- What kinds of books do you want to write? Do you aspire to write one picture book or three in the coming year? A picture book and a middle-grade novel? Do you want to branch out into plays or mix books with short stories? Add parenting articles to the mix?

- How many submissions or queries do you want to send out each week, month?

- How do you deal with rejection when a submission is declined, and how long does it take you to get back on your horse?

- Can you set aside time to take a children's writing course, either at a local university or writing institute? Many places now offer online courses that allow you to have your work critiqued by class participants and the instructor.

Potential Publisher Form

My Book targets middle-grade girls and is a guide to surviving the middle school years.

Category	Publisher	Notes
Middle Grade Social Issues	Rubicon Publishing	Publisher for students in K–12. Publishes 30+ titles per year and accepts queries from freelance writers.
	Diversion Press	Small press offering books for children and young adults in many categories including middle grade NF on real-life issues.
	Innovative Kids	Mid-size publisher that offers titles for middle-grade readers in a variety of nonfiction subjects. Currently accepting queries.
	Prometheus Books	Independent publisher offering titles for children of all ages on contemporary and real-life issues.
Online search:	American Girl	*A Smart Girl's Guide to Middle School*, by Julie Williams Montalbano and Cathi Mingus (2014).
	Harvest House	*A Girls Guide to Making Good Choices*, by Elizabeth George (2013).

Time Management

Many writers live a dual existence, with a day job as they build their writing careers. They have families and other responsibilities. People doing freelance work such as writing have to be self-starters who know how to manage their time well. Here are some questions to help you determine how you might best use your time.

- How much time can you give to developing concepts, to research?

- How do you balance writing with kids, spouse/partner, day job and/or school?

- What are you willing to give up in order to give more time to your writing? Some television or computer time? Time-consuming meals? Lunch with friends or acquaintances? Volunteer work?

- How can you create a support group for your writing? From your family, fellow writers?

- What amount of time are you willing or able to devote to the business side of a writing career—creating and maintaining a website, networking, attending conferences, making appearances to support your books, tracking submissions, following up with editors, doing financial tasks, and so on?

Use a calendar or smartphone to schedule your day, including making appointments with yourself to do the writing and the marketing.

Organization

The workspace: To accomplish your goals and manage your time, you need some practical mechanisms in place.

- Do you have a truly workable space—desk and files devoted to your writing?

- Is your research well-organized? Create a system, whether it's paper, electronic, or both. Make notes on sources.

- Do you have a system for tracking submissions and accounting for finances, like expenses and income?

- Is your technology working for you? Is the hardware in good shape, and does your software help you write and maintain the business side, too?

The writing: Everyone has their own techniques for writing. Some write straight through a chapter or section, and go back later for revisions. Others must begin with an outline for the whole piece. Some allow their voice and tone to flow. Others craft these elements carefully.

Award-winning young adult fiction author John Green does much of his writing work at his walking desk, using the treadmill below to walk countless miles while working on his novels and other written work. That method works for him, and it is important that you find the right environment and method that make you as productive as possible. Whether sitting or standing, playing music or enjoying the silence, everyone is different, and the way you optimize the quality and production of your writing might be completely unique to you.

Organization contributes to your platform. The presentation of your work—in your writing, your communications with editors and colleagues, on your website or blog, in speaking engagements—becomes part of your voice and professional persona.

Queried

When it comes to becoming a *published* writer, queries are essential. They represent the bridge from your creative endeavors to becoming a professional. Sure, some submissions require cover letters or website forms, but every writer must conquer the query above all. And the query is a key part of a writer's platform. This section will look at queries, cover letters, and the other elements that make up submission packages.

Queries

In addition to a great book, you also need a great query letter. The query letter is your

Does Your Manuscript Stand Out?

An editor is swamped with manuscripts on a daily basis. After perusing just the first few pages of a manuscript, he or she knows whether an idea is fresh and interesting—or stale as yesterday's bread. While there's no such thing as a completely original idea, there are ways to make sure that your story idea captures an editor's attention.

- *Don't follow a trend.* If you do, you're likely to lose your voice. Branch out and find new territory to write about.
- *Be honest.* Make sure your young characters talk and act like real kids. See the sidebar "Authentic Kids" on page 39 to find out more about what kids are like at different stages.
- *Don't preach.* All good books impart a message, but if your story is didactic, you'll turn off the reader. Make sure your theme is subtly drawn through your characterization and plot.
- *Stay away from anthropomorphic animals.* If you're going to include animals in your story, make sure they behave like real animals.
- *Be careful with rhyme.* It's very hard to rhyme as well as Dr. Seuss, so if you're writing picture books, try to give your text rhythm and incorporate wordplay without rhyming, unless you can do it well.
- *Have a vision.* Strong characters, and a unique way of approaching an idea, create a book with vision.

calling card. It's essentially a pitch. You know what it's like to read a great blurb on a book jacket? Think of your query letter as great jacket copy. Use it to sell your story and your talent.

The basic query consists of these parts:

- Introduction
- Pitch
- Writer (about yourself)
- Closing

Let's look at these four elements.

Introduction (paragraph 1)
This is where you state the basics about your project—the title and type of book. It's also where you mention whatever connection you may have to the editor to whom you're sending it (e.g., you met at a conference, were referred by a friend) and also state that the editor had requested the manuscript.

Pitch (paragraphs 2 and 3)
This is the most important part of the query. It is where you sell the idea to the editor. These paragraphs encapsulate the characters and plot of your story. You should establish that your idea is new and compelling and the right concept for that publisher. Indicate your

understanding of the marketplace and how your book fills a need within that marketplace.

Writer (paragraph 4)
This is where you'll describe any pertinent background information or writing credits.

Closing (paragraph 5)
Close gracefully and professionally by thanking the editor for his or her time and consideration. If you've included other materials requested by the publisher, mention that here. Send exactly what's required or requested.

What not to do:

- Don't over-talk or provide excess information. Publishers do not want to hear that your kids and friends love your book. This signals to publishers that you're a beginner.

- Don't misspell the editor's name. Misspellings and questionable grammar are surefire ways to turn off an editor.

- Don't use fancy fonts or paper (if the publisher is asking for a hard copy). Make sure your query is single-spaced and use a basic 12-point typeface.

Cover Letters

The technical difference between a cover letter and a query, both of which can take a variety of forms, is that the former accompanies a manuscript and the latter does not.

Good cover letters remain the most common accompaniment to fiction. They are simple in both senses of form: in their structure and in their custom or professional purpose. They are a courteous introduction, and when done properly, can lead you to acceptance.

A cover letter should give the basics, but not much more. If it is too long, an editor may see it as wastefully eating into time or as reflective of a writer who can't quite focus or self-edit. Cover letters should indicate:

- That a manuscript is enclosed.

- The basic facts: word length, genre, whether or not the manuscript is a simultaneous submission.

- Other attachments, such as your résumé or a bibliography for certain kinds of fiction.

- Your contact information.

Sample Query

Here's what a sample query letter might look like:

Dear Mr. Parker,

We recently met at the Society of Children's Book Writers and Illustrators conference in Los Angeles, where we discussed my book, *When I Get Angry.*

"I want to crush everything," says Jamie when her sister takes her stuffed bear away. She's so angry, in fact, that she kicks, screams, and eventually runs into the backyard where she climbs up to their treehouse, She looks out over the water, and feels better. Calm, she returns home, ready to participate in family life.

Tantrums and angry outbursts are common among preschoolers, but, unfortunately, there are very few books that treat this issue in a sensitive – and entertaining – way. *When I Get Angry* fills a need in the marketplace for real stories that can help small children process their feelings and to understand that anger is a natural emotion. This book will be useful not only to parents but also to educators or anyone who works with children and cares deeply about their emotional needs.

I am a member of the SCBWI and have studied my craft at the Institute of Children's Literature. I have had several short stories published in *Highlights* magazine for children.

If you are interested in reading the manuscript for *When I Get Angry,* I can send it upon request. I look forward to hearing from you.

Sincerely,

Your Name

Cover letters may also include:

- The particular needs met by the enclosed manuscript—a theme, topic, hole in the marketplace—and why it works for that publisher and a given readership.

- A short synopsis, perhaps a paragraph.

- Your publication history or relevant background.

- Any other information requested in the publisher's submission guidelines.

A cover letter may include a synopsis of a paragraph or two but technically remains a cover letter because it *covers* an attached manuscript. A query would not, but would ask an editor if the manuscript might be sent along. For book submissions, a longer synopsis is often attached to the cover and manuscript.

Proposals

A proposal is a form of submission package that goes beyond a query alone. Paying attention to writers' guidelines is essential in pulling a proposal together because publishers may have very specific

Sample Cover Letter

Address
Email Address
Date

Scholastic Publishing
557 Broadway
New York, NY 10012-3999

Dear Editor:

It was a pleasure to meet you at the 2007 RUCCL One-on-One Plus Conference, at which time you invited me to mail my picture book manuscript to your attention.

It's Spike's first day on the school bus and it looks big and scary! His mother assures him that a school bus buddy will make him forget his troubles. However, when Spike rides the bus, a bumpy ride and prickly quills get in the way of friendship. When Spike forgets about himself and thinks about someone else, he finds the perfect solution to his problem and a new friendship!

I have studied writing for children/children's literature for over four years through a B.A. degree program at Empire State College and Institute for Children's Literature. I am a full member of the SCBWI who has attended many SCBWI conferences. Recent publication credits include stories, rebuses, crafts and puzzles in Highlights for *Children, Babybug, Children's Playmate, SCBWI Bulletin, Hopscotch, Family Fun,* and more.

I hope that you will find HEDGEHOG GOES TO KINDERGARTEN endearing enough to add to your Fall list.

Very truly yours,

Lynne Marie Pisano

requirements. For those that don't, take hints from others that do. Here are some examples of what is requested by publishers listed in *Book Markets for Children's Writers 2021*.

- Bancroft Press requests a cover letter, résumé, and market analysis.
- Boyds Mills Press requests a detailed biography and a detailed explanation of competitive titles for nonfiction submissions.
- Charlesbridge, a trade publishing company, requests a proposal with synopsis, chapter outline, and first three chapters.
- Fire and Ice looks for queries with synopsis and three sample chapters.
- Greystone Kids requests queries with chapter outline, one sample chapter, and market analysis.

Synopsis: When publishers or agents request a synopsis—a summarizing narration of the story or of the information to be included in a book and how it is structured—they may want something as brief as a paragraph in a cover letter or as long as several pages. Some publishers request chapter-by-chapter summaries.

Synopses can be daunting. How much can you convey in so little a space that will present an impactful picture of your book in both substance and style? You must condense but represent, painting a miniature portrait of your work.

Fiction: For fiction, a synopsis should reveal the main characters, point-of-view, setting, basic plot line, conflict, motivation, and theme. Briefly describe pivotal scenes, and include the story's resolution. Convey your book's tone and voice, but do not make your protagonist or narrator speak. You are doing the talking, but write the synopsis in the third person.

Nonfiction: Cover all the major points of the book and let the synopsis make clear your primary purpose or approach in writing the book, the scope of your subject, and why you have structured the information the way you did. If you do this well, it should become clear why you are the right person to write the book.

Aim for clarity when putting together a synopsis, but without sacrificing a style that reflects your book. Look at the blurbs on book dust jackets for some inspiration. These are almost an art form, the purpose of which is to make a book's contents clear and highly appealing.

Outline: In general, publishers look for synopses for fiction and outlines for nonfiction. An outline is a more formal, enumerated list of topics and subtopics to be covered in a book. Outlines may vary by level of detail; in an annotated form they can be not dissimilar to chapter-by-chapter synopses.

Outlines highlight organization, and through that, substance. Whether or not they use the traditional school-taught Roman numeral structure, outlines indicate main thoughts or arguments (and sometimes counter-arguments), and supporting detail. Like synopses, they should indicate the theme, angle, or overall approach to the book and to each of the book's major parts, as well as the book's conclusions. As always, check a targeted publisher's submission requirements to see if they give guidance on the level of detail preferred.

Bibliography: As the children's book publishing industry grew over recent decades, its expectations of research quality increased, as discussed in earlier pages. A wise author will be sure that a substantial bibliography, or list of sources, accompanies nonfiction submissions, and some fiction as well (think historical fiction). A good bibliography need not be as scholarly as an accompaniment to a graduate school thesis, but it should be pointedly compiled, comprehensive, and accurate in its form. That is, you want to use high-quality sources that are relevant, and not just pile them on randomly to impress; they won't.

Build a strong bibliography (which reflects the quality of your proposed manuscript) with primary sources—original documents, expert interviews—carrying the most weight. Secondary sources should be solid. Avoid encyclopedias, with few exceptions.

Sample Outline

Title: Spies Yesterday and Today

Audience Age: 12+

Introduction

Chapter I. Good Spy, Bad Spy
    A. Why Spy?

Chapter II. Spies in History
    A. Ancient Egypt
    B. Ancient China
        1. Sun Tzu and The Art of War
    C. Elizabethan England
        1. Sir Francis Walsingham's Spy Network
    D. American Revolution
        1. Nathan Hale
        2. Benedict Arnold
    E. Intelligence Collection
        1. The Pinkerton Agency
    F. Writers Who Spied
        1. Chaucer
        2. Christopher Marlow
        3. T. E. Lawrence

Chapter III. Modern Espionage
    A. Wartime Spies
        1. World War I
        2. World War II
        3. Cold War
            a. CIA
            b. KGB
            c. Alger Hiss, Whittaker Chambers, and the Rosenbergs
            d. Gary Powers
    B. Peacetime Spies
    C. Counterintelligence
    D. When Spies Are Caught

Chapter IV. The Science of Spying
    A. Early Spy Techniques
    B. Spying in Space
    C. Modern Technology

Chapter V. Future of Espionage

Sample Synopsis

Foolish John

Synopsis

A retold folktale based on a Highlands legend.

There was once a king in ancient Ireland with three sons, the youngest named John. He was taken for a fool by many. When the king's eyes dimmed and he could not see to walk alone, the king sent his two older sons to bring three bottles of water from a well that was said to heal the eyes. John was left behind but decided to travel out on his own.

In the first town he reached, John came upon his two older brothers, who threatened to harm him if he did not return home. Afraid of being lost in the woods at night, John climbed a tree in a green glen, to be safe from the animals and his brothers. Soon, he saw a large brown bear coming toward him. The bear called to John to come down, but John said, "Do you, too, think me a fool?"

"Then let us chat," said the bear and they began to talk. John revealed that he was the king's son, and that he was very hungry. The bear hunted down a buck, and said, "For the son of the king of Ireland, here is a dinner to fill you and keep you warm." John was coaxed down. They roasted the deer and ate. John told the Bear of the Green Glen how his brothers would not let him gather the water to cure their father's sight. Soon, John was so full he fell asleep. He woke in the morning between the paws of the great bear.

The bear told John of the home of a giant who loved the king and would help him. When John and the Bear of the Green Glen told the giant of the king's blindness, the giant put out food that would attract a giant eagle with a painful growth on its head. The giant told John to draw his sword, cut off the growth, and the eagle would do John a service. The grateful eagle picked up John and flew him across the sea, to the Green Isle. There, John filled three bottles of blessed water, and met a girl as beautiful as a gem, called Gemma. After adventures on the Green Isle, the eagle flew John toward home. They saw the two brothers below them.

When the empty-handed brothers saw John on the back of an eagle, with the three bottles of water, they decided to steal the water and take credit for their father's cure, expecting to be given the kingdom to divide. The brothers threw John in a ditch where he stayed for three days. But the eagle, the Bear of the Green Glen, and Gemma, the daughter of the King of the Green Isle, came to John's aid. Gemma opened the water and washed the king's eyes until he could see almost across the sea to the Green Isle.

When the king of Ireland learned what the older sons had done, he asked John, "What are you willing to do to your two brothers?" John replied, "The very thing they wished to do to me." And from that day the brothers were known to be fools. John married the daughter of the king of the Green Isle, and when the ancient king died in peace, they ruled over Erin and the Green Isle together for seventy years and seven.

A strong bibliography convinces editors that you have done the research, thought through the project, and can back up what you've written. It indicates that you are likely to put a premium on accuracy, and that you can create your own book out of a synthesis of wide-ranging information. It reassures editors and their legal departments that plagiarism of ideas or language will not be an issue. In this age of James Frey, Jayson Blair, and others, that is an important concern across the industry.

The bibliography you send an editor may not be the one you include in an appendix in your finished book, but parts of it could be, depending on the age of your targeted audience. That's a plus.

Don't forget to use appropriate bibliographic formatting. See page 25 for a sample bibliography.

Résumés and author biographies: Your résumé or author biography should be well-constructed and regularly updated. Sure, your manuscript will ultimately be evaluated for itself, but a résumé or bio may be the token you pay to get it read. Editors judge résumés or author biographies not just for experience and qualifications, but for a writer's ability to present themselves.

Résumés should include your contact information (name, address, phone, email), work experience, education, and relevant professional organizations to which you belong. For writers, this might include the Society of Children's Book Writers and Illustrators (SCBWI). Résumés may also include an objective, which should highlight what you want to accomplish with your writing and especially the particular book or project you are proposing.

Tailor this résumé specifically to writing, even if you are employed in another field. One-size-fits-all does not work well. For your writing résumé, emphasize your relevant credentials and, depending on the book you are proposing, your background in given topics. For example, if you're looking to write a book on health for children, it's a plus if you've been trained as a nurse or dietitian.

An author biography is basically a narrative version of your background.

Some publishers want a very brief (one paragraph) biography included in the cover letter; others want a longer one (one or two pages), attached.

For writers who have been published, the résumé or author bio should be accompanied by a list of publishing credits. If you have credits in a wide variety of categories, tailor them to the work you are currently pursuing. So, if you've written middle-grade novels and articles for the local newspaper on zoning regulations and recent town elections, you don't need to include the latter.

Sample chapters or clips: If you have sent a query and been invited to forward sample chapters, or if the publisher you are targeting accepts proposal packages that include samples, select either those that the publisher requests—often, the first three chapters—or those that best represent your book and style of writing. If the book is still in the idea or outline stage, you might send clips. These too should be reflective of the kind of writing you are now proposing, in terms of target age, style, and subject.

Competitive titles and market research: Publishers increasingly ask prospective authors to look for competitive titles already published (see pages 13–14) and also for suggestions about where and how the proposed book may be sold, especially if it is a special interest title. A science title might be appropriate for gift shops at children's museums across the country; a regional novel should be marketed to local independent bookstores and regional Barnes & Noble stores; perhaps sports organizations would be interested in a baseball book.

Manuscript Formatting

Whether you send your manuscript electronically or by hard copy, formatting is an important issue for editors. They don't want to spend time adjusting their procedures to the idiosyncrasies of a writer's software or struggle through a manuscript that's hard to read because the type is too small or crowded or fuzzy.

Show your professionalism by always following the best manuscript formatting

Sample Bibliography

The Northwest Passage and Arctic Warming
Audience: Middle-grade

Arctic Drift. Clive Cussler and Dirk Cussler. Waterville, ME: Paragon, 2008.

Arctic Labyrinth: The Quest for the Northwest Passage. Glyn Williams. Berkeley, CA: University of California Press, 2011.

Arctic Passages: A Unique Small-boat Journey Through the Great Northern Waterway. John Bockstoce. New York: Hearst Marine Books, 1991.

Arctic Warming Unlocking A Fabled Waterway. Jackie Northam. First in a six-part series, National Public Radio. www.npr.org/2011/08/15/139556207/arctic-warming-unlocking-a-fabled-waterway.

Changes in the Arctic Environment and the Law of the Sea. Edited by Myron H. Nordquist, et al. Martinus Nijhof, 2010.

Interview with Dr. Vladimir Romanovsky of the Geophysical Institute, University of Alaska, Fairbanks, AK. January 2009. Arctic Warming, website collection of interviews with experts on Arctic warming. www.arcticwarming.net/node/70.

"The North Pole Is Melting." David Biello. *Scientific American*. September 21, 2007. www.scientificamerican.com/article.cfm?id=the-north-pole-is-melting.

The Northwest Passage. Documentary by Sprague Theobald. Hole in the Wall productions. Newport, Rhode Island, 2009.

The Search for the Northwest Passage, Great Journeys series. Jill Foran. Weigl Publishers, 2005.

Sample Résumé

Ellen Brooke
Address
Telephone Number
Email

Experience
- Published author of children's stories, articles, and books, and adult nonfiction articles
- Fifth-grade teacher, Mytown Intermediate School, 1998–present
- Sales associate, Baa Baa Black Sheep Bookstore, Mytown, Ohio, 1994-1998

Education
- B.A., English and Education, Greene College, cum laude, 1997
- M.F.A candidate, Greene College School of Fine Arts

Published Credits
- *Girls: Aces in Sports* (Kiddo Publishing, 2014)
- *A Secret Passage* (Fiction Company, 2016)
- "Circle the Wagons" (U.S. History for Kids Magazine, September 2015)
- "Why the Library's Children's Section Must Grow" (series of three articles, Mytown weekly paper, Spring 2013)
- "Teaching Etiquette in a Third-Grade Classroom" (Teachers Share Magazine, November 2010)

Professional Memberships
- Society of Children's Book Writers and Illustrators
- National Council of Teachers of English

Awards
- Kids' Choice Award, Ohio, for *A Secret Passage*

practices. See page 30 for an example of how to format a book, and follow these guidelines:

- Double-space manuscript text; leave 1- to 1½-inch margins on the top, bottom, and sides.

- Create a title page:
  - In the upper left corner, type your name, address, phone number, and email address.
  - In the upper right corner, indicate the page count, or for a picture book, the word count.
  - About 5 inches down, centered, type the title of your book in capital letters.
  - Two lines below the title, type your byline.

- Create a chapter opening page:
  - Type your last name, and the title (in shortened form, if necessary) in the upper left corner.
  - Type the page number in the upper right corner.
  - Start the chapter halfway down the page.

- On following pages, continue to include your name/title in the left corner and page number in the right corner.

Picture Book Formatting

Publishers who accept picture books usually request the complete manuscript, but editors do not expect—nor want—to see artwork unless the author is also the illustrator. If you are not a professionally trained artist, an editor will likely prefer to find the illustrator separately.

Picture book manuscripts may be prepared in the same way as other manuscripts, except you may begin the book on the title page, about four lines down from the byline. On following pages, continue to type the story without breaks.

Many publishers do not request picture book dummies, but some do. Send one only if requested. For a standard 32-page picture book, take eight sheets of paper, fold them in half, and number them as on page 28; this will not include the end papers that line the book's front and back cover. Lay out your text and a brief description of the accompanying illustrations, being sure that the words and pictures fit together as they should. Depending on the context, sometimes picture books also come in other lengths, from 16 to 64 pages.

If you are an author-illustrator and plan to submit artwork, never send the original art. If sending other than digital, send copies only, and the appropriate size self-addressed, stamped envelope (SASE) if you need the materials returned. Not all publishers return material, so check the guidelines before including an SASE.

Electronic or Hard Copy Submissions

Publishers today predominantly prefer electronic submissions, some requesting email with attachments, some with the manuscript pasted into the body of an email, and some using website forms. Other publishers prefer to continue receiving hard copies. Follow the submission guidelines closely. *Book Markets for Children's Writers 2021* includes extensive research on these preferences, but always double-check publisher websites for updates.

Electronic: Most publishers today prefer electronic submissions. As with any other submission, check whether the editor wants a query, complete manuscript, or proposal package.

Then, confirm what form is acceptable: email messages with no attachments, or, if attachments are allowed, what kind.

- Unless otherwise indicated in the publisher's submission guidelines, make the email message—your electronic cover letter—brief.

- Make sure that you check your spelling and grammar. Don't use fancy fonts or colors or anything that would complicate reading your email.

- Be sure to include your contact information: name, address, phone number. Your email address is already included when sending an electronic message.

Picture Book Dummy (Artwork placement for example only)

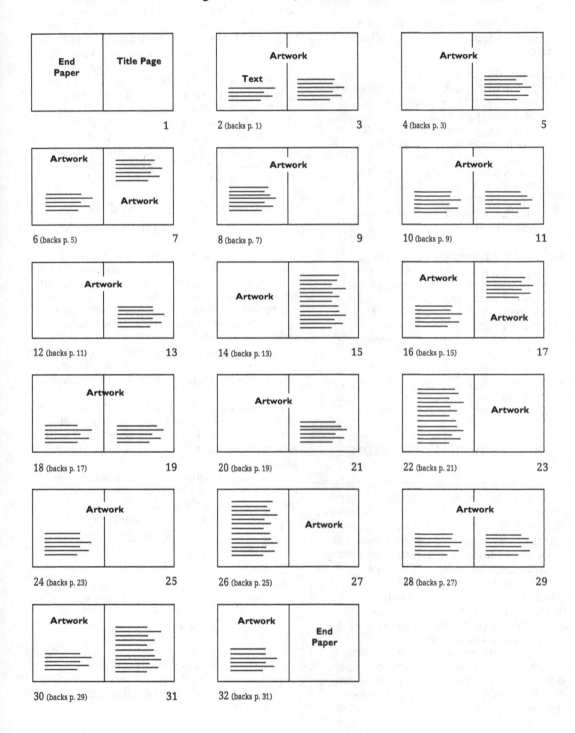

- Guidelines sometimes request specific information in the email subject line, for example: "Query, YA fiction."
- Don't be informal in style because you're sending an email. Remain professional.
- If attachments are preferable, confirm which kind: Microsoft Word documents (check if .doc and/or .docx is accepted); Adobe PDF; or RTF (Rich Text Format). Attach documents as directed by your email program.

Hard Copy: While not as common, some publishers still prefer to receive a hard copy submission package. With a cover letter on top, gather the pages. The first page of a manuscript should include your name and contact information, the word count of the article or story, the title, and your byline. The following pages should include your name, and the page number. Use a standard font such as Times Roman in 12-point type.

Do not staple the pages. To mail the manuscript, use a 9x12 or 10x13 manila envelope and send it First Class or Priority. Do not use certified or registered mail.

Sold

As exciting as it is to receive a positive response to a submission, your job is far from over once you've sold your idea or the book itself. You'll interact with an editor, abide by a contract, work on publicity. You will manage your own business concerns by developing online and print promotional materials; tracking your submissions and work that's been sold; monitoring income, taxes, office expenses; and so on. You'll be working on the whole package of being a published writer.

The Platform: Promote

Having a platform has been made much easier in the age of Twitter and Facebook. A platform is about your visibility to the world at large. Small as your credentials may seem at first, writers who truly want to find a market and be published must *brand* themselves today. Editors, marketing staff, agents, other writers, teachers, librarians, and especially your young readers should know who you are and what you write—and, of course, buy your books.

This is not to say you need to be friending and tweeting and linking every day. Begin building a platform gradually, after some self-examination as a writer. First, identify yourself with genres, subjects of interest, a style, a voice, a perspective, and eventually how these are expressed in your specific writing credits. Next, determine how best to communicate your abilities, what you have to offer, and why others should be interested. Finally, create ways, reflective of you, for others to find you and your work.

Submissions: Because your platform grows out of the writing you create, the materials you submit are core. They represent you and your capabilities. What is it that interests you in writing? What subjects, what form, what voice, what goals, what readers? How do you want to present yourself to editors and readers, and how do you match your work with editors who are likely to be responsive to your particular platform? How do you write that right query or proposal?

Electronic: Use the Internet to connect and promote in the form of a website, blog, online articles, social media, online forums and groups, even podcasts.

Websites: If a business doesn't have a website today, we may very well question its solidity. That is increasingly true for writers, too. A website is a virtual business card, a résumé, and a marketing tool rolled into one. Developing and maintaining an effective site will help draw readers to you by highlighting you and your books.

When developing a website, you will need to consider the creative side and the numbers side. Creatively, look at the information to include, the kind of design that represents you, what works on the landing/home page, how interactive it should be, whether you want to develop it yourself or hire someone with website design expertise. On the numbers side, you will want to know how much traffic the site gets, from where, the most popular features, the keywords that

Manuscript Format

Title Page

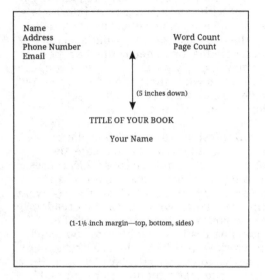

Name
Address
Phone Number
Email

Word Count
Page Count

(5 inches down)

TITLE OF YOUR BOOK

Your Name

(1-1½ inch margin—top, bottom, sides)

New Chapter

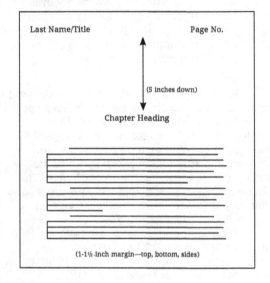

Last Name/Title   Page No.

(5 inches down)

Chapter Heading

(1-1½ inch margin—top, bottom, sides)

Following Pages

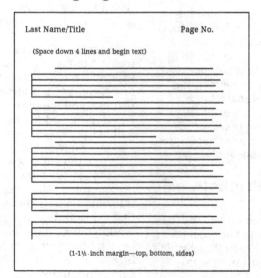

Last Name/Title   Page No.

(Space down 4 lines and begin text)

(1-1½ inch margin—top, bottom, sides)

best allow search engines to find you (SEO, or search engine optimization), and how much time you can give the site without taking away from your writing. Here are some other suggestions for your website:

- Include a brief biography, publishing credits, and contact information.

- Emphasize connection. Reflect your personality. Give the website some depth and make it well-rounded and easy to use.

- Consider including *extras*, especially for child or teacher use, such as games or activities related to your writing, or a free e-book or stories. Perhaps you might compose a free newsletter to which readers can subscribe. This will allow you to build an email list.

- Do you want a comments or forum page? A page of FAQs? Links to publishers' or other writers' websites?

- Remember to refresh or create new content regularly (good for SEO).

- When you publish a new title, add links to Amazon and other booksellers.

Blogs: If you're going to write a blog—potentially a great mechanism for a publishing platform—commit to doing it well.

- Decide what it should contain. Will it be all about your writing or your subjects of interest, or will it be more wide-ranging? Will it target readers of your books, other writers, and the publishing community? Teens, children, adults?

- Will you bring in content from other people by doing interviews, for example, with writers or editors?

- Consider participating on other writers' blogs or websites, and inviting them to contribute to yours.

- How often can you post to it—daily, weekly, biweekly?

Other high-tech routes: Many other technological means of promoting and building your platform are possible. Among them:

- Create a presence on Amazon.com for you and your book—set up your author page to promote yourself, or look into CreateSpace to self-publish.

- Use Facebook, Twitter, or other social media platforms to talk about your writing and publishing.

- Connect with other writers on online forums or sites dedicated to literature, writing, books, or publishing, such as Absolute Write.

- Check for blogs and other sites specifically about children's writing and keep up to date on people and publishers.

- Write online articles to showcase your areas of expertise, on sites such as About.com or Leaf Group. Upload to Scribd.com, "the world's largest social reading and publishing company."

Traditional: While electronic may trump print for promotion in some ways, there's no substitution for old-fashioned networking. Publishing promotion has long consisted of distributing print materials such as business cards, postcards, brochures, or bookmarks; attending conferences to network; doing bookstore readings, school visits, and other speaking engagements; participating in professional organizations; developing connections with the press, and so on.

- Join professional organizations. The premier children's writer group, SCBWI, has been mentioned earlier. Consider joining organizations related to your subject area. If you're a science writer for children, for example, look at the National Association of Science Writers (www.nasw.org). Mystery writers might join Mystery Writers of America (www.mysterywriters.org).

- Develop a presentation about your book and/or related subjects for schools, bookstores, and libraries.

- Print materials are still important when you attend conferences or speaking engagements, and for general personal networking. Have business cards, bookmarks, or flyers to hand out.

Make sure they are well-designed and professional in appearance. Ask local bookstores to make some of your materials available.

- When you've published a book, arrange school visits and bookstore or library readings, or speak at a writers' conference.

- Send press releases to local and regional publications or radio programs. Put together a press kit about your book, including a brief biography and credits if any, an excerpt from the book, synopsis, a picture of the cover, a picture of you, and your print promotional material (business card, postcard, etc.) with information on price and availability. If you have reviews, add those. Offer these to local reporters and editors and let them know you're available for an interview.

- Some writers cross-promote with groups of other writers: "You talk about my book on your blog or when you're at a conference, and I'll do the same." So, network away with a critique group, online groups, and so on.

- Between your online connections (website, blog, forums, social networking, etc.) and your real-time connections (critique group, conferences, presentations, school visits, etc.), start letting people know they can stay up-do-date with your books (or if you start a newsletter or have a book signing) by opting in to your email list. Don't add people—it's considered rude, and if you're using a professional service like MailChimp or ConstantContact, it's not legal. In the Institute for Writers online course, How to Create Your Author Platform Module #3 is "Creating Your Platform Using Email," for more detailed information. At https://instituteforwriters.teachable.com/p/how-to-create-your-author-platform.

The Business: Rights, Contracts, and Payment

Before you're fully promoting your sold book, you will have been offered and signed a contract. It will include the purchase of certain rights, payment, deadlines, and other legal issues. New writers signing book contracts without the aid of a literary agent would be wise to seek legal or other business advice from someone who specializes in intellectual property law and knows the publishing industry. At the very least become well-read on the subject, should you go into contract negotiations on your own. Another place to get advice is the Authors Guild (www.authorsguild.org), whose legal staff will review book contracts as part of Guild membership benefits. For a discussion and list of agents, see pages 303-338.

Here are the basics of book contracts.

Copyright: Even without registering, you own the copyright to your book. Unless the publisher is offering to buy the book outright (unlikely) or it was commissioned as a work-for-hire (see page 33), you hold the copyright. Once your book is sold, however, the publisher often registers the copyright and pays the fee for you.

Rights granted: The contract will include language that says you guarantee your book is completely original. You grant the publisher certain rights to your book, including the primary right to produce and distribute it as a bound book, whether hardcover or paperback, trade or mass-market, or, increasingly today, electronic.

Subsidiary rights include reprint rights, foreign rights, electronic rights, audio rights, film/TV/dramatic rights, merchandising rights, and book club rights. Subsidiary rights should be handled very carefully. Among the most argued issues in publishing today is electronic rights. As new publishing formats like electronic readers have developed, publishers have tried to extend their reach under contracts signed before the media even existed.

The kind of book you've written will affect the rights you'll be asked to convey, and at what payment rate. You won't be selling film rights for a concept book, but you might just hit the jackpot and see your teen novel become a TV show, like Cecily von Ziegesar with *Gossip Girl*. Picture books with great characters could give rise to product licensing arrangements. Think *Olivia* and *Fancy Nancy*.

Remember that picture book authors may have different arrangements because they split rights and royalties with an illustrator.

Rights generally may be held as long as the copyright, which under U.S. law is the lifetime of the author plus 70 years.

Payment: For the right to produce and sell your book, you receive a payment in return. For books, this usually means a royalty, and sometimes an advance. The royalty may be a single percentage across the life of the book (7.5, 10, 12.5, or 15 percent of the cover price), or it may be graduated—a sliding scale that depends on the number of books sold (10 percent for the first 5,000, and 12.5 percent for the next 5,000). Royalties vary between paperbacks and hardcovers, trade and mass-market.

An advance is "taken against royalties." That is, the author is given an amount before the book goes on sale that is subtracted from the royalties earned from actual sales.

The contract will include when and how often royalties are paid. They may be paid quarterly, semi-annually, or annually.

Finally, note that the royalty system can be quite complicated and varies among publishers. Royalty calculations may include printer costs, discounts to booksellers, returns, and sometimes other costs. This is another reason to have legal and business advice when negotiating a book contract.

Reversion and out-of-print clauses: The publisher's part under the contract is to print, produce, and distribute the book. If it does not perform these tasks, it has not honored the contract and the rights may revert to the author. A reversion clause includes a time frame for publication, and if that deadline is not met, the author may also usually keep any advance.

If a publisher produces a book but lets it go out of print after some time, an out-of-print clause says the rights return to the author, who may take the book to another publisher for reprint. Many authors make an effort to find new publishers for out-of-print books or to offer them in another form. Today, that can mean self-publishing through print-on-demand (POD), or offering an electronic version through an e-book publisher.

Option clause: The option clause gives the publisher the right to have the first opportunity to read the author's next book and make an offer to publish it, within a reasonable amount of time. This clause has many variations, and many people are cautious about it. Some argue it is unnecessary.

Electronic rights: Electronic rights are changing practically before authors' and publishers' eyes, as the pace of technology continues to quicken and e-book publishing has begun to overtake print publishing. In May 2011, Amazon sold more Kindle books than print books for the first time ever.

Electronic rights have been at the center of arguments between authors and publishers of many kinds, from newspaper publishers to book publishers, for a long time now. New book contracts handle these rights more directly, but the question "What is a book?" is still being hammered out. Get good legal advice about selling these rights; the Authors Guild has a strong viewpoint and some basic recommendations:

- An author should be fairly compensated whether his or her work is in print, an e-book, on the Internet, in a database, or in any other digital form.

- Check the Grant of Rights clause to see how it covers electronic rights. Publishers try to get the broadest rights they can.

- Check the royalty clause to see if electronic formats have a different payment structure than print.

- Publishers may want to assign digital versions of your book to another company. Decide whether that is in your best interest.

For more advice from the Authors Guild on this complex topic, go to https://www.authorsguild.org/member-services/legal-services/#.

Work-for-hire: Some publishers want to purchase books outright, with the author surrendering any claim to copyright. Educational publishers in particular may assign books in series to authors, and want to retain the rights to all the titles in the series. Books written as works-for-hire are developed

Websites, Blogs, and Social Media

Webhosting
- Bluehost.com
- Dreamhost.com
- Godaddy.com
- GreenGeeks.com
- HostGator.com
- Justhost.com
- InMotionHosting.com
- Yahoo: www.webhostingconsumer.com

Blog Platforms
- Blogger.com (Google)
- Tumblr.com
- Squarespace.com
- Weebly.com
- Wix.com
- Wordpress.org

Miscellaneous Writing and Publishing Sites
- Absolute Write: http://absolutewrite.com
- AdvicetoWriters.com
- All Freelance Writing: www.allfreelancewriting.com
- Cynsations: www.cynthialeitichsmith.com
- DailyWritingTips.com
- Gather.com
- Goodreads.com
- Verla Kay: www.verlakay.com
- ProBlogger.com
- Fantasy Author's Handbook: https://fantasyhandbook.wordpress.com
- Kidlit.com
- Kidlit411.com
- The Purple Crayon: www.underdown.org
- Writing for Children Podcast: https://www.instituteforwriters.com/podcast/

Social Media:
- Facebook.com
- Twitter.com
- YouTube.com
- LinkedIn.com
- Pinterest.com
- Instagram.com

either by employees as part of their job, or by freelancers (independent contractors) who are specifically commissioned and must sign a specific work-for-hire agreement.

The advantage of work-for-hire arrangements can be that a writer is asked to do a series of books for a publisher. Another advantage is that, because all rights are being purchased, the payment—a flat, project fee in many cases—may be relatively high. Unlike a royalty arrangement, payment is received on completion of the project, rather than as books are sold. Many authors consider this possibility an assurance of steady income.

Self-publishing, subsidy, and POD: If you're considering self-publishing, understand that you will assume the cost and responsibility of printing, publishing, and promoting your book. You can write your book, design it, find a printer, work out a marketing plan, and sell it. As difficult as it is, there have been some major self-publishing success stories, including *Eragon*.

Ebook self-publishing is growing rapidly. Amazon is at the forefront with its Digital Text Platform (DTP), but other companies are also making strides in this field. They include CreateSpace, Lulu, Scribd, and Smashwords.

Some companies—subsidy publishers—will take on some of these tasks for a fee; they produce the book, and do a limited degree of marketing and distribution.

Print-on-demand (POD) publishers will print and ship limited numbers of your book, and may handle a few other services, for a fee. The advantage of POD is that costs can be controlled through limited printings. Even some mainstream publishing companies are now using POD.

While these publishing choices may be viable for writers who are committed to seeing their work in print, self-publishing, subsidy publishing, and POD publishing all have pitfalls. Be cautious. (See Sidebar Pitfalls of Self-Publishing on page 38.) Authors may be taken advantage of, or end up taking on more than they know how to handle. Do extensive research on what services companies offer (whether an independent printer down the street or a full-blown subsidy publisher) and what they don't, and costs. Have any contracts reviewed by a lawyer or a knowledgeable business advisor.

Revised

It's the end of the day: You've sold an editor on an idea and the manuscript, and you've signed a contract. You're ready to turn to revisions. Any successful writer will tell you how important they are. Revisions are the last step before putting a polished book—your best efforts—out into the world. The revision process is also important in terms of your career: Developing a strong writer-editor relationship can mean the difference between being a one-hit wonder and extending your publishing success.

Many authors suggest putting the manuscript down for a while before beginning revisions. At times, authors become too close with their manuscript, and editing your own words can be a difficult process. A few days and a fresh mind will allow you to look at the manuscript more objectively.

One suggestion is to read the manuscript out loud to check for sentence flow.

Sometimes hearing it spoken out loud allows you to hear when things are too wordy.

So now you've been inspired. You've researched. You've devised your book and queried. The book sold and the revisions are done. You've put together a complete creation and others will soon share it. On to the next . . . and a promising writing career.

Plusses + Pointers: The Benefits of Self-Publishing

Not all that long ago, self-publishing was viewed as a last resort for writers who'd been turned away by traditional book publishers. You'd likely also been told that the editor at big publishing houses will know almost immediately whether your pearly prose is going to sell . . . important to know before you invest more time and hard work into it.

Sounds good, but try telling that to J.K. Rowling. She was rejected by an even dozen publishers before being picked up . . . and only then reportedly because one book editor's daughter liked what she saw and wanted more.

Why and When
The reality is that, today, even previously published authors often add self-publishing to the mix. Here are several reasons why, and when, it may make sense for you, too.
And, to help you decide, we also offer a glance into some of the nuts and bolts of the self-publishing process.

First, some of the plusses:

• **Speed.** Your book was just accepted for publication. More often than not, you won't see it in print for 18+ months. Self-publish, however, and you can be talking months or even weeks. E-books, are of course, the fasted to turn around.

• **$$$.** Faster turnaround translates to quicker cash. And sometimes more cash. If you self-publish, even with a giant like Amazon, you get the lion's share of the list price.

• **Control.** This is one reason previously published authors say they like self-publishing, especially electronic self-publishing. They, and you, can control most everything from start to finish—not just content per se, but art, cover design, format, marketing, and more.

• **Character/Story Development.** And, speaking of content, when you sell your book to a traditional publisher, they can also make you change anything they want . . . plot, characters, etc. That can be a tough trade-off.

• **Rights.** If you're fortunate enough to hit it big, self-publishing means you keep the rights for any adaptation to other forms . . . film, etc. Regardless, you won't have to deal with the constraints that traditional publishing houses place on authors.

Key Considerations
Until printing on demand (POD) became possible in the '90s, thanks to advances in technology, most people looking to self-publish needed to pair up with what was called a "vanity" house. That's all changed, however.

And, it's made self-publishing even more popular. If you're ready to consider giving it a try, here are some of the things you need to consider:

• **Format.** Do your homework to decide which is better for you . . . POD (publishing on demand) or an ebook. Either way, the cheapest mode is, of course, to self-publish on your own, using freelance help only as needed.

• **POD.** If you do want some help, today's custom printing service options are reasonable, and they alleviate the historic problem of sitting, as a self-publisher, with unsold copies in every corner. Instead, have an order? Get it printed then. No warehouse. No minimum print-run orders. Be sure, however, to thoroughly research any POD service you're considering.

• **Services.** Just like picking a traditional publisher, however, it's important to make sure you're happy with any POD publishing service you are considering. Here's a glance at three of the majors, each with different benefits:

> √ IngramSpark, the self-publishing arm of the country's biggest book wholesaler, Ingram Content Group.
> √ KDP Print, which is now the self-publishing branch of Amazon.
> √ BookBaby, known for its author-friendly services, is considered a good platform for beginners.

• **Reality Check.** Unless you go freelance, you'll likely use some sort of service to get you from A to Z. A good help-for-many service does, however, take money out of your pocket.

On the plus side, most of these services have multiple packages. If you decide to go this route, check your options to determine which best meets your needs or whether you want to go the freelance-help route.

Some services will just charge a set fee up front as opposed to taking a percent of sales. Before you sign, also be sure to check there are no stipulations—e.g., rights to your work You may even decide to go it completely on your own, but don't forget that if you can't manage all the soup-to-nuts steps yourself, you may need to pay a middleman to pave the road between printing and distribution.

• **E-Books.** There's no question that most self-publishing revenue comes from the sale of e-books. And, though it's probably no surprise, more than 80% of those e-book sales are made through one company . . . Amazon. And one key benefit, which is why many publishing services groups are seeing dollars drop, is that it's easy and cost-effective to deal with online vendors like Amazon. Don't forget, though, that which of their services you use will determine your royalty.

• **Other Options.** Some agents offer services for self-publishing . . . for a fee. And some services now position themselves as what's referred to hybrid publishers. For some services, it's just a fancier title. For others, their services provide a good, though more costly option. As always, do your homework. And check it twice!

Whatever route you choose, self-publishing has very real benefits. And, lasting, bottom-line ones, too.

The Pitfalls of Self-Publishing

There are many great advantages to self-publishing. You can get your book out much faster than with a traditional publisher, where the process might take up to two years. You also retain complete control over your content, layout, and cover. However, there are also some common pitfalls that many authors fall into. Here are three of the snares hidden in the self-publishing world, and how you can avoid them.

1. A Lack of All Trades

When you self-publish, suddenly you need to master more skills than just writing. Not only do you need a fantastic and gripping story, but it needs to be presented in a way that is reader-friendly. This includes brushing up on margin spacing, suitable fonts, and layouts, all of which work together to produce a professional book that your readership can enjoy. The same can be said for the front cover. While you wish the saying "Don't judge a book by its cover" was always applied, sadly an off-putting or poorly designed cover can cause readers to skim over the title without even picking it up. If you know that your design or editing skills are not up to snuff, the best thing you can do is outsource these jobs to experts who can really bring your book to life in a way that truly does the story justice.

2. Jumping the Gun

When you have completed your first manuscript of a new book, it can be the most exciting feeling in the world. All you want is to get it out there for the world to read and enjoy. However, publishing too soon is a serious pitfall that can cost you dearly. There is a reason why traditional publishing takes so long; there are countless edits and changes that are made to the original draft to make it ready for publishing. Whether it is poor character development, tedious twists, or gaping plot holes, there are some mistakes that you might miss but may bring your whole story crashing down. Even a typo or two within your text can really make your reader question the quality of the book. Take time to send your book to some trusted editors and make sure it is ready for publishing before you dive in.

3. Getting Taken for a Ride

Perhaps the scariest of self-publishing pitfalls is the prospect of being scammed. Sadly, it is all too common, and so the most important place to start when self-publishing is with a reputable publishing house. There are a few red flags to look out for when choosing your publisher. If a self-publisher makes grand claims, informing you that they will make your book a best-seller and get it into every bookstore in the country, this should set off alarm bells in your head. Similarly, a publisher that is positively begging for your business, employing excessive flattery, may also be cause for concern. Another necessity is reading through your contract very carefully. Some publishers will hide clauses in there that they can use to take advantage of you later. If you struggle to understand the terms, ask an attorney to read it through for you and check everything is in order.

Authentic Kids

If you're going to write for kids, it's crucial that your child characters talk and act like real kids. Young people want to read about kids their own age (or just a little older) and they want to read about kids they can relate to, even if those characters live in a fantasy world or somewhere in the past.

To make your kids authentic, you'll have to do some research. Children's books are usually separated into various age categories. Here are some very basic developmental outlines about those ages:

Ages 0-3

Babies are naturally egocentric. They can't see things from someone else's point of view, and they don't yet have the language skills to express their needs. Babies and toddlers aren't quite ready for full-blown stories with vivid characterization. They care more for colors, shapes, and sounds in their books.

Ages 3-5

Preschoolers are beginning to use more complicated sentences and to learn that they can use specific words to say what they mean. "No" and "why" become important words. They are fascinated by everything. Where does milk come from? What makes a shadow? How do birds fly? Family is their world, but they are also growing aware of people outside their family—teachers, the other kids in nursery school, their neighbors and friends.

Ages 5-8

Kids in this age range are taking on more independence. They go to school, participate in sports, and learn to read and write and ride bicycles without training wheels. They now realize they are no longer the center of the universe. They move from being more concrete thinkers to more reflective ones, as they begin to look at causes and ask more challenging questions. School age kids feel alternatively dependent, resistant, or rebellious toward their parents. Friends become important. They enjoy telling jokes, appreciate puns, and love to be silly.

Ages 8-12

Kids this age are developing specific interests, and they're eager to learn all about them, whether it's sports or music or movies. This is when their lives outside the home start to compete with their lives inside the home. Kids in this age range are becoming aware of hierarchies at school and who is okay to hang out with and who isn't. This is also when the opposite sex becomes more intriguing.

Ages 12-16

Puberty sets in during this stage, and kids' bodies seem to change overnight. This is also when the center of activity shifts fully away from home, over to school and activities and hanging out with friends. To their dismay, parents find they've become uncool and often a source of embarrassment to the child who was once attached to them like flies to flypaper. Some other kids are uncool, too, and social status and being in the right clique becomes all consuming. And for the older teens, so does getting into the right college. For a lot of kids, the teen years can be filled with pressure and angst.

2020 Children's Book Award Winners

John Newbery Medal: *New Kid*, written and illustrated by Jerry Craft (HarperCollins).

Randolph Caldecott Medal: *The Undefeated*, illustrated by Kadir Nelson (Versify).

The Coretta Scott King (Author) Book Award: *New Kid*, by Jerry Craft (HarperCollins).

The Coretta Scott King (Illustrator) Book Award: *Undefeated*, illustrated by Kadir Nelson; written by Kwame Alexander (Schwartz & Wade Books).

The Coretta Scott King/John Steptoe New Talent Author Award: *Genesis Begins Again*, by Alicia D. Williams (Atheneum).

The Michael L. Printz Award: *Dig*, by A. S. King (Dutton Books for Young Readers).

The Margaret A. Edwards Award: Steve Sheinkin. His books include: *Bomb: The Race to Build—and Steal—the World's Most Dangerous Weapon; The Port Chicago 50: Disaster, Mutiny, and the Fight for Civil Rights;* and *The Notorious Benedict Arnold: A True Story of Adventure, Heroism, & Treachery* (Macmillan).

Children's Literature Legacy Award: Kevin Henkes, whose award-winning works include *Julius,the Baby of the World, Olive's Ocean,* and *Waiting* (Greenwillow Books).

The Theodor Seuss Geisel Award: *Stop! Bot!* written and illustrated by James Yang (Viking).

The 2019 Morris Award: *The Field Guide to the North American Teenager*, by Ben Philippe (Balzer + Bray).

The Mystery Writers of America 2018 Edgar Awards:

Juvenile category: *Me and Sam-Sam Handle the Apocalypse*, by Susan Vaught (Paula Wiseman Books).

Young Adult category: *Catfishing on Catnet*, by Naomi Kritzer (Tor Teen).

2020 Irma Simonton Black and James H. Black Award: *The Crayon Man, by* Natascha Biebow (Houghton Mifflin Harcourt).

The NCTE Orbis Pictus Award for Outstanding Nonfiction for Children: *A Place to Land: Martin Luther King Jr. and the Speech that Inspired a Nation*, by Barry Wittenstein (Holiday House).

The Scott O'Dell Award: *Butterfly Yellow*, by Thannh´a Lai (HarperCollins).

Articles

Let's Talk About Plot

Getting from Beginning to End

By Jamie K. Schmidt

Many writers struggle with plot.

New writers struggle with plot.

Even published writers can struggle with plot.

In fiction, plot is the form that story assumes. Some folks confuse plot and theme. And some folks confuse plot and premise. Some even confuse plot and character. And that's understandable because the elements of story aren't really as compartmentalized as we might like.

Plot functions because of character needs and desires. Plot explores theme. Plot takes place in premise. So all these elements mix and blend when we think about plot. Thus, confusion is understandable.

What Is Plot?

Plot is the way the story happens. Plot is how Winnie the Pooh got himself stuck in Rabbit's doorway and eventually was freed. Plot is how we get from "Once upon a time" to "they lived happily ever after." Plot is how Trixie lost her Knuffle Bunny and how she got it back. It is the specific journey taken in a book to get from the beginning where everything is status quo and through the catastrophic to the end where something has been changed and we know the characters will be living with that change.

Plot differs from theme and premise because plot is very specific to one book. There maybe be hundreds of books that explore the theme of maturing friendships, but each one will take a different story journey to do that exploration. There may be dozens of books with the premise of schools for magical or super kids, but each one will follow a different path within that premise. And that path is plot.

Plot is exactly how the journey happens in the story. And if you have skills and imagination, your plot will not be exactly like anyone else's, nor will it be just like any other story you've written. This second part is quite important because it's really easy to fall in love with a plot and just keep telling that story over and over.

Say, you write a story about a superhero who lives in a city where there is a super villain. And that super villain can turn dark emotion into evil villainy. So one of the superhero's friends gets really furious with her, and the super villain uses that to turn the friend into a monster, which the superhero must defeat without harming her friend (and make up for the fight they had). So she does. You love the story. And all your readers love the story. So in the next story, you have the superhero's mom get hurt feelings and the super villain turns the mom into a monster because of her hurt feelings. And the superhero now has to defeat the mom monster without hurting her (and make up for hurting her mom's feelings).

Do You See the Problem Here?

You've told the same story twice. And if the next time it's her brother or a teacher or the school librarian, it's still going to be the same story because it's the same journey. If you'd like to see how this works in action, just catch the first few seasons of The Miraculous Ladybug on Netflix. In the series, every episode follows the exact same plot journey even though the characters change and the theme changes.

Plot Begins with Character

Let's use our superhero plot example to boil down what plot is. We will start with a main character (which is probably best if you're fairly new to writing, but if you decide to use more than one main character, do try to avoid hopping from one character's viewpoint to another character's viewpoint too often). A single main character gives your plot more focus and helps readers become attached to the character.

So, let's suppose you have a character with good and bad qualities (because this makes the character feel more real as we are all a mix of good and bad qualities). The character is interesting in some way. In our superhero plot, she's interesting because she's a superhero. But she must also be interesting for something more. So she is an incredible seamstress (which I've often thought must be a useful quality in a superhero as those outfits tend to show some impressive tailoring) and socially awkward. (Okay, aren't we all at some point? But that has become almost a cliche in main characters. Where are all the socially successful main characters who haven't been made evil by popularity?) And the character's actions and decisions drive the action of the story. This is essential. A character that bobs along on the actions of others tends not to be so interesting.

Make Your Character's Life Difficult

Not every plot has to be a tale of vicious misery. In fact, none of the plots I've ever written and few of the plots I enjoy reading are tales of misery. But you do have to complicate your main character's life. In our superhero plot, she and her best friend clearly must have some sort of fight if her best friend ends up furious. So even before the evil villain steps in, the main character's life has become complicated. She has a problem. At some point when you're working on your plot (and potentially at several points if you're writing a longer short story or a novel) you should be able to look at a spot and say, "my main character has a problem." The problem needs to be one that applies pressure to act.

The concept of "pressure to act" is an important one in plotting. The character's actions grow out of pressure that cannot be ignored. Having a huge fight with your best friend will apply pressure to act. No one wants to be on the outs with a best friend, and if you feel that you've completely destroyed the relationship,

you're not going to shrug something like that off. You're going to do things that are driven by that problem. You might not do the right things, but you're going to be driven to act. If the actions of your characters aren't being driven by the conflicts and challenges popping up in the characters' lives, then you are not building an effective plot.

Crafting Action from Conflict

The bigger the problem, the more pressure a character will feel to act. And the more likely the character is to choose an action that maybe makes things worse. So a character who has just had an argument with her best friend might try to fix it too quickly, while the friend is still really mad. And that attempt might drive the character from anger to fury. And in our superhero story, this gives an opening to the super villain who turns the friend into a monster.

This upping of the problem is a common function of plot. The character has a problem, so what might she logically do that will unintentionally make it worse? And how might circumstances (in this case, a handy evil villain) do to make things even worse than it already is? Worsening problems are another aspect of plot. Nothing should be too easy. And the new, worsened problem will make it even less likely that the main character can simply walk away. Something must be done. (And of course you know that something catastrophic to a toddler might be shrug-worthy to a teen, so you need to tailor your problem accordingly.)

Don't Ignore the Obvious

One thing some plots fail to do is consider human nature. Say you've gone into a haunted house. You're not really expecting a monster in there. Not really. You're really expecting the place to be creepy and for you to have an adventure you can tell friends about. But along comes the monster. So what do you logically do? Do you stay and try to defeat the monster? Or do you run very fast with a determination never to go back into that house again? Humans run. It's basic survival. So if you intend to make a character do something that doesn't fit normal human nature, you have to give the main character a reason to stay. A reason that we believe. Now, a really naturally brave and really loyal person might stay until she can get her friend out with her. Maybe. But why not simply run outside and call for help on your ubiquitous cell phone? Would you really stay? Really?

So the best friend probably isn't enough. And you really do have to keep in mind that real people have real life choices, like the cell phone. If you're going to keep the person in the house, you're going to have to deal with the phone. And with the motivation. Traditionally, escape has been blocked by the house itself, or the person maybe stays because the secondary character is someone they flatly could not leave behind (a little sister, maybe). But whatever you do in the story, the choices you make must grow logically out of the circumstances. Don't make a choice because it is convenient for you if it ignores what a real life person would do in that situation.

Resolution Sometimes Comes from Weakness

Sometimes the thing that makes the main character the weakest or most vulnerable or gets the main character in trouble in the first place is the thing that saves the day. Say your main character is being punished for taking the classroom clock apart to see how it worked. Your character is made to stay behind during recess and follows another naughty kid on an adventure where they end up locked in a closet. When you reach the worst moment of the story, where the main character absolutely must get them out of there, what do you do? You have a character with a long history of tinkering and taking things apart. So he knows how hinges work and gets them out of the closet. Or he takes apart the door handle. Or you find another way to use that initial weakness as a strength, because that's often how plot works. Weaknesses can be strengths depending on the situation and the way you look at them.

Now once you've solved the problems (big and small) you have to get out of the story. So the superhero keeps her friend from destroying the city and restores her to being a normal kid again, possibly by calling upon their friendship somehow? Or by using the thing they fought about in the first place. So now you just have two

kids again who end the story by doing something symbolic to affirm their friendship (ice cream maybe?) and you're done. You must resist the urge to go on and on once there are no more problems. An ending that is clever or witty is always nice too. Gives a nice bit of pizzazz, but the real key is to make sure it's satisfying. You do that by revealing (as subtly as you're able) that things have been changed by the story. The friendship is now on stronger ground than ever before or some such. Some kind of change because story is all about change. You don't end up back exactly where you began. It might look as if you do at first glance, but upon reflection you realize the story did change the characters.

So that's plot. It's a journey to change. It's one dang thing after another. It's ruining someone's life and bringing them to wholeness through it. It's an adventure. So good luck on yours.

USA Today bestselling author Jamie K. Schmidt writes erotic contemporary love stories and paranormal romances. Her steamy romantic comedy, *Life's a Beach*, reached #65 on *USA Today*, #2 on Barnes & Noble and #9 on Amazon and iBooks. Her Club Inferno series from Random House's Loveswept line has hit both the Amazon and Barnes & Noble top one hundred lists. The first book in the series, *Heat*, put her on the *USA Today* bestseller list for the first time, and is a #1 Amazon bestseller. Her book *Stud* is a 2018 Romance Writers of America Rita® Finalist in Erotica. Her dragon paranormal romance series has been called "fun and quirky" and "endearing." Partnered with *New York Times* bestselling author and actress Jenna Jameson, Jamie's hardcover debut, *SPICE*, continues Jenna's FATE trilogy.

This article was reprinted with permission by InstituteForWriters.com.

Tips for Getting Past the Gatekeeper
10 Reasons Manuscripts Are Automatically Rejected

By Jan Fields

Some writers love revision. In fact, for many, the rough draft is something to be rushed through to get to the real "fun," the revision.

I'm Not One of Those Writers.

I do a lot of revising, but it's not the part I most enjoy. And since I'm not as much of a workaholic as folks tend to think, revision can be something I would skimp on if I didn't enter into revision with a plan.

Create the Plan as You Write

When I'm writing, I'll often think of things that would make the plot work better. Or I'll wish I'd made a character act a little differently early on, to clue the reader in on something, so that a later action will feel more believable. Those kinds of thoughts are in my head a lot. And what I used to do is stop and make the change, and then try to get back into the flow at the point I'd left off. Sometimes that worked, but a lot of times, it didn't. I'd lose the thread of where I was when I stopped. And I would often end up slowing a book down so much that I'd give up on it before it was done. I needed a new method. Of course, I also didn't want to leave those corrections undone as they would show up as glaring errors to an editor.

So, what I do now is to begin the revision plan while I'm writing. In this plan, I include those ideas that pop in my head as I'm writing. I keep track of all those things that need fixing, in a bulleted list.

This same list also contains the name of every single character in the book. As soon as I add a new character, I jot the name in the revision plan. That sets the character's name and spelling. Then a character named Philip in the beginning of the book won't become Phillip in the end of the book simply because I forget what I called him and how I spelled it.

List My Weaknesses

Some things are always in my revision plan because they're always in my writing. I have a definite writer's voice that has strong similarities to my speaking voice. So I will overuse some perfectly good words (like "lovely"). And I will tend to overuse some gestures (nodding, for instance). I will pick up temporary pet words that plague a book or two (like "actually"). And then there are all the little words that are commonly overused by everyone (such as "so" and "just" and "very"). All of these things go into my revision plan. When the time comes to do the revision, I will use my writing program's search function to find all the instances of these overused bits and I'll curb them down to a less obtrusive number. We're not talking about things that are wrong, just overused. An overused word pulls the reader's attention away from my story and onto my technique. I want my technique to be invisible, and revision plays a part in that.

List Common Mistakes

Some things always need to be fixed. Typos need cleaning up. Verb tenses need to be checked for consistency (and to be certain of using the right tense in the right spot). If it's a book with chapters, I need to make sure my format for starting new chapters (or giving chapter titles) is consistent. If it's a shorter nonfiction book with headings, I need to be sure my format for handling headers is consistent. As I add these items to my revision plan, I help ensure my book will be clean. (Or as clean as I can make it. I'm human, and I will always miss things.)

Pet sentence structures need to be varied. I tend to write very direct sentences, which can be good for very young readers, but more than a little dull when it's the only sentence structure in a book for fluent readers. So, I need to check into that. Many writers fall in love with starting sentences with an -ing phrase like this: "Ringing the bell, the teacher called the students in from play." That structure is wonderful to use for variety, but if it appears in every paragraph (or even more than once in every paragraph), then you have a pet sentence structure that will eventually pull attention away from the story and onto the mechanics.

Working the Plan

When my rough draft is done, I begin to work my revision plan. I work from the big things to the little things. So, I'll begin with all those notes about changes I need to make to motivation or action or other such things that would require rewriting of sentences, paragraphs, or even whole scenes. This is really the only fun part of revision for me since I'm still writing and not just checking for mistakes.

Once I have the big things, then I begin my focused revision "passes." This is where I go down my list and fix them one at a time for the whole book. I don't try to fix all the things in one pass, because I'll nearly always forget things if I do that. So, I just do my revising in pass after pass after pass. By the time the revision process is done, I will have read the manuscript dozens of times as I work through the revision steps.

Getting a Change of View

The final thing I do in any revision is change the font for the whole thing to something VERY different. Then I read though the manuscript in this "new look." This sometimes allows me to fix mistakes that I've somehow overlooked during all the other passes. Of course, after I finish this final pass, I switch back to the "correct" font and read the book one last time.

Does that sound like a lot of work? It is. And it's not work I particularly enjoy. But I do enjoy selling books. So, I do the work.

What does your plan look like?

With a career that began in the early 1980s, **Jan Fields** has written for newspapers, magazines, testing companies, book publishers, and even a toy company. She's produced over 100 books, mostly series fiction. Her chapter books for children tend to be humorous action adventure for the educational market, while her adult novels are all cozy mysteries. She also speaks at schools and leads workshops at writing conferences around the country.

This article was reprinted with permission by InstituteForWriters.com.

Listings

Listings Key

Sterling Children's Books

1166 Avenue of the Americas, Floor 17, New York,
NY 10036.
http://www.sterlingpublishing.com/childrens-books.html — **Website**

Children's Book Editor ———————————— **Contact**

Sterling Children's Books' list includes picture books, joke books, classics, novelty formats, and board books, as well as middle-grade and young adult fiction. Sterling is interested in reviewing submissions that fit these categories.

Profile of Publisher & Readership

Freelance Potential: Publishes 4 titles annually: 15% developed from unsolicited submissions; 15% by agented authors. Receives 100–150 unsolicited manuscripts monthly.

Number of Books Published and Freelance Statistics

Fiction: Toddler books, early picture books, early readers, story picture books. Genres: contemporary, fairy tales, fantasy, ghost stories, animal stories, myth.

Categories of Current Titles

Nonfiction: Toddler books, early picture books, early readers, middle-grade, YA. Topics include history, biography, early learning, animals, nature, science, holidays, seasons, crafts, activities, games.

Recent Titles to Study

Submissions and Payment: Guidelines and catalogue available on website. Send complete manuscript with author's biography, special qualifications in the subject area, and publishing history. Accepts hard copy. Accepts simultaneous submissions if identified. SASE. Response time varies. Publication in 1 year. Royalty; advance.

How to Submit

★ New Listing

🌐 Overseas Publisher

🍁 Canadian Publisher

🤝 Agented Submissions Only

🔒 Not Accepting Submissions

How to Use the Listings

One of the most essential—and we believe, useful—qualities of *Book Markets for Children's Writers 2021* is the division of publisher listings into sections: trade, classroom/educators, parents, regional, religious, and of interest. These listings number 622 in total, with 260 trade markets and 102 educational/classroom publishers. This edition also lists 87 literary agents and 45 contests and awards.

You can approach this book three ways:

(1) Use the alphabetical index beginning on page 388 to find a particular publisher, agent, or contest listing.

(2) Browse through a given section of the book to review the needs of the companies of most interest to you. (Maybe you want to write a religious picture book, for example, so you would begin with the religious section of the listings.)

(3) Go to the category index, page 349, and search out publishers in specific genres and categories.

We have reviewed and updated every listing in the book through research, and multiple rounds of surveys and fact-checking. Also included are cross-references among parent companies, their divisions, and imprints, to help you hone in on exactly the right place for your submissions. Note, however, that it is not uncommon for contact names, addresses, and editorial needs to change suddenly. After deciding to approach a company, agent, or contest you've found in *Book Markets for Children's Writers 2021*, follow the advice often given in the book: Check the publisher's website for updates to guidelines before submitting a query letter or manuscript.

To help you judge a publisher's receptivity to submissions, we include a Freelance Potential section in each listing. This is where you'll find the number of titles published yearly, and other figures available about unpublished writers, authors new to the publishing house, and agented authors. We also provide numbers of query letters and unsolicited manuscripts received.

Use this information and the other information included in the listing to locate publishers that are looking for the type of material you have written or plan to write. Become familiar with the style and content of the house by studying its catalogue and several recent titles.

Children's Trade Publishers

Trade publishers are the companies that most people think of when they think of books in general, and children's books in particular. Trade publishers sell their books primarily through bookstores or other profit-making businesses, and target the general consumer market. This is in contrast to classroom or educational publishers, who sell their books to the institutional market made up of schools and libraries.

The big companies with large lists and well-known titles, including many best-sellers, are usually trade publishers: Scholastic with *Hunger Games*, HarperCollins with *Fancy Nancy*, Abrams Books with the *Wimpy Kid* series. But small, *independent* publishers may be trade publishers as well, as long as they sell through the same consumer publishing channels.

The larger trade companies can be difficult to break into, and often work with agented writers primarily. But this is far from universal. Some big houses remain open to unsolicited submissions. Smaller publishers are often more open, but they can also be more limited in what they publish. Study the listings in this section to become more informed about the publishing industry in general, which is very important for a writer serious about selling a book. You will begin to learn about the extraordinary range of publishers, their needs, the styles of their books, their editorial perspectives—and where you might fit in. Every publisher wants to find a gem of a new writer.

Abbeville Family

655 Third Ave, Suite 2520, New York, NY 10017. www.abbeville.com

Editorial Director: Susan Costello

Abbeville has produced art, photography, and lifestyle books of the utmost quality, as well as several titles for children and parenting since its beginnings in 1977. It has long been a mainstay in the art book publishing world, and is currently making strides into the digital realm. The imprint also publishes parenting manuals and a variety of fun and educational books for kids. It is not accepting submissions at this time.

Freelance Potential: Publishes 10–12 titles annually: about 30% by authors who are new to the publishing house.

Fiction: Toddler books, early picture books, picture books, story picture books, middle-grade. Genres: multicultural, fairy tales, folklore, mystery.

Nonfiction: Concept books, board books, novelty books, toddler books, preschool, picture books, story picture books, middle-grade, YA. Topics: animals, the arts, counting, letters, dinosaurs, vehicles, families. Also publishes parenting books.

Submissions and Payment: Catalogue available on website. Not accepting queries or manuscripts at this time because its list is full for the next several seasons. Check the website for policy changes.

Abrams Appleseed

195 Broadway, 9th Floor, New York, NY 10007. www.abramsbooks.com/imprints/abramsappleseed

Publishing Director: Cecily Kaiser

Abrams Appleseed creates books that appeal to the youngest of readers by pairing the comfort of familiar objects with the introduction of something new or unexpected. Each book from this imprint of Abrams Publishing is artfully conceived and developmentally appropriate. Due to the large volume of manuscripts it receives, at this time Abrams Appleseed is only accepting submissions from literary agents.

Freelance Potential: Publishes approximately 20 books annually.

Fiction: Board books, novelty books, picture books.

Nonfiction: Board books, novelty books, picture books.

Submissions and Payment: Agented authors only. Responds to queries in 2–4 months, to manuscripts in 3–6 months. Publication period varies. Royalty; advance.

Abrams Books for Young Readers

195 Broadway, 9th Floor, New York, NY 10007. www.abramsbooks.com/abramskids/

Editor: Maggie Lerman

Publishing books of the highest quality for the preschool through middle grade audience is what this imprint from Abrams does. Abrams was the first company in the United States to specialize in publishing art and illustrated books. Its fellow imprints include Amulet Books, which focuses on middle-grade and YA, and Appleseed Books, which publishes books for infants to age five.

Freelance Potential: Publishes 50–75 titles annually: 100% by agented authors; 10–25% by authors who are new to the publishing house; 10–25% by previously unpublished writers. Receives 100 queries monthly.

Fiction: Early picture books, picture books, early readers, middle-grade. Genres: adventure, fantasy, contemporary, multicultural, historical, horror, humor, mystery, fairy tales, stories about nature and animals, graphic novels, poetry.

Nonfiction: Early picture books, picture books, early readers, middle-grade, YA. Topics: animals, the arts, biography, nature, science, holidays, activity books.

Submissions and Payment: Guidelines and catalogue available on website. Not accepting unsolicited fiction submissions (picture books or novels) at this time. For nonfiction picture books of up to 20 pages, send complete manuscript. For longer nonfiction, query with table of contents, sample chapter, and chapter-by-chapter synopsis. Include your biography with all submissions, indicating what makes you qualified to write the proposed book, and a list of competitive titles and what will distinguish your book.

AdventureKEEN

2204 1st Avenue South, Suite 102, Birmingham, AL 35233. www.AdventureWithKeen.com

Submissions Editor

Specializing in the nonfiction market, AdventureKEEN publishes books on a wide range of subjects including adventure, outdoors, travel, nature, local history, sports, and more. The company also advises potential writers to review its catalogue for existing series that could be expanded.

Freelance Potential: Unavailable.

Fiction: Story picture books, early readers, middle-grade, YA. Genres: adventure and mystery set in the great outdoors.

Nonfiction: PreK, picture books, early readers, middle-grade, YA. Topics: animals, birds, the outdoors, nature, wilderness skills and recreation.

Submissions and Payment: Catalogue available on website. Query with cover letter, sample chapter, and outline, or send complete manuscript. Also include target audience and author credentials. Accepts email submissions to submissions@adventurewithkeen.com (include "submission" in the subject line). Also accepts hard copy. Submissions not returned. Responds in 6 months. Publication period varies. Royalty.

Aladdin

Simon & Schuster Children's Publishing, 1230 Avenue of the Americas, New York, NY 10020. http://simonandschusterpublishing.com/aladdin/

Assistant Editor: Alyson Heller

Inspired by the dreams of its authors and readers, Aladdin publishes for a diverse community of readers with books that are enduring and culturally relevant. This imprint from Simon & Schuster has something for everyone. It prides itself on building worlds that kids won't want to leave and establishing characters that feel like old friends. Aladdin accepts submissions from agents only.

Freelance Potential: Publishes 100 titles annually: 100% by agented authors.

Fiction: Early readers, story picture books, chapter books, middle-grade. Genres: contemporary, historical, suspense, mystery, fantasy, adventure, graphic novels.

Nonfiction: Picture books, middle-grade. Topics: America's national monuments, natural wonders, biographies of world figures, humor.

Submissions and Payment: Catalogue available on website. Agented authors only. Offers some work-for-hire assignments on certain series. Response time, publication period, and payment policy vary.

Allison & Busby

11 Wardour Mews, London W1F 8AN England. www.allisonandbusby.com

Editor

The goal of this publisher is to offer a little something for everyone. Since 1969, Allison & Busby have been publishing high-quality books from outstanding writers. Featuring a wide range of genres including women's fiction, YA, historical fiction, contemporary fiction, and fantasy, Allison & Busby accepts submissions from agents only.

Freelance Potential: Publishes 35+ titles each year: 100% by agented authors.

Fiction: YA, adult. Genres: Fantasy, historical fiction, literary fiction, mystery, science fiction.

Nonfiction: YA, adult. Topics: Writing guides, military, history, biographies, memoirs, travel guides, cookbooks.

Submissions and Payment: Catalogue available on website. Accepts submissions from agented authors only. Responds in 6 months if interested. Materials are not returned. Publication in 12–24 months. Payment policy varies.

Alma Little

8362 Tamarack Village, Suite 119-106, St. Paul, MN 55125. http://www.elvaresa.com/almalittle.html

Acquisitions: Elizabeth Snow

Alma Little's mission is to bring children a diverse world of possibilities, opportunities, and wonder. It publishes beautiful, meaningful children's books and donates a portion of all book sales to charity. It is the children's imprint of Elva Resa.

Freelance Potential: Publishes about 5 titles annually: 10–25% developed from unsolicited submissions; 75–100% assigned; 25–50% by authors who are new to the publishing house; 10–25% by previously unpublished writers. Receives 100–150 queries, 15+ manuscripts monthly.

Fiction: Story picture books, chapter books, middle-grade. Genres: contemporary, historical, inspirational.

Nonfiction: Chapter books, middle-grade. Topics: self-help, current events, activities, biography, politics, inspirational, real life/problems, religious, reference, parenting, military life.

Submissions and Payment: Guidelines and catalogue available on website. Accepts submissions on a call-for-manuscripts basis only; check website for updates. Query with outline. Accepts email queries (Word or PDF attachments) to submissions@elvaresa.com. Accepts queries for work-for-hire assignments. Responds in 3–6 weeks. Publication in 12–24 months. Royalty; advance. Flat fee.

Amberjack Publishing

P.O. Box 1667, Eagle, ID 83616. www.amberjackpublishing.com

Acquisitions

Amberjack Publishing is committed to sharing award-winning fiction that moves readers. According to Amberjack Publishing they publish stories that "promise the joy of discovery and the celebration of flawed characters who help readers connect to humanity." This small publishing house offers middle-grade, young adult, literary, and commercial fiction. It also looks to promote female authors of narrative nonfiction and memoirs. At this time Amberjack is closed to submissions to catch up on backlog. Check the website for changes to this policy.

Freelance Potential: Publishes 20–24 titles annually.

Fiction: Middle-grade, YA. Genres: fantasy, contemporary, science fiction, humor, horror.

Nonfiction: YA. Topics: memoir, social issues, health.

Submissions and Payment: Guidelines and catalogue available on website. At this time Amberjack is closed to submissions. Response time, publication period, and payment policy vary.

Amistad Press

10 E. 53rd St., New York, NY 10022. www.harpercollins.com

Editorial Director: Tracy Sherrod

Multicultural fiction and nonfiction are the mainstays of this publisher. This renowned imprint showcases award-winning novelists, celebrated cultural figures, and esteemed critics and scholars. This African-American imprint from HarperCollins is the oldest publisher devoted to multicultural voice. Amistad only accepts submissions through literary agents.

Freelance Potential: Publishes about 20 titles annually.

Fiction: Picture books, chapter books, middle-grade. Genres: multicultural, historical, contemporary, social issues.

Nonfiction: Picture books, chapter books, middle-grade. Topics: biography, history, sports, social issues.

Submissions and Payment: Guidelines and catalogue available on website. Accepts submissions through literary agents only. Publication in 18–36 months. Royalty; advance.

AMP! Comics for Kids

1130 Walnut Street, Kansas City, MO 64106. www.ampkids.com

Book Submissions

AMP! Comics for Kids is the graphic novel imprint from Andrews McMeel that targets middle-grade readers. This imprint encourages reading by publishing high quality graphic novels. The line began with a combination of original work and material adapted from already published titles. New titles include digital versions of its titles with interactive elements.

Freelance Potential: Publishes about 5 titles annually. Andrews McMeel publishes about 250 titles each year.

Fiction: Middle-grade. Genre: comics.

Submissions and Payment: Guidelines and catalogue available on website. Query with cover letter describing manuscript, target audience, and why AMP! is the best publisher for it, 1 or 2 sample chapters, brief author bio, and completion schedule for the manuscript. Prefers hard copy. SASE. Responds if interested. Publication period and payment policy vary.

Amphorae Publishing Group

4168 Hartford St., St. Louis, MO 63116. www.amphoraepublishing.com

Acquisitions: Laura Robinson

Established in 2014, Amphorae Publishing offers titles that are passionate, progressive, inclusive, empowering, and experimental. Amphorae Publishing Group is a woman- and veteran-owned business with a focus on good, well told stories that make readers think. The company is made up of three divisions: Blank Slate Press, which offers historical fiction, mystery, and contemporary fiction; Walrus Publishing, which offers science fiction, fantasy, romance, and humor; and its children's imprint, Treehouse Publishing Group.

Freelance Potential: Publishes 25+ titles annually.

Fiction: Early picture books, early readers, story picture books, middle-grade, YA. Genres: historical, contemporary, multicultural, fantasy, science fiction, steampunk.

Nonfiction: Story picture books, middle-grade, YA. Topics: history, social studies, and social skills.

Submissions and Payment: Catalogue and guidelines available on website. Query or send complete manuscript. Accepts agented submissions only through email to acquisitions@amphoraepublishing.com. Responds in 10–12 weeks. Publication period and payment policy varies.

Amulet Books

115 West 18th Street, 6th Floor, New York, NY 10011. www.amuletbooks.com

Editor: Erica Finkel

Amulet Books publishes novels, graphic novels, and nonfiction for young adults and middle-grade readers from a stellar roster of authors. This division of Abrams Books accepts submissions from agents only.

Freelance Potential: Publishes 150 titles annually: 100% by agented authors; 10–25% by authors who are new to the publishing house; 10–25% by previously unpublished writers.

Fiction: Chapter books, middle-grade, YA. Genres: contemporary, historical, science fiction, fantasy, suspense, mystery, humor, graphic novels, poetry.

Nonfiction: Middle-grade, YA. Topics: art, multicultural, ethnic, history, natural history, the environment, nature, self-help.

Submissions and Payment: Guidelines and catalogue available on website. Only accepts submissions from agents at this time. Publication period varies. Royalty; advance.

Andersen Press

20 Vauxhall Bridge Road, London SW1V 2SA United Kingdom. www.andersenpress.co.uk

Picture Book Submissions Editor, Fiction Submissions Editor

Founded in 1976, Andersen Press publishes some of the most well known and best loved names in the world of children's books. It is a specialist in award-winning children's titles including picture books, juvenile fiction, and older fiction. Andersen Press is actively looking for juvenile fiction submissions.

Freelance Potential: Publishes about 90 titles annually: 10% by agented authors. Receives 100 unsolicited manuscripts monthly.

Fiction: Early picture books, early readers, story picture books, chapter books, middle-grade, YA. Genres: historical, contemporary, humor, adventure, fantasy, folktales, horror, mystery, suspense, romance, animals, sports.

Submissions and Payment: Guidelines and catalogue available on website. Query with synopsis and 3 sample chapters. Send complete manuscript for picture books only (500–1,000 words). Accepts hard copy. Label envelope with Picture Book Submission Department or Fiction Submissions Department. SASE. Responds in 2 months. Publication period and payment policy vary.

Andrews McMeel Publishing

1130 Walnut Street, Kansas City, MO 64106. http://publishing.andrewsmcmeel.com

Submissions Editor

Andrews McMeel Publishing (AMP) offers an individualized, flexible approach to publishing success by respecting the author's vision as the primary source of inspiration. It is passionate about discovering authors and creators who have a distinct point of view. It is a leading publisher of humor, inspiration, poetry, and middle-grade children's books. They are always looking for new ideas and authors for books and calendars. This publisher considers work from both agented and unagented authors.

Freelance Potential: Publishes 20 titles annually. Receives 10+ unsolicited manuscripts monthly.

Fiction: Middle-grade. Genres: contemporary, multicultural, animal and family stories, humor.

Nonfiction: Middle-grade. Topics: animals, concepts, families, toys, holidays, real life issues.

Submissions and Payment: Catalogue available on website. Send 1–2 sample chapters, cover letter, outline, and author bio. Prefers email to booksubmissions@amuniversal.com. Will accept hard copy. Responds in 90 days. Publication period and payment policy vary.

Annick Press

15 Patricia Avenue, Toronto, Ontario M2M 1H9 Canada. www.annickpress.com

Editor: Katie Hearn

Annick Press is committed to publishing diverse authors and illustrators and believes strongly in publishing content that reflects its readers' own experiences while broadening their perspectives. It publishes books for toddlers through young adults. It is recognized as one of the most innovative and cutting-edge publishers of fiction and nonfiction for children and young adults. The publisher strives to create educational, entertaining books that will spark a lifelong love affair with the written word. At this time, Annick Press is open to submissions in teen and middle-grade fiction, picture books, and nonfiction. Check the website for updates to this policy.

Freelance Potential: Publishes 28 titles annually: 50% by authors who are new to the publishing house; 30% by previously unpublished writers. Receives 350 queries monthly.

Fiction: Picture books, middle-grade, YA. Genres: contemporary, fantasy, humor.

Nonfiction: Middle-grade, YA. Topics: culture, history, science, biography, pop culture, contemporary issues.

Submissions and Payment: Canadian authors only. Guidelines and catalogue available on website. Query with synopsis and sample chapter. Accepts hard copy and email to submissions@annickpress.com. Response time, publication period, and payment policy vary.

Arbordale Publishing

612 Johnnie Dodds., Suite A2, Mount Pleasant, SC 29464. www.arbordalepublishing.com

Associate Editor: Katie Hall

Arbordale Publishing's mission is to get children excited about science and math through fun-to-read picture book stories. They are looking for fiction or narrative nonfiction stories with science or math woven into the story. It publishes hardcover, paperback, and electronic books. Its titles are used to promote oral language skills, vocabulary, and reading comprehension. It is not seeking books about counting, ABCs, fairytales, fantasy, or YA titles. Arbordale's picture books are designed from the ground up to introduce young children to science and math. Fictional stories have facts scattered in the text or the nonfiction stories have "cuddle factors" so parents can read to children snuggled in their laps. Each book then includes 2–6 pages of its signature "For Creative Minds" nonfiction information presented in engaging activities for adults to help the children learn more about the underlying subject in the story. All books are translated into Spanish. It publishes hardcover, paperback, Spanish paperbacks, and dual-language digital books. See submission guidelines for their current interests.

Freelance Potential: Publishes approximately up to 14 books annually.

Fiction: Picture books, no more than 1,000 words. Genres: science, animals, folktales, nature/environment, math-related.

Submissions and Payment: Catalogue and guidelines available on website. Accepts email submissions to submissions@arbordalepublishing.com. Include a 300–400 word biography, and how you envision the marketing of the book. Include bibliography to indicate research for underlying science or math within story (even fiction). Response time and publication period varies. Royalty; advance.

Archipelago Books

232 Third Street #A111, Brooklyn, NY 11215. www.archipelagobooks.org

Archipelago is always striving to find visionary international writers whom American readers might not otherwise encounter. It is devoted to publishing high-quality translations of classic and contemporary world literature. Its list includes more than 120 titles in more than 30 languages. It recently launched its children's imprint Elsewhere Editions.

Freelance Potential: Publishes 8–10 titles yearly.

Fiction: Middle-grade, YA. Genres: mystery, adventure, historical fiction, folktales.

Submissions and Payment: Catalogue available on website. Query. Accepts email queries to info@archipelagobooks.org. Response time varies. Payment rates and policies vary.

Atheneum Books for Young Readers

Simon & Schuster Children's Publishing, 1230 Avenue of the Americas, New York, NY 10020. http://imprints.simonandschuster.biz/atheneum

Editorial Director: Caitlyn Dlouhy
Editor: Juston Chanda

Atheneum Books is committed to publishing commercial books with outstanding literary merit. Known for publishing enduring literary middle-grade, teen, and picture book titles, it offers hardcover and paperback books for children and teens. It is known for its literary picture books and award-winning middle-grade and teen fiction, as well as a selection of graphic novels, nonfiction, and poetry. Simon & Schuster accepts agented manuscripts only.

Freelance Potential: Publishes 50–75 titles annually: most are by agented authors; some are by previously unpublished writers. Receives 2,500 queries monthly.

Fiction: Concept books, toddler books, early picture books, story picture books, chapter books, middle-grade, YA. Genres: fantasy, mystery, adventure, fairy tales, historical, graphic novels.

Nonfiction: Story picture books, chapter books, middle-grade, YA. Topics: adventure, biography, the environment, science, nature, sports, history, multicultural issues.

Submissions and Payment: Catalogue available on website. Guidelines available. Accepts agented manuscripts only. Publication period varies. Royalty.

August House

3500 Piedmont Road NE, Suite 310, Atlanta, GA 30305. www.augusthouse.com

Editorial Department

August House focuses on world folktales, stories from the oral tradition, stories from diverse cultures, and scary stories, as well as resource books relating to storytelling or using stories in the classroom. For over 30 years, August House has curated a highly acclaimed, award-winning selection of picture books, story collections, and resource books from the word's greatest oral traditions.

Freelance Potential: Publishes 4–6 titles annually.

Fiction: Picture books, story picture books, early readers, middle-grade. Genres: folktales, animal fables, multicultural, social issues, ethics.

Submissions and Payment: Guidelines and catalogue available on website. Query or send manuscript with author biography and publishing history. For multi-chapter or multi-story books, send query or proposal with sample chapters (at least 40 pages) rather than complete manuscript; descriptive outline or table of contents; estimate of final manuscript pages or word count; and completion date. Give sources for folktales. Accepts hard copy only. Accepts simultaneous submissions. SASE for manuscript receipt. Responds in 5 months if interested. Publication period and payment policy vary.

Baen Books

P.O. Box 1188, Wake Forest, NC 27588. www.baen.com

Editor: Toni Weisskop

Baen Books publishes science fiction and fantasy only. It is looking for science fiction submissions with powerful plots and solid scientific and philosophical underpinnings and fantasy books with a magical system that is both rigorously coherent and integral to the plot. While many of its adult titles would be of interest to YA readers, it has recently started publishing titles specifically for young adults. Although it is an independent press, Baen's titles have long been distributed by Simon & Schuster.

Freelance Potential: Publishes 36–48 titles annually; publishes 2 to 3 new authors annually.

Fiction: YA and adult. Genres: fantasy, historical, hard science fiction, military science fiction, space opera, urban fantasy.

Submissions and Payment: Guidelines and catalogue available on website. Prefers mss between 100,000–130,00 words. Send complete manuscript. Prefers electronic submissions using submission form at http://baen.com/slush/index/submit No email submissions. Accepts hard copy. Responds in 9–12 months. Publication period and payment policy vary.

Bailiwick Publishing

309 East Mulberry Street, Fort Collins, Colorado 80524. www.bailiwickpress.com

Submissions

Bailiwick wants kids to love reading. It is an innovative micropress that creates books and other products that inspire and tell great stories. It believes all forms of reading are essential. It strives to provide children with the cognitive challenge they need to construct meaning from fully developed stories. Bailiwick's books for kids inform, inspire, and delight.

Freelance Potential: Publishes several books annually.

Fiction: Picture book, board books, early readers, chapter books, middle-grade, YA. Genres: comic novels, animals.

Nonfiction: Picture books, early readers, middle-grade, YA. Topics: concept books.

Submissions and Payment: Catalogue and guidelines available on website. Accepts submissions through the website only. Response time and publication period vary. Payment policy varies.

Bala Kids

https://www.shambhala.com/childrens-books/

Editor

Bala Kids is the new children's imprint from Shambhala Publications that draws on the Buddhist principles of compassion, empathy, and mindfulness. It is dedicated to publishing books that inspire and teach the values of compassion and wisdom to young readers. This imprint features titles for children ages birth through eight.

Freelance Potential: Plans to publish 4–6 titles annually.

Fiction: Toddler books, early picture books, picture books, story picture books. Genres: multicultural, fairy tales, folklore, mystery.

Nonfiction: Concept books, board books, toddler books, preschool, picture books, story picture books. Topics: mindfulness, Buddhism, meditation, and yoga.

Submissions and Payment: Catalogue available on website. Send complete manuscript with cover letter, author bio, and summary. Accepts email submissions to balakids@shambhala.com; include Bala Kids Submission in the subject line. Response time varies. Payment policy varies.

Balzer & Bray

HarperCollins Children's Books, 10 E. 53rd St., New York, NY 10022. http://www.harpercollinschildrens.com/Home/ChildrensImprints.aspx

Co-Publishers: Alessandra Balzer, Donna Bray

Bold, creative, groundbreaking picture books and novels that appeal to kids in a fresh way are what this imprint from HarperCollins specializes in. It allows authors to have the freedom to take risks and fulfill their unique visions. Balzer & Bray accepts submissions from agents only.

Freelance Potential: Publishes 25 titles annually; 100% by agented authors.

Fiction: Picture books, chapter books, middle-grade, YA. Genres: adventure, contemporary, historical, multicultural, mystery/suspense, nature, science fiction, fantasy, sports.

Nonfiction: Picture books, chapter books, middle-grade, YA. Topics: biography, history, the arts, nature, multicultural.

Submissions and Payment: Agented submissions only. Publication in 18 months. Royalty; advance.

Bancroft Press

P.O. Box 65360, Baltimore, MD 21209-9945. www.bancroftpress.com

Editor: Bruce Bortz

Bancroft Press publishes books in virtually every genre. If you have the ability to tell a good story that enlightens the reader, Bancroft Press will consider it. It prides itself as being a small publishing company without a niche. It looks for fiction and nonfiction titles that connect with readers and encourage a love of reading.

Freelance Potential: Publishes 4–6 titles annually: 50% by authors new to the publishing house; 30% by previously unpublished writers. Receives 170 queries, 800 unsolicited manuscripts monthly.

Fiction: Middle-grade, YA. Genres: mystery, history, sports, contemporary, multicultural.

Nonfiction: YA. Topics: sports, biography. Also publishes parenting and self-help books for adults.

Submissions and Payment: Guidelines and catalogue available on website. Query with résumé and 4–5 sample chapters; or send complete manuscript with cover letter, market analysis, and résumé to bruceb@bancroftpress.com. Responds in 6 months. Publication period varies. Royalty; advance.

Beach Lane Books

http://imprints.simonandschuster.biz/beach-lane-books

Editor: Andrea Welch

Beach Lane Books publishes books for all ages and across all genres, with a primary focus on lyrical, emotionally engaging, highly visual picture books for young children. Founded in 2008, this imprint from Simon & Schuster only accepts submissions from literary agents.

Freelance Potential: Publishes about 20 books annually.

Fiction: Board books, novelty books, picture books, early readers, middle-grade. Genres: animals, adventure, fairy tales, multicultural.

Nonfiction: Board books, novelty books, picture books, early readers, middle-grade. Topics: animals, dinosaurs, concepts, multicultural.

Submissions and Payment: Catalogue available on website. Simon & Schuster imprints accept agented submissions only. Publication period and payment vary.

Bebop Books

95 Madison Avenue, Suite 1205, New York, NY 10016. www.leeandlow.com

Submissions Editor

This imprint from Lee & Low Books offers books in English and Spanish that support literacy learning content for beginning readers in guided reading and intervention settings—all with the same commitment to diversity and cultural authenticity that sets all Lee & Low Books apart. Bebop Books are carefully leveled texts that appeal to children's interests and provide the supports they need as they face challenges in their development as readers. Appealing texts and pictures by outstanding authors and illustrators of diverse backgrounds engage young readers and support their efforts as they begin their journey to become successful, independent readers. Check the website for details and updates of current needs.

Freelance Potential: Publishes about a dozen titles annually: 15–25% developed from unsolicited submissions; 15% by agented authors; about 40% by authors who are new to the publishing house; 25% by previously unpublished writers. Receives approximately 85 unsolicited manuscripts monthly.

Fiction: Story picture books, chapter books. Genres: realistic, historical, contemporary, multicultural, ethnic.

Nonfiction: Story picture books. Topics: multicultural and ethnic issues and traditions, biography.

Submissions and Payment: Guidelines and catalogue available on website. Send complete manuscript. Early readers may be between 100 and 2500 words, depending on reading level. Chapter books are between 4,000 and 13,000 words, again depending on reading level. For longer work, send a query with story synopsis, chapter outline, and first 3 chapters. Include cover letter with brief author biography and publishing history; note whether manuscript is an exclusive or simultaneous submission. Accepts hard copy. Responds in 6 months if interested. Materials not returned. Publication in 2–3 years. Advance against royalty.

Bell Bridge Books

P.O. Box 300921, Memphis, TN 38130. www.bellebooks.com

Acquiring Editor: Debra Dixon

Bell Bridge Books is known for nurturing emerging fiction voices as well as being the "second home" for many established authors who continue to publish with major publishing conglomerates. Some of its notable authors include Sharon Sala, Anne Bishop, and Cheryl Reavis. Its list features books for children and young adults, as well as titles for adults. It is currently not accepting submissions. Check the website for updates to this policy.

Freelance Potential: Publishes 60–70 titles annually.

Fiction: Middle-grade, YA. Genres: mystery, suspense, horror, fantasy, science fiction, humor, urban fantasy.

Submissions and Payment: Guidelines and catalogue available on website. Not currently accepting middle-grade submissions. Query with full ms, brief synopsis and writer's credentials. See website for specific editor needs and requirements. Accepts email only to queries@bellebooks.com. Responds in 1–3 months, publication period 12+ months. Royalty; advance.

Bellerophon Books

P.O. Box 21307, Santa Barbara, CA 93121. www.bellerophonbooks.com

Editor

Bellerophon Books specializes in books that are interactive and provide an alternative learning resource for children and adults. It publishes low-cost educational books with a focus on history, art, and more. Children from around the world have grown up with the books from this publisher. Its titles are visually appealing and entertaining. It also offers many coloring books with historical themes.

Freelance Potential: Publishes several titles annually.

Nonfiction: Story picture books, middle-grade, YA. Topics: animals, history, nature, science, music, nautical, air and space.

Submissions and Payment: Catalogue available on website. Query. Accepts queries through the website only. Responds if interested. Publication period and payment policies vary.

Beyond Words

20827 NW Cornell Rd, Suite 500, Hillsboro, OR 97124. www.beyondword.com

Acquisitions Editor

Beyond Words is always looking for new authors to become part of its family. It aims to inspire by anticipating trends in the evolution of consciousness and the intersection of science and spirituality. It has a mission of partnering with authors and filmmakers to help produce and disseminate information that can help make a difference in people's lives. One of its core values is to create miracles. It publishes and distributes books at the convergence of science and spirituality. It offers titles for children, young adults, and adults.

Freelance Potential: Publishes 10–15 titles annually.

Nonfiction: Early readers, middle-grade, YA. Topics: spirituality, health, science, history.

Submissions and Payment: Guidelines and catalogue available on website. Accepts electronic submissions through email to Michele@beyondword.com. Responds in 3–4 weeks. Publication period varies. Royalty. Flat fee.

Big Picture Press

99 Dover Street, Somerville, MA 02144. www.candlewick.com

Editorial Director: Liz Bicknell

Big Picture Press's mission is to create and publish the very best stories for children and young readers on the market. It creates highly illustrated books for the incurably curious. It is an imprint of Candlewick Press. It reviews work from agents or through conference appearances where editors meet authors. Check the website for changes to this policy.

Freelance Potential: Parent company Candlewick publishes 200 titles annually: almost all by agented authors; 1–10% by authors who are new to the publishing house; 1–10% by previously unpublished writers. Receives about 500 queries monthly.

Fiction: Toddler books, early picture books, early readers, picture books. Genres: multicultural, fantasy, adventure, mystery, humor, poetry.

Nonfiction: Concept books, early picture books, story picture books. Topics: history, nature, science, the environment, geography, biography, music, visual arts, and activity books.

Submissions and Payment: Agented authors only. Catalogue available on website. Response time, publication period, and payment policy vary.

Black Bed Sheet Books

7865 Valley Quail Ct., Antelope, CA 95843. www.downwarden.com; https://blackbedsheetbooks.com/

Acquisitions

Black Bed Sheet Books offers titles for children, young adults, and adults. It specializes in fiction, especially dark fiction, fantasy, and thrillers. Its titles appear both in print and online.

Freelance Potential: Publishes 10–20 titles annually.

Fiction: Middle-grade, YA. Genres: Mystery, fantasy, dark fiction.

Submissions and Payment: Catalogue and guidelines available on website. Query with brief synopsis of manuscript and author publishing credits (if any). Accepts email submissions to BBSAdmin@ downwarden.com. Responds if interested. Publication period and payment policies vary.

Blink

5300 Patterson Ave SE, Grand Rapids, MI 49530. http://blinkyabooks.com

Editor

Blink is home to some of the most engrossing teen publishing anywhere. Readers will see themselves in all facets of Blink's literature and will find new levels of entertainment that enrich and uplift. The literature published by Blink is a positive reflection of what is inspiring and heartening. Bringing true stories and fiction to young adult readers is what Blink does. Blink publishes clean young adult fiction and nonfiction.

Freelance Potential: Publishes 5–6 titles annually.

Fiction: YA. Genres: social issues, contemporary, mystery, fantasy, dystopian, paranormal.

Submissions and Payment: Guidelines and catalogue available on website. Agented submissions only. Manuscripts may also be uploaded on HarperCollins' writing community site, Authonomy.com, for consideration. Publication period and payment policy, unknown.

Bloomsbury Children's Books USA

1385 Broadway, New York, NY 10018. www.bloomsburyusa.com, www.bloomsburykids.com

Submissions Editor

Established in 1986, Bloomsbury USA has four divisions: Bloomsbury Academic and Professional, Bloomsbury Information, Bloomsbury Adult Publishing, and Bloomsbury Children's Publishing. Bloomsbury Children's Books publishes books for readers of all ages. It also publishes an extensive list of education books. This publishers accepts submissions from agents only.

Freelance Potential: Publishes about 75 titles annually: all by agented authors; 1–10% by previously unpublished writers. Receives 300 queries monthly.

Fiction: Concept books, toddler books, early picture books, early readers, story picture books, chapter books, middle-grade, YA. Genres: adventure, fantasy, mystery, contemporary, science fiction, multicultural.

Nonfiction: Early picture books, middle-grade, YA. Topics: multicultural, ethnic, biography.

Submissions and Payment: Guidelines and catalogue available on website. Accepts agented submissions only. Responds in 6 months if interested. Publication period varies. Royalty; advance.

Blue Apple Books

515 Valley Street, Suite 180, Maplewood, NJ 07040. www.blueapplebooks.com

Submissions

Blue Apple Books has published hundreds of books since its beginning in 2003. It publishes board books, picture books, activity books, and more for babies through age 14. The Publisher is Harriet Ziefert. Its books are distributed by Consortium.

Freelance Potential: Publishes about 50 titles annually: most from agented authors. Receives 300+ unsolicited manuscripts monthly.

Fiction: Board books, picture books, concept books, early readers. Genres: social skills, education, animals, family.

Nonfiction: Board books, picture books, concept books, early readers. Topics: numbers, colors, letters, language arts.

Submissions and Payment: Catalogue available on website. Accepts submissions from agents only. Response time, publication period, and payment policy vary.

Blue Dot Kids Press ★

www.bluedotkids.press.com

Submissions Editor

Blue Dot Kids Press publishes stories that connect us to each other and to the Earth. The company hopes to empower the next generation of global citizens with empathy, resilience, creativity, and the shared value of nature and its stewardship. It publishes fiction and narrative nonfiction for children ages three to eight and board books for ages zero to three.

Freelance Potential: Publishes 10 titles each year.

Fiction: Picture books, board books, early readers, story picture books. Genres: social issues, realistic fiction, nature.

Nonfiction: Story picture books, board books, picture books, early readers. Topics: STEAM, science, crafts, conservation, emotional intelligence, and creative problem solving.

Submissions and Payment: Catalogue and guidelines available on the website. Accepts complete manuscripts by email only to hello@BlueDotKidsPress.com. Does not accept queries. Include the title in the subject line. Include a summary, author bio, and contact information. Manuscripts must be in Word of PDF format. Response time varies. Payment policies vary.

Blue Sky Press

Scholastic, 557 Broadway, New York, NY 10012-3999. www.scholastic.com

Editorial Director

This imprint at Scholastic produces a wide variety of children's fiction and nonfiction with the goal of inspiring students and cultivating their minds. It aims to both challenge and entertain its readers. It features titles for children of all ages, from birth to YA. Products are designed to help enhance readers' understanding of the world around them. Among its best-selling titles are No, David books by Dav Pilkey.

Freelance Potential: Parent company Scholastic publishes more than 600 titles a year: all by agented authors.

Fiction: Toddler books, early picture books, easy readers, story picture books, chapter books, middle-grade, YA. Genres: historical, contemporary, multicultural, folklore, fairy tales, fantasy, humor, adventure.

Nonfiction: Story picture books, middle-grade. Topics: nature, environment, history.

Submissions and Payment: Agented authors only. Response time and publication period vary. Royalty.

Blue Swan Publishing

10509 Sedgegrass Dr., Indianapolis, IN 46235. www.blueswanpublishing.com

Acquisitions

Blue Swan is actively seeking sweet, traditional romance with strong, irresistible characters for the young adult market. It is an imprint of Ten West Publishing that publishes inspirational stories in a variety of genres. It prefers manuscripts with sweet themes; think Little House on the Prairie. This can include romance, mystery, science fiction, and fantasy.

Freelance Potential: Publishes about 10 titles yearly: most are developed from unsolicited submissions.

Fiction: YA. Genres: Inspirational, real life problems, fantasy, science fiction.

Submissions and Payment: Guidelines and catalogue available on website. Send complete manuscript with synopsis. Accepts email to submissions@blueswanpublishing.com (Word or RTF files). Accepts simultaneous submissions if identified. Responds in 3–4 months. Publication period varies. 40% royalty on sales.

Bold Strokes Books

648 S. Cambridge Rd, Bldg A, Johnsonville, NY 12094. www.boldstrokesbooks.com

Selections Director: Len Barot

Bold Strokes Books aims to aid excellent authors in honing their skills in an environment of mutual respect. Since its inception in 2004, their mission has remained unchanged: to bring quality queer fiction to readers worldwide and to support committed authors in developing their craft and reaching an ever-growing community of readers via print, digital, and audio formats. Its titles promote quality and diversity in LGBTQ literature. All trade fiction genres are accepted.

Freelance Potential: Publishes 120 titles annually.

Fiction: All trade fiction genres (45,000–120,000 words).

Submissions and Payment: Catalogue and guidelines available at www.boldstrokesbooks.com. Accepts unagented submissions. Does not accept simultaneous submissions. Send complete manuscript. Only accepts submissions by email to submissions@boldstrokesbooks.com (Word or RTF files). Include a one-page synopsis, author bio, working title, and category or genre. Responds in 16 weeks. Publication period and payment policy vary.

Bookouture

www.bookouture.com

Acquisitions

This digital publisher connects stories and readers globally. It is looking for entertaining fiction with a distinctive voice. It looks for unique and creative storytelling that stands out from the crowd. It is very open to working with unagented authors. Everyone is considered on a level playing field at Bookouture. They are especially interested in young adult, fantasy, and dystopian titles.

Freelance Potential: Publishes about 150 titles yearly: most are developed from unsolicited submissions.

Fiction: YA; Genres: Inspirational, real life problems, fantasy, science fiction, romance, thriller, women's fiction, contemporary, and paranormal romance.

Submissions and Payment: Guidelines and catalogue available on website. Send complete manuscript with synopsis. Accepts submissions through the website. Responds in 2 months. Publication period varies. 45% royalty of net receipts on all digital sales in e-book and audio, and 7.5% of net receipts for print-on-demand (POD) paperback sales.

Boyds Mills & Kane

300 Park Ave., New York, NY 10022. https://boydsmillsandkane.com

Submissions Editor

Exceptionally crafted titles designed to entertain, inform, and engage children of all ages is what this publisher looks for. With its May 2019 acquisition of the trade book division of Highlights for Children, Kane Press officially changed its name to Boyds Mills & Kane. In addition to its Kane Press titles, it will now publish under the imprints of Boyds Mills Press, Calkins Creek, and WordSong. The company's new trade imprint, StarBerry Books, focuses on diverse, imaginative stories with bright, colorful illustrations. StarBerry titles aim to encourage children's natural curiosity, inquisitiveness, and sense of adventure, and to let their imaginations soar through the joy of reading. Excellent writing and the ability to stand out in the market will get this publisher to notice you.

Freelance Potential: Publishes 15+ titles annually.

Fiction: Story picture books, early readers, chapter books; primary series.

Nonfiction: Narrative story books, picture book biographies, early readers. Genres: contemporary, historical, multicultural, mystery, social skills, math, literature, science, social studies, animal stories.

Submissions and Payment: Boyds Mills & Kane books are written for children ages 2–11. It is actively seeking submissions for the StarBerry trade imprint. Books in the Kane Press educational line are series-based, with an educational underpinning. While the educational line is not currently seeking submissions for titles in ongoing series, editors are open to discussing ideas for new series. Due to the volume of submissions received, this publisher responds only to manuscripts of interest. If you have not heard back after three months, you may assume your project is not the right fit. All manuscripts should be submitted by email: submissions@bmkbooks.com.

Boyds Mills Press

300 Park Ave., New York, NY 10022. www.boydsmillspress.com

Executive Editor: Elizabeth Van Doren

Now an imprint of Boyds MIlls & Kane, Boyds Mills Press publishes a wide range of high-quality fiction and nonfiction titles for picture book, middle grade, and young adult audiences. They are actively seeking submissions.

Freelance Potential: Publishes 25 titles annually. Receives about 85 queries monthly.

Fiction: Story picture books, middle-grade, YA. Genres: adventure, contemporary, historical, multicultural, humor, seasonal, folktales, humor.

Nonfiction: Concept books, early picture books, early readers, story picture books, chapter books, middle-grade. Topics: history, science, nature, crafts, activities, reference.

Submissions and Payment: Catalogue and guidelines available on website. For middle-grade and YA fiction, query with first 3 chapters and plot summary. Send complete manuscript for picture books and poetry books only. Nonfiction should have a strong narrative quality. For nonfiction, send the manuscript, a detailed bibliography, an expert's review of the manuscript, and a detailed explanation of competitive titles. Send cover letter with all submissions. Accepts hard copy. SASE. Responds in 3 months. Publication in 2-3 years. Royalty; advance.

Buster Books 🌐

Michael O'Mara Books, 16 Lion Yard, Tremadoc Road, London SW4 7NQ United Kingdom. www.mombooks.com/buster

Managing Director: Lesley O'Mara
Publisher: Philippa Wingate

Brimming with titles that spark imagination, Buster Books loves to create books for curious and creative children. Its list encourages exploration with books that will satisfy the keenest of puzzle masters, budding artists, and the deepest of thinkers.

Freelance Potential: Publishes 60–70 titles annually.

Fiction: Picture books, middle-grade, YA. Genres: commercial, fantasy, contemporary.

Nonfiction: Activity, puzzle, and reference books for ages 5–12. Topics: art, doodling, drawing, science, geography.

Submissions and Payment: Guidelines and catalogue available on the website. Accepts hard copy and email to buster.submissions@mombooks.com. Responds if interested. Publication period and payment policy vary.

Calkins Creek Books

300 Park Ave., New York, NY 10022. https://boydsmillsandkane.com

Manuscript Submissions

Calkins Creek titles present multiple points of view through original and extensive research. It publishes both nonfiction and historical fiction that introduces children to the many people, places, and events that have shaped US history. Each of its books uses primary sources, such as timelines, bibliographies, and historical notes.

Freelance Potential: Publishes about 7 titles annually. Receives 4 unsolicited manuscripts monthly.

Fiction: Story picture books, chapter books, middle-grade, YA. Genres: historical.

Nonfiction: Story picture books, chapter books, middle-grade, YA. Topics: US history.

Submissions and Payment: Catalogue and guidelines available on website. Query or send complete manuscript with cover letter, and detailed bibliography for historical fiction and nonfiction. Accepts hard copy. SASE. Responds in 3 months. Publication period varies. Royalty.

Candlewick Press

99 Dover Street, Somerville, MA 02144. www.candlewick.com

Editorial Director: Liz Bicknell

Candlewick Press has one simple aspiration: creating and publishing the very best stories for children and young readers on the market. With a reputation for high-quality nonfiction and fiction, this independent publisher produces books for all ages. It publishes board books, e-books, and cutting edge fiction. Candlewick Press reviews work from agents or through conference appearances where editors meet authors. Check the website for changes to this policy.

Freelance Potential: Publishes 200 titles annually: almost all by agented authors; 1–10% by authors who are new to the publishing house; 1–10% by previously unpublished writers. Receives about 500 queries monthly.

Fiction: Toddler books, early picture books, early readers, picture books, chapter books, middle-grade, YA. Genres: contemporary, multicultural, historical, science fiction, fantasy, adventure, mystery, humor, poetry.

Nonfiction: Concept books, early picture books, story picture books, middle-grade, YA. Topics: history, nature, science, the environment, politics, geography, biography, music, visual arts.

Submissions and Payment: Agented authors only. Catalogue available on website. Response time, publication period, and payment policy vary.

Candlewick Studio

99 Dover Street, Somerville, MA 02144. www.candlewick.com

Editorial Director: Liz Bicknell

Candlewick Studios features books for book lovers of all ages. Featuring titles from around the globe and targeting readers across the world is what this publisher aims to do. It reviews work from agents or through conference appearances where editors meet authors. Check the website for changes to this policy.

Freelance Potential: Parent company Candlewick publishes 200 titles annually: almost all by agented authors; 1–10% by authors who are new to the publishing house; 1–10% by previously unpublished writers. Receives about 500 queries monthly.

Fiction: Toddler books, early picture books, early readers, picture books, middle-grade, YA. Genres: contemporary, multicultural, historical, fantasy, adventure, mystery.

Nonfiction: Concept books, early picture books, picture books, middle-grade, YA. Topics: history, nature, science, the environment, politics, geography, biography.

Submissions and Payment: Agented authors only. Catalogue available on website. Response time, publication period, and payment policy vary.

Carolrhoda Books

Lerner Publishing, 241 First Avenue North, Minneapolis, MN 55401. www.lernerbooks.com

Editorial Director: Andrew Karre

Since 1969, Carolrhoda has been publishing award-winning, high-quality picture books and fiction titles. Carolrhoda Books believes all children should be able to find themselves in the pages of a book. With a joyful approach to storytelling, its authors are distinguished by their exceptional voices and imaginative writing.

Freelance Potential: Publishes 20–25 titles annually.

Fiction: Story picture books, middle-grade, YA. Genres: contemporary, historical, multicultural, mystery, real life/problems.

Nonfiction: Early readers, middle-grade. Topics: history, biography, contemporary.

Submissions and Payment: Guidelines and catalogue available on website. Does not accept unsolicited submissions. Does seek targeted submissions at specific reading levels and for certain subject areas. Also puts out periodic calls for submissions that it posts on its website and blog (http://carolrhoda.blogspot.com). Response time, publication period, and payment policy vary.

Carolrhoda Lab

Lerner Publishing Group, 1251 Washington Ave N, Minneapolis, MN 55401. www.carolrhodalab.com

Editorial Director: Andrew Karre

Tackling relevant issues through a wide variety of genres, Carolrhoda Lab offers thought-provoking stories told by fresh voices. Unflinching, voice-driven narratives that enthrall and challenge teen readers are the backbone of this publisher. Books that probe and examine teenage life from many different perspectives and give YA readers opportunities to explore new and surprising ways of thinking about themselves and the world around them is the mainstay of this imprint of Lerner Publications.

Freelance Potential: Publishes 6–8 titles annually.

Fiction: YA. Genres: contemporary, realistic, coming-of-age, paranormal.

Submissions and Payment: Guidelines and catalogue available on website. Periodically open to submissions from unagented authors; check the blog (http://carolrhoda.blogspot.com) for updates. Email manuscript with brief cover letter to carolrhodasubmissions@lernerbooks.com. (Put "Query" in subject line; RTF attachments.) Other than occasional submission calls, accepts through agents and by author referral only. Accepts simultaneous submissions. Responds in 6 months. Publication period varies. Royalty; advance.

Cartwheel Books

Scholastic Inc., 557 Broadway, New York, NY 10012. www.scholastic.com

Editor

Cartwheel Books publishes innovative books for children up to age 8 and is an imprint of Scholastic Trade Division. It only accepts submissions from agents.

Freelance Potential: Publishes 100+ titles annually.

Fiction: Toddler books, concept books, picture books, early readers, story picture books, chapter books. Genres: humor, contemporary, friendship, family, animals, multicultural.

Nonfiction: Concept books, toddler books, picture books, early readers, story picture books. Topics: science, mathematics.

Submissions and Payment: Accepts submissions from agents and previously published authors only. Response time varies. Publication period and payment policies vary.

Charlesbridge Publishing

9 Galen Street, Watertown, MA 02472. www.charlesbridge.com

Submissions Editor

Charlesbridge has a goal of creating lifelong readers and lifelong learners. Its books for children and teens encourage reading and discovery in the classroom, library, and home.

Freelance Potential: Publishes about 45 titles annually: 1–10% developed from unsolicited submissions; 75% by agented authors. Receives 200–300 unsolicited manuscripts monthly.

Fiction: Toddler books, early picture books, early readers, middle-grade, YA. Genres: contemporary, nature, bedtime stories, multicultural, the arts, poetry.

Nonfiction: Concept books, toddler books, early picture books, easy readers, story picture books, chapter books, middle-grade, YA. Topics: nature, history, social studies, science, math, multicultural themes.

Submissions and Payment: Guidelines and catalogue available on website. Send cover letter and complete manuscript for picture books and shorter "bridge" books. For fiction longer than 30 manuscript pages, send a detailed synopsis, chapter outline, and 3 chapters. For nonfiction longer than 30 manuscript pages, send a detailed proposal, chapter outline, and 1–3 chapters. Accepts hard copy only. No simultaneous submissions (must write "Exclusive Submission" on envelope and cover letter). Responds in 3 months only if interested. Publication in 2-5 years. Royalty.

Charlesbridge Teen

9 Galen Street, Watertown, MA 02472. www.charlesbridge.com

Submissions Editor

Charlesbridge Teen is always seeking new voices, new visions, and new directions. It features storytelling that presents new ideas and an evolving world. Its carefully curated stories give voice to unforgettable characters with unique perspectives. This new imprint from Charlesbridge looks to inspire teens to cheer, sigh, laugh, or reflect, but ultimately, pick up another book. Its mission is to make reading irresistible.

Freelance Potential: Publishes about 3–5 titles annually.

Fiction: YA. Genres: contemporary, folktales, nature, multicultural, mystery, thriller, adventure.

Nonfiction: YA. Topics: nature, history, multicultural themes, social issues, cooking.

Submissions and Payment: Guidelines and catalogue available on website. Send cover letter and complete manuscript for picture books and shorter "bridge" books. For fiction longer than 30 manuscript pages, send a detailed synopsis, chapter outline, and 3 chapters. For nonfiction longer than 30 manuscript pages, send a detailed proposal, chapter outline, and 1–3 chapters. Accepts hard copy or email to YAsubs@charlesbridge.com. No simultaneous submissions (must write "Exclusive Submission" on envelope and cover letter). Responds in 3 months only if interested. Publication in 2–5 years. Royalty.

Children's Book Press

95 Madison Avenue, Suite #1205, New York, NY 10016. www.leeandlow.com

Submissions Editor

Children's Book Press publishes high-quality bilingual books help build a solid foundation to achieve literacy in any language while validating a child's identity, culture, and home language. It was the first independent press in the United States to focus on publishing children's literature by and about people of color. This imprint of Lee & Low Books promotes the shared experiences of cultures that have been historically underrepresented or misrepresented in literature for children. It is the largest multicultural children's book publisher in the country. Children's Book Press especially looks for books that promote bilingualism, literacy, and education.

Freelance Potential: Publishes 5 titles annually. Receives 100 unsolicited manuscripts monthly.

Fiction: Board books, story picture books. Genres: contemporary, ethnic, multicultural, humor.

Nonfiction: Picture books. Topics; history, multicultural and ethnic.

Submissions and Payment: Guidelines and catalogue available on website. Send complete manuscript with cover letter that includes brief author biography and publishing history; note whether manuscript is an exclusive or simultaneous submission. Accepts hard copy. Responds in 6 months if interested. Materials not returned. Publication in 2–3 years. Royalty; advance.

Chronicle Books

Children's Division, 680 Second Street, San Francisco, CA 94107. www.chroniclebooks.com

Children's Division Editor

Chronicle Books publishes inspiring and enduring books. It looks for projects that have a unique bent and lend their list a distinctive flair. It publishes an eclectic mixture of traditional and innovative children's books. Based in San Francisco, it is an independent publisher dedicated to sparking the passions of others through reading. Its list includes children's books and interactive formats, young adult books, cookbooks, and books on fashion, spirituality, pop culture, and relationships.

Freelance Potential: Publishes 100 titles annually. Receives 20 queries, 1,000 unsolicited manuscripts each month.

Fiction: Toddler books, board books, early picture books, easy readers, story picture books, chapter books, middle-grade, YA. Genres: contemporary, historical, science fiction, adventure, humor.

Nonfiction: Concept books, toddler books, board books, early picture books, early readers, story picture books, chapter books, middle-grade, YA. Topics: art, crafts, nature, geography, history.

Submissions and Payment: Guidelines and catalogue available on website. Send complete manuscript for toddler books and picture books. For books for older children, query with synopsis and 3 sample chapters. Accepts hard copy and simultaneous submissions, if identified. Responds in 6 months only if interested; materials are not returned. Publication in 2 years. Payment policy varies.

Clarion Books

Houghton Mifflin Harcourt, 3 Park Avenue, 19th Floor, New York, NY 10016. www.hmhbooks.com/kids

Vice President/Publisher: Dinah Stevenson

Clarion Books, a division of Houghton Mifflin Harcourt, began publishing children's fiction and picture books in 1965 and has published many award-winning titles throughout the years. It creates engaging, dynamic, and effective educational content and experiences from early childhood to K–12, and beyond the classroom. The mission at Clarion Books is to change people's lives by fostering passionate, curious learners. It is currently not reviewing unsolicited submissions. Check the website for changes to this policy.

Freelance Potential: Publishes 30–40 titles annually: 8% developed from unsolicited submissions; 70% by agented authors; 30% by authors who are new to the publishing house; 8% by previously unpublished writers. Receives 40 queries, 300 unsolicited manuscripts monthly.

Fiction: Toddler books, early picture books, early readers, story picture books, chapter books, middle-grade, YA. Genres: fantasy, adventure, folklore, fairy tales, historical, multicultural, science fiction.

Nonfiction: Early readers, story picture books, chapter books, middle-grade, YA. Topics: animals, nature, science, history, holidays, biography, multicultural and ethnic issues.

Submissions and Payment: Guidelines and catalogue available on website. Send complete manuscript for fiction. Query with synopsis and sample chapters for nonfiction. Accepts hard copy. Responds in 12 weeks only if interested; materials are not returned. Publication in 2 years. Royalty.

Creston Books

P.O.Box 9369, Berkeley, CA 94709. www.crestonbooks.co

Publisher: Marissa Moss

Creston Books is dedicated to producing quality picture books that can be enjoyed for ages. It is author driven, with talented authors given more editorial control than other publishers. Creston Books looks for strong writing in whatever form it appears. Potential writers are encouraged to visit this publisher's website to familiarize themselves with the types of books it publishes. The company values strong writing and powerful illustration combined into picture books.

Freelance Potential: Publishes 8 titles annually.

Fiction: Picture books, middle-grade, YA. Genres: animals, holidays, inspirational, concept.

Nonfiction: Picture books, middle-grade, YA. Topics: science, nature, social issues, social skills.

Submissions and Payment: Guidelines and catalogue available on website. Send digital submissions (no more than one project per month) to submissions@crestonbooks.co (no attachments). Accepts multiple submissions. Response time and payment policy vary.

Curiosity Quills Press

Whampa, LLC, P.O. Box 2160, Reston, VA 20195. www.curiosityquills.com

Acquisitions Editors

Curiosity Quills Press is a publisher of hard-hitting dark sci-fi, speculative fiction, and paranormal work aimed at young adults and adults. It looks for thought-provoking books that will take readers on a roller-coaster ride. It is currently looking for books that challenge the mind and turn the world upside down.

Freelance Potential: Publishes 75 titles annually: 65% developed from unsolicited submissions.

Fiction: YA (45,000–75,000 words). Genres: speculative fiction, science fiction, paranormal.

Submissions and Payment: Guidelines and catalogue available on website. Accepts submissions from the website only. Response time, 2-4 months. Publication period varies. Royalty: print, 30%; e-book, 50%.

Darby Creek Publishing

1251 Washington Avenue North, Minneapolis, MN 55401. www.lernerbooks.com

Editorial Director: Andrew Karre

Darby Creek makes reading an adventure instead of a challenge or a chore. It publishes series fiction for emerging, striving, and reluctant readers ages 8 to 18. It offers younger readers stories filled with hilarious escapades, tales of magic, monsters, warriors, and more. Teen readers can experience spine-tingling brushes with the supernatural, gripping survival stories, game-changing stakes for athletes, and more. This imprint of Lerner Books also publishes some titles as e-books.

Freelance Potential: Publishes 10–15 titles annually.

Fiction: Early readers, chapter books, middle-grade, YA. Genres: contemporary, fantasy, science fiction, high-interest subjects.

Submissions and Payment: Accepts agented submissions only. Puts out occasional calls for submissions on website; check website for changes to this policy. Publication period and payment policy vary.

Dawn Publications

12402 Bitney Springs Road, Nevada City, CA 95959. www.dawnpub.com

Editor: Carol Malnor

Now an imprint of Sourcebooks, Dawn Publications is dedicated to inspiring in children a deeper understanding and appreciation for all life on Earth. Dawn's "nature awareness" titles—almost always picture books—are intended to inspire children as well as educate them. They pursue quality over quantity and limit themselves to only a half dozen or so titles a year.

Freelance Potential: Publishes about 6 titles annually: most developed from unsolicited submissions; about 50% by authors who are new to the publishing house; about 30% by previously unpublished writers. Receives about 170 unsolicited manuscripts monthly.

Nonfiction: Early readers, story picture books, middle-grade. Topics: the environment, conservation, ecology, rainforests, animal habitats, the water cycle, seasons, family relationships, personal awareness, multicultural and ethnic issues.

Submissions and Payment: Guidelines available on website. Send complete manuscript with cover letter describing yourself, your vision for the book, and other books you have published, if any. Accepts email submissions (put "Manuscript Submission" followed by the title of your manuscript in subject line) to submission@dawnpub.com (Word or PDF attachments), and hard copy. SASE. Responds in 2 months. Publication in 18–24 months. Royalty; advance.

Dial Books for Young Readers

Penguin Young Readers Group, 375 Hudson Street, New York, NY 10014-3657. http://www.penguin.com/publishers/dialbooksforyoungreaders/

Publisher: Lauri Hornik

Dial cares deeply about diversity and artistic excellence. Its books encourage, enrich, and entertain readers age 2 through teen. This imprint of the Penguin Group was an early pioneer of titles for the very young.

Freelance Potential: Publishes 75 titles annually: 75% by agented authors; 25% by authors who are new to the publishing house; 10% by previously unpublished writers. Receives 100 queries, 100 unsolicited manuscripts monthly.

Fiction: Board books, concept books, early picture books, early readers, story picture books, chapter books, middle-grade, YA. Genres: contemporary, historical, science fiction.

Nonfiction: Concept books, toddler books, early picture books, early readers, story picture books, middle-grade, YA. Topics: animals, science, social issues.

Submissions and Payment: Guidelines and catalogue available on website. Accepts hard copy submissions only. Send complete manuscript for picture books. Query with synopsis, 10 manuscript pages, and publishing credits for longer works. Materials are not returned. Responds in 4 months if interested. Publication period and payment policy vary.

Doubleday Children's Books

Random House Children's Books UK, 61-63 Uxbridge Road, London W5 5SA, England. http://www.randomhousekids.com/about-us/

Submissions

This imprint of Random House Children's Publishers UK publishes books for children of all ages. It features an array of commercial fiction, literary fiction, and serious nonfiction titles. This publisher only accepts submissions from literary agents.

Freelance Potential: Publishes 10–20 titles annually: Receives numerous queries monthly.

Fiction: Board books, picture books, early readers, chapter books, middle-grade, YA. Genres: contemporary, adventure, mystery, social issues, historical, fantasy, humor.

Submissions and Payment: Guidelines and catalogue available on website. Only accepts agented submissions. Response time, publication period, and payment policy vary.

Dover Publications

31 East 2nd Street, Mineola, NY 11501-3582. www.doverpublications.com

Editorial Department

Dover Publications produces a variety of coloring and activity books that include hands-on projects for a wide variety of topics including science, nature, history, art, world cultures, crafts, and holidays. Dover does not accept submissions for original fiction, music, or poetry, but they do welcome all other submissions.

Freelance Potential: Publishes 500 titles annually: 3%–4% by authors who are new to the publishing house. Receives about 100 submissions monthly.

Nonfiction: Middle-grade, YA. Topics: science, natural history, wildlife, environment, history, biology, hobbies, crafts, activities.

Submissions and Payment: Guidelines and catalogue available on website. Query with outline, table of contents, sample chapter, and art sample if available. Accepts hard copy. Responds only if interested; materials are not returned. Publication period and payment policy vary.

Dramatic Publishing

311 Washington Street, Woodstock, IL 60098. www.dramaticpublishing.com

Submissions Editor: Kevin Wright

Since 1885, Dramatic Publishing has been a source for plays and musicals. Dramatic Publishing embraces plays that ultimately challenge audiences, actors, producers, students, and educators to examine their beliefs on controversial topics. Dramatic Publishing publishes original full-length, one-act, and 10-minute plays and musicals of every genre. It has an open submissions policy and is interested in receiving new plays.

Freelance Potential: Publishes about 40 titles annually: about 30% by authors who are new to the publishing house. Receives about 40 unsolicited manuscripts monthly.

Fiction: Full-length and one-act plays, monologues, and anthologies. Genres: drama, humor, fairy tales, musicals.

Nonfiction: YA. Topics: stagecraft, stage dialects, playwriting, production techniques, audition presentations, teaching theater arts.

Submissions and Payment: Guidelines and catalogue available on website. Prefers electronic submissions using form on the website, but will accept hard copy. Send complete manuscript with résumé, synopsis, production history, reviews, cast list, and set and technical requirements; include CD or audio cassette for musicals. SASE for response only; material not returned. Responds in 6 months. Publication in 18 months. Payment policy varies.

Dundurn

500-3 Church Street, Suite 500, Toronto, Ontario M5E 1M2 Canada. www.dundurn.com

Managing Editor: Kathryn Lane

Dundurn Press is a leading independent, inclusive publisher offering Canadian books from every corner of the country. It is currently looking for middle-grade and young adult submissions from Canadian authors.

Freelance Potential: Publishes 100–120 titles annually: 5–15% developed from unsolicited submissions; 5–10% assigned; 10–25% by agented authors; 10–25% by authors who are new to the publishing house; 10–20% by previously unpublished writers. Receives 20–30 queries, 40–50 unsolicited manuscripts monthly.

Fiction: Chapter books, middle-grade, YA. Genres: multicultural, contemporary, historical, regional, fantasy, mystery, suspense, humor, animals, nature, environment, coming-of-age.

Nonfiction: Hi-lo, reluctant readers, middle-grade, YA. Topics: biography, current events, history, humor, social issues, nature, environment, the arts, Canada.

Submissions and Payment: Guidelines and catalogue available on website. Canadian authors only. Query with a cover letter, résumé with past publishing experience, synopsis (include table of contents for nonfiction), 3 sample chapters (first 3 for fiction), word count of complete manuscript, and marketing plan. Accepts email to submissions@dundurn.com and simultaneous submissions. Responds in 6 months if interested. Materials not returned. Publication in 12–24 months. Payment policy varies.

Dutton Children's Books

Penguin Young Readers Group, 345 Hudson Street, New York, NY 10014. http://us.penguingroup.com

Queries Editor

Dutton is one of the oldest continually operating children's book publishers in the United States. Exceptional literary works with distinctive narrative voices and strong commercial appeal are the heart of the current Dutton list. It is a boutique imprint within the largest English-language publisher in the world. Its titles target middle-grade and young adult readers.

Freelance Potential: Publishes 50 titles annually: 2% by previously unpublished writers. Receives 85+ queries monthly.

Fiction: Concept books, early picture books, early readers, story picture books, middle- grade, YA. Genres: contemporary, adventure, mystery, fantasy, humor.

Nonfiction: Toddler books, picture books, YA. Topics: animals, history, nature, science.

Submissions and Payment: Catalogue, guidelines, and editor list with specific genres they seek, available on website. Send 1-page query letter only; include brief synopsis of manuscript and author publishing credits (if any). Accepts hard copy. SASE required. Responds in 4 months if interested. Publication in 1+ years. Royalty; advance.

Eifrig Publishing

P.O. Box 66, 701 Berry Street, Lemont, PA 16851. www.eifrigpublishing.com

Editor: Penelope Eifrig

This publisher's main focus is on books that promote social and environmental consciousness and empower children as they grow in their communities. Its selection includes children's titles on themes of environmentalism, self-esteem, and body image, non-traditional roles for girls, as well as empowering tales of animal rescue and protection, historical preservation, love, and kindness. It has an additional focus on educational books with innovative ideas. It is currently seeking books that feature diversity and inclusion.

Freelance Potential: Publishes 8 titles annually: 70% by authors who are new to the publishing house, 70% by previously unpublished authors. Receives 60 queries yearly.

Fiction: Story picture books, early readers, chapter books, middle-grade, YA. Genres: contemporary, literary, historical, mystery, religious, social issues.

Nonfiction: Adult. Topics: Parenting, social issues, community.

Submissions and Payment: Guidelines and catalogue available on website. Submit a proposal (3–7 pages) that includes working title, summary, target audience, market and competition analysis, outline, and project status; along with sample chapters and author bio or résumé. Accepts electronic submissions through website and email queries to submissions@eifrigpublishing.com. Response time, 4–6 weeks. Publication in 1 year. Payment policy varies.

Eldridge Plays and Musicals

P.O. Box 4904, Lancaster, PA 17604. www.histage.com, www.95church.com

New Plays Editor: Susan Shore

A leading play publisher since 1906, Eldridge Publishing offers hundreds of full-length plays, one-acts, melodramas, holiday, religious plays, children's theatre plays, and musicals of all kinds. It accepts work suitable for performance by community theatres, junior/senior high schools, and churches. While it welcomes shows on all subjects, shows with explicit adult content or graphically defined situations do not fit its market. For musicals, include an audio sample of several songs and a few pages from the score. It is strongly recommended that your script be workshopped, read, or performed before submitting. Plays and musicals should have a minimum running time of 30 minutes.

Freelance Potential: Publishes 35 titles annually: 85% developed from unsolicited submissions; 15% by authors who are new to the publishing house. Receives 40 unsolicited manuscripts monthly.

Fiction: Full-length plays, skits, musicals for grades 6–12 to perform. Genres: classical, contemporary, humor, folktales, melodrama, Western, religious themes. Also publishes plays and musicals for adults.

Submissions and Payment: Guidelines and catalogue available on website. Send complete manuscript with cover letter briefly describing the work, its running time, performance history, and author background/writing experience. If submitting a musical, include CD of at least several songs and sample pages from score. Accepts simultaneous submissions, email to NewWorks@histage.com (cover letter in body of email, play in Word or PDF attachment). Responds in 2 months. Publication in 6–12 months. Royalty, 50% performances, 10% copy sales.

Ellysian Press

www.ellysianpress.com

Submissions

Ellysian Press believes that a passion for books is a necessary element in the publishing process. It offers high quality books with engaging stories and believable characters. It is home to a wide range of titles including young adult, fantasy, science fiction, romance, paranormal, and horror.

Freelance Potential: Publishes 6-8 titles annually: about 25% by authors who are new to the publishing house.

Fiction: YA. Genres: mystery, horror, fantasy.

Submissions and Payment: Catalogue and guidelines available on website. Query with synopsis and first 10 pages of your manuscript in the body of an email (no attachments). Accepts queries by email only to submissions@ellysianpress.com. Responds in 1 month.

Elm Books

www.elm-books.com

Publisher: Leila Monaghan

Elm Books is interested in books that feature children of color that will grab readers' attention. It is actively seeking middle-grade and young adult books. Its titles include mysteries, romance, science fiction, and disability literature. It also has a multicultural line of children's books for grades 2 through 12.

Freelance Potential: Publishes 5–10 titles annually.

Fiction: Early reader, middle-grade, YA. Genres: multicultural fiction, romance, mystery, science fiction.

Submissions and Payment: Guidelines and catalogue available on website. Send outline and first three chapters of novel by email only to Leila.Elmbooks@gmail.com. Responds in 4–8 weeks if interested. Publication period varies. Royalty.

Elsewhere Editions

Archipelago Books, 232 Third Street #A111, Brooklyn, NY 11215. www.archipelagobooks.org

Visionary children's books from around the world make up the catalogue from this publisher. Elsewhere Editions is devoted to translating imaginative works of children's literature from all corners of the world. Its hope is that these titles will enrich children's imaginations and cultivate curiosity about other cultures, as well as delight book lovers of all ages with their humor, art, and playful spirit.

Freelance Potential: Publishes titles from freelance writers.

Fiction: Early readers, picture books, chapter books. Genres: mystery, fairytales, folktales.

Submissions and Payment: Catalogue available on website. Query. Accepts email queries to info@archipelagobooks.org. Response time varies. Payment rates and policies vary.

Entangled Publishing

www.entangledpublishing.com

Submissions Editor

Entangled Publishing is an independent publisher of romantic fiction, in both the adult and young adult markets. Fresh voices with high-concept plots are what this publisher is looking for. Whether they're dark and angsty or fun and sassy, contemporary, fantastical, or futuristic, Entangled Publishing has exactly what teen readers want. Entangled Publishing is committed to acquiring diverse books and books written by diverse authors. It is currently interested in YA books for ages 13 to 19 and for the following genres: historical, thrillers, science fiction, contemporary, paranormal, fantasy, and urban fantasy. All manuscripts must have strong romantic elements. It accepts agented and unagented submissions.

Freelance Potential: Publishes approximately 24 print and 360 digital titles annually: 60% by agented authors, 40% by authors who are new to the publishing house, 50% by previously unpublished writers. Receives 2,000 queries yearly.

Fiction: YA. Genres: fantasy, contemporary, historical, science fiction, thriller, paranormal, fantasy, and urban fantasy, all with romantic themes.

Submissions and Payment: Guidelines and catalogue available on website. YA novels, 70,000–120,000 words. Send one-page query with genre, word count, brief synopsis, writing credentials, links to your website, and first 5 manuscript pages or complete manuscript. Accepts submissions via centralized system on website. Responds in 30 days. Publication period and payment policy vary.

Epic Reads Impulse

195 Broadway, New York, NY 10007. www.harperteen.com; http://www.epicreads.com/features/impulse/

Editorial Department

Epic Reads Impulse looks for the latest in teen books. It publishes works from both new and established authors. This digital first imprint offers new releases every month from HarperCollins. It accepts submissions from literary agents only.

Freelance Potential: Publishes 60 titles annually.

Fiction: YA. Genres: contemporary, fantasy, science fiction, humor, mystery, romance.

Submissions and Payment: Catalogue available on website. Accepts submissions through literary agents only. Publication in 18–36 months. Royalty; advance. HarperCollins also features an online community, Figment, which connects authors, agents, editors, publishers, and readers and allows writers to get feedback on works in progress.

Fantagraphics Books

7563 Lake City Way NE, Seattle, WA 98115. www.fantagraphics.com

Submission Editor

Fantagraphics Books publishes comics for thinking readers—readers who like to put their minds to work, who have a sophisticated understanding of art and culture, and appreciate personal expression. It looks for independently created, publishable work. Originality and diversity are sure to get you noticed. Fantagraphics has published and championed many of the finest cartoonists working today. It gained an international reputation for its literate and audacious editorial standards and its exacting production values. It has been a leading proponent of comics as a legitimate form of art and literature since it began publishing the critical trade magazine *The Comics Journal* in 1976.

Freelance Potential: Publishes 80 titles annually.

Fiction: YA. Genres: fantasy, contemporary, science fiction, thriller, paranormal, fantasy, urban fantasy.

Nonfiction: YA. Topics: biography, travel, horror, real life.

Submissions and Payment: Guidelines and catalogue available on website. Submit a minimum of 5 pages of completed art and text, synopsis, and projected final page count. Accepts hard copy only. Responds if interested. Publication period and payment policy, unknown.

Farrar, Straus & Giroux Books for Young Readers

120 Broadway, New York, NY 10271. http://us.macmillan.com/fsgyoungreaders.aspx

Editorial Director: Grace Kendall

Renowned for its international list of literary fiction, nonfiction, poetry, and children's books, this publisher is committed to publishing books of the highest literary quality for children and teenagers. This publisher is known for its award-winning list of children's fiction, nonfiction, and picture books. Farrar, Straus & Giroux is an imprint from Macmillan. Its goal is to help create books that positively impact the lives of young people; books that make them laugh and think and wonder and question and dream.

Freelance Potential: Publishes about 80 titles annually: all by agented authors.

Fiction: Toddler books, early picture books, picture books, early readers, story picture books, chapter books, middle-grade, YA. Genres: contemporary, adventure, fairy tales, fantasy, horror, humor, mystery, suspense, science fiction, graphic novels.

Nonfiction: Concept books, toddler books, picture books, middle-grade. Topics: biography, families, early learning concepts, science, history, nature.

Submissions and Payment: Accepts submissions through agents only. Response time, publication period, and payment policy vary.

Fey Publishing

www.feypublishing.com

Submissions

Cutting edge stories that push boundaries are what this publisher looks for. Pushing boundaries aside and aiming for something unique, the mission at Fey Publishing is to produce quality books that are different from the mainstream. Young Fey is its newest brand, focusing on quality middle-grade and YA fiction. It is currently seeking YA submissions outside the genre of romance.

Freelance Potential: Publishes 10+ titles annually.

Fiction: Middle-grade, YA. Genres: mystery, thriller, paranormal, science fiction, contemporary, coming-of-age, adventure, fantasy.

Submissions and Payment: Guidelines and catalogue available on website. Send complete manuscript only. Accepts submissions through the website only. Include a short bio. Responds in 1–2 months if interested. Publication period varies. Royalty.

David Fickling Books

31 Beaumont Street Oxford OX1 2NP United Kingdom. www.davidficklingbooks.co.uk

Submissions: Matilda Johnson

Publishing with enthusiasm and commitment, David Fickling Books is now an independent publisher that publishes fiction for toddlers through young adults across a variety of genres. It also publishes children's comic books. This publisher also offers a yearly contest that is open for submissions. Visit the website for more details.

Freelance Potential: Publishes 12–20 titles annually: 1–10% by authors who are new to the publishing house. Receives 40+ queries monthly.

Fiction: Toddler books, story picture books, chapter books, middle-grade, YA. Genres: contemporary, historical, science fiction, adventure, drama, fairy tales, fantasy, humor, romance, poetry.

Submissions and Payment: Guidelines and catalogue available on website. Accepts submissions from agents only. Publication in 1–2 years. Royalty; advance.

Fire and Ice

www.fireandiceya.com

Acquistions

Fire and Ice looks for stories with strong openings, great characterization, and intriguing storylines. Publishing in both e-book and print format, this publisher is looking for books that are free of sex, foul language, violence, drugs, alcohol, or smoking by main characters. Fire and Ice will put out submission calls for specific topics; check the website for current needs. While it is still not accepting submissions of middle-grade fiction, it is currently seeking dystopian tales for ages 16 and up.

Freelance Potential: Publishes 25–35 titles annually.

Fiction: YA. Genres: historical, romance, paranormal, Western, contemporary.

Submissions and Payment: Guidelines and catalogue available on website. Send synopsis and first three chapters. Accepts email to nancy@melange-books.com (doc or docx format). Please title your manuscript DOC or DOCX in the following format: "Date-TITLE-by-AUTHOR NAME." Responds in 12–20 weeks. Publication period varies. Royalty; 40% net royalties on digital; 20% on print.

Fitzhenry & Whiteside

195 Allstate Parkway, Markham, Ontario L3R 4T8 Canada. www.fitzhenry.ca

Children's Book Editor: Sharon Fitzhenry

Fitzhenry & Whiteside specializes in history, biography, children's fiction and nonfiction, young adult fiction and nonfiction, and books for mid-level readers. It publishes books that represent the breadth and depth of Canadian content and authors, from far and wide.

Freelance Potential: Publishes 10–12 titles annually: 30% by agented authors. Receives 80+ unsolicited manuscripts monthly.

Fiction: Early picture books, story picture books, chapter books, middle-grade, YA. Genres: contemporary, historical, multicultural, mystery, suspense, adventure, coming-of-age, humor, poetry.

Nonfiction: Early picture books, story picture books, middle-grade, YA. Topics: global citizenship, animals, history, biography, nature, the environment, educational.

Submissions and Payment: Guidelines and catalogue available on website. Send cover letter and synopsis/proposal plus 3 sample chapters for nonfiction and novels; complete manuscript for picture books. Accepts hard copy only. SASE. No simultaneous submissions. Responds in 4–6 months. Publication in 1-2 years. Royalty; advance.

Floris Publishing ⊙

2A Robertson Avenue, Edinburgh EH11 1PZ Scotland. www.florisbooks.co.uk

Commissioning Editors: Sally Polson and Eleanor Collins

This independent British publisher features beautiful children's books from the United Kingdom and across the world, as well as adult nonfiction with an alternative viewpoint. See www.florisbooks.co.uk for the full range. Potential writers should familiarize themselves with this publisher's guidelines before submitting material.

Freelance Potential: Publishes 60 titles annually: 5% developed from unsolicited submissions; 20% by agented authors; 10% by authors who are new to the publishing house; 10% by previously unpublished writers. Receives 50 unsolicited manuscripts monthly.

Fiction: Board books, picture books, chapter books, middle-grade, YA, Adult.

Nonfiction: YA, Adult. Titles that draw on the work of Rudolf Steiner are of interest to the Steiner-Waldorf community (e.g. biodynamics, Steiner-inspired education and parenting, anthroposophical texts).

Submissions and Payment: Full guidelines and catalogue available on website. Children's fiction submissions: currently only accepting unsolicited manuscripts from under-represented perspectives (BAME; low socioeconomic background; disability or illness; LGBTQIA). Adult nonfiction submissions: open. Submit via online form or post. Responds in about 3 months. Royalty.

Flux

North Star Editions, 2297 Waters Drive, Mendota Heights, MN 55120. www.fluxnow.com

Editor: Mari Kesselring

Flux, an imprint of North Star Editions, is dedicated to guiding readers towards a love of lifetime reading. It aims to produce high-quality fiction for teens. Its tagline is "Where Young Adult Is a Point of View, Not a Reading Level." Its books relate to the issues and challenges teens encounter and present a teen's point of view whether a story is comic, tragic, or a journey of discovery. You won't find condescension or simplification here.

Freelance Potential: Publishes about 25 titles annually: about 60% by authors who are new to the publishing house; about 50% by previously unpublished writers. Receives about 60 queries, 40 unsolicited manuscripts monthly.

Fiction: YA. Genres: contemporary, realistic, coming-of-age, fantasy, thrillers.

Submissions and Payment: Guidelines and catalogue available on website. Query with plot synopsis (1–2 paragraphs), author bio, and 3–5 comparative titles. Email to submissions@northstareditions.com. Publication in 18–24 months. Royalty; advance.

Flyaway Books

100 Witherspoon Street, Louisville, KY 40202 www.flyawaybooks.com

Manuscript Submissions

Hardcover, illustrated picture books with themes of compassion, community, emotional growth, and social justice fill the catalogue from Flyaway books. It is currently seeking manuscripts that feature its priorities of diversity, inclusivity, and care for the world.

Freelance Potential: Will publish 8 titles in 2021.

Fiction: Story picture books, picture books, early readers. Genres: multicultural, realistic, inspirational, and contemporary.

Nonfiction: Picture books, early readers, middle-grade, YA. Topics: human rights, social justice, religion, diversity.

Submissions and Payment: Guidelines and catalogue available on website. Send complete manuscript including intended audience, age level, author bio, and relevant promotional activities you engage in. Also accepts submissions from agents. Accepts email submissions to submissions@flyawaybooks.com. Responds in 6 weeks, if interested. Advance, royalty.

Formac Publishing

5502 Atlantic Street, Halifax, Nova Scotia B3H 1G4 Canada. www.formac.ca

Acquisitions Editor

Formac Publishing aims to produce the most beautiful, most innovative, most challenging, most technologically sophisticated books. Its goal is to publish books about Canada's Maritime provinces or by Maritime Canadian authors. Featuring a children's list with a national aim, Formac is open to new book proposals and is looking for beginner chapter novels that offer realistic and funny stories on themes like teasing, friendship, diversity, and bullying. The protagonists are ages 6 to 9; the length is about 4,000 words.

Freelance Potential: Publishes about 50 titles annually.

Fiction: Early readers, chapter books, middle-grade, YA. Genres: adventure, humor, regional, social issues.

Nonfiction: Middle-grade, YA. Topics: history, regional, multicultural, the environment.

Submissions and Payment: Canadian authors only. Guidelines and catalogue available online. Query with cover letter describing book idea, a brief outline, writing sample, schedule for completion, estimated final word count, and résumé. Accepts hard copy. Responds only if interested. Publication in 1–2 years. Royalty.

Walter Foster Jr.

6 Orchard, Suite 100, Lake Forest, CA 92630. www.quarto.com

Editorial Director: Pauline Molinari

Walter Foster Jr. titles cover a wide range of subjects, including art, edutainment, history, craft, nature, preschool concepts, and more. It publishes fun and imaginative books and kits for children of all ages. As a creator of content for children and families, Walter Foster Jr. strives to bring out that childlike wonderment in all of us and inspire lifelong interests.

Freelance Potential: Publishes 25 books annually.

Nonfiction: Early readers, middle-grade, YA. Topics: art, history, crafts, gardening.

Submissions and Payment: Catalogue and guidelines available on website. Accepts email proposals to Pauline.Molinari@quarto.com. Include an author bio, detailed description of subject/content, artwork, market information, and a signed Submission Agreement (available at the website). Response time, publication period, and payment policies vary.

4RV Publishing

2912 Rankin Terrace, Edmond, OK 73013. www.4rvpublishing.com

Submissions

4RV Publishing offers fiction and nonfiction in a broad range of categories and is currently accepting submissions for tween novels, YA, and adult fiction. It offers titles for children, tweens, teens, and adults. This publisher does not accept poetry, violence, or graphic sexual content.

Freelance Potential: Publishes 10–20 titles annually.

Fiction: Picture books, early readers, chapter books, middle-grade, YA, and novels. Genres: fantasy, contemporary, historical, science fiction, social issues, social skills.

Nonfiction: Middle-grade, YA. Topics: history, animals, social issues.

Submissions and Payment: Guidelines and catalogue available on website. Does not expect to open submissions for picture books until late 2020. For all other categories, send cover letter indicating genre, audience age, content level, marketing/promotion plans, and whether an artist is needed (2-page limit); synopsis of book (4-page limit); and first 3 chapters of manuscript. Send complete manuscript for children's books. Accepts electronic submissions only with each component as a separate Word attachment to President@4rvpublishingllc.com with copies to vp_operations@4rvpublishingllc.com and to managing-vp@4rvpublishingllc.com. Responds in 3 months if interested. Publication period varies. Royalty paid when it reaches over $25.00.

Free Spirit Publishing

6325 Sandburg Road, Suite 100, Golden Valley, MN 55427. www.freespirit.com

Acquisitions Editor

Free Spirit Publishing provides children and teens with the tools to think for themselves and make good decisions. It is a leading publisher of self-help books for children and teens and also offers learning materials that are practical, positive, and solution-focused. Free Spirit is particularly interested in submissions for early childhood readers and educator resources. This publisher advises that potential authors familiarize themselves with its writers' guidelines for detailed information on submitting work.

Freelance Potential: Publishes 15–20 titles annually.

Nonfiction: Board books, toddler books, early picture books, early readers, story picture books, middle-grade, YA. Topics: social skills, stress management, conflict resolution, character building, relationships, self-esteem. Also publishes adult titles about teaching methods, behavior issues, bullying prevention, learning differences, service learning, child development, special education, gifted education, and parenting books related to specific youth development issues.

Submissions and Payment: Guidelines and catalogue available on website. Does not accept unsolicited queries. Accepts complete manuscript submissions and proposals that include a cover letter, at least 2 sample chapters (or entire text for picture book submissions), market analysis, and author résumé. See additional details in submission guidelines on the website. Responds in 2–6 months. Publication in 1–3 years. Royalty.

Samuel French

235 Park Avenue South, 5th Floor, New York, NY 10003. www.samuelfrench.com

Literary Director: Amy Rose Marsh

Making theatre happen and celebrating the ability to bring a group of people together to see a show, Samuel French is committed to respecting the history of the theatre. Samuel French strives to cultivate and expand its catalogue in ways that meet the artistic needs of all theatres. It is also leading the industry with new technological advancements and cutting edge literature.

Freelance Potential: Publishes 20–30 titles annually: 1–10% developed from unsolicited submissions; 50–100% by agented authors. Receives 25–75 queries, 16 manuscripts monthly.

Fiction: Full-length and one-act plays for both amateur and professional theater groups. Samuel French also reviews YA and children's plays. Genres: musicals, drama, comedy, farce, mystery.

Submissions and Payment: Guidelines and catalogue available on website. Website contains most current closed areas and submission requirements. Accepts queries only to publications@samuelfrench.com. Put "Query Submission" and title of play in the subject line. Attach PDF document with the following: title of play, contact info, one-page synopsis, casting requirements, genre, plot, list of upcoming productions, author bio, and 10-page sample of the play or musical. Responds in 4–6 months, if interested. Payment policy varies.

Fulcrum Publishing

4690 Table Mountain Drive, Suite 100, Golden, CO 80403. www.fulcrum-books.com

Submission Editor

Fulcrum Publishing strives to create books that inspire readers to live life to the fullest and to learn something new every day. At this time, the house seeks nonfiction manuscripts that explore US or Native American history, nonfiction-based graphic novels, and conversation-oriented material. It does not accept fiction manuscripts.

Freelance Potential: Publishes 16–20 titles annually: 10% by agented authors, 15% by authors who are new to the publishing house; 30% by previously unpublished authors. Receives 7 queries monthly.

Nonfiction: Middle-grade, YA. Topics: conservation, ecology, natural history, Native American culture, African-American history, outdoor recreation, the American West.

Submissions and Payment: Accepts email queries only to acquisitions@fulcrumbooks.com. Guidelines and catalogue available on website. Query with synopsis, 2–3 sample chapters, author bio, intended audience, competition analysis, and marketing suggestions. Responds in 3 months, if interested. Publication in 18–24 months. Royalty.

Gibbs Smith, Publisher

P.O. Box 667, Layton, UT 84041. www.gibbs-smith.com

Editorial Assistant: Debbie Uribe

Gibbs Smith is currently accepting submissions for children's activity books, board books, and picture books. Enriching and inspiring humankind, the books from Gibbs Smith focus on lifestyle topics, popular culture, arts and crafts, and gift books for adults. For children, it offers fiction and nonfiction picture books and activity books. Its subjects range from offbeat fiction to crafts and educational topics.

Freelance Potential: Publishes about 60 titles annually: 1–10% by authors who are new to the publishing house; 1–10% by previously unpublished writers. Receives 85 queries monthly.

Fiction: Story picture books. Genres: adventure, Western, fantasy, folktales, humor, animal stories, nature, the environment.

Nonfiction: Activity books. Topics: drawing, crafts, the outdoors, holidays, science.

Submissions and Payment: Guidelines and catalogue available on website. Query with detailed outline and writing sample for activity books. Accepts email submissions only to DUribe@gibbs-smith.com. Responds in 3 months if interested. Publication in 1–2 years. Royalty; advance.

David R. Godine, Publisher

15 Court Square, Suite 320, Boston, MA 02108-2536. www.godine.com

Editorial Department

David R. Godine is determined to prove that the day of elegant books has not vanished. As the trend moves away from the printed word in favor of electronic editions, this publisher continues to publish well-made, often beautifully illustrated books. With a deliberately eclectic list, this independent publisher aims to identify the best work and produce it in the best way possible. Godine's list includes original fiction, nonfiction translations, children's books, and poetry.

Freelance Potential: Publishes 30–40 titles annually: all by agented authors; 25% by authors who are new to the publishing house. Receives about 85 queries monthly.

Fiction: Story picture books, chapter books. Genres: mystery, Western, historical, nature, animal stories.

Nonfiction: Story picture books, chapter books, YA. Topics: study skills, camping, crafts, activities, history, biography.

Submissions and Payment: Guidelines and catalogue available on website. Query through literary agent. For consideration or freelance work in copyediting, proofreading, or indexing, send cover letter and résumé by email to info@godine.com. Response time, publication period, and payment policies vary.

Goosebottom Books ★

543 Trinidad Lane, Foster City, CA 94404.
www.goosebottombooks.com

Editor: Shirin Yim Bridges

Shirin Yim Bridges founded Goosebottom Books with her own series of middle-grade books, Thinking Girl's Treasury of Real Princesses, to reach girls and help them be determined and creative, but not confrontational. That series was followed by Thinking Girl's Treasury of Dastardly Dames, with books written by Mary Fisk Pack, Gretchen Maurer, Janie Havemeyer, Liz Hockinson, and Natasha Yim. Goosebottom Books wants to inspire girls with the stories of real women.

Freelance Potential: Publishes 6 books annually: 60% by authors who are new to the publishing house, 30% by previously unpublished writers. Receives 300 queries annually.

Nonfiction: Middle-grade. Topics: women, history.

Submissions and Payment: Catalogue and guidelines available on website. All topics/books are assigned. Accepts writing samples only to submissions@goosebottombooks.com. No hard copy. Responds if interested.

Graphia

Houghton Mifflin Harcourt, 222 Berkeley Street, Boston, MA 02116. www.graphiabooks.com

Submissions: Julie Richardson

Graphia serves today's teens: sophisticated, funny, confused, smart, provocative, scared, and hopeful. Its titles run the gamut from fiction to nonfiction, poetry to graphic novels. With a belief that teens deserve books that reflect their lives, Graphia offers books that include relatable characters and familiar situations and dilemmas that today's teens face.

Freelance Potential: Publishes 10–15 titles annually: 20–30% by authors who are new to the publishing house. Receives up to 50 queries, 85 unsolicited manuscripts monthly.

Fiction: YA. Genres: contemporary, historical, science fiction, mystery, suspense, humor, graphic novels.

Nonfiction: YA. Topics: history, multicultural issues.

Submissions and Payment: Guidelines and catalogue available on website. Send complete manuscript for fiction. Query with synopsis and sample chapters for nonfiction. Accepts hard copy only. No SASE; materials not returned. Responds in 3 months, if interested. Publication period varies. Royalty; advance.

Graphix

557 Broadway, New York, NY 10012. www.scholastic.com

Editor

Graphix is dedicated to publishing engaging, age-appropriate graphic novels for children and teens. Graphix produces creator-driven graphic novels that bring exceptional art and strong storytelling to realistic fiction, memoir, fantasy, and beyond. Graphix is an imprint of Scholastic and only accepts queries from agented authors and writers who have worked with the company in the past.

Freelance Potential: Parent Company Scholastic publishes 600+ titles annually: all by agented authors.

Fiction: Middle-grade, YA. Graphic novels, fantasy, realistic fiction, memoir.

Submissions and Payment: Accepts queries from agented authors only. Publication in 1–2 years. Royalty; advance.

Greene Bark Press

P.O. Box 1108, Bridgeport, CT 06601-1108. www.greenebarkpress.com

Editor

Greene Bark Press is constantly in search of books with originality, imagery, and colorfulness. It has the intention of capturing a child's attention, firing up young imaginations, and sparking the desire to read and explore the world through books. It publishes books that add some value and growth to the learning process of young readers.

Freelance Potential: Publishes about 1 title annually: 75–100% by previously unpublished writers. Receives 25–50 unsolicited manuscripts monthly.

Fiction: Board books, early picture books, early readers, picture books, story picture books. Genres: contemporary, animal stories, social issues, social skills.

Submissions and Payment: No agented authors. Guidelines available. Catalogue available on website. Send complete manuscript. Availability of artwork improves chance of acceptance. Accepts hard copy. Accepts simultaneous submissions if identified. SASE. Responds in 6–12 months. Publication in 18 months. Royalty, 10%.

Greenwillow Books

HarperCollins Children's Books, 195 Broadway, New York, NY 10007. www.harpercollinschildrens.com

Editor: Virginia Duncan

Greenwillow Books is an imprint of HarperCollins that publishes stories for children of every age created by authors and artists whose work is full of honesty, emotion, and depth. Like all HarperCollins imprints, Greenwillow does not accept unsolicited submissions. It works through literary agents only.

Freelance Potential: Publishes 45 titles annually.

Fiction: Picture books, early readers, story picture books, chapter books, middle-grade, YA. Genres: contemporary, fantasy, science fiction, mystery.

Nonfiction: Picture books, early readers, story picture books. Topics: nature, animals, science, holidays, seasons.

Submissions and Payment: Guidelines and catalogue available on website. Accepts agented submissions only. Payment rates and policy vary.

Greystone Kids

343 Railway Street, Suite 302, Vancouver, BC, V6A 1A4 Canada. www.greystonekids.com

Editor

Greystone Kids' books inspire, engage, and connect with readers of all backgrounds around the world. It is the first children's imprint from parent company Greystone Books. It focuses on a variety of subjects for which Greystone is already internationally recognized. This new imprint is committed to publishing distinctive, ambitious material from talented writers.

Freelance Potential: Plans to publish several titles each year.

Nonfiction: Picture books, middle-grade. Genres: sports, the environment, science, social justice, natural history.

Submissions and Payment: Guidelines and catalogue available on website. Query explaining why you'd like to publish your book with Greystone Kids. Include a chapter outline, one sample chapter, market analysis, and author bio. Prefers email queries to submissions@greystone.com. Publication period varies. Royalty; advance.

Groundwood Books

128 Sterling Road, Lower Level / Toronto, ON M6R 2B7, Canada. www.groundwoodbooks.com

Assistant Editor: Emma Sakamoto

Groundwood Books is an independent Canadian children's publisher based in Toronto. It publishes high-quality, character-driven literary fiction. It is dedicated to the production of children's books of the highest possible quality for all ages, including fiction, picture books, and nonfiction. It is always looking for new authors of novel-length fiction for children of all ages. It does not generally publish stories with an obvious moral or message, or genre fiction such as thrillers or fantasy.

Freelance Potential: Publishes 20–25 titles annually: 1–10% developed from unsolicited submissions; 10–25% by agented authors; 10–25% by authors who are new to the publishing house; 1–10% by previously unpublished writers. Receives 15–40 queries monthly.

Fiction: Board books, picture books, middle-grade, YA. Genres: contemporary, bilingual, coming-of-age, historical, realistic, multicultural, adventure, humor, folktales, nature, graphic novels, poetry.

Nonfiction: Board books, chapter books, middle-grade, YA. Topics: the arts, biography, Canada, history, current events, real life/problems, religion, social issues, social studies, sports, technology.

Submissions and Payment: Guidelines and catalogue available on website. Not currently accepting unsolicited submissions for picture books. For longer works, query with synopsis and several sample chapters. Accepts electronic submissions via email to submissions@groundwoodbooks.com. Accepts simultaneous submissions if identified. Responds in 6 months. Publication in 2 years. Royalty.

Guardian Angel Publishing

12430 Tesson Ferry Road, #186, St. Louis, MO 63128. www.guardianangelpublishing.com

Publisher: Lynda S. Burch

Guardian Angel Publishing believes we can change the world by investing in children, one child at a time. Guardian Angel Publishing is both an e-book publisher and print publisher. Guardian Angel Publishing creates a safe environment for children to learn and grow with its books. Guardian Angel is open to submissions at different times throughout the year. Check website for open submission periods.

Freelance Potential: Publishes 50–75 titles annually: 10–25% developed from unsolicited submissions; 1–10% by agented authors; 10–25% by authors who are new to the publishing house; 50–75% by previously unpublished writers.

Fiction: Toddler books, early picture books, early readers, picture books, story picture books, chapter books, middle-grade. Genres: adventure, contemporary, historical, regional, inspirational, bilingual, multicultural, fairy tales, sports, humor, nature, poetry.

Nonfiction: Concept books, toddler books, picture books, reluctant readers, hi/lo. Topics: animals, nature, holidays, seasons, recreation, science, social skills, social studies, math, language arts, health, and fitness.

Submissions and Payment: Guidelines and catalogue available on website. Send complete manuscript with cover letter containing genre and approximate word/page count between May 1 and September 1. Accepts email submissions only to editorial_staff@guardianangelpublishing.com (.doc, RTF, or .wpd attachments only). Responds in 2–3 months. Publication in 12–18 months. Royalty, 30%.

Hachette Book Group

237 Park Avenue, New York, NY 10017. www.hachettebookgroup.com

CEO: Michael Pietsch

Publishing great books well is the mission of this publisher. Hachette Book Group is a leading US trade publisher and a division of the third largest trade and educational book publisher in the world. This international publishing company is part of the France-based Lagardère, with an American division. They foster creativity and encourage risk-taking and innovation. Its divisions and imprints include Little, Brown and Company and its imprints LB–Kids, LB–Teens, and Poppy, which publishes for teen girls; Orbit Books, a science fiction and fantasy imprint; and Yen Press.

Freelance Potential: Publishes 250+ children's titles, 900+ adult titles annually.

Fiction: Toddler books, concept books, picture books, early readers, chapter books, YA. Genres: adventure, fantasy, contemporary, multicultural, sports, humor, graphic novels, manga.

Nonfiction: Concept books, story picture books, middle-grade, YA. Topics: sports, biography, animals, history, families, nature/environment, science, art, activities.

Submissions and Payment: Guidelines and catalogue available on website. Accepts agented submissions only.

   Hachette Imprints: Little, Brown and Company Books for Young Readers, Orbit Books, Worthy Kids.

Happy Fox

903 Square Street, Mount Joy, PA 17552. www.foxchapelpublishing.com

Submissions Editor

According to Vice President of Content Christopher Reggio, "Happy Fox Books will educate, excite, and help children understand the world around them." The imprint focuses on children ages 0 to 10.

Freelance Potential: Plans to publish 5–10 titles yearly.

Fiction: Early reader, middle-grade. Genres: adventure.

Nonfiction: Early reader, middle-grade. Topics: concepts, geography, activity books.

Submissions and Payment: Catalogue and guidelines available on website. Send 1–2 sample chapters, brief synopsis, market analysis, author bio, and title suggestion. Accepts to acquisitions@ foxchapelpublishing.com. Responds if interested. Publication period and payment policy vary.

Harcourt Children's Books

Houghton Mifflin Harcourt, 215 Park Avenue South, New York, NY 10003. www.hmhbooks.com/kids

Submissions Editor

This publisher's mission is to publish authors and illustrators across all platforms to entertain, inform, and connect with readers everywhere. Helping groundbreaking voices find a home, Harcourt Children's Books offers fiction and nonfiction picture books and contemporary and historical fiction for early readers up through young adult. Aiming to spark a lifelong love of learning in every individual they touch, it has been publishing for more than 90 years and has established a reputation for producing fine literature for children.

Freelance Potential: Publishes 30–60 titles annually: by agented and non-agented authors.

Fiction: Board books, toddler books, early picture books, early readers, story picture books, chapter books, middle-grade, YA. Genres: contemporary, historical, multicultural, mystery, fantasy, suspense, sports stories, poetry.

Nonfiction: Picture books. Topics: nature, the environment, biography, animals, world cultures.

Submissions and Payment: Guidelines and catalogue available on website. Send complete manuscript for picture books and novels. Accepts hard copy; materials not returned. Responds in 12 weeks only if interested. Royalty; advance.

HarperChapters

10 East 53rd Street, New York, NY 10022. www.harpercollinschildrens.com

Senior Editor: Maria Barbo

Launched in 2020, this imprint from HarperCollins targets newly independent readers who are beyond easy readers, but not quite ready for standard chapter books. Its titles blend shorter blocks of text with illustrations and interactive elements. This publisher accepts submissions from agents only.

Freelance Potential: Publishes 15–20 titles annually: all by agented authors.

Fiction: Early chapter books. Genres: mystery, adventure, fantasy.

Submissions and Payment: Guidelines and catalogue available on website. Agented authors only. Royalty; advance.

HarperCollins

10 East 53rd Street, New York, NY 10022. www.harpercollins.com

Editorial Departments

HarperCollins Publishers is respected worldwide for publishing quality books for children and home to many classics of children's literature. It is the second-largest consumer book publisher in the world. At HarperCollins, authors and their work are at the center of everything they do. It has many specialized divisions and imprints ranging from commercial and literary to academic, business, and religious. They are proud to provide their authors with unprecedented editorial excellence, marketing reach, long-standing connections with booksellers, and industry-leading insight into reader and consumer behavior. Its imprints for children and teens include Balzer & Bray, Amistad, Greenwillow Books, HarperFestival, and HarperCollins Children's Books.

Freelance Potential: Publishes thousands of titles annually: most by agented authors.

Fiction: Children, teens, and adults, across all genres.

Nonfiction: Children, teens, and adults, across all genres.

Submissions and Payment: Guidelines and catalogues for the various divisions and imprints available on website. Agented authors only. HarperCollins does feature an online writing community, Authonomy, which offers tips and opportunities for authors who want to get books published.

HarperCollins Imprints: AMACOM Books, Amistad Press, Balzer & Bray, Blink, Collins, Epic Reads Impulse, Greenwillow Books, HarperChapters, HarperCollins Children's Books, HarperCollins Christian Publishing, HarperFestival, Harper Voyager, Heartdrum, Inkyard Press, Thomas Nelson Children's Books and Education, Quill Tree Books, Katherine Tegen Books, Walden Pond Press.

HarperCollins Children's Books

10 East 53rd Street, New York, NY 10022. www.harpercollinschildrens.com

Associate Editor: Alyson Day

Authors and their work are at the center of everything this publisher does. Respected worldwide for publishing quality books for children and home to many classics of children's literature, it also employs digital technology to create unique reading experiences. Its list includes high-quality fiction and nonfiction for children from preschool through high school. HarperCollins Children's Books, like all of its sister imprints, works with agented authors only.

Freelance Potential: Publishes 500 titles annually: all by agented authors.

Fiction: Story picture books, early readers, chapter books, middle-grade, YA. Genres: contemporary, historical, multicultural, science fiction, adventure, drama, humor, fantasy, folktales, mystery, horror, suspense, Western.

Nonfiction: Story picture books, early readers, chapter books, middle-grade, YA. Topics: animals, science, history, geography, social studies, biography.

Submissions and Payment: Guidelines and catalogue available on website. Agented authors only. Royalty; advance.

HarperFestival

10 East 53rd Street, New York, NY 10022. www.harpercollinschildrens.com

Editorial Department

HarperFestival is home to books, novelties, and merchandise for the youngest of children. Its list is comprised of board books, picture books, and character-based programs like the Biscuit, Little Critter, and Berenstain Bears series. Consistent with the policy of all imprints of HarperCollins, HarperFestival reviews submissions from agented authors only.

Freelance Potential: Publishes 120 titles annually.

Fiction: Toddler books, novelty books, picture books, story picture books, early readers. Genres: contemporary, family, friends, animal stories.

Submissions and Payment: Guidelines and catalogue available on website. Accepts queries through literary agents only. Royalty; advance.

Harper Voyager

10 East 53rd Street, New York, NY 10022. www.harpercollins.com

Executive Editor, U.S: Diana Gill

Harper Voyager is a thriving global imprint dedicated to science fiction and fantasy. The imprint's successful digital-first platform, Harper Voyager Impulse, has launched a wide variety of new and exciting speculative fiction talent. Harper Voyager publishes some of the most notable names in science fiction, epic fantasy, and urban fantasy, including worldwide bestselling authors R.A. Salvatore, J.R.R. Tolkien, Isaac Asimov, and more.

Freelance Potential: Publishes 60 titles annually.

Fiction: YA, adult. Genres: science fiction, epic, high-tech, urban fantasy, space opera, historical fantasy, gothic, romance, paranormal, horror, dystopian, thrillers.

Submissions and Payment: Catalogue available on website. Accepts submissions through literary agents only. Publication in 18–36 months. Royalty; advance.

Harvest Kids

Harvest House Publishers, P.O. Box 26311, Eugene, OR 97402. www.harvesthousepublishers.com

Editor

Harvest House Publishers has a goal to help the hurts of people everywhere. It is a Christian publisher that includes the imprint of Harvest Kids. It publishes books that are affordable, trustworthy, and practical. It creates a wide variety of products that promote biblical values, spark imagination, and encourage readers up to the age of 12 to develop a lifelong love of Jesus Christ. This imprint includes Bibles, picture books, and devotionals, with a special focus on resources for children 8–12.

Freelance Potential: Parent company Harvest House publishes 150 titles yearly.

Fiction: Picture books, middle-grade, YA. Genres: inspirational, religious.

Nonfiction: Picture books, middle-grade, YA. Topics: religion, devotionals.

Submissions and Payment: Guidelines and catalogue available on website. Accepts manuscripts through Christian Manuscript Submissions at ChristianManuscriptSubmissions.com only. No unsolicited submissions. Publication period and policies vary.

HCI Books

1700 NW 2nd Avenue, Boca Raton, FL 33432. www.hcibooks.com

Editorial Committee

HCI seek high-caliber authors who produce original material that appeals to a broad readership. It looks to continue their tradition of excellence in publishing. Dedicated to bringing readers quality books, HCI Books has been changing the lives of its readers one book at a time. The company carefully selects its authors, who inspire readers to achieve their dreams, live lives of abundance, and experience consolation when needed. Most of its authors are experts in their field.

Freelance Potential: Publishes 60 titles annually: 1–10% developed from unsolicited submissions; 90% by agented authors; 15% by authors who are new to the publishing house; 1–10% by previously unpublished writers. Receives 40 queries monthly.

Fiction: YA. Genres: contemporary, fantasy.

Nonfiction: YA. Topics: teen issues, health, fitness, relationships. Also publishes parenting titles.

Submissions and Payment: Guidelines available on website. Send proposal with author information, including credentials and publishing credits; detailed marketing data that includes target audience and promotion ideas; book summary; competing titles and sales figures; specific information that is not provided by comparable titles; a detailed outline; table of contents; introduction; and 2 sample chapters. Accepts hard copy or electronic submissions to editorial@hcibooks.com. SASE. Responds in 6 months. Publication in 6–12 months. Payment policy varies.

Heartdrum ★

10 East 53rd Street, New York, NY 10022. www.harpercollinschildrens.com

Editorial Director: Cynthia Leitich Smith

Launching in 2021, this new imprint from HarperCollins is devoted to publishing books by Native American authors and showcase books that feature Native protagonists and showcase the present Indian Country. As part of its mission, Heartdrum will make an annual donation to the We Need Diverse Books Native Fund, to be used for writing workshops.

Freelance Potential: Plans to publish 10 titles in its first year: all by agented authors.

Fiction: Picture books, middle grade, young adult. Genres: Mullticultural, realistic and historical fiction.

Submissions and Payment: Guidelines and catalogue available on website. Agented authors only. Royalty; advance.

Heuer Publishing

P.O. Box 248, Cedar Rapids, IA 52406. www.heuerpub.com

Editor: Geri Albrecht

Heuer is one of the oldest US publishing houses serving the educational and community theater markets. It is a pioneer in commissioning and publishing unique works from a broad range of playwrights. For the middle-grade and young adult set, it publishes short, full-length, and 10-minute plays and monologues, as well as musicals, which are entertaining yet thought provoking. Its current needs include classic, 10-minute, social, family, interactive, and dinner theater. It no longer publishes theater resources or texts.

Freelance Potential: Publishes 40–50 titles annually: 50–75% developed from unsolicited submissions; 1–10% by agented authors; 10–25% by authors who are new to the publishing house; 1–10% by unpublished writers. Receives more than 200 unsolicited manuscripts monthly.

Fiction: Middle-grade, YA. Genres: dramas, plays, monologues, musicals.

Submissions and Payment: Guidelines and catalogue available on website. Send complete manuscript with production history, synopsis, cast list, running time, and set requirements. Accepts submissions through the website only (Word, Adobe, or RTF formats). Responds in 4–6 months (10–12 months for plays without production history). Publication in 3–6 months. Payment policy varies.

Hogs Back Books 🌐

Chateau D'Anglers, Anglers Juillac, 46140, France. http://www.hogsbackbooks.com

Submissions: K. Stevens

Hogs Back Books publishes picture books for readers aged up to 10 years. It produces quality books for children to enjoy and treasure by matching great stories with fresh and original illustrations.

Freelance Potential: Publishes 5 titles each year.

Fiction: Early picture books, picture books. Genres: Animals, folktales, nature, adventure.

Submissions and Payment: Catalogue available on website. Accepts hard copy or email. Send complete manuscript along with cover letter by email to submissions@hogsbackbooks.com. Responds in 3 months. Publication period and payment policies vary.

Holiday House

425 Madison Avenue, New York, NY 10017. www.holidayhouse.com

Acquisitions Editor

Holiday House publishes quality books that entertain, enlighten, and educate children. Completely devoted to its authors and illustrators, Holiday House is an independent publisher of children's books. It specializes in quality hardcovers, from picture books to young adult fiction and nonfiction. Its books target children ages 4 and up. Most of its titles are also aligned with Common Core standards. It does not publish mass-market books.

Freelance Potential: Publishes 70 titles annually: most by agented authors; 1–10% by authors who are new to the publishing house; 1–10% by previously unpublished writers. Receives 100 unsolicited manuscripts monthly.

Fiction: Early picture books, early readers, story picture books, chapter books, middle-grade, YA. Genres: contemporary, historical, multicultural, humor, mystery, fantasy.

Nonfiction: Early picture books, early readers, story picture books, middle-grade, YA. Topics: history, social issues, biography, science.

Submissions and Payment: Guidelines and catalogue available on website. Send complete manuscript. Though not necessary, include copies of artwork if available. Accepts hard copy. No SASE; materials not returned. Responds in 4 months, if interested. Publication period varies. Royalty; advance.

Henry Holt Books for Young Readers

Macmillan, 175 Fifth Avenue, New York, NY 10010.
http://us.macmillan.com/holtyoungreaders.aspx; http://henryholt.tumblr.com/

Submissions Editor

Founded in 1866, this imprint of Macmillan continues to carry on the house's long history of publishing books of high quality that appeal to a diverse and substantial readership. Henry Holt and Company has for almost a century and a half published writers that define their era and endure far beyond it. The house is known for publishing high-quality picture books, chapter books, novels, and nonfiction for children from preschool through high school. Although the genres and subjects it publishes are diverse, the common denominators are quality writing and engaging story lines. Henry Holt accepts submissions through literary agents only.

Freelance Potential: Publishes about 40 titles annually. Receives 1,000 queries monthly.

Fiction: Toddler books, early picture books, early readers, story picture books, chapter books, middle-grade, YA. Genres: contemporary, historical, multicultural, ethnic, adventure, drama, fantasy, poetry.

Nonfiction: Story picture books, chapter books, middle-grade. Topics: biography, history, ethnic issues, mythology.

Submissions and Payment: Guidelines and catalogue available on website. Accepts submissions through literary agents only. Publication period and payment policy vary.

Hot Key Books

80-81 Wimpole Street, W1G 9RE, London, England. www.hotkeybooks.com

Acquisitions Editor

Hot Key Books, a division of Bonnier Publishing, publishes stand-out, quality fiction that people like to talk about. It publishes original and thought-provoking books for children ages 9 to 19. The company focuses on top-notch author care and connecting with readers who love books as much as they do.

Freelance Potential: Publishes 10–20 books annually

Fiction: Middle-grade, YA. Genres: contemporary, historical, humor, mystery, fantasy, realistic, futuristic.

Submissions and Payment: Guidelines and catalogue available on website. Send cover letter with author info and complete manuscript along with a full synopsis to enquiries@hotkeybooks.com (prefers Word or PDF attachments). Accepts email only. Responds in 3 months.

Houghton Mifflin Books for Children

Houghton Mifflin Harcourt, 222 Berkeley Street, Boston, MA 02116-3764. http://hmhbooks.com/kids

Submissions Coordinator

This publisher publishes some of the world's most renowned fiction and nonfiction children's books. Timeless classics and fresh new titles that your family will want to read again and again make up the catalog from Houghton Mifflin Books for Children. It is interested in the highest caliber books. Its goal is to foster curious learners and to excite and nurture dedicated readers. It is interested in increasing the number of titles available electronically and eventually acquiring original e-content.

Freelance Potential: Publishes 60 titles annually: most by agented authors. Receives 100 queries, 1,700 unsolicited manuscripts monthly.

Fiction: Toddler books, early picture books, early readers, story picture books, middle-grade, YA. Genres: contemporary, historical, multicultural, adventure, animal stories.

Nonfiction: Middle-grade, YA. Topics: history, science, nature, the environment, biography.

Submissions and Payment: Guidelines and catalogue available on website. Send complete manuscript for fiction. Query with synopsis and sample chapters for nonfiction. Accepts hard copy. No SASE; materials not returned. Responds in 12 weeks if interested. Publication period varies. Royalty; advance.

Houghton Mifflin Harcourt

Houghton Mifflin Harcourt, 222 Berkeley St., Boston, MA 02116. www.hmhco.com

Submissions Coordinator

Houghton Mifflin Harcourt values enabling and promoting the curiosity of others, resulting in remarkable discoveries and new ideas. Inspiring the thinkers and doers of tomorrow and bringing learning to every moment, Houghton Mifflin Harcourt helps people find success. It publishes educational materials under its School Division, and trade books for adults and children.

Freelance Potential: Publishes hundreds of titles annually across its divisions.

Fiction: Children, teens, and adults, across most genres.

Nonfiction: Children, teens, and adults, across most genres.

Submissions and Payment: Accepts unsolicited submissions by mail for the children's division, but only responds if interested. Royalty; advance.

> **Houghton Mifflin Imprints:** Clarion Books, Graphia, Harcourt Children's Books, Houghton Mifflin Books for Children, MeeGenius.

Hungry Tomato

1251 Washington Avenue North, Minneapolis, MN 55401. https://www.hungrytomato.com

Editorial Director: Shaina Olmanson

Hungry Tomato publishes accessible and entertaining books with brilliant art and design to hold young readers' attention page by page. It offers high-interest nonfiction for ages 8 to 12 that combines gripping text and eye-catching images. The books from this imprint begin at the first-grade level, with the majority at a third- to fifth-grade level, designed to engage even the most reluctant readers.

Freelance Potential: Publishes 15–20 titles annually.

Nonfiction: Middle-grade, YA. Topics: animals, history, the environment, and nature.

Submissions and Payment: Accepts solicited submissions only. Puts out occasional calls for submissions on website; check website for changes to this policy. Publication period and payment policies vary.

Igloo Books ⊙

Igloo Books Limited, 251 Park Ave. S., New York, NY, 10010. www.igloobooks.com

Editor

Acquired by Bonnier Publishing in 2014, Igloo Books is a leading international mass-market publisher specializing in creating value-driven books. Its catalogue is filled with children's books, books on food and drinks, reference books, and hobby and interest titles. Its philosophy is to inspire, educate and "edutain!"

Freelance Potential: Publishes hundreds of books annually.

Fiction: Board books, early picture books, picture books, toddler books. Genres: animals, nature.

Nonfiction: Board books, early picture books, picture books, toddler books, concept books. Topics: counting, colors, activities.

Submissions and Payment: Catalogue available on website. Accepts proposals by email to submissions@igloobooks.com. Response time varies. Payment rates and policies vary.

Imagine That Publishing ⊙

www.topthatpublishing.com

Submissions Editor: Josh Simpkin-Betts

Imagine That publishes three distinct imprints, each with a separate focus, and each forming an important contribution. Its list takes children on a creative journey of reading and learning, focusing on interactive and stunning novelty and activity books. Imagine That is an award-winning, independent children's publisher with a mission to create books that inspire children to read, learn, play, and create. The distinctive Imagine That imprints sell more than 11 million books and kits per year, in over 70 countries around the world. Its imprints include Imagine That Publishing, Willow Tree Books, and Top That.

Freelance Potential: Publishes 15+ titles each year.

Fiction: Early readers, picture books, middle-grade, YA. Genres: animals, folktales, nature, myth.

Nonfiction: Preschool, early readers, concept books, picture books, middle-grade, YA. Topics include: animals, humor, activity books, cookbooks,

Submissions and Payment: Guidelines and catalogue available on website. Query or send complete manuscript. Accepts submissions by email to josh@imaginethat.com. Responds 8 weeks, if interested. No simultaneous submissions. Publication period varies. Payment rates and policies vary.

Immedium

P.O. Box 31846, San Francisco, CA 94131. www.immedium.com

Submissions Editor

Immedium publishes engaging characters and entertaining stories that scratch the surface of possibility. It publishes innovative, influential, and insightful books and collaborates with authors who have the same goals. It values fresh ideas, dynamic perspectives, and can-do creativity. It is open to children's picture books and titles for young adults and adults on Asian-America and arts and culture.

Freelance Potential: Publishes 4 titles annually: 65% from unsolicited submissions.

Fiction: Picture books, story picture books. Genres: adventure, animals.

Nonfiction: Picture books, YA. Topics: Asian culture, social trends, lifestyle.

Submissions and Payment: Guidelines and catalogue available on website. Send complete manuscript for picture books. Query for YA and adult titles. Proposal should include a cover letter with relevant background experience, target market and reader, comparable titles, and samples of your work. Response time, 2-4 months. Publication period varies. Royalty: 5%.

Inkyard Press

195 Broadway, 24th Floor; New York, NY 10279. www.inkyardpress.com

Editorial Director: Natashya Williams; Editor: T.S. Ferguson; Associate Editor: Lauren Smulski

In January 2019, Harlequin TEEN rebranded and relaunched as Inkyard Press. It is passionate about publishing diverse voices and relevant stories that appeal to older teens and an adult crossover audience. It continues to publish books for young adult readers across a variety of genres—from contemporary and mainstream to genre fiction, including horror, fantasy, mystery, romance, and thriller. It is important that readers see themselves reflected in the books it publishes, and it is proud to represent authors from diverse backgrounds and communities. As part of its commitment to publish exceptional books, it is working to broaden its publishing portfolio with an inclusive, diverse list of authors and stories. This publisher is always looking for fresh voices, including writers with unique perspectives and experiences to share. Inkyard Press is an imprint of Harlequin—a division of HarperCollins Publishers. Inkyard Press accepts submissions through literary agents only.

Freelance Potential: Harlequin publishes 100s of titles annually.

Fiction: YA. Genres: contemporary, literary, historical, fantasy, science fiction, coming-of-age, horror, genre blends.

Submissions and Payment: Agented authors only. Agents may submit a partial or complete manuscript with full synopsis. Accepts email to Natashya.Wilson@harpercollins.com; TS.Ferguson@harpercollins.com; Lauren.Smulski@harpercollins.com (Word attachments). Response time, publication period, and payment policies vary.

Interlink Publishing Group

46 Crosby Street, Northampton, MA 01060-1084. www.interlinkbooks.com

Editorial Director

Interlink Publishing is a Massachusetts-based independent publishing house that offers a global perspective. Interlink aims to change the way people think about the world. It specializes in producing titles that expand its readers' view of the world, including world travel, art, world history, and children's books from around the world. Authors should familiarize themselves with the books currently in Interlink's catalogue prior to submitting material. At this time, Interlink is closed to children's book submissions. Check website for updates to this policy.

Freelance Potential: Publishes 50 titles annually: about 35% by authors who are new to the publishing house; 15% by previously unpublished writers. Receives 150 queries monthly.

Fiction: Toddler books, early picture books, story picture books. Genres: multicultural, contemporary, myths, folktales, stories from other countries.

Nonfiction: Concept books, toddler books, early picture books, story picture books. Topics: nature, animals, cultures of the world.

Submissions and Payment: Guidelines and catalogue available on website. Publication in 18–24 months. Royalty, 6–7% of retail; small advance.

Jabberwocky

Sourcebooks, 1935 Brookdale Road, Suite 139, Naperville, IL 60563.
http://www.sourcebooks.com/spotlight/jabberwocky.html

Editor: Annie Berger

Focused on all things children's fiction, Jabberwocky delivers unique voices, education, and entertainment to the next generation of picture and board book readers. Jabberwocky believes in engaging children in the pure fun of books and the wonder of learning new things. This children's imprint of Sourcebooks publishes notable fiction and nonfiction with the hopes of engaging children. It features stories and characters for children in preschool through the middle grades that find that special place where children can grow and have fun. Young adult fiction is accepted by its sister imprint, Fire. At this time, Jabberwocky is only accepting submissions through agents.

Freelance Potential: Sourcebooks publishes 300+ titles annually: 1–10% developed from unsolicited submissions; 1–10% assigned; 50–75% by agented authors; 50–75% by authors who are new to the publishing house; 10–25% by previously unpublished writers.

Fiction: Toddler books, early picture books, early readers, story picture books, chapter books, middle-grade. Genres: contemporary, humor, historical, mystery, adventure.

Nonfiction: Chapter books, middle-grade. Topics: history, biography.

Submissions and Payment: Guidelines and catalogue available on website. Accepts submissions through literary agents only. Responds in 8–12 weeks. Publication in 1 year. Royalty; advance.

Jolly Fish Press

2297 Waters Drive, Mendota Heights, MN 55120. www.jollyfishpress.com

Editor: Mari Kesselring

This imprint of North Star Editions, Inc. is dedicated to promoting exceptional, unique new voices in middle-grade fiction and jump-starting writing careers. It is currently seeking middle-grade contemporary fiction. Potential writers should have a strong one-line pitch that focuses on what is unique about their manuscript.

Freelance Potential: Publishes 10–15 titles annually: 30% by agented authors, 70% by contracted, work-for-hire writers. Receives 50–100 submissions monthly.

Fiction: Middle-grade. Genres: contemporary, fantasy, humor, graphic novels, action adventure, science fiction, mystery, sports fiction, historical.

Submissions and Payment: Guidelines available on website. Accepts email submissions only to jfp-submit@northstareditions.com. Publication period and payment rates vary.

Just Us Books

P.O. Box 5306, East Orange, NJ 07017. www.justusbooks.com

Editorial Director: Cheryl Willis Hudson

Just Us Books remains one of the nation's few Black-owned publishers. Just Us Books focuses primarily on the culture, history, and contemporary experiences of African-Americans. It is the nation's premier independent publisher of Black-interest books for young people. Its catalogue includes fiction, nonfiction, and biographies for young children through young adults, but currently it is accepting only queries for chapter books and middle-grade titles. Its new imprint, Marimba, publishes multicultural children's titles.

Freelance Potential: Publishes 4–6 titles annually. Receives 85+ queries monthly.

Fiction: Concept books, picture books, early readers, story picture books, chapter books, middle-grade, YA. Genres: contemporary, historical, multicultural, ethnic, adventure, mystery—all featuring African-American characters or themes.

Nonfiction: Middle-grade. Topics: African-American history, culture, social issues, biography.

Submissions and Payment: Guidelines and catalogue available on website. Currently open to chapter books and middle-grade fiction only. Query with 1–2 page synopsis, 3–5 sample pages, and author biography that includes publishing credits. Accepts hard copy. Send SASE for response. Responds in 6 months. Publication period varies. Royalty.

Kane Miller

10302 E. 55th Place, Tulsa, OK 74146. www.kanemiller.com

Editorial Department

Kane Miller is interested in great stories with engaging characters, especially the kinds that reflect our diverse world, and also books on American subjects. They are committed to expanding their picture book list and are interested in great stories with engaging characters. It offers the most exciting, engaging, and educational books on the market today. Its titles are high-quality, innovative, and lavishly illustrated. Its titles come from all over the world to bring a different feel, culture, or just a silly story that kids everywhere can enjoy. Kane Miller has a preference for stories written from a firsthand experience.

Freelance Potential: Publishes about 75–100 titles annually: 1–10% developed from unsolicited submissions; 1–10% by agented authors; 45% by authors who are new to the publishing house; 10% by previously unpublished writers. Receives 100+ unsolicited manuscripts monthly.

Fiction: Concept books, toddler books, early picture books, story picture books, chapter books, middle-grade. Genres: historical, multicultural, adventure, humor, mystery, animal stories.

Submissions and Payment: Guidelines and catalogue available on website. Send complete manuscript or query with synopsis and 2 sample chapters to "the editors." Accepts only email submissions to submissions@kanemiller.com. Responds in 3 months. Publication in 1–2 years. Royalty; advance.

KCP Loft

Kids Can Press, Corus Quay, 25 Dockside Drive, Toronto, Ontario M5A 0B5, Canada. www.kidscanpress.com

Acquisitions Editor: Kate Egan

KCP Loft works with Canadian writers only. It is the first imprint from Kids Can Press specifically targeting teen readers. The company prefers books that promote a world view, and consistently delivers high-quality print books that are loved by parents, teachers, librarians, and children.

Freelance Potential: Kids Can Press publishes about 30 titles annually. Receives 300+ queries and unsolicited manuscripts monthly.

Fiction: YA. Genres: Mystery, adventure, coming-of-age.

Nonfiction: YA. Topics: social issues, technology, education.

Submissions and Payment: Canadian authors only. Guidelines and catalogue available on website. Send complete manuscript for picture books. Query with synopsis and 3 sample chapters for all other books. Accepts hard copy. Accepts simultaneous submissions, if identified. No SASE; materials are not returned. Responds in 6 months, if interested. Publication period varies. Royalty; advance.

Kensington Publishing

119 West 40th Street, New York, NY 10018. www.kensingtonbooks.com

Editorial Director: Alicia Condon

Kensington Publishing is known as "America's Independent Publisher." It provides hardcover, trade paperback, mass market, and digital titles. Its list features New York Times best-selling authors, including Fern Michaels, Lisa Jackson, Joanne Fluke, and William W. Johnstone. Kensington's diverse imprints include Zebra, Pinnacle, Dafina, and Lyrical Press, which are well known for providing readers with a range of popular genres such as romance, women's fiction, African-American, young adult, and nonfiction, as well as true crime, Western, and mystery titles. It currently seeking 80,000-word contemporary romance, Amish and inspirational romance, women's fiction, romantic suspense, and historical romance. At this time, it is not accepting manuscripts for children or teens.

Freelance Potential: Kensington publishes about 600 books a year; the new KTeen imprint publishes about 12 titles annually.

Fiction: Contemporary romance—either sexy or sweet, Amish and inspirational romance, women's fiction, romantic suspense, historical romance with unusual settings, cozy mysteries, psychological mysteries/thrillers. Not currently accepting children's, middle-grade, young adult, or poetry submissions.

Submissions and Payment: Do not submit to more than one editor (full list of editors on Kensington's website). Will accept queries only by email to acondon@kensingtonbooks.com; no manuscripts or attachments. Will respond in 3 months if interested. Please send a query only in the body of the email. Do not attach manuscripts or proposals to e-mail queries. An editor will respond if he or she is interested in seeing your material based on your query. Due to the volume of submissions, editors may only respond to projects they wish to further consider. Requested manuscripts should be Word documents unless otherwise specified, typed in 12-point font, double-spaced, and paginated. Include title and author in file name.

Kids Can Press

Corus Quay, 25 Dockside Drive, Toronto, Ontario M5A 0B5 Canada. www.kidscanpress.com

Acquisitions Editor

Kids Can Press consistently delivers high-quality print books that parents, teachers, librarians, and children around the world have come to expect. It looks for quality picture books and nonfiction manuscripts for children, as well as chapter books for ages 7–10. It is the largest Canadian-owned children's publisher in the world. It produces a variety of fiction and nonfiction books for children in preschool through high school. Its titles include picture books, poetry, and science books. It prefers books that promote a world view, and works with Canadian writers only. It currently leads the way in Canada with the most children's illustrated e-books in the market.

Freelance Potential: Publishes about 30 titles annually. Receives 300+ queries and unsolicited manuscripts monthly.

Fiction: Toddler books, early readers, story picture books, chapter books, middle-grade, YA. Genres: contemporary, historical, folklore, mystery, suspense, animal stories.

Nonfiction: Early readers, middle-grade. Topics: animals, crafts, hobbies, nature, history, biography, science.

Submissions and Payment: Canadian authors only. Guidelines and catalogue available on website. Currently not seeking YA fiction. Send complete manuscript for picture books. Query with synopsis and 3 sample chapters for all other books. Accepts hard copy. Accepts simultaneous submissions, if identified. No SASE; materials are not returned. Responds in 6 months, if interested. Publication period varies. Royalty; advance.

Jessica Kingsley Publishers

400 Market Street, Suite 400, Philadelphia, PA 19106. www.jkp.com

Editorial Manager: Victoria Peters

Jessica Kingsley Publishers publishes books that make a difference. This publisher has a range of graphic novels across subject areas, and books for children on issues including bereavement, depression, and anger. It is well known for its long-established lists on the autism spectrum, social work, and arts therapies. Its list also includes titles on mental health, counseling, and practical theology. Some of its titles target children and teens.

Freelance Potential: Publishes 15–20 titles each year.

Nonfiction: YA, Educators. Topics: autism, special education, art therapy, social skills, mental health, anxiety, real life issues.

Submissions and Payment: Guidelines and catalogue available on website. Submit book proposal (form available on website), curriculum vitae/resume. Prefers electronic submissions through Submittable on their website. Will accept hard copy. Responds in 3–6 months. Publication period varies. Payment rates and policies vary.

Klutz/Klutz Jr

568 Broadway St., Suite 503, New York, NY 10012. www.klutz.com

Publisher

Klutz and Klutz Jr. are imprints from Scholastic that specialize in hands-on books. It creates book-based activity kits that stimulate creativity and critical thinking in kids of all ages. They target children ages 4 and up with craft and activity kits ranging from knitting tutorials, to doodle journals, to creating fashion jewelry. While its use of freelancers is limited, it is always open to new ideas that will excite children and encourage them to explore new areas of their creativity.

Freelance Potential: Publishes 20+ craft kits per year.

Nonfiction: Early readers, middle-grade, YA. Topics: crafts and activities.

Submissions and Payment: Guidelines and catalogue available on website. Query. Accept hard copy. Responds in 6–8 weeks. Publication in 18–24 months. Payment policy varies.

Alfred A. Knopf Books for Young Readers

Random House, 1745 Broadway, 8th Floor, New York, NY 10019. www.randomhouse.com/kids

Submissions Editor

Known for the caliber of its authors and artists this publisher offers distinguished, high-quality books for children of all ages. It publishes books intended to entertain, inspire, and endure. This imprint is deeply committed to creating books that children and adults who read to children will love for years to come.

Freelance Potential: Publishes 60–75 titles annually: 1–10% developed from unsolicited submissions; 50% by agented authors; 1–10% by authors who are new to the publishing house.

Fiction: Toddler books, picture books, chapter books, middle-grade, YA. Genres: contemporary, adventure, fantasy, suspense, mystery, science fiction, animal stories.

Nonfiction: Story picture books, chapter books, middle-grade, YA. Topics: biography, history, real life issues.

Submissions and Payment: Catalogue available on website. Like most Penguin Random House imprints, submissions are accepted through a literary agent. Responds in 6 months if interested. Publication period and payment policy vary.

Kokila

Penguin Young Readers Group, 375 Hudson Street, New York, NY 10014-3657. https://www.penguin.com/publishers/kokila/

Editor: Joanna Cárdenas

By centering stories from the margins and making space for storytellers to explore the full range of their experiences, Kokila delivers books that inspire and entertain readers. Kokila, an imprint of Penguin Young Readers, brings together an inclusive community of authors and illustrators, publishing professionals, and readers to examine and celebrate stories that reflect the richness of our world.

Freelance Potential: Plans to publish 15–20 books yearly.

Fiction: Picture books, middle-grade, YA. Genres: multicultural, social issues, real life problems.

Nonfiction: Picture books, middle-grade, YA. Topics: social issues, multicultural.

Submissions and Payment: Guidelines and catalogue available on website. Accepts hard copy submissions only; no electronic submissions. Send complete manuscript for picture books. Query with synopsis, 10 manuscript pages, and publishing credits for longer works. Materials are not returned. Response time, publication period, and payment policies vary.

Lantana Publishing

www.lantanapublishing.com

Submissions

Lantana changes the game and publishes inclusive books that celebrate our differences, no matter what they are. This award-winning London-based publishing house accepts submissions from authors of BAME (Black, Asian, and Minority Ethnic) heritage. It is a young, independent house that aims to open up a space for diversity and inclusion in children's publishing. Its current focus is on picture books for children ages 4–8 and narrative nonfiction for children ages 7–11.

Freelance Potential: Publishes up to 12 titles annually.

Fiction: Picture books (to 500 words).

Nonfiction: Narrative nonfiction (to 1,000 words).

Submissions and Payment: Advance and royalty payments. Guidelines and catalogue available on website. Send complete manuscript for picture book submissions. Accepts email submissions to submissions@lantanapublishing.com. Responds in 12 weeks. More information available at www.lantanapublishing.com/submissions.

Lee & Low Books

95 Madison Avenue, Suite 1205, New York, NY 10016. www.leeandlow.com

Submissions Editor

Lee & Low takes pride in nurturing new authors. It has earned a reputation for high-quality and groundbreaking books for young readers, with many of their titles winning major awards and honors. Known as the largest multicultural children's book publisher in the country, Lee & Low Books and its imprints Children's Book Press, Tu Books, Shen's Books, and Bebop Books have a special interest in realistic and historical fiction, and in nonfiction with a distinct voice or unique approach. Its mission is to publish contemporary, diverse stories that all children can enjoy. It is seeking picture book and chapter book manuscripts at this time.

Freelance Potential: Publishes about a dozen titles annually: 25% developed from unsolicited submissions; 30% by agented authors; about 50% by authors who are new to the publishing house; 50% by previously unpublished writers. Receives approximately 85 unsolicited manuscripts monthly.

Fiction: Story picture books, chapter books, middle-grade, YA. Genres: realistic, historical, contemporary, multicultural, ethnic.

Nonfiction: Story picture books, middle-grade, YA. Topics: multicultural and ethnic issues and traditions, biography.

Submissions and Payment: Guidelines and catalogue available on website. See website for details and updates of current needs. It is seeking middle-grade, YA, and picture book submissions at this time. For middle-grade manuscripts of more than 10,000 words, query with story synopsis, chapter outline, and first 3 chapters. Include cover letter with brief author biography and publishing history; note whether manuscript is an exclusive or simultaneous submission. Accepts hard copy. Materials not returned. Responds in 6 months if interested. Publication in 2–3 years. Advance against royalty.

     Lee & Low Imprints: Bebop Books, Children's Book Press, Shen's Books, Tu Books.

Little Bee Books

251 Park Avenue South, Floor 12, New York, NY 10010. www.littlebeebooks.com

Editor

Little Bee Books offers a variety of board books, picture books, activity books, nonfiction, and novelty books. It is a children's book publisher dedicated to making high-quality, creative, and fun books for the youngest of readers up to age 12. This imprint of Bonnier Publishing USA offers titles that inform, educate, delight, and inspire. This publisher accepts submissions from agents only.

Freelance Potential: Publishes 10 titles annually.

Fiction: Concept books, early picture books, early readers, story picture books, middle-grade. Genres: nature, reluctant readers, animals.

Nonfiction: Toddler books, story picture books, early readers, middle-grade. Topics: animals, nature, science.

Submissions and Payment: Catalogue available on website. Accepts submissions through agents only. Publication period and payment policies vary.

Little, Brown and Company Books for Young Readers

Hachette Book Group, 237 Park Avenue, New York, NY 10017. www.lb-kids.com, www.lb-teens.com

Publisher: Megan Tingley

Publishing a diverse, carefully curated list of the finest books for young readers of all ages and backgrounds is the goal of this publisher. Since 1926, the children's division of Little, Brown and Company has featured a core list of picture books and hardcover and paperback fiction and nonfiction for middle-grade and young adult readers. It only reviews submissions that are made through literary agents.

Freelance Potential: Publishes 135 titles annually: all by agented authors.

Fiction: Toddler books, concept books, novelty books, picture books, early readers, chapter books, YA. Genres: adventure, fantasy, contemporary, multicultural, holiday stories, sports, humor, graphic novels, manga.

Nonfiction: Concept books, story picture books, middle-grade, YA. Topics: sports, biography, animals, history, families, nature/environment, science, art, and activities.

Submissions and Payment: Guidelines and catalogue available on website. Accepts submissions from agented authors only. Publication period varies. Royalty; advance.

Little Simon

Simon & Schuster Children's Publishing, 1230 Avenue of the Americas, New York, NY 10020. http://imprints.simonandschuster.biz/little-simon

Submissions

Little Simon publishes innovative books for young children. This imprint from Simon & Schuster publishes books for young children with colorful picture books, board books, pop-up and lift-the-flap books, and other novelty formats. Its goal is to make reading fun for both young children and their parents. Due to the volume of submissions received, it is unable to review any submissions that do not come through literary agents.

Freelance Potential: Publishes 65 titles annually: 100% by agented authors.

Fiction: Concept books, board books, novelty books, toddler books, picture books. Genres: animal stories, holidays, trucks, automobiles, families, friendship.

Submissions and Payment: Accepts queries through literary agents only. Publication in 2 years. Royalty; advance. Flat fee.

Little Tiger Press 🌐🔒

1 The Coda Centre, 189 Munster Road, London SW6 6AW, United Kingdom.
http://www.littletiger.co.uk

Submissions Editor: Mara Alperin

Creating warm, bright, bold, and appealing picture books, Little Tiger Press blends humor, drama and imagination to captivate young minds. Helping children develop a love of reading for over thirty years, Little Tiger has been discovering and nurturing exceptional writing talent with whom they create humorous, touching, and imaginative picture books which provide a satisfying reading experience for child and parent alike. It was recently acquired by Penguin Random House. It features a diverse list of award-winning books. Its brightly illustrated titles share exciting stories and inspiring messages with young readers as they develop and grow in confidence. At this time, it is not accepting manuscripts. Check website for updates to this policy.

Freelance Potential: Publishes 60+ titles annually: 1–10% by authors who are new to the publishing house; 1–10% by previously unpublished writers. Receives 300 unsolicited manuscripts monthly.

Fiction: Concept books, board books, early picture books, story picture books. Genres: contemporary, classical.

Submissions and Payment: Guidelines and catalogue available on website. Not currently accepting submissions. Publication period and payment policy vary.

Lonely Planet Kids

124 Linden St., Oakland, CA 94607. http://www.lonelyplanet.com/kids

Lonely Planet has put travelers at the heart of everything they do. Lonely Planet Kids, an imprint of the world's leading travel authority Lonely Planet, published its first book in 2011. Building on parent brand Lonely Planet's 45 years of experience inspiring millions to travel, Lonely Planet Kids encourages the next generation of global citizens to learn about the world around them with engaging books on culture, sociology, geography, nature, history, space, and more. Whether at home, in school, or on the road, every day can be an adventure. Its books share the love of travel, a sense of humor, and a continual fascination with what makes the world a diverse place.

Freelance Potential: Publishes 20 titles annually.

Nonfiction: Middle-grade. Topics: travel.

Submissions and Payment: Lonely Planet posts freelance author, editor, and photographer opportunities on its website. Check regularly for current needs. At press time the company was not accepting book proposals. Response time, publication period, and payment policy vary.

James Lorimer & Company

117 Peter Street Suite 304, Toronto ON M5V 0M3 Canada. www.lorimer.ca

Children's Book Acquisitions: Robin Studniberg

James Lorimer & Company proudly continues on its mission to find and publish Canadian authors who speak to a distinctly Canadian youth audience. Publishing books that encourage even the most reluctant of readers to read, James Lorimer focuses on books that deal with contemporary social issues in a way that engages kids and teens. James Lorimer & Company began its journey in children's publishing in 1975. Lorimer publishes series fiction, nonfiction, self-help, and stand-alone fiction titles for kids and teens. It does not publish speculative fiction, picture books, or holiday books. Lorimer works only with Canadian authors.

Freelance Potential: Publishes 30 titles annually: 50% developed from unsolicited submissions; 25% by agented authors; 50% by authors who are new to the publishing house; 20% by previously unpublished writers. Receives 5+ queries monthly.

Fiction: Chapter books, middle-grade, YA. Genres: contemporary, realistic, sports, social issues.

Nonfiction: Middle-grade. Topics: sports biographies, Canadian history, self-help, social issues.

Submissions and Payment: Canadian authors only. Guidelines and catalogue available on website. Send complete manuscript with cover letter, author biography with a list of previously published works, word count, and plot synopsis that includes setting and characters. Accepts hard copy only. SAE/IRC. Responds in 3–4 months if interested. Publication in 1–2 years. Royalty.

Macmillan

175 Fifth Avenue, New York, NY 10010. http://us.macmillan.com

Editor

The company publishes a broad range of quality works, including award-winning fiction and nonfiction, and inspired and much-loved children's books. Macmillan is a global publisher that has many divisions and imprints. It is a distinctive group of publishing companies that has a rich history in the book industry. Note that Macmillan/McGraw-Hill and Gale's Macmillan Reference are not part of the same company; they are divisions of an earlier company sold to other corporations.

Freelance Potential: Publishes hundreds of books annually.

Fiction: All ages and genres across a variety of imprints.

Nonfiction: All ages and genres across a variety of imprints.

Submissions and Payment: Submission policies vary by division or imprint, although most acquisitions are via agents.

> **Macmillan Imprints:** Farrar, Strauss & Giroux Books for Young Readers, Greenhaven Press, Henry Holt Books for Young Readers, Kingfisher, Odd Dot, Roaring Brook Press, Starscape, Tor Books.

March 4th Press

www.littlepicklepress.com

Publisher

Dedicated to creating media and products that foster kindness in young people, March 4th Press is creating a new universe for young people. It is one filled with characters whose stories entertain while instilling qualities such as bravery, honesty, empathy, and patience. It has three imprints: Little Pickle Stories (0–10 years); Big Dill Stories (11–14 years); and Relish Stories (15+). Its titles do not shy away from controversial subjects.

Freelance Potential: Publishes 20 titles annually: 10% developed from unsolicited submissions.

Fiction: Early reader, middle-grade, YA. Genres: adventure, real-life stories, social issues, multicultural, mystery.

Submissions and Payment: Guidelines and catalogue available on website. Manuscripts can be submitted through the website through the Author.me form-building process, which allows you to attach your first three chapters and full manuscript to your submission. Documents must be in Word or PDF. Responds in 4 months. Publication period varies. Royalty.

Marimba Books

P.O. Box 5306, East Orange, NJ 07017. http://justusbooks.com

Submissions

Marimba Books is a multicultural children's book imprint that shares contemporary stories for young people. It is dedicated to publishing titles that reflect our country's diversity. Marimba Books focus on the richness, rhythm of language, and contemporary multicultural stories. It features board books, picture books, and chapter books for middle-grade readers. At this time, it is only accepting queries for middle-grade chapter books. Check the website for updates to this policy.

Freelance Potential: Publishes 2–3 titles annually.

Fiction: Board books, early picture books, story picture books, chapter books, reluctant readers, middle-grade. Genres: contemporary, historical, multicultural, social issues, social skills, religious.

Submissions and Payment: Guidelines and catalogue available on website. Currently accepting queries for chapter books only. Query with 1- to 2-page synopsis, 3–5 sample pages, and author biography that includes publishing credits. Accepts hard copy. Send SASE for response. Responds in 4–6 months. Publication period varies. Royalty.

Mayhaven Publishing, Inc.

803 E. Buckthorn Circle, P.O. Box 557, Mahomet, IL 61853. www.mayhavenpublishing.com

Editor/Publisher: Doris Replogle Wenzel

Mayhaven Publishing aims to produce interesting and unique books. Mayhaven Publishing offers books for children, young adults, and adults. It includes both fiction and nonfiction titles. It looks for high-quality submissions on a variety of subjects.

Freelance Potential: Publishes 2–5 children's titles annually: 98% developed from unsolicited submissions; 1–5% by agented authors; 70% by authors who are new to the publishing house; 30% by previously unpublished writers. Receives 20 queries, 10 unsolicited manuscripts monthly.

Fiction: Early reader books, picture books, story picture books, chapter books, middle-grade, YA. Genres: contemporary, multicultural, historical, realistic, science fiction, romance, fairy tales, humor, mystery, adventure, sports, animals.

Nonfiction: Early readers, picture books, story picture books, chapter books, middle-grade, YA. Topics: biography, educational, history, pop culture, reference, travel, contemporary issues, poetry. Also publishes books on parenting and crossover titles of interest to both children and adults.

Submissions and Payment: Catalogue available on website. Query or send complete manuscript. Accepts hard copy and email submissions to mayhavenpublishing@mchsi.com (Word or PDF attachments). SASE. Response time varies. Publication period varies. Royalty.

Margaret K. McElderry Books

Simon & Schuster, 1230 Avenue of the Americas, New York, NY 10020. http://imprints.simonandschuster.biz/margaret-k-mcelderry-books

Submissions Editor

This publisher is a leader in acquiring properties from foreign publishers as well as being known for attracting and nurturing talent from other countries. Recognized internationally as a publisher of literary, author-driven fiction and nonfiction for the teen, middle-grade, picture book, and poetry markets, this boutique publisher is an imprint from Simon & Schuster's Children's Division. It accepts submissions through literary agents only.

Freelance Potential: Publishes 50 titles annually: all by agented authors.

Fiction: Picture books, story picture books, middle-grade, YA. Genres: contemporary, historical, fantasy, poetry, animals, nature stories.

Nonfiction: Middle-grade, YA. Topics: history, nature, natural history, mythology.

Submissions and Payment: Agented authors only. Publication in 2–4 years. Royalty; advance.

McSweeney's McMullens

849 Valencia Street, San Francisco, CA 94110. www.mcsweeneys.net

Publisher: Dave Eggers
Editor and Art Director: Brian McMullen

McSweeney's exists to champion ambitious and inspired new writing, and to challenge conventional expectations about where it's found, how it looks, and who participates. McSweeney's discovers things they love, help them find their most resplendent form, and imagine new ways to bring them to you.

McSweeney's is a publishing company that also offers a daily humor website and publishes a quarterly book of stories, as well as an ever-growing selection of books. It is currently not accepting submissions for children's books.

Freelance Potential: Publishes 10 books annually.

Fiction: Picture books, middle-grade. Genres: adventure, mystery, family, social skills.

Submissions and Payment: Guidelines and catalogue available on website. McSweeney's McMullens is open to book submissions from new and established authors, agented and unagented. At this time it is not accepting submissions for children's books. Check the website for changes to this policy. Accepts submissions with cover letter that includes a brief synopsis; submit through submishmash at mcsweeneysbooksubmissions.submishmash.com/submit. Response time, publication period, and payment policy vary.

MeeGenius

www.hmhco.com

Editor

Part of Houghton Mifflin Harcourt, MeeGenius, is a reading app that digitalizes children's stories. The books have digital features, such as highlighting, professional narration, and read-along technology. It is open to submissions from authors of works to be published in this manner.

Freelance Potential: Publishes 50 titles yearly.

Fiction: Picture books, story picture books, toddlers, early readers. Genres: animals, real life, adventure, social skills.

Nonfiction: Picture books, story picture books, toddlers, early readers. Topics: animals, weather, real life, social skills, inspirational, holiday.

Submissions and Payment: Guidelines and catalogue available on website. Query or send complete manuscript with author bio. Accepts email to publish@meegenius.com. Responds in 2 weeks. Publication period, unknown. Payment policy varies.

Meriwether Publishing

Pioneer Drama Service, Inc., P.O. Box 4267, Englewood, CO 80155.
www.pioneerdrama.com; http://meriwether.com/

Editor

A division of Pioneer Drama Service, Meriwether Publishing publishes how-to books and instructional videos for stage, television, and film acting students, aspiring theatre professionals. Several Meriwether Publishing theatre arts books are widely accepted as classroom textbooks or supplements for acting and drama classes from middle school to college level. It also publishes monologue and scene books, theatre anthologies, speech and drama curriculum books, and resources for theatre arts educators.

Freelance Potential: Publishes 3–5 titles annually: 10–20% developed from unsolicited submissions;

50% by authors who are new to the publishing house; about 10% by previously unpublished writers. Receives 20 queries, 10–15 unsolicited manuscripts monthly.

Nonfiction: Middle-grade, YA, Trade. Topics: acting, directing, auditioning, improvisation, public speaking, interpersonal communication, debate, mime, storytelling, costuming, stage lighting, sound effects, theatre curriculum. Also publishes collections of monologues, scenes, and short plays.

Submissions and Payment: Guidelines and catalogue available on website: www.pioneerdrama.com. Query with a synopsis, outline, sample chapters, market analysis, publishing credits, and payment expectations. Accepts hard copy and email to Books@pioneerdrama.com. Accepts simultaneous submissions if identified. SASE. Responds in 4–6 weeks. Publication in 12+ months. Royalty.

Milet Publishing

814 North Franklin Street, Chicago, IL 60610. www.milet.com

Editorial Director

Milet is known for its thoughtful, beautiful, high quality books and for its steadfast commitment to diverse voices and visions. It combines artistic innovation with linguistic excellence in books and multimedia resources that are both educational and entertaining. It has a mission of expanding the scope and look of bilingual and multicultural books for children and young adults. It is also a groundbreaking publisher of literature in translation, bringing into English works by international authors of children's books.

Freelance Potential: Publishes about 10 titles annually: 10% by agented authors; 20% by authors who are new to the publishing house.

Fiction: Board books, picture books, middle-grade. Genres: multicultural, fantasy.

Nonfiction: Board books, picture books, middle-grade. Topics: world cultures, language.

Submissions and Payment: Guidelines and catalogue available on website. Query with cover letter that includes author credentials, brief description of the work, target audience, and competing titles; synopsis of the work (one page or less); and sample text or chapters. Accepts email to info@milet.com. Responds in 3 months, if interested. Publication period and payment policies vary.

Milkweed Editions

1011 Washington Avenue South, Open Book, Suite 300, Minneapolis, MN 55415-1246. www.milkweed.org

Editor: Joy McGarvey

Milkweed Editions takes risks on debut and experimental writers, they invest significant time and care in the editorial process, and they enable dynamic engagement between authors and readers. It is an independent publisher of fiction, nonfiction, and poetry. It seeks to be a site of metamorphosis in the literary ecosystem. This independent publisher's mission is to identify, nurture, and publish transformative literature, and build an engaged community around it. It does not publish picture books or children's nonfiction. It is currently closed for submissions; check the website for changes in this policy.

Freelance Potential: Publishes 18–20 titles annually: about 5% developed from unsolicited submissions; 25% by agented authors; 30% by authors who are new to the publishing house; 15% by previously unpublished writers. Receives 250 unsolicited manuscripts monthly.

Fiction: Middle-grade, YA. Genres: contemporary, historical, multicultural, ethnic, nature stories.

Submissions and Payment: Guidelines and catalogue available on website. Query from January to March and July to September only, with the first 3 chapters. Prefers submissions through the website's Submissions Manager. Accepts hard copy. Responds in 4–6 months during reading periods. Publication in 2 years. Royalty, 6% of list price; advance varies.

Denene Millner Books

Simon & Schuster Children's Publishing, 1230 Avenue of the Americas, New York, NY 10020. https://www.simonandschuster.com

Editorial Director: Denene Millner

Launching in spring 2020, this new imprint from Simon & Schuster is under the direction of award-winning journalist and author Denene Millner. It will publish titles written by African-American writers for readers of all ages.

Freelance Potential: Published 5 titles in 2020.

Fiction: Concept books, toddler books, early picture books, story picture books, chapter books, middle-grade, YA. Genres: fantasy, mystery, adventure, fairy tales, historical, contemporary, graphic novels.

Nonfiction: Story picture books, chapter books, middle-grade, YA. Topics: adventure, biography, the environment, science, nature, sports, history, multicultural issues.

Submissions and Payment: Catalogue available on website. Guidelines available. Accepts agented manuscripts only. Publication period varies. Royalty.

MIT Kids ★

www.candlewick.com

Aquisitions

MIT Kids is one of two new imprints from an innovative publishing project between MIT Press and Candlewick Press. The imprint will publish engaging and ambitious books for children covering STEAM topics ranging from planetary science to the internet and the environment. MIT Press and faculty will help identify prospective writers, as well as check submissions for scientific validity.

Freelance Potential: MIT Kids will debut their first list in 2021.

Nonfiction: Concept books, early readers, middle-grade. Topics: science, math, planets, environment, nature.

Submissions and Payment: Agented authors only. Catalogue available on website. Response time, publication period, and payment policy vary.

MIT Teens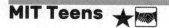

www.candlewick.com

Aquisitions

MIT Teens is a new STEAM imprint that is part of a collaboration between MIT Press and Candlewick Press. The imprint will target teens with a range of nonfiction and fiction centering on science, technology, engineering, arts, and mathematics. MIT Press and faculty will help identify prospective writers, as well as check submissions for scientific validity. This imprint will review submissions from agents only.

Freelance Potential: MIT Teens will debut their first list in 2021.

Fiction: YA. Genre: fiction that deals with STEAM topics.

Nonfiction: YA. Topics: science, math, planets, environment, nature.

Submissions and Payment: Agented authors only. Catalogue available on website. Response time, publication period, and payment policy vary.

Move Books

P.O. Box 183, Beacon Falls, CT 06403. www.move-books.com

Editor: Eileen Robinson

Move Books wants boys to become emotionally invested, finding the books they love. Its vision is to grow and sustain boys' appetite for reading—to move them to read for the long term. Publishing boy-centered books that are able to stand on their own is the main goal of Move Books. It stands behind the fact that boys do read when presented with materials that interest them. It wants boys to be compelled and inspired to read on their own because the stories and experiences mean something to them. It is currently accepting middle-grade submissions only.

Freelance Potential: Publishes 2–6 titles annually.

Fiction: Chapter books, middle-grade. Genres: fantasy, contemporary, historical, humor, adventure.

Submissions and Payment: Guidelines available on website. Query with synopsis and the first 25 pages of your manuscript. Accepts hard copy. Responds if interested. Publication period and payment policy varies.

Muddy Boots

Globe Pequot, 246 Goose Lane, P.O. Box 480, Guilford, CT 06437. www.globepequot.com; http://www.muddybootsbooks.com/

Executive Editor: Rick Rinehart

Globe Pequot launched its first children's imprint, Muddy Boots, in 2016 inviting kids of all ages to go further, dig deeper, think bigger. Designed to help children ages 12 and under engage with the outdoors, the imprint brings together bestselling authors from imprints of the parent company, Rowman & Littlefield, including Linda Kranz and Carmen LaVigna Coyle.

Freelance Potential: Publishes 15 titles each year.

Nonfiction: Early readers, middle-grade. Topics: outdoor life, camping, hiking, nature, animals, travel, recreation, sports, regional, pets, biography, cooking, current events, home and garden.

Submissions and Payment: Guidelines and catalogue available on website. Globe is currently closed to unsolicited manuscript and proposal submissions but is still offering freelance work. To be considered, send résumé, writing credits, and 3 brief writing samples. Accepts hard copy. Responds in 3 months. Publication in 18 months. Royalty, 8–12%; advance, $500–$1,500.

MuseItUp Publishing

14878 James, Pierrefonds, Quebec H9H 1P5 Canada. www.museituppublishing.com

Acquisition Editor: Lea Schizas

This publisher looks for well-written fiction that pulls them in from the beginning, stories that surprise at the end, and characters readers connect with. MuseItUp is an epublisher specializing in fiction for middle-graders, young adults, and adults. It welcomes new writers in many genres, but is especially interested in young adult romance, middle-grade historical fiction, and stories for boys. It now has imprints specifically for children, middle-grade, and young adults titled MuseIt Kids, MuseIt Young, and MuseIt YA.

Freelance Potential: Publishes 150–200 titles annually: 50–70% developed from unsolicited submissions; 1–10% by agented authors; 25–50% by previously unpublished writers. Receives approximately 100 unsolicited manuscripts monthly.

Fiction: Middle-grade, YA. Genres: contemporary, fantasy, historical, inspirational, adventure, sports, mystery, romance, paranormal, Western.

Submissions and Payment: Guidelines and catalogue available on website. Send complete manuscript with synopsis and cover letter that includes brief author bio, title, genre, and word count during open submission periods (check website for dates). Accepts email submissions to musesubs@gmail.com (Word or RTF attachments). Accepts simultaneous submissions, if identified. Responds in 3–4 months. Publication in 1 year. Royalty, 40%.

Namelos

www.namelos.com

Publisher: Stephen Roxburgh

Namelos publishes titles simultaneously in hardcover, paperback, and e-book formats. It offers high quality children's and young adult fiction and nonfiction books. This publisher accepts unsolicited submissions with a required evaluation fee. Each submission receives a written evaluation and a phone or email follow-up with the goal of preparing a manuscript for submission to an agent or editor. Evaluation fee is refunded if the manuscript is accepted.

Freelance Potential: Publishes 6–10 titles annually. Receives 20 queries and 15 unsolicited manuscripts monthly.

Nonfiction: Middle-grade, YA. Topics: social issues, culture, history, poetry.

Fiction: Middle-grade, YA. Genres: historical, social issues, fantasy, Western, mystery, contemporary.

Submissions and Payment: Catalogue and guidelines available on website. Send a cover letter with author bio, up to 10,000 words of a manuscript, and $250 fee to info@namelos.com (Word attachments). Responds in 2 weeks. Publication period and payment policy vary.

National Geographic Society

National Geographic Children's Books, 1145 17th Street NW, 6th Floor, Washington, DC 20036-4688. http://kids.nationalgeographic.com/explore/publishing/

Associate Editor: Kate Olesin

National Geographic is the ultimate destination for kids of all ages who are curious about their world and how it works. National Geographic is the leading nonfiction publisher in the world. It sparks curiosity and inspires kids to learn about the world. It creates and distributes print and digital works that inspire, entertain, teach, and give readers access to a world of discovery and possibility. At this time, it is not accepting submissions from authors.

Freelance Potential: Publishes 70 titles annually: 5% by authors who are new to the publishing house. Receives 20 queries monthly.

Nonfiction: Early readers, story picture books, activity books, chapter books, middle-grade, YA. Topics: the sciences, American and world cultures, myth, history, animals, geography, biography.

Submissions and Payment: Guidelines and catalogue available on website. It is not currently accepting submissions. Check website for changes to this policy.

Tommy Nelson Kids

501 Nelson Place, P.O. Box 141000, Nashville, TN 37214. www.tommynelson.com

Acquisitions Editor

Tommy Nelson kids, the children's division of Thomas Nelson, Inc., publishes a wide variety of high-quality products that are consistent with the teachings found in the Bible. The products from Tommy Nelson are designed to expand children's imaginations and nurture their faith while pointing them to a personal relationship with God.

Freelance Potential: Publishes 50–75 titles annually: 100% by agented authors. Receives 20 queries each month.

Fiction: Board books, concept books, toddler books, early picture books, early readers, story picture books, middle-grade. Genres: religious, real life/problems, contemporary, inspirational, adventure, fantasy, humor, science fiction, dystopian, mystery, of interest to girls.

Nonfiction: Board books, picture books, Bible storybooks, middle-grade, YA, devotionals. Topics: the Bible, Christianity, inspirational, biography.

Submissions and Payment: Catalogue available on website. Accepts proposals through literary agents only. Also recommends christianmanuscriptsubmissions.com. Response time and publication period vary. Royalty; advance.

NorthSouth Books

600 Third Avenue, 2nd Floor, New York, NY 10016. http://northsouth.com

Editor: Beth Terrill

NorthSouth Books offers fresh, original fiction and nonfiction picture books targeting readers ages 3–8. It features books with lovable characters, fun and thoughtful themes that resonate with kids and parents around the world, and incredible artwork that opens minds and hearts. It is currently interested in picture book submissions from US–based authors and illustrators.

Freelance Potential: Publishes 30 titles annually: 95% by agented authors, 30% by authors who are new to the publishing house, 3% by previously unpublished writers.

Fiction: Board books, novelty books, toddler books, early picture books, early readers, story picture books, chapter books. Genres: contemporary, multicultural, adventure, drama, fairy tales, folklore, humor, nature stories.

Nonfiction: Concept books, early picture books, chapter books. Topics: early learning, holidays, animals, hobbies, crafts, humor, nature, religion, science, technology, social issues, sports, multicultural and ethnic issues.

Submissions and Payment: Catalogue available on website. Fiction and nonfiction, to 1,000 words. Prefers complete ms. Accepts email submissions to submissionsnsb@gmail.com. Publication period and payment policy vary.

Norton Young Readers

500 Fifth Avenue, New York, NY 10110. http://books.wwnorton.com/books/index.aspx

Norton Young Readers publishes a full range of picture books, narrative fiction and nonfiction, and graphic novels. This new imprint is the first children's imprint for W.W. Norton & Company. According to publishing director Simon Boughton, "We're cultivating a broad range of books, both in terms of age and category." Nonfiction is at the center of its program.

Freelance Potential: Publishes several titles each year.

Nonfiction: Early readers, middle-grade, YA, Adult. Topics: science, history, multicultural, health.

Submissions and Payment: Catalogue available on website. Accepts submissions through literary agents only. Responds 3–6 months. Publication period, payment rates, and policies vary.

Nosy Crow 🌐

The Crow's Nest, 14 Baden Place, London SE1 1YW United Kingdom. http://nosycrow.com

Editorial Director: Camilla Reid
Head of Picture Books: Louise Bolongaro
USEditor, Candlewick Press: Joan Powers

Making well-designed physical books is important to Nosy Crow. It publishes high-quality commercial fiction and nonfiction books for children ages 0–12 by well-known authors and illustrators and by new talent. It is a small, award-winning independent company and one of the country's fastest growing publishing companies. Looking for "parent-friendly" books, it publishes all of its fiction work in e-book format as well as print. In the United States, the Nosy Crow imprint publishes under the umbrella of Candlewick Press.

Freelance Potential: Publishes 25 books and apps annually.

Fiction: Preschool, board books, novelty books, picture books, middle-grade, young YA, apps. Genres: adventure, humor, fairy tales, contemporary, historical, mystery.

Nonfiction: Preschool, board books, novelty books, picture books. Topics: animals, transportation, work, nature.

Submissions and Payment: Guidelines available on website. For board, novelty, or picture books/apps, send full text and any supporting visual material (not original artwork). For longer fiction or nonfiction, send a cover letter with relevant information about you and the work, a short synopsis, and first chapter. Prefers email to submissions@nosycrow.com (Word or PDF files). Put "Submission to Nosy Crow" in the subject line. Accepts hard copy. SASE. Responds in 3+ months.

Odd Dot

120 Broadway, 24th Floor, New York, NY 10271. www.odddot.com

Editorial Assistant: Kate Avino

Gift books and definitive, interactive nonfiction in unique categories and formats for people of all ages fill the catalogue from Odd Dot. It is an imprint of Macmillan that focuses on sound pedagogy, visual, and format-focused ideas. Odd Dot also publishes novelty books with toy-like experiences, ranging from trade workbooks to craft kits and beyond.

Freelance Potential: Publishes 30 titles annually: many by freelance authors.

Fiction: Concept books, novelty books, story picture books.

Nonfiction: Concept books, novelty books, workbooks. Topics: science, English, math, coding, crafts.

Submissions and Payment: Catalogue available on website. Query with detailed synopsis. Accepts email queries to kate.avino@odddot.com. Response time, publication period, and payment policies vary.

Orca Book Publishers

1016 Balmoral Road, Victoria, British Columbia V8T 1A8 Canada. www.orcabook.com

Editor

Orca publishes everything from beautifully illustrated board books and picture books to middle-grade and young-adult fiction. Orca prides itself on publishing Canadian authors and bringing them to a wider market. It is an independently owned Canadian children's book publisher of award-winning, best-selling books in a number of genres. Accepting work from Canadian authors only, its titles are sorted into divisions, each serving a specific type of reader or content.

Freelance Potential: Publishes 80+ titles annually: 50% developed from unsolicited submissions; 50% by agented authors; 55% by authors who are new to the publishing house; 20% by previously unpublished writers. Receives 166 queries, 42 unsolicited manuscripts monthly.

Fiction: Board books, toddler books, early picture books, early readers, story picture books, chapter books, reluctant readers, graphic novels, middle-grade, YA. Genres: regional, historical, contemporary, mystery, fantasy, adventure, sports stories.

Nonfiction: Middle-grade, YA. Topics: nature, history.

Submissions and Payment: Canadian authors only. Guidelines and catalogue available on website. Send cover letter and complete manuscript for picture books, historical fiction, and graphic novels. Query for all others. (Refer to guidelines for submission details and current needs for each division.) Accepts hard copy. SASE. Responds in 4 months if interested. Publication in 18–24 months. Royalty, 10% split; advance.

Orchard Books

Scholastic Inc., 557 Broadway, New York, NY 10012. www.scholastic.com

Editorial Director

Founded in 1986, Orchard Books is a part of Scholastic's Trade Division. It offers the very best in children's books for all ages. From the young, bright, and bold to the edgy, glamorous, and intense, Orchard Books has something of interest to kids of all ages.

Freelance Potential: Publishes 15–20 titles annually.

Fiction: Concept books, toddler books, early picture books, early readers, story picture books. Genres: historical, contemporary, multicultural, fairy tales, folktales, fantasy, humor, sports, animal, and nature stories.

Submissions and Payment: Agented authors only. Publication period varies. Royalty; advance.

Page Street Publishing

27 Congress Street, Suite 103, Salem, MA, 01970. www.pagestreetpublishing.com

Submissions

Page Street Publishing inspires readers with thoughtful stories. It is growing every year. It searches out creative people whose passions and exceptional talents have earned them many fans. It is focused on creating top-quality content for children and teens featuring believable, diverse characters and riveting stories that resonate with readers. Its books are distributed through Macmillan.

Freelance Potential: Publishes 120 titles yearly.

Fiction: Early readers, middle-grade, YA. Genres: animals, humor, real-life problems, folktales.

Nonfiction: Early readers, middle-grade, YA. Topics: biography, history, science, cooking, self-help, nature.

Submissions and Payment: Catalogue and guidelines available on website. For picture book submissions: include a query and attach the manuscript as a word document or a pdf sketch dummy, 32–40 pages, in spread layouts. Your query must contain: 1) synopsis, pitch, age range; and 2) an author bio that describes your publishing history, social media presence, and any other relevant information that pertains to your manuscript. If you are an illustrator, also include your website. Accepts email submissions to childrensubmissions@pagestreetpublishing.com with the title of your manuscript in the subject line. For YA fiction: include a 1-page query with the first three chapters of your manuscript in the body of your email. Your query must contain: 1) a book synopsis that includes your novel's pitch, word count, and classification (literary, historical, fantasy, mystery, etc.); and 2) an author bio that describes your occupation, publishing history, social media presence, and any other relevant information that pertains to your manuscript (including any endorsements, if applicable). If you are represented by an agent or plan to be, please note this in your author bio. Ideally, your manuscript's length is 60–90K words and your protagonist is 15–18 years old. Accepts submissions by email to yasubmissions@pagestreetpublishing.com with the title of your manuscript in the subject line. For nonfiction: include an author bio, a short synopsis of the book concept and approach, samples of your work (recipes/projects/writing sample) if applicable, and any notable media hits or press features. If you are represented by an agent or plan to be, please note that they need to be part of the conversation from the start. Accepts submissions by email to submissions@pagestreetpublishing.com with the title of your manuscript in the subject line. If you are an agent, write AGENTED in the subject line as well. Responds only if interested. Publication period varies. Royalty.

Pajama Press ☆

181 Carlaw Avenue, Suite 207, Toronto, ON, Canada. www.pajamapress.ca

Publisher: Gail Winskill
Editor: Ann Featherstone

Pajama Press is looking for manuscripts from authors of diverse backgrounds. Stories about immigrants are of special interest. It accepts submissions from Canadian authors only. It is a small literary press with high editorial and production standards. It publishes picture books—both for the very young and for school-aged readers—as well as early chapter books, novels for middle-grade readers, and contemporary or historical fiction for pre–high school aged YA readers aged 12–14. Its nonfiction titles typically contain a strong narrative element.

Freelance Potential: Publishes 18–20 titles annually.

Fiction: Picture books, middle-grade, YA. Open to genres.

Nonfiction: Picture books, middle-grade. Open to all topics.

Submissions and Payment: Guidelines and catalogue available on website. For permission to send manuscript, email query with a brief summary of the book and 1–2 sample pages of the finished book to annfeatherstone@pajamapress.ca. Also include link to online published writings. No hard copy. Simultaneous submissions discouraged. Response time, publication period, and payment policies vary.

Pants On Fire Press

www.pantsonfirepress.com

Editor: Becca Goldman

Pants on Fire is looking for strong writers who are excited about marketing their stories and building a following of readers. This award-winning boutique publisher loves big story ideas and meaty characters. It offers middle-grade, young adult, and fictional books for adults in both print and e-book formats. It is open to working with new writers.

Freelance Potential: Publishes 10 titles annually.

Fiction: Middle-grade, YA. Genres: Adventure, mystery, science fiction, thriller, horror, humor, fantasy, historical, romance, Christian.

Submissions and Payment: Guidelines and catalogue available on website. Accepts electronic submissions to submission@pantsonfirepress.com. Royalty; advance.

Peachtree Publishers

1700 Chattahoochee Avenue, Atlanta, GA 30318-2112. www.peachtree-online.com

Acquisitions Editor: Helen Harriss

From picture books to young adult fiction and nonfiction, to health, education, and parenting, you can find it all in the catalogue from Peachtree. It creates books that educate, entertain, and endure. Peachtree Publishers' mission is to create books that captivate young and old readers alike, with well-crafted words and pictures.

Freelance Potential: Publishes 25 titles annually: 5% from unsolicited submissions; 15% by authors who are new to the publishing house. Receives 1,600 manuscripts monthly.

Fiction: Early picture books, early readers, story picture books, chapter books, middle-grade, YA. Genres: contemporary, regional, historical, multicultural.

Nonfiction: Early picture books, story picture books, middle-grade. Topics: nature, sports, biography.

Submissions and Payment: Guidelines and catalogue available on website. Send complete ms for picture books. For all others, send complete manuscript or query with table of contents and 3 sample chapters. For all submissions, include author biography and publishing credits. Accepts hard copy only. SASE. Responds in 6–9 months. Publication period and payment policy vary.

Penguin Random House Children's Books USA

1745 Broadway, New York, NY 10019. www.penguinrandomhouse.com

Editor

Penguin Random House is the international home to nearly 250 editorially and creatively independent publishing imprints. Penguin Random House's mission is to foster a universal passion for reading by partnering with authors to help create stories and communicate ideas that inform, entertain, and inspire, and to connect them with readers everywhere. It publishes stories that can take you anywhere. It is committed to expanding its role as a cultural institution that serves society not only with the books it publishes, but also by making investments in new ideas and diverse voices.

Freelance Potential: Publishes hundreds of books annually.

Fiction: All ages and genres across a variety of imprints.

Nonfiction: All ages and genres across a variety of imprints.

Submissions and Payment: Guidelines and catalogue available on website. Submission policies vary by division or imprint, although many acquisitions are made via agents. For details, see http://us.penguingroup.com/static/pages/aboutus/pyrg-subguides.html.

> **Penguin Random House Imprints:** Dial Books for Young Readers, DK Publishing, Dutton Children's Books, Alfred A. Knopf Books for Young Readers, Kokila, Penguin Random House UK, Penguin Workshop, Philomel Books, Price Stern Sloan, Puffin Books, G. P. Putnam's Sons Books for Young Readers, Random House Graphic, Random House Studio, Razorbill, Rise, Anne Schwartz Books, Viking Children's Books, WaterBrook Multnomah.

Penguin Random House UK Children's Books

20 Vauxhall Bridge Road, London SW1V 2SA United Kingdom. www.randomhouse.co.uk/browse/children

Picture Books: Hannah Featherstone. Fiction: Naomi Wood

This publisher exists to connect the world with the words that matter, through books that spark thoughts, dreams, conversations, and learning. The world's leading trade publisher brings to the field creative formats that bring ideas and stories to life in compelling and contemporary ways and capturing the attention of the world for the stories, ideas, and writing that matter. It seeks out and champions diverse author voices and brings their stories to readers everywhere. Most imprints accept submissions from agented authors only.

Freelance Potential: Publishes 200+ titles annually: all by agented authors. Receives 250 queries each month.

Fiction: Toddler books, early picture books, early readers, picture books, story picture books, chapter books, middle-grade. Genres: contemporary, multicultural, historical, fantasy.

Submissions and Payment: Catalogue and guidelines available on website. Accepts submissions from agented authors only. Publication in 1–2 years. Royalty; advance.

Penguin Workshop

Penguin Young Readers Group, 1745 Broadway, New York, NY 10019.
http://www.penguin.com/publishers/penguinworkshop/

Editorial Director: Francesco Sedita

Penguin Workshop replaces the Grosset & Dunlap imprint at Penguin. Penguin Workshop makes great books for every kind of reader from birth through age 12. Its list includes unique board books, picture books, chapter books, and best-selling series. It also features Penguin's award-winning leveled reader program. Material will no longer be accepted through the Grosset & Dunlap imprint.

Freelance Potential: Publishes several titles each year. Plans to publish 30 titles annually.

Fiction: Early picture books, early readers, story picture books, chapter books, middle-grade. Genres: mystery, science fiction.

Submissions and Payment: Guidelines and catalogue available on website. Mailed submissions only; no electronic submissions. Send complete manuscript for picture books. Query with synopsis, 10 manuscript pages, and publishing credits for longer works. Materials are not returned. Responds in 4 months if interested. Publication period and payment policy vary.

Peter Pauper Press

202 Mamaroneck Avenue, Suite 400, White Plains, NY 10601-5376. www.peterpauper.com

Children's Editor

Fine gift books, humor books, compact references, travel guides, unique journals, quality stationery, holiday cards, and innovative children's activity books make up this publisher's catalogue.

Freelance Potential: Publishes 100 titles annually: 15% developed from unsolicited submissions, 10% by agented authors, 10% by authors who are new to the publishing house, 5% by previously unpublished writers. Receives 120 mss yearly.

Fiction: Story picture books, story-based activity books. Genres: humor, fantasy, adventure.

Nonfiction: Story-based activity books, puzzle books. Topics: biography, history, nature, science.

Submissions and Payment: Guidelines and catalogue available on website. Query with letter describing the work as a whole, the intended market, and how the project differs from the competition; author credentials; 2 sample chapters and artwork samples, if applicable, or the complete manuscript. Accepts electronic submissions through the website and hard copy. SASE. Responds in 3 months. Publication period varies. Payment varies.

Phaidon Press

Regent's Wharf, All Saints Street, London N1 9PA United Kingdom. www.phaidon.com

Editorial Submissions

Phaidon takes pride in publishing some of the most beautiful books in the world. It publishes for children ages 0–8 in the categories of board book, novelty book, and picture book. It is the premier global publisher of the creative arts with over 1,500 titles in print. It offers books for adults on art, architecture, music, theater, film, and the performing arts. Though it has offices in New York, editorial submissions are accepted through the London office. Phaidon operates a global sales and distribution network, selling in over 100 countries and publishing books in multiple languages.

Freelance Potential: Publishes 20+ titles annually: 50% developed from unsolicited submissions. Receives 10–20 queries monthly.

Fiction: Early picture books, board books, early readers, story picture books. Genres: contemporary, multicultural, social skills.

Nonfiction: Early picture books, story picture books. Topics: cooking, the arts, crafts, games.

Submissions and Payment: Guidelines and catalogue available on website. Query with resume and a short synopsis. Accepts email only to submissions@phaidon.com. Responds in 3 months if interested. Publication period varies. Royalty; advance.

Philomel Books

Penguin Group, 345 Hudson Street, New York, NY 10014.
http://us.penguingroup.com http://www.penguin.com/publishers/philomel/

Editorial Assistant

Philomel specializes in books that are lyrical, beautiful in concept and form, and fine enough to be celebrated as gifts. Whatever the genre, Philomel strives to foster a love of reading in children and young adults. It produces high-quality picture books for young readers as well as middle-grade books and young adult titles. This publisher takes pride in its ability to reach the reluctant reader. Philomel accepts submissions from agents only.

Freelance Potential: Publishes 40–50 titles annually: 1–10% developed from unsolicited submissions; 90% by agented authors. Receives 50 queries monthly.

Fiction: Early picture books, story picture books, chapter books, reluctant readers, middle-grade, YA. Genres: fantasy, contemporary, historical, multicultural, science fiction.

Nonfiction: Story picture books, YA. Topics: biography and first-person narratives.

Submissions and Payment: Guidelines and catalogue available on website. Prefers submissions from literary agents. Responds in 4 months if interested. Publication in 1–2 years. Royalty.

Piccadilly Press ⊙

5 Castle Road, London, NW1 8PR, England. http://www.piccadillypress.co.uk

Submissions Editor

Piccadilly Press publishes well-written stories for 5–12 year olds. Fun, family-oriented fiction makes up the catalogue from this publisher. Their books include exciting stories for young readers, engaging novels for teens, and nonfiction books for young adults. It is not accepting picture book submissions at this time.

Freelance Potential: Publishes about 25 titles annually.

Fiction: Toddler books, early picture books, early readers, story picture books, chapter books, middle-grade, YA. Genres: historical, contemporary, mystery, fantasy, adventure, humor.

Nonfiction: Story picture books, middle-grade, YA. Topics: real life, social issues.

Submissions and Payment: Guidelines and catalogue available on website. Send cover letter and complete manuscript for picture books. For longer manuscripts, include a cover letter, synopsis, and a few sample pages. Accepts email submissions only to hello@bonnierbooks.co.uk. Responds in 6 weeks. Publication period and payment policy, unknown.

Piñata Books

Arte Público Press, University of Houston, 4902 Gulf Freeway, Building 19, Rm 100, Houston, TX 77204-2004. www.artepublicopress.com

Submissions

Piñata Books has made giant strides in filling the void that exists in American publishing and literature: books that accurately reflect themes, characters, and customs unique to US Hispanic culture. Literary treats are spilling out of Piñata Books, an imprint of Arte Público Press. Its catalogue includes bilingual picture books for children and entertaining novels for young adults.

Freelance Potential: Publishes about 20–25 titles annually.

Fiction: Picture books, middle-grade, YA. Genres: contemporary, historical, multicultural.

Nonfiction: Picture books, middle-grade, YA. Topics: biography, social issues, self-help.

Submissions and Payment: Guidelines and catalogue available on website. Query with sample chapters or send complete manuscript in English or Spanish. Accepts electronic submissions through form on website (Word or RTF files only). Responds in 2–6 months. Publication period and payment policies vary.

Pixel+Ink

425 Madison Avenue, New York, NY 10017. www.pixelandinkbooks.com

Editor-in-Chief: Bethany Buck

Pixel+Ink was launched in 2019 by Trustbridge, parent company of Holiday House and Peachtree Publishing. It publishes everything from picture books to chapter books to middle grade and graphic novels. Every one of its offerings is full of heart and humor. Its list targets children ages 3–13.

Freelance Potential: Its inaugural list will publish in 2020.

Fiction: Early readers, story picture books, chapter books, middle-grade, graphic novels. Genres: contemporary, multicultural, humor, mystery, fantasy.

Submissions and Payment: Guidelines available on website. Send complete manuscript. Though not necessary, include copies of artwork if available. Accepts email submissions to info@tbridgemedia.com. Responds in 4 months if interested. Publication period varies. Royalty; advance.

Playwrights Canada Press

202–269 Richmond Street West, Toronto, Ontario M5V 1X1, Canada. www.playwrightscanada.com

Submissions Editor

This publisher of Canadian plays looks for well-written literary works with engaging dialogue, interesting characters, and strong themes that incite discussion and analysis, and that focus on contemporary issues. It publishes new plays, both drama and comedies, written by Canadian authors only. It caters to drama production and theater groups by offering plays of all types, as well as books on topics such as stage management and acting technique. It also publishes plays for young audiences and French plays by Canadian authors in English translation, and includes theatre for young audiences. Announcements regarding the occasional call for material for anthologies and drama festivals will be posted on the website.

Freelance Potential: Publishes 30 titles annually: 1–10% developed from unsolicited submissions. Receives 8–10 queries monthly.

Fiction: Dramatic plays for elementary, middle school, and high school students.

Nonfiction: Middle-grade, YA. Topics: acting, play production. Also publishes theater resources for drama teachers.

Submissions and Payment: Canadian authors only. Guidelines and catalogue available on website. Send complete manuscript. Plays must include first production information, including cast and crew. Accepts email to submissions@playwrightscanada.com (Word or PDF attachments) and hard copy. SASE. Responds in 6–8 months. Publication in 5 months. Royalty.

Polis Books

www.polisbooks.com

Editor

Polis Books is an independent publishing company actively seeking new and established authors for its growing list. It aims to introduce readers to brand new voices, as well as reinvigorate the careers of talented authors who deserve a wider readership. It publishes books in both print and electronic formats.

Freelance Potential: Publishes 40 titles annually.

Fiction: YA. Genres: Fantasy, science fiction, romance, horror.

Nonfiction: YA. Topics: Sports, biography, pop culture.

Submissions and Payment: Guidelines and catalogue available on website. Send query with 3 sample chapters and author bio. Accepts email queries only to submissions@polisbooks.com (no attachments). Responds if interested. Publication period, 6–9 months. Advance against royalties.

POW!

32 Adams Street, Brooklyn, NY 11201. www.powkidsbooks.com

Editor

An imprint of PowerHouse Books, POW! publishes projects that combine an offbeat or humorous sensibility with outstanding design to make books that delight children and grownups equally. It is a book producer and co-edition publisher of innovative, stylish books and book-plus products for both the adult and children's markets. It publishes visually driven, imagination-fueled books for kids. It is actively seeking manuscripts that represent diverse characters, cultures, and points of view.

Freelance Potential: Publishes 10–15 titles annually.

Fiction: Early readers, picture books, middle-grade. Genres: Nature, adventure.

Nonfiction: Early readers, concept books, middle-grade. Topics: Geography, science, travel.

Submissions and Payment: Guidelines and catalogue available on website. Send complete manuscript with brief author bio and illustrations (if available). Accepts hard copy or email submissions to info@powbooks.com. Attach Word document or include submission in the body of the email; no links. Responds if interested. Payment policy varies.

Price Stern Sloan

Penguin Young Readers Group, 345 Hudson Street, New York, NY 10014. http://us.penguingroup.com

Editorial Department

Quirky, unique books and products make up this publisher's catalogue. Price Stern Sloan, an imprint of Penguin Young Readers Group, publishes fun and engaging books in a variety of formats, including board books, doodle books, activity books, and novelty titles. Well-known characters and licenses include Mad Libs, Adventure Time, and Mr. Men Little Miss. It offers both fiction and nonfiction titles. It is accepting submissions in all book formats except picture books and Mad Libs.

Freelance Potential: Publishes about 70 titles annually.

Fiction: Board books, activity and doodle books, middle-grade. Genres: contemporary, humor, horror.

Nonfiction: Activity and doodle books. Topics: humor, holidays, crafts.

Submissions and Payment: Catalogue and guidelines available on website. Not accepting picture books at this time. Query with summary and first 1–2 chapters for all other works. Accepts hard copy. No SASE; materials will not be returned. Response time and payment policies vary.

Puffin Books

Penguin Group, 345 Hudson Street, New York, NY 10014. http://us.penguingroup.com

Manuscript Submissions

Puffin Books was founded on a strong literary tradition and a commitment to publishing a successful mix of classic children's fiction and the best new literature. Over the years, Puffin has transformed from a small yet distinguished paperback house into one of the largest, most diverse, and successful children's publishers in business, publishing everything from picture books to ground-breaking middle-grade and teen fiction. The best way to put your idea in front of this publisher is through a literary agent, but a truly great proposal will be noticed whether you are agented or not. Puffin is not currently accepting picture book submissions.

Freelance Potential: Publishes 225 titles annually. Receives 40+ queries monthly.

Fiction: Novelty books, early picture books, early readers, story picture books, chapter books, middle-grade, YA. Genres: contemporary, historical, science fiction, mystery, sports, adventure, romance.

Submissions and Payment: Guidelines and catalogue available on website. Not accepting submissions for picture books. Query with a maximum of 30 sample pages for longer works and novels. Accepts hard copy. Novel submissions must include SASE. Responds in 4 months if interested. Publication in 12–18 months. Royalty, 2–6%.

G. P. Putnam's Sons Books for Young Readers

Penguin Group, 345 Hudson Street, New York, NY 10014.
http://www.penguin.com/publishers/gpputnamssonsbooksforyoungread/

Manuscript Editor

G. P. Putnam's Sons publishes some of the best fiction for middle-grade and young adult readers. The catalogue from G. P. Putnam's Sons is filled with lively, accessible picture books and some of today's strongest voices in fiction. It is an imprint of Penguin Random House. Among its distinguished authors are Dave Barry, Tom Clancy, and Robin Cook.

Freelance Potential: Publishes 50 titles annually: 1–10% developed from unsolicited submissions; 50–60% by agented authors; 30% by authors who are new to the publishing house; 1–10% by previously unpublished writers. Receives 125 queries, 600 unsolicited manuscripts monthly.

Fiction: Toddler books, early picture books, early readers, story picture books, chapter books, middle-grade, YA. Genres: contemporary, multicultural, fantasy, mystery, humor.

Submissions and Payment: Guidelines and catalogue available on website. Send complete manuscript for picture books. For longer works, query with a maximum of 10 pages from the opening chapter(s) of the manuscript and a cover letter briefly describing the plot, genre, intended age group, and author's publishing credits, if any. Accepts hard copy. No SASE; materials not returned. Responds in 4 months if interested. Publication period varies. Royalty; advance.

Pyr Books

59 John Glenn Drive, Amherst, NY 14228-2197. www.pyrsf.com

Editor

Pyr publishes in many areas of speculative fiction including steampunk, epic fantasy, sci-fi blends, and near future thrillers. Its mission is to provide books of a consistently high quality. It published its first book for young adults in 2011 and has continued to make YA a priority. Pyr Books, an imprint of

Prometheus Books, is a leader in publishing science fiction and fantasy novels. It has set the bar high for creativity, intelligence, and quality. This publisher accepts submissions from agents only.

Freelance Potential: Publishes 30 titles (6 YA) annually.

Fiction: YA, adult. Genres: science fiction; fantasy; sub-genres of speculative fiction including epic fantasy, sword and sorcery, contemporary/urban fantasy.

Submissions and Payment: Guidelines and catalogue available on website. Accepts email to rsears@prometheusbooks.com (Word or RTF attachments). Agented submissions only. Send 1–3.

QED

6 Blundell Street, N7 9BH, London, United Kingdom. www.qed-publishing.co.uk

Associate Publisher: Maxime Boucknooghe

QED is always on the lookout for authors with creative ideas that enhance and broaden its publishing list of children's books. Creating fresh, informative, high-quality books that appeal to children, parents, and teachers alike is what QED does. Each book from QED Publishing has been specifically designed to make learning exciting, stimulating, and fun for children. Its diverse range of titles covers everything from entertaining, innovative facts for the classroom to beautifully illustrated fiction that kids will want to take home.

Freelance Potential: Publishes 80 titles annually: 1–10% by authors who are new to the publishing house; 20% by previously unpublished writers. Receives 4–8 queries monthly.

Fiction: Toddler books, early picture books, early readers, picture books, chapter books, middle-grade. Genres: contemporary.

Nonfiction: Concept books, toddler books, early readers, picture books, story picture books, middle-grade. Topics: early learning, animals, science, nature, games, geography, history, math, religion, technology.

Submissions and Payment: Catalogue available on website. Query with clips. Accepts hard copy and email queries to amandaa@quarto.com. Availability of artwork improves chance of acceptance. Response time and publication period vary. Royalty. Flat fee.

Quill Tree Books ★🖐

10 East 53rd Street, New York, NY 10022. www.harpercollinschildrens.com

Editorial Director: Rosemary Brosnan

This new imprint from HarperCollins focuses on publishing authors with a strong point of view, as well as those that are often underrepresented. Books with a fresh point of view, a strong narrative, and something worthwhile to say to young people are of interest at this imprint. This imprint accepts submissions from agents only.

Freelance Potential: Publishes 15–20 titles annually: all by agented authors.

Fiction: Picture books, graphic novels, middle grade, young adult. Genres: mystery, adventure, fantasy, multicultural, social issues.

Submissions and Payment: Guidelines and catalogue available on website. Agented authors only. Royalty; advance.

Quirk Books

215 Church Street, Philadelphia, PA 19106. http://quirkbooks.com

Associate Publisher/Creative Director: Jason Rekulak

Quirky Philadelphia publisher Quirk Books creates innovative and fun books with a resume that includes cookbooks, children's books, art books, gag gifts, pop culture titles, and more. Always looking to set the next trend, Quirk delivers books and stories that are bold, unprecedented, beautifully designed, and affordable. Publishing books across a broad range of categories with the goal of delivering innovative books to discerning readers, Quirk Books features titles with unique angles and irreverent treatments of topics. The company is best known as the creator of the Worst-Case Scenario Survival Handbook series and the Pride and Prejudice and Zombies series, but it publishes titles on a broad range of nonfiction topics, from parenting to history to crafts, as well as horror, science fiction, and mysteries for adults and children. It is always on the lookout for strikingly unconventional manuscripts and book proposals.

Freelance Potential: Publishes 25 titles annually.

Fiction: Picture books, middle-grade, YA. Genres: fantasy, contemporary, science fiction, humor, horror.

Nonfiction: Picture books, middle-grade, YA. Topics: cooking, humor, family.

Submissions and Payment: Guidelines and catalogue available on website. Send 1-page query describing the project and 1–2 sample chapters. See guidelines for specific editors and interests. For most YA and middle-grade submissions, email jason@quirkbooks.com. Also accepts hard copy. SASE. Response time, publication period, and payment policies vary.

Ramsey & Todd

445 Park Avenue, 9th Floor, New York, NY 10022. www.turnerpublishing.com

Acquisitions

Ramsey & Todd, part of the Turner Publishing Group, is a children's imprint that publishes more than 3,000 titles yearly. The company is in the top 101 independent publishing companies in the United States. Its books are currently sold in more than 55 countries and its market continues to grow.

Freelance Potential: Publishes about 10–12 annually: most are developed from unsolicited submissions. Receives 20 queries monthly.

Fiction: Early readers, middle-grade, YA. Genres: Real life problems.

Nonfiction: Middle-grade, YA, adults. Topics: self-help, social skills, health, entertainment.

Submissions and Payment: Guidelines and catalogue available on website. Query with proposal containing an overview, chapter-by-chapter outline, approximate length, illustrations and other features, author biography, and market analysis. Accepts hard copy, or email to submissions@turnerpublishing.com. Accepts simultaneous submissions if identified. SASE. Responds in 3–4 months. Publication in 1–2 years. Royalty.

Random House Graphic ★

Random House, 1745 Broadway, 8th Floor, New York, NY 10019. www.randomhouse.com/kids

Submissions Editor

Random House launched its highly anticipated Random House Graphic imprint this year with a mission of discovering new talent. Its graphic novels offer adventure and fun accompanied with beautiful artwork. Its list targets young and middle grade readers. Like most Random House imprints, Random House Graphic accepts submissions from literary agents.

Freelance Potential: Plans to 12 titles each year.

Fiction: Graphic novels. Genres: adventure, mystery, interactive fiction.

Submissions and Payment: Catalogue soon to be available on website. Like most Penguin Random House imprints, submissions are accepted through a literary agent. Responds in 6 months if interested. Publication period and payment policies vary.

Random House Studio ★

Random House, 1745 Broadway, 8th Floor, New York, NY 10019. www.randomhouse.com/kids

Submissions Editor

This new imprint is spearheaded by Lee Wade, one of the former directors of the Schwartz & Wade imprint at Random House. Random House Studio is looking for "fresh, original, child-pleasing books, with an eye to what's going on in the world—aesthetically, politically, and culturally." This imprint accepts submissions from agents only.

Freelance Potential: Plans to publish several titles each year.

Fiction: Picture books, middle grade, young adult. Genres: adventure, fantasy, suspense, mystery, science fiction, animal stories.

Nonfiction: Picture books, middle-grade, YA. Topics: biography, history, real life issues.

Submissions and Payment: Catalogue soon to be available on website. Like most Penguin Random House imprints, submissions are accepted through a literary agent. Responds in 6 months if interested. Publication period and payment policies vary.

Razorbill

Penguin Group, 345 Hudson Street, 15th Floor, New York, NY 10014.
http://www.penguin.com/publishers/razorbill/

Submissions

Razorbill, an imprint of Penguin Random House, is always on the lookout for YA and middle grade fiction with diverse and memorable voices, interesting hooks, and vivid settings, as well as nonfiction. It is dedicated to publishing the very best in middle-grade and young adult books. Taking risks and finding new ways to tell stories, Razorbill chooses books that will speak to readers on their level and present them with stories and characters with whom they can relate.

Freelance Potential: Publishes about 40 titles annually. Receives 40 queries monthly.

Fiction: Middle-grade, YA. Genres: contemporary, science fiction, mystery, suspense, fantasy, humor.

Nonfiction: Middle-grade, YA. Topics: pop culture.

Submissions and Payment: Catalogue and guidelines available on website. Not currently accepting manuscripts for picture books. For middle-grade and YA, query with a maximum of 30 sample pages and a cover letter describing the plot, genre, target audience, and publishing credits, if applicable. Accepts hard copy. SASE. Responds in 4 months if interested. Publication period varies. Advance.

Red Deer Press

195 Allstate Parkway, Markham, Ontario L3R 4T8 Canada. www.reddeerpress.com

Children's Editor: Peter Carver

Red Deer Press publishes upscale children's picture books, including illustrated children's Aboriginal titles, contemporary juvenile YA fiction, adult fiction and nonfiction. Red Deer Press is looking for quality writing for children across the ages, from picture books to YA fiction and nonfiction. It produces creative and contemporary books by enlisting a balance of established and emerging authors and illustrators. It is owned by Fitzhenry & Whiteside and works only with Canadian authors and illustrators.

Freelance Potential: Publishes 14–18 titles annually: 25% by authors who are new to the publishing house; 12% by previously unpublished writers. Receives 165+ unsolicited manuscripts monthly.

Fiction: Story picture books, middle-grade, YA. Genres: regional, contemporary, adventure, fantasy, mystery, suspense, science fiction.

Nonfiction: Middle-grade, YA. Topics: activities, field guides, biography, Canadian nature, wildlife, First Nations, history, sports.

Submissions and Payment: Canadian authors only. Guidelines and catalogue available on website. Accepts hard copy or email to rdp@reddeerpress.com. Send complete manuscript for picture books. For fiction, send query letter or 3 sample chapters; for nonfiction, submit query letter or sample chapter with outline. SASE. Accepts multiple submissions. Responds in 4–6 months.

Red Rock Press

205 West 57th Street, Suite 8B, New York, NY 10019. www.redrockpress.com

Creative Director: Ilene Barth

This independent book publisher produces beautiful, handsome, and entertaining gift books for adults and for children. It prefers manuscripts from agents, but will look at unsolicited proposals. It publishes books for children under its Red Pebble imprint.

Freelance Potential: Publishes 6 titles annually: 2 developed from unsolicited submissions; 1 by a previously unpublished writer. Receives 67 unsolicited manuscripts monthly.

Fiction: Picture books, story picture books. Genres: contemporary, adventure, historical, multicultural.

Submissions and Payment: Guidelines and catalogue available on website. Prefers agented submissions. Send complete manuscript with marketing plan. Accepts hard copy. SASE. Responds in 2–4 months. Publication in 18 months. Royalty; advance. Flat fee.

Regnery Publishing

300 New Jersey Avenue NW, Suite 500, Washington, DC 20001. www.regnery.com

Editor

Regnery Kids books are non-partisan, entertaining, and brilliantly written and illustrated by award-winning authors and artists. Regnery Kids, an imprint of Regnery, provides charming stories and beautiful illustrations while teaching children about history, science, and culture. Its publishing program also includes Little Patriot Press, a series of educational books for young readers.

Freelance Potential: Publishes 6–8 titles annually.

Fiction: Picture books, story picture books. Genres: contemporary, adventure, historical.

Nonfiction: Picture books, story picture books. Topics: history, biography, science, animals, patriotism.

Submissions and Payment: Catalogue available on website. Accepts only agented submissions. Publication period and payment policy, unknown.

Rise ★

Penguin Young Readers Group, 1745 Broadway, New York, NY 10019.
http://www.penguin.com/publishers/penguinworkshop/

Editorial Director: Cecily Kaiser

This new imprint from Penguin Young Readers Group will feature a list of varied titles that empower children to feel smart, capable, safe, and important. Its mission is to help children develop empathy, resilience, and compassion through its line of board books and early picture books.

Freelance Potential: Publishes several titles each year. Plans to publish 30 titles annually.

Fiction: Early picture books, board books

Nonfction: Early picture books, board books.

Submissions and Payment: Guidelines and catalogue available on website. Mailed submissions only; no electronic submissions. Send complete manuscript for picture books. Query with synopsis, 10 manuscript pages, and publishing credits for longer works. Materials are not returned. Responds in 4 months if interested. Publication period and payment policies vary.

Roaring Brook Press

Macmillan, 175 Fifth Avenue, New York, NY 10010. http://us.macmillan.com/RoaringBrook.aspx

Editor: David Langva

Roaring Brook Press believes their authors' talent defines them. An imprint of Macmillan, it is a publisher of high-quality literature for young readers, from toddlers to teens, in all categories: picture books, fiction, and nonfiction. Since its first list was published in 2002, many of its titles have received prestigious awards, including the Caldecott Medal and Newbery Honor award.

Freelance Potential: Publishes about 40 titles annually.

Fiction: Picture books, early readers, middle-grade, YA. Genres: adventure, contemporary, fantasy, history, humor, multicultural, nature/environment, poetry, religion, science fiction, sports, suspense/mystery, graphic novels.

Nonfiction: Picture books, early readers, middle-grade, YA. Topics: history, politics, biography, social issues, sports, reference, geography, culture.

Submissions and Payment: Guidelines and catalogue available on website. Agented submissions only.

Running Press Kids

2300 Chestnut Street, Suite 200, Philadelphia, PA 19103-4399. www.runningpress.com

Submissions Editor

High quality, exciting books and book-related kits are what Running Press provides. Its imprints Running Press Kids and Running Press Teens feature engaging and thought-provoking titles for children of all ages.

Freelance Potential: Publishes 80 titles annually: 4% by authors who are new to the publishing house; 10% by previously unpublished writers.

Fiction: Board books, novelty books, early picture books, early readers, picture books, chapter books, middle-grade, YA. Genres: multicultural, mystery, coming-of-age, animal stories.

Nonfiction: Board books, picture books, story picture books, middle-grade. Topics: history, nature, biography, activities.

Submissions and Payment: Guidelines and catalogue available on website. Currently only accepting submissions from agents. Check website for changes to this policy.

Salaam Reads

Simon & Schuster Children's Publishing, 1230 Avenue of the Americas, New York, NY 10020. www.salaamreads.com

Executive Editor: Zareen Jaffery

Salaam Reads, which takes its name from the Arabic word for peace, publishes books for young readers of all ages. It is an imprint that aims to introduce readers of all faiths and backgrounds to a wide variety of Muslim children and families and offer Muslim kids an opportunity to see themselves reflected positively in published works.

Freelance Potential: Publishes 10–20 titles annually.

Fiction: Early readers, story picture books, chapter books, middle-grade, YA. Genres: contemporary, historical, religious, multicultural, suspense, mystery, fantasy, adventure.

Nonfiction: Picture books, middle-grade, YA. Topics: biography, multicultural, history, religion.

Submissions and Payment: Catalogue available on website. Accepts submissions from both agented and unagented authors. Will consider unsolicited submissions by email to SalaamReads@ simonandschuster.com. Response time, publication period, and payment policies vary.

Salina Bookshelf

1120 West University Ave., Suite 102, Flagstaff, AZ 86001. www.salinabookshelf.com

Submissions Editor

Authentic depictions of Navajo life, both contemporary and traditional, are what this publisher looks for. Salina Bookshelf is an independent publishing house with a regional and topical emphasis on Navajo content. This publisher specializes in dual language Navajo/English books. It has a focus on fiction (realistic and historical) and nonfiction centering on Navajo or Native American children/people for readers ages 0–5 and 6–12. Salina Bookshelf is an independent publisher of multicultural materials that include textbooks, children's picture books, informational texts, reference books, audio books, and language learning materials.

Freelance Potential: Publishes 10 titles annually: 50% developed from unsolicited submissions; 60% by authors who are new to the publishing house; 20% by previously unpublished writers. Receives 10–12 unsolicited manuscripts monthly.

Fiction: Toddler books, early picture books, early readers, story picture books. Genres: folklore, folktales, multicultural and ethnic fiction, and stories about nature and the environment.

Nonfiction: Middle-grade, YA. Topics: Navajo history and culture, biography.

Submissions and Payment: Guidelines and catalogue available on website. Query with sample chapter or send complete manuscript. Accepts hard copy. SASE. Accepts electronic submissions by email to submissions@salinabookshelf.com. Responds in 6 months. Publication in 1 year. Royalty varies; advance varies.

Scholastic Children's Books UK

Euston House, 24 Eversholt Street, London NW1 1DB United Kingdom. www.scholastic.co.uk

Editorial Department

This publisher believes that independent reading is a critical part of children's learning and growth. Getting children to read and enjoy it is what the UK Division of Scholastic aims to do. This children's publisher creates books that educate, entertain, and motivate children of all ages. It believes that finding the right book at the right time can light an emotional spark within children that motivates them to read more, understand more, and read joyfully. It accepts agented submissions only.

Freelance Potential: Publishes 200 titles annually: most by agented authors. Receives 30–33 unsolicited manuscripts monthly.

Fiction: Concept books, toddler books, early picture books, early readers, chapter books, middle-grade, YA. Genres: contemporary, historical, adventure, mystery, suspense, drama, fantasy.

Nonfiction: Chapter books. Topics: geography, history, math, sports.

Submissions and Payment: Guidelines and catalogue available on website. Send cover letter and first 3 chapters for trade books. For educational projects, send query with the idea and sample activities or sections to the Education Division. No electronic submissions. Responds in 6 months. Publication period and payment policy vary.

Scholastic Focus

Scholastic, 557 Broadway, New York, NY 10012-3999. www.scholastic.com

Editorial Director

This imprint's publishing philosophy underscores the relevance of values that have long guided humanity; the profound effects of invention, inspiration, and revolution; and the importance of introducing a diversity of perspectives and identities. Scholastic Focus is dedicated to middle-grade and young adult narrative nonfiction that will change the way the world is read. It encourages readers to draw connections between historical events and contemporary issues.

Freelance Potential: Parent company Scholastic publishes more than 600 titles a year: all by agented authors. Scholastic Focus plans to publish 6–9 new titles yearly.

Fiction: Toddler books, early picture books, easy readers, story picture books, chapter books, middle-grade, YA. Genres: historical, multicultural, folklore, fairy tales, fantasy, humor, adventure.

Nonfiction: Middle-grade, YA. Topics: history, biography, social issues, technology.

Submissions and Payment: Agented authors only. Response time and publication period vary. Royalty.

Scholastic Inc.

557 Broadway, New York, NY 10012. www.scholastic.com

Editor

A leader in education and publication for over 100 years, Scholastic's divisions encompass trade and educational publishing, licensing, and media. Scholastic is the largest children's book and magazine publisher and distributor in the world. Its trade publishing division includes a variety of imprints that market hardcover and paperback books in many genres for the very youngest readers through young adults. Scholastic only accepts queries from agented authors and writers who have worked with the company in the past.

Freelance Potential: Publishes 600+ titles annually: all by agented authors.

Fiction: Toddler books, early picture books, picture books, chapter books, middle-grade, YA. Genres: contemporary, science fiction, historical, adventure, fantasy, humor, mystery.

Nonfiction: Story picture books, chapter books, middle-grade, YA. Topics: history, nature, biography, humor, the environment, multicultural subjects.

Submissions and Payment: Accepts queries from agented authors only. Publication period varies. Royalty; advance.

>**Scholastic Trade Imprints:** Blue Sky Press, Cartwheel Books, Children's Press, Graphix, Klutz/Klutz Jr., Arthur A. Levine Books, Orchard Books, Push, Scholastic Focus, Scholastic Books UK.

Anne Schwartz Books ★

Random House, 1745 Broadway, 8th Floor, New York, NY 10019. www.randomhouse.com/kids

Submissions Editor

Formerly part of the Schwartz & Wade imprint at Random House, Anne Schwartz now has her own imprint at the company. Its list will include picture books, middle-grade, and young adult fiction and nonfiction. Schwartz is looking to work with undiscovered talent. Already signed on to publish with the imprint are Candace Fleming, April Harrison, and David Ezra Stein. This imprint accepts submissions through agents only.

Freelance Potential: Plans to publish several titles each year.

Fiction: Picture books, middle-grade, young adult. Genres: adventure, fantasy, suspense, mystery, science fiction, animal stories.

Nonfiction: Story picture books, middle-grade, YA. Topics: biography, history, real life issues.

Submissions and Payment: Catalogue soon to be available on website. Like most Penguin Random House imprints, submissions are accepted through a literary agent. Responds in 6 months if interested. Publication period and payment policies vary.

Seagrass Press

6 Orchard, Suite 100, Lake Forest, CA 92630. https://www.quartoknows.com/Seagrass-Press

Publisher: Josalyn Moran

Seagrass Press nurtures and grows childrens' imaginations with informative and entertaining titles that show kids the world around them. Beautifully illustrated picture books and readers feature unforgettable characters and relatable stories from this imprint of The Quarto Group. Seagrass Press aims to help children learn about the fascinating world around them with nonfiction titles written by award-winning children's authors.

Freelance Potential: Plans to publish 5–10 titles annually.

Fiction: Early readers, picture books. Stories about animals, nature.

Nonfiction: Early readers, picture books. Topics: animals, nature.

Submissions and Payment: Catalogue and guidelines available on website. Accepts email proposals to Josalyn.Moran@quarto.com. Include an author bio, detailed description of subject/content, artwork, market information, and a signed Submission Agreement (available at the website). Response time, publication period, and payment policies vary.

Seven Stories Press

140 Watts Street, New York, NY 10013. www.sevenstories.com

Acquisitions

Seven Stories Press publishes, in English or other languages, works of the human imagination—sometimes in the form of fiction and literature, sometimes in the form of political nonfiction, and sometimes in a hybrid form that has elements of both. Seven Stories Press believes that publishers have a special responsibility to defend free speech and human rights wherever they can. It is widely known for its books on politics, human rights, and social justice, but also publishes books for children and young adults.

Freelance Potential: Publishes 20–30 titles annually; 4–8 juvenile.

Fiction: Story picture books, early readers, middle-grade, YA. Genres: contemporary, realistic, coming-of-age, historical, graphic novels.

Nonfiction: Picture books, early readers, middle-grade, YA. Topics: history, the women's movement, human rights, social justice, gender equality, science, the environment, social issues.

Submissions and Payment: Guidelines and catalogue available on website. Query only with cover letter and no more than 2 sample chapters. Accepts hard copy. SASE. Responds in 2–4 months. Publication in 18 months. Royalty.

Simon & Schuster

Simon & Schuster Children's Publishing, 1230 Avenue of the Americas, New York, NY 10020. www.simonandschuster.com

Submissions Editor

Simon & Shuster is dedicated to bringing an extensive cross-section of first-class information and entertainment in all printed, digital, and audio formats to a worldwide audience of readers. As a major international publishing company, Simon & Schuster publishes many titles globally, and its products—hardcovers, trade and mass market paperbacks, children's books of every format, electronic books, audiobooks of bestselling and critically acclaimed fiction and nonfiction for readers of all ages and every conceivable taste—are distributed in more than 200 countries around the world.

Freelance Potential: Publishes 2,000 titles annually.

Fiction: Children, teens, adults, across all genres.

Nonfiction: Children, teens, adults, across all categories.

Submissions and Payment: Guidelines and catalogues available on website. Most imprints accept submissions through literary agents only.

> **Simon & Schuster Imprints:** Aladdin, Atheneum Books for Young Readers, Beach Lane Books, Little Simon, Margaret K. McElderry Books, Denene Millner Books, Moonbot Books, Salaam Reads, Simon & Schuster Books for Young Readers, Simon Pulse, Paula Wiseman Books.

Simon & Schuster Books for Young Readers

Simon & Schuster Children's Publishing, 1230 Avenue of the Americas, New York, NY 10020. http://www.simonandschusterpublishing.com/bfyr/

Submissions Editor

Simon & Shuster Books for Young Readers publishes acclaimed and best-selling books in a variety of formats for children ages preschool through teen. Committed to publishing a wide range of contemporary, commercial, award-winning fiction and nonfiction that spans every age of children's publishing, Simon & Schuster Books for Young Readers is the flagship imprint of the Simon & Schuster Children's Division. It publishes a wide array of picture books, chapter books, and novels for teens and tweens in a variety of genres, while also offering nonfiction, biographies, and anthologies. It accepts submissions from agented authors only. Its publishing program's eclecticism, elasticity, and sensibility to the ever-changing marketplace make it the home for a vast array of blockbuster children's titles.

Freelance Potential: Publishes 90 titles annually: most by agented authors. Receives 830 queries each month.

Fiction: Novelty books, board books, toddler books, early picture books, early readers, story picture books, chapter books, middle-grade, YA. Genres: contemporary, historical, multicultural, mystery, fantasy, folklore, fairy tales.

Nonfiction: Story picture books, middle-grade, YA. Topics: social issues, science, nature, math, history, biography.

Submissions and Payment: Guidelines and catalogue available on website. Accepts submissions through literary agents only. Responds in 2 months. Publication in 2–4 years. Royalty; advance.

Simon Pulse

Simon & Schuster Children's Publishing, 1230 Avenue of the Americas, New York, NY 10020. http://simonandschusterpublishing.com/simonpulse/

Submissions Editor

Simon Pulse publishes books that teens want to read, delivering fresh, bold voices that inspire compulsive reading for teens and beyond. With a focus on high-concept commercial fiction, this imprint of Simon & Schuster is known for pushing boundaries. It publishes single titles, series, and select nonfiction. Publisher Bethany Buck heads Simon Pulse, and Annette Pollert is Editor. They look for dynamic books—from cult classics to electrifying debuts that embrace escapism and get people talking.

Freelance Potential: Publishes 100+ titles annually: 10% by authors who are new to the publishing house.

Fiction: YA. Genres: contemporary, inspirational, ethnic, multicultural, historical, mystery, myth, romance, suspense, science fiction, fantasy, dystopian, horror.

Nonfiction: YA. Topics: Social issues, relationships.

Submissions and Payment: Catalogue available on website. Accepts agented submissions only. Response time, publication period, and payment policies vary.

Simply Read

501-5525 West Boulevard, Vancouver, British Columbia V6M 3W6, Canada. www.simplyreadbooks.com

Submissions

Simply Read introduces contemporary books with a fresh, modern appeal and fresh outlook, and offers a careful selection of timeless stories that link the past with the present. It specializes in high-quality, unique picture books and fiction. The approach that Simply Read Books takes to producing its children's books follows the finest publishing tradition and spirit with inspired content, extraordinary artwork, and outstanding graphic design. It is currently seeking manuscripts for picture books, early readers, chapter books, middle-grade fiction, and graphic novels.

Freelance Potential: Unavailable.

Fiction: Board books, story picture books, toddler, early readers, chapter books, middle-grade, YA. Genres: fantasy, contemporary, classics, folktales, fairy tales, social issues, real life, nature.

Submissions and Payment: Guidelines and catalogue available on website. Query or send complete manuscript with a cover letter that includes a short synopsis and author information. Accepts hard copy only. SASE. Responds in 5 months if interested. Publication period and payment policies vary.

Skyhorse Publishing

307 West 36th Street, 11th Floor, New York, NY 10018. www.skyhorsepublishing.com

Editor, Sky Pony Press: Julie Matysik

Skyhorse is dedicated to publishing books that make people's lives better. It is one of the fastest-growing independent book publishers in the United States. Its catalogue includes titles on outdoor sports, adventure, team sports, nature, politics, and military history.

Freelance Potential: Publishes 250 books (15–20 juvenile) annually.

Fiction: Picture books, early readers, middle-grade, YA. Genres: contemporary, social issues, animals, coming-of-age, special needs.

Nonfiction: Middle-grade. Topics: sports, activities, outdoors, nature/environment, horses, art, autism. For adults, travel, home, health, history, games and gambling, horses, pets and animals, nature, science, food and wine, aviation, true crime, current events.

Submissions and Payment: Guidelines available on website. Query or send complete manuscript with author bio, publishing credits, and qualifications to write in the subject area of your submission. Accepts email for each imprint. Visit the website for complete information. Response time, publication period, and payment policies vary.

Sky Pony Press

307 West 36th Street, 11th Floor, New York, NY 10018. www.skyhorsepublishing.com

Editor, Sky Pony Press: Julie Matysik

The goals of Sky Pony Press is to provide books for readers with a wide variety of interests. Open to any genre and style, Sky Pony Press is always looking for something new and different. Launched in 2011, Sky Pony Press is the children's imprint of Skyhorse Press. Its list is comprised of fiction, picture books, educational books, novelty books, and titles for middle-grade readers.

Freelance Potential: Publishes 15–20 juvenile annually.

Fiction: Picture books, early readers, middle-grade, YA. Genres: contemporary, social issues, animals, coming-of-age, special needs.

Nonfiction: Middle-grade. Topics: sports, activities, outdoors, nature/environment, horses, art, autism.

Submissions and Payment: Guidelines and catalogue available on website. Query or send complete manuscript with author bio, publishing credits, and qualifications to write in the subject area of your submission. Accepts email submissions to skyponysubmissions@skyhorsepublishing. com. Visit the website for complete information. Response time, publication period, and payment policies vary.

Smart Pop Books

10300 North Central Expressway, Suite 530, Dallas, TX 75231. www.smartpopbooks.com

Editor-in-Chief: Leah Wilson

Smart Pop is a line of smart, fresh, engaging nonfiction titles on the best of pop culture, TV, books, and film, with a particular focus on science fiction and fantasy television and literature. It has a mission of enriching readers' experience of the shows and books they love. It is the pop culture imprint of independent publisher BenBella Books.

Freelance Potential: Publishes 8–10 titles annually, large anthologies of 12–15 essays each.

Nonfiction: Middle-grade, YA, adult. Topics: biography, pop culture, books, movies, television shows, cooking.

Submissions and Payment: Guidelines and catalogue available on website. Email proposal or query or writing sample and author bio to be considered for essay writing for anthologies to leah@benbellabooks.com. Response time, publication period, and payment policy vary.

Soho Teen

853 Broadway, New York, NY 10003. www.sohopress.com

Editorial Director: Daniel Ehrenhaft

Soho Teen looks for exciting voices in the world of YA. It looks for books of adolescent identity and self-discovery, especially those with a unique format. Soho Teen began with YA mysteries and thrillers. It has since evolved to include a broad range of categories, including dystopian and paranormal. All books feature a 14- to 17-year-old protagonist with stories and characters that reflect the entire spectrum of the teen experience. It is only accepting submissions from agents, but check the website for updates to this policy.

Freelance Potential: Publishes 7–10 titles annually: 70% by authors who are new to the publishing house; 80% by agented authors; 25% by previously unpublished writers. Receives 30 queries monthly.

Fiction: YA mystery. Genres: adventure, thriller, dystopian, paranormal, contemporary.

Submissions and Payment: Guidelines and catalogue available on website. Even though not currently accepting unagented submissions (check website for updates to this policy), the following guidelines are available. Query with cover letter, a paragraph pitch, 2- to 3-page synopsis (including the ending), and the first 50 pages of the book. Not currently interested in acquiring series, but if a stand-alone title has series potential, include future plots in the synopsis. Accepts email to rkowal@sohopress.com (Word attachments). Publication period and payment policies vary.

Sourcebooks

1935 Brookdale Road, Suite 139, Naperville, IL 60563. www.sourcebooks.com

Editorial Submissions

Sourcebooks believes in authorship; they work with authors to develop great books that reach wide audiences. Sourcebooks' mission is to reach as many people as possible with books that will enlighten their lives. Under its children's division, Sourcebooks Kids, are the imprints Sourcebooks Jabberwocky (the flagship fiction imprint that publishes picture books and board books), Sourcebooks eXplore (children's nonfiction), Sourcebooks Wonderland (proprietary, customized, and regional), and Sourcebooks Young Readers (middle-grade). Its young adult imprint, Sourcebooks Fire, publishes the best new voices for the next generation of book lovers. Sourcebooks also publishes in all areas of adult fiction and nonfiction under the following imprints: Sourcebooks Landmark (fiction), Sourcebooks (nonfiction), Simple Truths (business), Poisoned Pen Press (mystery), and Sourcebooks Casablanca (romance). It accepts agented submissions only for all imprints except adult nonfiction and romance. See website for details.

Freelance Potential: Publishes 300+ titles annually: 1–10% developed from unsolicited submissions; 1–10% assigned; 50–75% within house; 10–25% by previously unpublished writers. Receives 200+ queries, 200+ manuscripts monthly.

Fiction: Early picture books, early readers, story picture books, chapter books, middle-grade, YA, adult fiction. Genres: contemporary, historical, adventure, romance, mystery, fantasy, coming-of-age, realistic, humor, horror, book club.

Nonfiction: Chapter books, middle-grade, YA, prescriptive nonfiction, adult nonfiction. Topics: history, biography, humor, social science, science, business. Also publishes titles on parenting, college, careers.

Submissions and Payment: Guidelines available on website. Primarily accepts submissions from agents only, except in adult nonfiction and romance. Responds in 8–12 weeks. Publication in 1 year. Royalty; advance.

Sourcebooks eXplore

1935 Brookdale Road, Suite 139, Naperville, IL 60563. www.sourcebooks.com

Editorial Director: Kelly Barrales-Saylor

Sourcebooks eXplore is the new children's nonfiction imprint from Sourcebooks that is dedicated to entertaining and educating young readers on a variety of subjects. It currently accepts submissions only from agents and experts in the children's literature field.

Freelance Potential: Sourcebooks publishes 300+ titles annually: 1–10% developed from unsolicited submissions; 1–10% assigned; 50–75% by agented authors; 50–75% by authors who are new to the publishing house; 10–25% by previously unpublished writers. Receives 200+ queries monthly.

Nonfiction: Early readers, concept books. Topics: animals, science, health, technology.

Submissions and Payment: Guidelines and catalogue available on website. Accepts submissions from agents only. Responds in 8–12 weeks. Publication in 1 year. Royalty; advance.

Sourcebooks Fire

1935 Brookdale Road, Suite 139, Naperville, IL 60563. www.sourcebooks.com

Submissions: Aubrey Poole

Sourcebooks Fire is one of the most powerful voices in the young adult category. Sourcebooks Fire is passionate about producing books with authentic teen voices that create and validate the teen experience in all of its diversity. It produces quality break-out fiction and nonfiction for young adults. This imprint from Sourcebooks targets young adults with contemporary and realistic fiction, mysteries, and romance, as well as nonfiction titles ranging from health to dating. It also offers titles for the tween age group.

Freelance Potential: Sourcebooks publishes 300+ titles annually: 1–10% developed from unsolicited submissions; 1–10% assigned; 50–75% by agented authors; 50–75% by authors who are new to the publishing house; 10–25% by previously unpublished writers. Receives 200+ queries monthly.

Fiction: Middle-grade, YA. Genres: contemporary, historical, coming-of-age, realistic, fantasy, mystery, romance, science fiction.

Nonfiction: Middle-grade, YA. Topics: health, relationships, real life problems, social issues.

Submissions and Payment: Guidelines and catalogue available on website. Accepts submissions from agents only. Responds in 8–12 weeks. Publication in 1 year. Royalty; advance.

Sourcebooks Young Readers

1935 Brookdale Road, Suite 139, Naperville, IL 60563. www.sourcebooks.com

Editorial Director: Steve Geck

This publisher is guided by its continuing commitment to reaching readers with books that will illuminate, inspire, and enlighten their lives. This new imprint from Sourcebooks features titles for middle-grade readers. The company made the decision to split apart its middle-grade titles from its Jabberwocky imprint to focus solely on middle-grade fiction and nonfiction. Its editors believe in promoting accessible, fun, and new voices for this important age group. At this time it is only open to submissions from agents.

Freelance Potential: Sourcebooks publishes 300+ titles annually: 1–10% developed from unsolicited submissions; 1–10% assigned; 50–75% by agented authors; 50–75% by authors who are new to the publishing house; 10–25% by previously unpublished writers. Receives 200+ queries monthly.

Fiction: Middle-grade. Genres: contemporary, historical, coming-of-age, realistic, fantasy, mystery, romance, science fiction.

Nonfiction: Middle-grade. Topics: health, relationships, real life problems, social issues.

Submissions and Payment: Guidelines and catalogue available on website. Accepts submissions from agents only. Responds in 8–12 weeks. Publication in 1 year. Royalty; advance.

Speeding Star

29 East 21st Street, New York, NY 10010. www.speedingstar.com

Acquisitions Editor

Speeding Star is looking for authors who can create books and content that appeal to boys' interests. The mission at Speeding Star is to keep boys reading whether it's zombies or sports cars. It seeks easy-to-read, engaging fiction and informational nonfiction geared to boys from third grade to high school. Writing should be on a fourth-grade level. It prefers male protagonists for fiction, and strong secondary characters. Each book will be either 48, 64, or 96 pages and available in print and digital formats.

Freelance Potential: Publishes about 15 titles annually.

Fiction: Middle-grade, YA. Genres: fantasy, science fiction, thriller/mystery, adventure, sports.

Nonfiction: Middle-grade, YA. Topics: Sports, cars, of interest to boys.

Submissions and Payment: Guidelines available on website. For nonfiction, send query, résumé, and a sample chapter or other writing sample. For fiction, send complete ms (between 5,000 and 12,000 words), along with résumé or list of published works. Accepts electronic submissions only through the website. Response time, publication period, and payment policies vary.

Spencer Hill Press

27 West 20th St., Ste. 1102, New York, NY 10011. www.spencerhillpress.com

Lead Editor: Patricia Riley

Spencer Hill Press is an independent publishing house specializing in YA and adult contemporary romance literature. It believes in the power of books and the ability to deliver engaging and well-written stories to readers. It publishes a diverse range of titles in addition to an ever-growing collection of YA and adult contemporary romance. Its imprints are Spencer Hill Press, Spencer Hill Contemporary, Spencer Hill Middle Grade, and Spence City. Currently, it is seeking YA and contemporary romance.

Freelance Potential: Publishes about 10 titles annually.

Fiction: Middle-grade, YA. Genres: science fiction, historical, contemporary, mystery, fantasy, paranormal, romance.

Submissions and Payment: Guidelines and catalogue available on website. Accepts agented and open queries at all times. Go to submission link on website: https://www.spencerhillpress.com/contact-us/submission-guidelines/. Response time varies. Publication period and payment policies unknown.

Splashdown Books

www.splashdownbooks.com

Founder: Grace Bridges

Giving you stories that refresh and surprise you, shake you and energize you is what Splashdown Books does. Splashdown Books is an independent publisher out of New Zealand specializing in speculative fiction. Enter new worlds and experience the altered state of being that comes from reading a good book. It offers both family-friendly and mature material with a focus on science fiction and fantasy.

Freelance Potential: Publishes about 8 titles annually.

Fiction: YA. Genres: fantasy, science fiction, supernatural, paranormal.

Submissions and Payment: Guidelines and catalogue available on website. Submit brief description, author bio, and first 500 words electronically through form on the website. Response time and publication period vary. Royalty.

StarBerry Books

300 Park Ave., New York, NY 10022. www.kanepress.com

Submissions Editor

StarBerry Books is a line of diverse and imaginative picture books created by authors and artists around the globe. This new trade imprint from Boyds Mills & Kane focuses on diverse, imaginative stories with bright, colorful illustrations. Its titles aim to encourage children's natural curiosity, inquisitiveness, and sense of adventure, and to let their imaginations soar through the joy of reading. Excellent writing and the ability to stand out in the market will get this publisher to notice you.

Freelance Potential: Publishes 15+ titles annually.

Fiction: Story picture books, early readers, picture books.

Submissions and Payment: Guidelines and catalogue available. Send complete manuscript. Accepts email submissions to submissions@kanepress.com. Responds only if interested. If you do not receive a response within 3 month, you can assume your project is not a good fit for our company.

Star Bright Books

13 Landsdowne Street, Cambridge, MA 02139. www.starbrightbooks.org

Submissions

Star Bright Books are particularly interested in books that are entertaining, meaningful, and sensitive to the needs of all children. It recognizes that to inspire a life-long love of books, it is important for children to begin building that relationship at the earliest possible age. It welcomes submissions for picture books and longer works, both fiction and nonfiction. Offering children's books in over 24 different languages, the catalogue from Star Bright Books reveals its focus on diversity and multiethnic views, with books featuring subjects and characters of varying cultural backgrounds and physical and mental abilities. Star Bright is particularly interested in math-infused stories that represent diverse backgrounds of children and family.

Freelance Potential: Publishes 15–20 titles annually: 25–50% developed from unsolicited submissions; 1–5% by agented authors; 25–50% by authors who are new to the publishing house; 25–50% by previously unpublished writers. Receives 1–10 queries, 50–75 unsolicited manuscripts monthly.

Fiction: Toddler books, early picture books, early readers, story picture books. Genres: contemporary, multicultural, bilingual, educational, folktales, stories about children with disabilities.

Nonfiction: Concept books, board books, toddler books, early picture books, chapter books. Topics: biography, families, animals, history, holidays, mathematics, science, seasons.

Submissions and Payment: Guidelines and catalogue available on website. Query or send complete manuscript.

Starfish Bay Children's Books 🌐

P.O. Box 1058, Unley, SA 5061 Australia. www.starfishbaypublishing.com.au

Editor

Starfish Bay places an emphasis on discovering new talent and supporting unpublished authors. It publishes imaginative and intriguing children's books from around the world. Using vibrant visuals to help children engage in and appreciate the magic of books, language and reading, Starfish Bay Publishing is dedicated to creating quality books for children. They hope to capture children's imagination and maintain their interest with a thoughtful story. Based out of Australia, its list targets readers ages 3–8. The company is now expanding its reach into the United States.

Freelance Potential: Publishes 10 titles each year.

Fiction: Early picture books, early readers, picture books. Topics: Animals, folktales, nature, humor, adventure.

Submissions and Payment: Guidelines and catalogue available on website. Query with one-sentence summary and a 300-word synopsis. Send complete manuscript for picture books. Author-illustrators should not include artwork. Accepts email to submissions@starfishbaypublishing.com.au. Responds in 3 months. Publication in 18–24 months. Payment policy varies.

Starscape

Tom Doherty Associates, 175 Fifth Avenue, New York, NY 10010. www.tor-forge.com

Acquisitions Editor, Children's/YA

Starscape strives to encourage critical discoveries by making the very best science fiction and fantasy literature available to young readers. This imprint of Tor Books, part of the Macmillan Group, brings the best of science fiction and fantasy to middle-grade readers ages 10 and up. It focuses on titles that are age- and theme-appropriate. Its sister imprint, Tor Teen, publishes similar books for young adults.

Freelance Potential: Publishes 30 titles annually. Receives thousands of submissions monthly.

Fiction: Middle-grade, YA. Genres: fantasy, science fiction, horror.

Submissions and Payment: Guidelines and catalogue available on website. Send a proposal that includes first 3 chapters (up to 60 pages); 3- to 10-page synopsis; and dated cover letter with contact information, title of submitted work, its genre, any author qualifications that pertain to book, and publishing credits, if any. Do not send query letter. SASE for reply only; materials not returned. Responds in 4–6 months. Publication in 18–24 months. Royalty; advance.

Stemmer House Publishers

34 Production Ave, Keene, NH 03431. www.stemmer.com

Editor: Becky Dalzell

Stemmer House's fiction list features "timeless" stories, poetry, and nature tales. It publishes fiction and nonfiction for preschool, elementary, and middle-grade readers. Encyclopedia books on nature and science topics comprise its nonfiction list. It is currently not accepting submissions; check website for updates to this policy.

Freelance Potential: Publishes 3 titles annually: 65% developed from unsolicited submissions; 65% by authors who are new to the publishing house; 35% by previously unpublished writers. Receives 15 queries, 20 unsolicited manuscripts monthly.

Fiction: Picture books, early readers, story picture books. Genres: contemporary, historical, multicultural fiction, nature stories.

Nonfiction: Early readers, picture books, story picture books, chapter books, middle-grade. Topics: nature, animals, science, natural history, art, music, geography.

Submissions and Payment: Guidelines available. Catalogue available on website. Send complete manuscript for picture books. Query with outline, synopsis, and 2 sample chapters for longer works. Accepts hard copy. Accepts simultaneous submissions if identified. SASE. Responds in 2 weeks. Publication in 1–3 years. Royalty; advance.

Sterling Children's Books

1166 Avenue of the Americas, Floor 17, New York, NY 10036. http://www.sterlingpublishing.com/childrens-books.html

Children's Book Editor

Sterling Children's Books' list includes picture books, joke books, classics, novelty formats, and board books, as well as middle-grade and young adult fiction. Sterling is interested in reviewing submissions that fit these categories.

Freelance Potential: Publishes 4 titles annually: 15% developed from unsolicited submissions; 15% by agented authors. Receives 100–150 unsolicited manuscripts monthly.

Fiction: Toddler books, early picture books, early readers, story picture books. Genres: contemporary, fairy tales, fantasy, ghost stories, animal stories, myth.

Nonfiction: Toddler books, early picture books, early readers, middle-grade, YA. Topics include history, biography, early learning, animals, nature, science, holidays, seasons, crafts, activities, games.

Submissions and Payment: Guidelines and catalogue available on website. Send complete manuscript with author's biography, special qualifications in the subject area, and publishing history. Accepts hard copy. Accepts simultaneous submissions if identified. SASE. Response time varies. Publication in 1 year. Royalty; advance.

Storey Publishing

#210 MASS MoCA Way, North Adams, MA 01247. www.storey.com

Editorial Director: Deborah Balmuth

Storey publishes practical books for creative self-reliance. A community of doers who love to grow, build, create, and explore the world comprise Storey Publishing. This publisher features books on subjects that include animals, gardening, crafts such as sewing and woodworking, health and well-being, and food. It also publishes a selection of children's activity and how-to books.

Freelance Potential: Publishes 5 juvenile books annually.

Nonfiction: Board books, early readers, middle-grade. Topics: animals, activities, games and puzzles, crafts, gardening, sewing, farming, equestrian, cooking.

Submissions and Payment: Guidelines and catalogue available on website. Send a proposal consisting of a letter of introduction, 1-paragraph description of the book, why the book is needed and who the readers are, a list of competitive titles and why your book is different, a 1-paragraph author bio with credentials, table of contents with chapter descriptions, proposed book length and possible art, writing sample, and sample chapter from the proposed book. Accepts hard copy. SASE. Response time, publication period, and payment policies vary.

Sunbird Books ★

8501 W. Higgins Road, Suite 300, Chicago, IL 60631. www.sunbirdbooks.com

Acquisitions Editor

Sunbird Books, the new imprint from Phoenix International Publishing, is the home for innovative and original books for children. From board books to storybooks (and everything in between!), forthcoming titles represent strong, lively, and diverse voices which reflect children's realities and feed their imaginations as well as nurturing up-and-coming writers and illustrators from around the world.

Freelance Potential: Plans to publish 10 titles in 2020 and 15 titles in 2021.

Fiction: Children's picture books, board books, early readers, graphic novels.

Nonfiction: Picture books, board books, concept books, early readers.

Submissions and Payment: Query or send complete manuscript to hello@sunbirdkidsbooks.com. Response time varies. Payment rate and policies varies.

Sweet Cherry Publishing ◯

www.sweetcherrypublishing.com

Submissions

This independent children's publisher's books feature engaging characters and worlds that children will want to revisit over and over again. It specializes in fiction series. It publishes a diverse selection of genres including action, fantasy, and coming-of-age. This publisher prefers to work with authors living in the United Kingdom but will accept submissions from US authors who explain why they feel Sweet Cherry is the right fit for their book.

Freelance Potential: Publishes 3–10 titles annually.

Fiction: Picture books, early readers, middle-grade, YA. Genres: historical fiction.

Submissions and Payment: Guidelines available on website. Query with the first two chapters or 3,000 words of your manuscript along with synopsis, author bio, and cover letter. Accepts email submissions to submissions@sweetcherrypublishing.com. No hard copy submissions accepted. Response time varies. Payment policy varies.

SynergEbooks

www.synergebooks.com

Editor: Debra Staples

SynergEbooks is an electronic publisher that offers both fiction and nonfiction for adults, as well as books for young adults and a line of children's e-books. It welcomes new writers and publishes most genres. This digital publisher accepts submissions in all genre and age ranges, but at the time of press was currently seeking nonfiction, self-help, paranormal, New Age, and spirituality.

Freelance Potential: Publishes about 24–36 titles annually: 50% by authors who are new to the publishing house; 60–75% by previously unpublished writers. Receives 50 unsolicited manuscripts each year.

Fiction: YA. Genres: fantasy, mystery, paranormal, horror, adventure, magic, romance, suspense, Western, Native American.

Nonfiction: YA. Topics: self help, spirituality.

Submissions and Payment: Guidelines and catalogue available on website. Check website for open submission periods. Query with brief synopsis (up to 300 words), genre, brief author bio that includes writing credits (up to 300 words), and why you think your book is a good fit for SynergEbooks, all contained in the body of the email. Attach first 3 chapters (Word only) in one attachment. Manuscript should be complete at time of query. Accepts email to synergebooks@camcatpublishing.com. Will accept hard copy but will only respond via email. Responds in 60 days. Publication in 6–12 months. Royalty, percentages vary by genre and format; see website for specifics.

Teen Crave

www.entangledpublishing.com

Submissions Editor

Teen Crave looks for irresistible first-love stories that feature a contemporary romance with a paranormal twist. One of Entangled's first teen category romance imprints, Teen Crave is all about engaging, irresistible first-love stories set during the characters' teen years with an out-of-this-world, trope-driven bend. It offers print and digital romance novels featuring characters ages 16–18. It is seeking sci-fi, paranormal, fantasy, dystopian, and cyberpunk romances and teen romances that follow the traditional category romance format. Novels in third person point of view, with light or dark tones, are preferred.

Freelance Potential: Publishes approximately 50 titles annually: 60% by agented authors, 40% by authors who are new to the publishing house, 50% by previously unpublished writers. Receives 300 queries yearly.

Fiction: YA. Genres: fantasy, contemporary, historical, science fiction, thriller, fantasy, and paranormal, all with romantic themes.

Submissions and Payment: Guidelines and catalogue available on website. YA novels, 45,000–60,000 words. Send 1-page query with genre, word count, brief synopsis, writing credentials, links to your website, and first 5 manuscript pages or complete manuscript. Accepts submissions via centralized system on website. Responds in 30 days. Publication period and payment policies vary.

Teen Crush

www.entangledpublishing.com

Submissions Editor

Teen Crush specializes in heart-stopping feelings and never-ending drama, ranging from funny to emotional, flirty to dark. Engaging, irresistible first-love stories are the backbone of this publisher. All of its titles feature teen characters ages 16–18.

Freelance Potential: Publishes approximately 50 titles annually: 60% by agented authors, 40% by authors who are new to the publishing house, 50% by previously unpublished writers. Receives 300 queries yearly.

Fiction: YA. Genres: fantasy, contemporary, historical, science fiction, thriller, fantasy, and paranormal, all with romantic themes.

Submissions and Payment: Guidelines and catalogue available on website. YA novels, 45,000–60,000 words. Send 1-page query with genre, word count, brief synopsis, writing credentials, links to your website, and first 5 manuscript pages or complete manuscript. Accepts submissions via centralized system on website. Responds in 30 days. Publication period and payment policies vary.

Katherine Tegen Books

10 East 53rd Street, New York, NY 10022. www.harpercollinschildrens.com

Editorial Director: Katherine Tegen

Katherine Tegen Books specializes in high-quality fiction that is both literary and commercial for children and teens: thought-provoking and entertaining stories that reach a wide audience. As with the policy all imprints of HarperCollins, Katherine Tegen Books reviews submissions from agented authors only.

Freelance Potential: HarperCollins publishes hundreds of titles annually.

Fiction: Early readers, picture books, middle-grade, YA. Genres: contemporary, family, friends, animal stories, real life stories, romance, mystery.

Submissions and Payment: Guidelines and catalogue available on website. Accepts queries through literary agents only. Royalty; advance.

Templar Books

99 Dover Street, Somerville, MA 02144. www.candlewick.com

Editorial Director: Liz Bicknell

Templar Books creates award-winning picture books and action packed novelty titles along with interactive baby books. This imprint of Candlewick reviews work from agents or through conference appearances where editors meet authors. Check the website for changes to this policy.

Freelance Potential: Candlewick publishes 200 titles annually: almost all by agented authors; 1–10% by authors who are new to the publishing house; 1–10% by previously unpublished writers. Receives about 500 queries monthly.

Fiction: Toddler books, early picture books, early readers, picture books, middle-grade. Genres: contemporary, multicultural, historical, fantasy, adventure, mystery.

Nonfiction: Concept books, early picture books, picture books, middle-grade. Topics: history, nature, science, the environment, politics, geography, biography.

Submissions and Payment: Agented authors only. Catalogue available on website. Response time, publication period, and payment policies vary.

Templar Publishing

107-109 The Plaza, 535 Kings Road, Chelsea Harbor, London SW10 0SZ. www.templarco.co.uk

Submissions Editor

The Templar Books imprint delivers cleverly conceived publishing with an emphasis on paper innovation, stylish design, and contemporary illustration for an international audience. It is celebrated for producing award-winning, innovative, illustrated children's preschool, picture books, nonfiction, and novelty titles. It is a leading UK children's publisher.

Freelance Potential: Publishes 60 titles annually: 2% developed from unsolicited submissions; 20% by agented authors; 20% by authors who are new to the publishing house; 10% by previously unpublished writers. Receives 34 unsolicited manuscripts monthly.

Fiction: Board books, baby books, novelty books, picture books, story picture books, middle-grade. Genres: contemporary, fantasy, animal stories.

Nonfiction: Story picture books, middle-grade. Topics: science, animals, natural history, nature.

Submissions and Payment: Guidelines and catalogue available on website. Send complete manuscript. Accepts hard copy. SAE/IRC. Responds in 3–4 months. Publication period and payment policies vary.

Theytus Books

154 En'owkin Way, RR 2, Site 50, Comp. 8, Penticton, British Columbia V2A 6J7 Canada. www.theytus.com

Submissions: Ann Doyon

Theytus Books is a leading North American publisher of Indigenous voices. It is recognized and respected internationally for its contributions to Aboriginal literature. Its catalogue includes books for children in grades K through 12, as well as books for use in universities and colleges.

Freelance Potential: Publishes 10 titles annually: 33% by authors who are new to the publishing house; 10–20% by previously unpublished writers. Receives 2 queries, 3–5 unsolicited manuscripts each month.

Fiction: Story picture books, middle-grade, YA. Genres: contemporary, historical, literary fiction, folktales, adventure, drama, humor, poetry.

Nonfiction: YA. Topics: Aboriginal history, policy, social issues.

Submissions and Payment: Canadian Aboriginal authors only. Guidelines and catalogue available on website. For children's books, send complete manuscript with synopsis and intended age group. For young adult books, query with synopsis, intended age group, and 4 sample chapters. All submissions must be accompanied by a cover letter and author biography that includes tribal affiliation and previously published works. Accepts hard copy. No simultaneous submissions. SASE. Responds in 6–8 months. Publication in 1–2 years. Pays $200 on publication, then 10% royalty.

Thistledown Press

410 2nd Avenue, Saskatoon, Saskatchewan SK S7K 2C3 Canada. www.thistledownpress.com

Publisher: Allan Forrie

Thistledown Press's mission is to encourage innovation and excellence in the literary arts through the development of its literary publishing program. Its catalogue features literary fiction, nonfiction, and poetry for adults. Working exclusively with Canadian authors, this Canadian publisher offers fiction for young adult readers. It no longer publishes books for the 8–12 age range. At this time, it is accepting YA novels and nonfiction submissions. Check the website for updates.

Freelance Potential: Publishes 18 titles annually: 55% by authors who are new to the publishing house; 39% by previously unpublished writers. Receives 50 queries monthly.

Fiction: Chapter books, YA. Genres: contemporary, multicultural, fantasy, mystery.

Submissions and Payment: Canadian authors only. Guidelines and catalogue available on website. Review guidelines for submission requirements for each genre. Accepts hard copy. SASE. No simultaneous submissions. Responds in minimum of 4 months. Publication in 1 year. Royalty.

TOON Books

RAW Junior, 27 Greene Street, New York, NY 10013. www.toon-books.com

Editorial Director: Francoise Mouly

TOON Books are the first high-quality comics designed for children ages 3 and up. A whole new approach to books for beginning readers, TOON Books publishes comics for early or emerging readers, as well as TOON Graphics, for ages 8–12 and grades 3–6. In addition to the graphic novels themselves, TOON supports classroom use of the books with teacher guides and other materials. TOON Books (32–48 pages) are divided into 3 reading levels: First Comics for Brand-New Readers (K–grade 1); Easy-to-Read for Emerging Readers (grades 1–2); and Chapter Book Comics for Advanced Beginners (grades 2–3). The books follow specific word length, vocabulary, and syntactical guidelines. TOON Graphics vary from 48 to 160 pages.

Freelance Potential: Publishes 4–6 books annually.

Fiction: Early readers, chapter books, reluctant readers. Genres: graphic novels/comics.

Submissions and Payment: TOON Books has occasionally (but very rarely) accepted unsolicited submissions from cartoonists. Responds only if interested. Query or send complete manuscript to mail@toon-books.com. Response time, publication and payment policies vary.

Topaz Books

www.topazpublishingllc.com

Acquisitions: Marilyn L. Godfrey

Topaz Books provides sweet, Christian, and inspirational romance, children's, preteen's, and young adult books. Helping young minds journey to faraway places, its books are designed to enhance positive behaviors. It is currently closed to submissions.

Freelance Potential: Publishes 10–15 titles annually.

Fiction: Early readers, middle-grade, YA. Genres: contemporary, romance, adventure, fantasy.

Nonfiction: Early readers, middle-grade, YA. Topics: biography.

Submissions and Payment: Guidelines and catalogue available on website. It is currently closed to submissions. Check the website for changes to this policy.

Tradewind Books

202-1807 Maritime Mews, Vancouver, British Columbia V6H 3W7 Canada.
www.tradewindbooks.com

Publisher

Tradewind Books has been publishing prize-winning picture books, novels, and poetry for children of all ages for over 20 years. It is a strictly Canadian publisher. It celebrates the work of authors from diverse cultures within Canada and around the world. Its books are distributed through Fitzhenry & Whiteside Limited.

Freelance Potential: Publishes 7–8 titles annually: 10–25% developed from unsolicited submissions; 10–25% by agented authors; 10–25% by authors who are new to the publishing house; 15% by previously unpublished writers. Receives 50–75 unsolicited manuscripts monthly.

Fiction: Picture books, early readers, chapter books, middle-grade, YA. Genres: contemporary, multicultural, mystery, folktales, fairy tales, poetry.

Submissions and Payment: Guidelines and catalogue available on website. Send complete manuscript for picture books. Query with first 3 chapters, a chapter outline, and plot summary for longer works. For poetry, send book-length collection of poems. With all submissions send a cover letter that shows you have read at least 3 books published by Tradewind in the genre in which you are submitting; also include author bio and publishing credits. Accepts hard copy only. SAE/IRC. Responds in 3 months. Publication in 3 years. Royalty, 10%.

Treehouse Publishing Group

4168 Hartford St., St. Louis, MO 63116. www.amphoraepublishing.com

Editor

Treehouse Publishing Group looks for children's books, picture books, middle-grade, and young adult books that have great writing, intriguing characters, and a little extra something to stand out in the crowd. Passionate, progressive, and inclusive, this publisher is particularly interested in historical fiction, contemporary stories, and science fiction and fantasy featuring strong female characters. It also welcomes multicultural submissions.

Freelance Potential: Publishes 15 titles annually.

Fiction: Early picture books, early readers, story picture books, middle-grade, YA. Genres: historical, contemporary, multicultural, fantasy, science fiction, steampunk.

Nonfiction: Story picture books, middle-grade, YA. Topics: history, social studies, and social skills.

Submissions and Payment: Catalogue and guidelines available on website. Query or send complete manuscript. Accepts submissions through the online submission form at the website. Responds in 10–12 weeks. Publication period and payment policies vary.

Triangle Square

140 Watts Street, New York, NY 10013. www.sevenstories.com

Acquisitions

Triangle Square offers fiction and nonfiction for young readers through young adults on a wide range of topics. It is the newest imprint from Seven Stories Press and targets the next generation of skeptical young readers.

Freelance Potential: Publishes 4–8 titles annually.

Fiction: Story picture books, early readers, middle-grade, YA. Genres: contemporary, realistic, coming-of-age, historical, graphic novels.

Nonfiction: Picture books, early readers, middle-grade, YA. Topics: history, the women's movement, human rights, social justice, gender equality, science, the environment, social issues.

Submissions and Payment: Guidelines and catalogue available on website. Query only with cover letter and no more than 2 sample chapters. Accepts hard copy. SASE. Responds in 2–4 months. Publication in 18 months. Royalty.

Tu Books

Lee & Low Books, 95 Madison Avenue, Suite 1205, New York, NY 10026. https://www.leeandlow.com/imprints/3

Submissions Editor

Tu Books believes the present and the future belong to everyone and to limit this reality is a fantasy. Diverse middle-grade and young adult books make up the catalogue from this publisher. Tu Books is an imprint of Lee & Low Books that is dedicated to publishing high-quality middle-grade and young adult novels that spark imagination, move the spirit, and keep teens turning pages. With a readership that is unconventional by choice, that dares to imagine the unimaginable, this imprint is now focused on all genres of fiction and nonfiction including novel and graphic novel forms. Novels in verse are also welcome.

Freelance Potential: Publishes 6–8 titles annually.

Fiction: Middle-grade, YA. Genres: fantasy, science fiction, mystery.

Submissions and Payment: Guidelines and catalogue available on website. Send cover letter that includes author biography and publishing credits, synopsis, and first 3 chapters. Accepts hard copy. Also accepts submissions electronically through the website. Accepts simultaneous submissions if identified. No SASE; materials not returned. Responds in 6 months if interested. Advance against royalties.

Tumblehome Learning

201 Newton Street, Weston, MA 02493. www.tumblehomelearning.com

Submissions

The majority of Tumblehome Learning books are geared toward upper elementary and middle-school grades (approximately ages 8–12). Tumblehome Learning provides STEM-related books and the tools for students to become inspired to learn more about the natural and man-made worlds around them. A large majority of their books are fiction, and generally have adventure/mystery plots containing scientific facts, engineering design processes, and/or genuine historical STEM figures. Each book published comes with a set of physical and ultimately online activities that allow readers to reproduce and extend the science they read about.

Freelance Potential: Publishes 3–6 titles annually.

Fiction: Story picture books, chapter books, middle-grade, YA. Genres: fantasy, contemporary, historical, adventure, mystery, science fiction.

Nonfiction: Story picture books, chapter books, middle-grade, YA. Topics: biography, science, social issues.

Submissions and Payment: Guidelines available. Catalogue available on website. Send query with cover letter detailing qualifications to write on the topic and previous publishing experience, synopsis of entire book, and first 3 chapters. Accepts electronic submissions only (Word or PDF attachments) with "Submission: [Title]" in the subject line to submissions@tumblehomelearning.com. Response time and payment policies vary.

Tuttle Publishing

364 Innovation Drive, North Clarendon, VT 05759-9436. www.tuttlepublishing.com

Acquisitions Editor: Brandy LaMotte

Tuttle Publishing spans many diverse categories and topics and is always in search of talent to become part of its elite team. "Pioneering into the future while building upon our past" is the motto of this publisher. Tuttle is regarded as the premier publisher and seller of books rooted in Asian culture. Its fundamental values are to discover, create, publish, and deliver best-in-class books and products that bring the world closer together one page turn at a time. Its children's line centers around Asian culture, crafts, and language.

Freelance Potential: Publishes 150 titles annually: 25–50% developed from unsolicited submissions; 1–10% assigned; 1–10% by agented authors; 25–50% by authors who are new to the publishing house; 75–100% by previously unpublished writers. Receives 10–25 queries, 10–25 unsolicited manuscripts monthly.

Fiction: Early readers, chapter books, middle-grade, YA. Genres: multicultural, fantasy, fairy tales, folktales, graphic novels, poetry.

Nonfiction: Activity books, early readers, story picture books, chapter books. Topics: Asian topics, animals, the arts, crafts, holidays, humor, language arts, multicultural topics, reference.

Submissions and Payment: Guidelines and catalogue available on website. Send proposal with cover letter, annotated table of contents, 1 or 2 sample chapters, target audience, and competition and market report. Prefers email to submissions@tuttlepublishing.com (Word or PDF attachments); will accept hard copy. Accepts simultaneous submissions if identified. Availability of artwork improves chance of acceptance. SASE. Responds in 3 months. Publication in 1 year. Royalty.

Viking Children's Books

Penguin Group, 345 Hudson Street, New York, NY 10014. http://us.penguingroup.com

Editorial Assistant: Joanna Cardenas

Throughout Viking's history, it has been known for innovation as well as for a dedication to quality that has created the rich backlist the house enjoys. Readers, both American and international, appreciate Viking for its depth, its breadth, its uniqueness, and its originality. Viking is a legendary imprint with a distinguished list of extraordinary writers in both fiction and nonfiction. Founded in 1933, this imprint from the Penguin Young Readers Group offers a wide variety of fiction and carefully chosen nonfiction titles, from picture books for young children to novels for teenagers.

Freelance Potential: Publishes about 75 titles annually: most by agented authors.

Fiction: Picture books, chapter books, middle-grade, YA. Genres: contemporary, historical, realistic, multicultural, science fiction, adventure, mystery.

Nonfiction: Middle-grade, YA. Topics: nontraditional.

Submissions and Payment: Guidelines and catalogue available on website. Agented authors preferred. Query with complete or partial manuscript. Accepts hard copy. SASE. Responds in 4 months if interested. Publication period varies. Royalty, 5–10%; advance. Flat fee.

Walden Pond Press

10 East 53rd Street, New York, NY 10022. www.harpercollinschildrens.com

Editor: Jordan Brown

Middle-grade classics that are fast-paced, funny, engaging, compulsively readable stories are the backbone of this imprint. Middle-grade classics are featured on the list of Walden Pond Books, which is a collaboration between HarperCollins and Walden Media. Many of its titles are available in audio format.

Freelance Potential: Publishes about 22 titles annually. Open to new talent.

Fiction: Middle-grade. Genres: fantasy, contemporary, historical, science fiction, sports, mystery, humor.

Submissions and Payment: Guidelines and catalogue available on website. Agented authors only. Royalty; advance.

Walker Books ★ 🌐

87 Vauxhall Walk, London SE11 5HJ www.walker.co.uk

Manuscript Submissions

This children's publisher was recently acquired by Trustbridge Global Media. Its catalogue is filled with picture books by authors and illustrators from around the world. It has worked with award-winning authors including Kate DiCamillo, Patrick Ness, and Jon Klassen.

Freelance Potential: Publishes 15–20 titles annually.

Fiction: Picture books on many different topics.

Submissions and Payment: Guidelines and catalogue available on website. Illustrated picture book submissions are accepted by email to editorial@walker.co.uk. Also accepts hard copy. Responds only if interested.

Wander 🤝

351 Executive Drive, Carol Stream, IL 60188. www.tyndale.com

Acquisitions Director: Linda Howard

Wander looks to fill a void in the Christian YA marketplace. Wander is the new young adult imprint from Tyndale. It features engaging stories with strong, positive messages that address today's current issues. This publisher accepts submissions from agents only.

Freelance Potential: Plans to publish 4 titles annually.

Fiction: YA. Genres: realistic and religious fiction.

Nonfiction: YA. Topics: Religion, spirituality, the Christian faith, real life/problems, devotionals, contemporary issues.

Submissions and Payment: Agented authors only. This publisher recommends that potential writers familiarize themselves with the online submissions service at www.christianmanuscriptsubmissions.com. No unsolicited manuscripts. Publication period varies. Royalty; advance. Flat fee.

West 44 Books

101 West 23rd Street, #240, New York, NY 10011. www.west44books.com

Editor

Diversity and inclusivity are top priorities at West 44 Books, so they are especially looking for own-voice stories. West 44 Books is the new hi/lo middle-grade and young adult fiction imprint from Enslow Publishing. Launched in the spring of 2019, it provides a platform for new, authentic voices and gripping stories. Its titles cover diverse subject matters that are relatable to readers of all backgrounds.

Freelance Potential: Publishes 6 titles each year..

Fiction: Middle-grade, YA. Genres: Realistic fiction, real-life problems, reluctant reader, social issues, coming-of-age.

Submissions and Payment: Catalogue available on website. Query with outline. Email to customerservice@enslow.com. Responds in 1–6 months. Publication in 1 year. Royalty; advance. Flat fee.

Albert Whitman & Company

250 South Northwest Highway, Suite 320, Park Ridge, IL 60068. www.albertwhitman.com

Editorial Director: Kelly Barrales-Saylorf

Albert Whitman is dedicated to continuing its tradition of creating award-worthy books for children. Its books help readers grow intellectually and emotionally. It has a long history of publishing books by talented and imaginative authors. The books from Albert Whitman & Company treat readers in a caring and respectful manner. Its catalogue features both fiction and nonfiction, and it has an extensive backlist that includes holiday books, concept books, and books in the classic Boxcar Children series. It also publishes books for parents. Albert Whitman is currently seeking fiction and nonfiction picture books for children ages 1–8.

Freelance Potential: Publishes 40 titles annually. Receives 25 queries, 375 unsolicited manuscripts each month.

Fiction: Board books, early picture books, chapter books, middle-grade, YA. Genres: historical fiction, humor, mystery, contemporary.

Nonfiction: Concept books, early picture books, chapter books, middle-grade, YA. Topics: social, multicultural, ethnic, and family issues; history; biography.

Submissions and Payment: Guidelines and catalogue available on website. Query with cover letter and 3 sample chapters; or send complete manuscript. Accepts hard copy and simultaneous submissions if identified. No SASE; materials not returned. Responds in 4 months if interested. Publication in 18–24 months. Royalty; advance.

Albert Whitman Teen

250 South Northwest Highway, Suite 320, Park Ridge, IL 60068. www.albertwhitman.com

Editor: Wendy McClure

Launched in 2011, this imprint aims to do for teens what its parent company does for younger children: publish books on issues that matter to its readers. This YA imprint of Albert Whitman and Company seeks titles that ask questions about the inner and outer worlds of teens. Stories should not just feature a teen protagonist, they should be about teen experiences and written for a teen audience. Editors are open to reality-bending, magic, or paranormal threads as long as they help the story, not define it. Albert Whitman is currently only publishing fiction but does not rule out nonfiction for the future.

Freelance Potential: Publishes about 5 titles annually.

Fiction: YA. Genres: fantasy, contemporary, historical, multicultural, real life/problems, coming-of-age, social issues.

Submissions and Payment: Guidelines available on website. Query with cover letter and 3 sample chapters; or send complete manuscript. Accepts email submissions to Submissions@albertwhitman.com. Accept simultaneous submissions if identified. No SASE; materials not returned. Responds in 4 months if interested. Publication in 18–24 months. Royalty; advance.

Windward Publishing

5995 149th Street West, Suite 105, Apple Valley, MN 55124. www.finneyco.coml

President: Alan E. Krysan

Windward offers nature and children's books on popular subjects including fishing, mammals, and birds. It is the home to most of Finney Company's children's books. Founded in 1973, Windward Publishing became a division of Finney Company in 2001.

Freelance Potential: Publishes 4–5 titles annually: 1–10% developed from unsolicited submissions; 1–10% by authors who are new to the publishing house; 1–10% by previously unpublished writers. Receives 15–20 queries monthly.

Fiction: Early readers, story picture books. Genres: nature stories.

Nonfiction: Early readers, story picture books, chapter books, middle-grade, YA. Topics: nature, flowers, birds, reptiles, amphibians, animals, fishing, seashells, sea life, space.

Submissions and Payment: Guidelines available on website. Query with letter explaining manuscript and author background/qualifications, 1-page overview, table of contents, introduction, at least 3 sample chapters, and short description of proposed market. Accepts hard copy. Accepts simultaneous submissions if identified. SASE. Responds in 10–12 weeks. Publication in 6–8 months. Royalty, 10% of net.

Paula Wiseman Books

Simon & Schuster, 1230 Avenue of the Americas, New York, NY 10020. http://imprints.simonandschuster.biz/paula-wiseman-books

Editors: Paula Wiseman and Alexandra Penfold
Associate Editor: Sylvie Frank

Paula Wiseman Books is an imprint of Simon & Schuster Children's Publishing that focuses on stories and art that are childlike, timeless, innovative, and centered in emotion. It strives to publish books that entertain while expanding the experience of the children who read them. Launched in 2003, it has since gone on to publish over seventy award-winning and bestselling books, including picture books, novelty books, and novels. It is interested in receiving submissions from new and published authors through agents and SCBWI conferences only.

Freelance Potential: Publishes 20–30 titles annually: 20% by authors who are new to the publishing house; 8% by previously unpublished authors.

Fiction: Novelty books, toddler books, early picture books, early readers, chapter books, middle-grade, YA. Genres: contemporary, multicultural, adventure, coming-of-age, humor.

Nonfiction: Board books, early readers, story picture books. Topics: animals, nature, sports, biography.

Submissions and Payment: Guidelines and catalogue available on website. Accepts submissions through literary agents or at conferences. Response time varies. Publication in 18–24 months. Royalty; advance.

Words & Pictures ⊚

The Old Brewery, 6 Blundell Street, London N7 9BH, UK. www.quartoknows.com/words-pictures

Publisher: Maxime Boucknooghe

A high-quality imprint for young children, Words & Pictures was started in 2012. Imagination, innovation, and inspiration define what this publisher sets out to do. Focusing on fun, imaginative books for children of all ages, it is always on the lookout for authors and artists with creative ideas that enhance and broaden its list of children's books.

Freelance Potential: Plans to publish 5–10 titles annually.

Fiction: Early readers, picture books. Stories about animals, nature.

Nonfiction: Early readers, picture books, middle-grade. Topics: animals, nature, social issues.

Submissions and Payment: Catalogue and guidelines available on website. Accepts email proposals to maxime.boucknooghe@quarto.com. Include an author bio, detailed description of subject/content, artwork, market information and a signed Submission Agreement (available at the website). Response time, publication period, and payment policies vary.

Workman Publishing

225 Varick Street, New York, NY 10014–4381. www.workman.com

Children's Department

Workman Publishing Company is an independently owned family of publishers including Algonquin Books for Young Readers, Storey Publishing, and Timber Press. The Workman imprint publishes exclusively nonfiction books for children and adults, as well as calendars. Known for its innovations that have stretched the boundaries of traditional books and calendars, Workman has produced a string of iconic bestsellers. It does not publish picture books or middle-grade/young adult fiction.

Freelance Potential: Publishes 40 titles annually: 15% by agented authors. Receives 25 unsolicited manuscripts monthly.

Nonfiction: Novelty books, concept books, baby books, chapter books, activity books, puzzle books. Topics: science, nature, animals, humor, hobbies, crafts.

Submissions and Payment: Guidelines and catalogue available on website. Query with proposal of no more than 30 pages. Include title and a subtitle, one-paragraph overview, author bio, table of contents, and market analysis. Children's manuscripts must specify "Children's Department." Prefers electronic submissions to submissions@workman.com (Word or PDF attachments). Accepts hard copy. SASE. Response time varies, usually 6 months or more. Publication period varies. Royalty; advance.

Worthy Kids

6100 Tower Circle, Suite 210, Franklin, TN 37067.
https://www.hachettebookgroup.com/imprint/hachette-nashville/worthy-books/

Submissions

Worthy Kids, part of Hachette Book Group, is an inspirational publisher for children and adults specializing in Christian authors and best-selling fiction and nonfiction. Worthy Kids accepts manuscripts only from agents.

Freelance Potential: Publishes 5–10 titles annually.

Fiction: Picture books, board books. Genres: general fiction stories for young children.

Nonfiction: Educational activity books for ages 3–8, board books, picture books. Topics: inspiration/faith, math, science, geography, cultures, history, cooking, arts and crafts, early learning topics.

Submissions and Payment: Guidelines and catalogue available on website. Send complete manuscript only; no queries. Accepts hard copy. Responds in 4–8 months if interested. Publication in 1–2 years. Royalty, some other payment arrangements; advance.

Yen Press

237 Park Avenue, New York, NY 10017. www.yenpress.com

Submissions

Yen Press publishes graphic novels and manga aimed at children and teens. It is open to project submissions from artists or writer/artist teams. It includes adaptations of popular novel series such as Twilight and Maximum Ride; English versions of Japanese, Korean, and other foreign works; and original titles. The books target many ages, from early readers to teens and adults. It is not currently seeking pitches from writers who are not already working with an illustrator.

Freelance Potential: Publishes 80–90 books annually.

Fiction: Early readers, middle-grade, YA, adult. Genres: adventure, fantasy, thrillers, historical fiction, humor, fairy tales.

Submissions and Payment: Guidelines and catalogue available on website. Send project summary, intended audience, plot outline with character descriptions, initial concept designs, and a minimum of 5–10 pages of sequential art. Accepts email to yenpress@hbgusa.com and hard copy. Responds only if interested. Publication period and payment policy vary.

Bettie Youngs Books

www.bettieyoungsbooks.com

Submissions

Bettie Youngs Books brings readers a carefully selected line of books about fascinating people and their remarkable life journeys. It seeks high-caliber authors who produce original material that appeals to its readers. With a reputation of excellence in publishing, Bettie Youngs Books focuses on memoirs of people who have lived interesting lives. This publisher's mission is to produce inspiring works to reawaken our passion for life and reaffirm our faith in the indomitability of the human spirit. It publishes a children's imprint, Kendhal House Press, and one for teens called Teen Town Press.

Freelance Potential: Publishes 4–6 titles yearly.

Nonfiction: Early readers, middle-grade, YA, adult. Topics: memoirs.

Submissions and Payment: Guidelines and catalogue available on website. Send a cover letter and proposal that includes target audience, promotion suggestions, summary and purpose, competition analysis, detailed outline, table of contents, introduction, 2 sample chapters, author credentials. Accepts email to info@bettieyoungsbooks.com. Publication period and payment policies vary.

Zest Books

2443 Filmore Street, Suite 340, San Francisco, CA 94115. http://zestbooks.net

Editorial Director: Daniel Harmon

Zest Books publishes smart, compelling, and evocative nonfiction for young adult readers. Zest titles are irreverent and edgy, spanning a variety of topics from dating and sexuality to illustrated travelogues and lifestyle advice. Readers can explore their own identities and ideas while engaging with and thinking critically about current events and a broader worldview.

Freelance Potential: Publishes about 8–12 titles annually.

Nonfiction: YA. Topics: biography, how-to, pop culture, health, careers, relationships, fashion.

Submissions and Payment: Guidelines and catalogue available on website. Send brief description of the book, table of contents, 1–5 sample pages, competition research, résumé, and 3–5 published writing samples. To be considered for author pool for in-house projects, send a cover letter stating interest and expertise in young adult nonfiction, résumé, and 3–5 writing samples. Accepts email to dan@zestbooks.net and hard copy. SASE. For graphic novels, the editors are looking for smart, edgy, compelling, and funny stories that are teen-friendly and different. Send a 3- to 5-page synopsis, including possible titles, character descriptions, and the story arc; a 5-page sample with finished panel art and text; a résumé; and SASE. Accepts hard copy or email to info@zestbooks.net, with "Graphic Novel Submission" in the subject line. Response time, publication period, and payment policy vary.

Zumaya Publications LLC

3209 South Interstate 35, #1086, Austin, TX 78741-6905. https://zumayatales.blog/category/zumaya-publications/

Acquisitions Editor: Rie Sheridan Rose

Zumaya Publishing stands apart from other publishers by limiting its list to only the highest quality titles. Zumaya Publications is an innovative publishing company with a goal of bringing the best fiction to the public. It is currently seeking Western fiction and LGBTQI fiction. If you have a well-written piece that stands apart from the crowd, you are encouraged to submit it.

Freelance Potential: Publishes 35 titles annually: 50% developed from unsolicited submissions; 20% by authors who are new to the publishing house; 15% by previously unpublished writers. Receives 70 queries monthly.

Fiction: Middle-grade, YA. Genres: fantasy, contemporary, science fiction.

Nonfiction: Middle-grade, YA.

Submissions and Payment: Guidelines and catalogue available on website. Most titles published as e-books initially unless author has a prepared marketing program requiring print or a proven sales record with print. Does not accept multiple submissions.

Classroom and Educational Publishing for Children

Approaching educational publishers and developing working arrangements with them can be quite different from approaching trade publishers. Companies that target schools and libraries—institutional markets—frequently publish in series, especially in nonfiction. They often look for particular expertise in subject matter and may even give weight to writers with classroom experience. Rather than pay royalties, educational publishers may use the work of freelancers on a per-project or work-for-hire basis, meaning they use *contract writers* or work *on assignment* only. What editors of classroom books look for reflects these arrangements. Some want full-blown proposals, including bibliographies, market analyses, and so on. Others prefer to receive author résumés and other information to help them evaluate whether writers are a good match for their company and might be brought into the *freelance stable* for assignments.

Classroom—school and library—markets are a strong choice for writers looking to create a career. A writer who can meet the needs of an editor in this part of the publishing industry, write to spec, and be creative too can establish a long-lasting editorial relationship and a writing portfolio to carry on to other publishers.

Children's writers may also be interested in writing books for those who educate and care for children and teens. These readers fill wide-ranging roles and often have an important place in the lives of young people.

The publishers listed in this section offer professional resources, classroom aids, and other materials in support of teachers, early childhood educators, librarians, principals, child psychiatrists, homeschoolers, those who work in gifted or special education, pediatric health, and many other areas. Some houses also publish books directed to children and teens themselves—books that educators, caregivers, and other adults might use with them.

While educational writers often have expertise or backgrounds in education, health, or other professional fields, they may also have personal experience that qualifies them to write books of this kind. Establishing a relationship with companies such as these can result in regular work, and a niche that extends a writing career.

ABC-CLIO

130 Cremona Drive, Suite C, Santa Barbara, CA 93117. www.abc-clio.com

Acquisitions Editor

For 65 years, ABC-CLIO has been providing reference, nonfiction, online curriculum, and professional development to inspire life-long learning for today's students and educators. With titles ranging from in-depth multi-volume encyclopedias to more precise handbooks, guides, and document collections, ABC-CLIO is an industry leader in the creation of innovative reference and professional development resources. ABC-CLIO is comprised of four imprints: ABC-CLIO/Greenwood, Praeger, Libraries Unlimited, and ABC-CLIO Solutions. They publish a comprehensive range of print and online materials that benefit learners, researchers, educators, librarians, and information specialists worldwide. The company has expanded its focus to include many disciplines and embrace the best of new technologies, but remains true to their original commitment to excellence, innovation, and meeting the needs of their customers. It offers reference and educational titles that cover history, humanities, and general interest topics that complement secondary and higher education curriculum.

Freelance Potential: Publishes 12 titles annually: 25% by authors who are new to the publishing house. Receives 10 queries monthly.

Nonfiction: Middle-grade, YA. Topics: technology, history, humanities, social issues, culture, geography.

Submissions and Payment: Guidelines and catalogue available at website. Query with author qualifications. Accepts email (see website for appropriate acquisitions editor) and hard copy. SASE. If interested, publisher will ask for proposal with working title, scope and purpose of book, an outline, methodology and presentation, and competitive titles. Responds in 8–10 weeks. Publication in 10–12 months. Royalty. For magazine articles, send complete manuscript (1,200–3,000 words) via email to appropriate editor (see website). Response time varies.

Abdo Publishing Company

1920 Lookout Drive, North Mankato, MN 56003. www.abdopublishing.com

Submissions Committee

ABDO is known throughout the industry for its high-quality design and content. Its goal is to bring new and exciting products to young readers everywhere. For over 30 years, ABDO has been publishing exceptional children's PreK–grade 12 educational titles for libraries and schools. While adapting to dynamic marketplaces and evolving its brand over the years, this Minnesota-based company is comprised of five divisions: Abdo Publishing, Magic Wagon, Spotlight, Abdo Kids, and Abdo Digital. Each book is leveled using grade-appropriate language and designed to be of high interest. Abdo Publishing Company works with contract writers only, and accepts résumés and clips; it does not accept unsolicited manuscripts. It is currently accepting fiction proposals only.

Freelance Potential: Publishes 600 titles annually: less than 10% developed from unsolicited submissions; less than 10% by authors who are new to the publishing house. Receives 30 queries each month.

Fiction: Early picture books, early readers, story picture books, chapter books, middle-grade, YA. Genres: adventure, animals, folklore, mythology, science fiction, seasonal, contemporary.

Nonfiction: Early picture books, early readers, story picture books, chapter books, middle-grade, YA. Topics: animals, nature, travel, geography, sciences, sports, history, biography, multicultural/ethnic.

Submissions and Payment: Catalogue available on website. Guidelines provided to writers under contract only. To be considered for writing assignments, send résumé with cover letter, area of expertise, and publishing credits. Accepts email to fiction@abdobooks.com. Response time varies. Publication period varies. Flat fee.

Academic Therapy Publications

20 Leveroni Court, Novato, CA 94949. www.academictherapy.com

Acquisitions Editor

As the field of special education continues to evolve and expand, Academic Therapy is excited about the future and looking forward to being there with you. Academic Therapy Publications was one of the first publishers to meet the needs of teachers, parents, and students in the field of special education and learning disabilities. Now, 50 years after its founding, ATP is still a family-owned business that is proud to continue producing relevant materials that can be used by special ed teachers, speech-language pathologists, occupational therapists, school psychologists, educational therapists, ESL teachers, parents, and specialists in all fields working with persons with reading, learning, and communication disabilities. Its High Noon imprint specializes in high/low reading material.

Freelance Potential: Publishes 15 titles annually: 10% developed from unsolicited submissions. Receives 50 queries monthly.

Nonfiction: Standardized tests and reference books, curriculum materials, teacher/parent references, and visual/perceptual training aids. Topics: speech/language, occupational therapy, rehabilitation, special education, school psychology.

Submissions and Payment: Catalogue available on website. Query with synopsis and author biography. Accepts hard copy. SASE. Response time varies. Publication period varies. Flat fee.

ALA Editions

American Library Association, 50 East Huron Street, Chicago, IL 60611-2729. www.alaeditions.org

Acquisitions Editor: Rachel Chance

ALA authors and developers are leaders in their fields, and their content is published in a growing range of print and electronic formats. ALA Editions and ALA Neal-Schuman publishes resources used worldwide by tens of thousands of library and information professionals to improve programs, build on best practices, develop leadership, and for personal professional development. It offers books, eCourses, and webinars for the library and information services community. ALA authors and developers are leaders in their fields, and their content is published in a growing range of print and electronic formats. Many of its authors are library information professionals, but ALA Editions is open to working with writers from other disciplines as long as the research is sound and the advice is practical. It is currently looking for submissions that include diversity.

Freelance Potential: Publishes 30–35 titles annually: nearly all by authors who have written for the publishing house before. Receives 4–5 queries monthly.

Submissions and Payment: Guidelines and catalogue available on website. Query with outline, 300-word synopsis, table of contents, author biography, and writing sample. Will request proposal if interested. Accepts email to rchance@ala.org. Responds in 6–8 weeks. Publication in 7–10 months. Royalty.

Allosaurus Publishing 🔒

886 110th Street, Suite 7, North Naples, FL 34108. www.allosauruspublishers.com

Editor

Allosaurus connects the past to the present through history, science, and reading comprehension. This independent publisher produces educational materials for students in grades K–12. All of its titles are teacher and student friendly and published in both print and e-book formats. At this time, it is not accepting submissions. Check the website for updates to this policy.

Freelance Potential: Publishes 20 titles yearly.

Fiction: Early readers, story picture books, middle-grade, YA. Genres: science and historical fiction.

Nonfiction: Story picture books, middle-grade, YA. Topics: history, science, regional titles on North Carolina, and workbooks.

Submissions and Payment: Catalogue, guidelines, and editor list with specific genres they seek available on website. Allosaurus is closed for submissions at this time. Check the website for updates to this policy.

Amicus Publishing

P.O. Box 1329, Mankato, MN 56002. www.amicuspublishing.us

Associate Publisher: Rebecca Glaser

Amicus knows that education is about more than good books. It's about relationships, life experiences, and understanding. Since 2010, Amicus has published books for children that educate, engage, inspire, and dig deeper. Their imprints respect the individuality of readers—for education and for life. The company is made up of four book lines: Amicus Readers (leveled nonfiction for grades K–2); Amicus Illustrated (fiction and nonfiction for PreK–grade 6); Amicus Ink (featuring board books, picture books, and paperbacks that encourage the exploration of facts and the examination of ideas); and Amicus High Interest (informational books with a high-interest presentation, grades 2–6). Amicus has recently added Amicus Digital, which offers the same great content as their print books with the convenience of online access. All of the books from Amicus promote critical thinking.

Freelance Potential: Publishes 100 titles annually.

Fiction: Picture books. Genres: contemporary, mysteries, all curriculum subject areas.

Nonfiction: Early readers, elementary. Topics: animals, science, social studies, health, careers, math, holidays, community, geography, sports, biology, technology, current events, social issues, nature/environment, economy.

Submissions and Payment: Catalogue available on website. Does not accept unsolicited manuscripts. Projects are work-for-hire. To be considered, send cover letter, résumé, and two unedited writing samples. Accepts email to submissions@amicuspublishing.us and hard copy. Response time varies.

AV2

350 Fifth Avenue, 59th Floor, New York, NY 10118. www.weigl.com; www.av2books.com

Managing Editor: Heather Hudak

Launched by Weigl in 2010, AV2 is the first and only media-enhanced book for the school market. Built-in digital features allow readers to dive even deeper into a topic through weblinks, videos, activities, and slideshows. They cover a wide range of topics within the categories of fiction, high interest, language arts, math, science, social studies, and sports. This publisher is always growing and expanding into new subject areas. It is currently adding fiction to its catalogue, as well as bilingual titles.

Freelance Potential: Publishes about 100 titles annually: 5% by authors who are new to the publishing house.

Fiction: Middle-grade. Genres include adventure and multicultural.

Nonfiction: Early readers, chapter books, middle-grade. Topics: global cultures, social and environmental issues, animal life, biography, sports, science, social studies, language arts.

Submissions and Payment: Catalogue available on website. All work is done on a work-for-hire basis. Send résumé, publishing history, and subject area of expertise only. No queries or unsolicited manuscripts. Accepts hard copy and email to av2books@weigl.com. SASE. Responds in 6–12 months. Publication in 2 years. Flat fee.

Barron's Educational Series

250 Wireless Boulevard, Hauppauge, NY 11788. www.barronseduc.com

Acquisitions Manager: Wayne Barr

For more than 80 years, Barron's has offered a large list of children's fiction and nonfiction, foreign language titles, and family and health books. Its editors remind potential authors that "not all picture books need to rhyme." They have been helping students succeed on more than 145 standardized tests.

Freelance Potential: Publishes 150–200 titles (60–85 juvenile) annually: 1–10% developed from unsolicited submissions; 1–10% assigned; 1–10% by agented authors. Receives 150–200 queries, 25–50 unsolicited manuscripts monthly; 200+ manuscripts yearly.

Fiction: Concept books, board books, toddler books, early picture books, early readers, story picture books, chapter books, middle-grade, YA. Genres: fairy tales, fantasy, adventure, retold stories, graphic novels, animals.

Nonfiction: Toddler books, early readers, story picture books, middle-grade, YA. Topics: art, activities, biography, concepts, prehistory, history, self-help, magic, bugs, cooking, pet memoirs, test prep guides, Spanish language.

Submissions and Payment: Guidelines and catalogue available on website. Prefers query with author credentials. Send complete manuscript with résumé for fiction. Query with table of contents, 2 sample chapters, market overview (including intended audience), and résumé for nonfiction. Accepts hard copy. SASE. Accepts simultaneous submissions if identified. Also accepts queries for work-for-hire assignments. Responds in 8 months. Publication in 6 months. Royalty; advance.

Bellwether Media

6012 Blue Circle Drive, Minnetonka, MN 55343. www.bellwethermedia.com

Founder: John Martin

Bellwether strives to publish the best nonfiction for beginning and reluctant readers. Publishing books for the grades K–6 range, Bellwether provides accessible and engaging books for libraries and classrooms that elevate research to an art form. All of its books are designed in accordance with the 5 tenets of effective reading instruction: Phonics, Fluency, Comprehension, Phonemic Awareness, and Vocabulary.

Freelance Potential: Publishes several titles each year.

Nonfiction: Early readers, reluctant readers, high/low, chapter books. Topics: Science, technology, sports, military, vehicles, careers, animals, geography, cultures, biography.

Submissions and Payment: Catalogue available on website. Works with freelancers on a work-for-hire basis. To be considered, send résumé and writing samples. Accepts hard copy and email to careers@bellwethermedia.com. Response time and payment policies, unknown.

Black Rabbit Books

P.O. Box 3263, Mankato, MN 56002. www.blackrabbitbooks.com

Editor: Jen Besel

"Every child is a reader . . . they just haven't found the right book yet," is the driving force of this publisher. Black Rabbit Books brings high-quality, unique and, most importantly, FUN books to readers. Its list is divided between BRB Kids (grades K–5) and BRB Teens (grades 6–12). Black Rabbit Books has multiple imprints: Arcturus Publishing (content-rich books for the upper grades); Brown Bear Books (high-interest books with primary sources); Cherrytree Books (nonfiction with unique features); New Forest Press (contemporary interests and strong photography); Sea-to-Sea Publications (specialty authors and classroom reading strategies); Smart Apple Media (nonfiction emphasizing point of view); Stargazer Books (creative takes on nonfiction, including stories); Walter Foster Library (drawing and craft books); and Zak Books (books by expert authors for classroom libraries).

Freelance Potential: Publishes hundreds of books annually.

Nonfiction: Beginning readers, early readers, middle-grade, YA. Topics: animals, nature, science, health, technology, the arts, language arts, geography, history, reference, social studies, sports.

Submissions and Payment: Catalogue available on website. Does not accept unsolicited manuscripts. Does offer work-for-hire writing and editing. To be considered, send cover letter, résumé, and 3 unpublished writing samples to info@blackrabbitbooks.com. Accepts hard copy. Response time and payment policies vary.

Bloomsbury Education

1385 Broadway, New York, NY 10018. www.bloomsbury.com/us

Submissions Editor

Bloomsbury Education specialises in the humanities and social sciences and publishes over 1,000 books and digital services each year. They publish a wide range of resources for students and researchers, from textbooks for initial teacher training to original studies, as well as amazing poetry, fiction, and nonfiction for school libraries or inspirational professional development. Many of its titles are available as downloadable e-books, and it also offers a wide range of digital subscription services.

Freelance Potential: Publishes about 1,400 titles annually: many by agented authors.

Nonfiction: Educators. Topics: education, reference, digital books.

Submissions and Payment: Guidelines and catalogue available on website. Accepts proposals to one of the editors listed on the second page of its catalogue; also accepts submission from agents. Responds in 6 months if interested. Publication period varies. Royalty; advance.

Bolchazy-Carducci Publishers, Inc.

1570 Baskin Road, Mundelein, IL 60060. www.bolchazy.com

Acquisitions Editor

Bolchazy-Carducci Publishers is proud to serve the classics community. It provides educational materials for Latin, Greek, and Classics teachers and students. It also offers titles on mythology and religion, as well as translations of children's classics.

Freelance Potential: Publishes approximately 14 books annually.

Fiction: Middle-grade, YA. Translations of children's classics, mythology, folklore.

Nonfiction: Middle-grade, YA, Educators. Latin, Greek educational material for teachers and students.

Submissions and Payment: Catalogue and guidelines available on website. Accepts hard copy email submissions manuscripts@bolchazy.com. Include a 25-page sample of book (Word document). Response time and publication period vary. Royalty; advance.

Britannica Educational Publishing

Rosen Publishing, 29 East 21st Street, New York, NY 10010. www.rosenpublishing.com

Editorial Director

Britannica Educational Publishing is an innovative publishing initiative of Encyclopedia Britannica and Rosen Publishing. Its titles serve as a thorough introduction to core subjects and events that shape the world. It is dedicated to publishing authoritative and comprehensive content that gives accurate background information as well as analysis on a wide variety of academic subjects. All its books are also available in e-book format.

Freelance Potential: Parent company Rosen Publishing publishes 700+ books annually over multiple imprints.

Nonfiction: YA. Topics: science, history, geography, current events, biography, literature, philosophy, math.

Submissions and Payment: Catalogue available on website. Contact Customer Service team via website for information about submissions. Responds in 3 months. Publication in 9–18 months. Flat fee.

Cambridge University Press

1 Liberty Plaza, Floor 20, New York, NY 10006. www.cambridge.org

Submissions Editor

Cambridge University Press enables people to achieve success by providing the best learning and research solutions. It is the printing and publishing house of the University of Cambridge, which is an integral part of the university. Its mission is to unlock people's potential with the best learning and research solutions. For centuries, the press has extended the research and teaching activities of the university by making available worldwide through its printing and publishing a remarkable range of academic and educational books, journals, examination papers, and Bibles.

Freelance Potential: Publishes about 50+ titles annually.

Nonfiction: Early readers, middle-grade, YA, educators. Topics: science, math, history, literature, education, reference, digital books.

Submissions and Payment: Guidelines and catalogue available on website. Accepts proposals through AuthorNet at Authornet.cambridge.org. Email proposal to appropriate editor listed on the site. Responds in 6 months if interested. Publication period varies. Royalty; advance.

Capstone

1710 Roe Crest Drive, North Mankato, MN 56003. www.capstonepub.com

Editorial Directors

Helping children develop a love of reading and learning, no matter their ability level, is at the heart of what Capstone does. Capstone's content comes in a variety of print and digital formats including board books, picture books, interactive books, apps, audio, and databases. Whether print, online, or new, yet-to-be-discovered formats, Capstone provides children and young adults with the content they love. Its nonfiction Capstone Press imprint specializes in emergent and reluctant readers and high-interest topics. Other imprints include Compass Point Books, Heinemann-Raintree, Picture Window Books, and Stone Arch Books. Capstone has launched a new trade line called Capstone Young Readers (CYR). It is always looking for fast, reliable, and talented authors that they can assign work-for-hire projects.

Freelance Potential: Publishes 700+ titles annually: 1–10% developed from unsolicited submissions; 75–100% assigned; 1–10% by agented authors; 10–25% by authors who are new to the publishing house; 1–10% by previously unpublished writers. Receives 10–25 queries monthly.

Fiction: Early picture books, early readers, story picture books, chapter books, middle-grade, graphic novels. Genres: adventure, science fiction, fairy tales, historical, humor, multicultural, realistic, sports.

Nonfiction: Concept books, early picture books, early readers, chapter books, graphic nonfiction, middle-grade. Topics: animals, arts, activities, games, crafts, biography, bilingual, education and career, current events, entertainment, social studies, history, geography, health, science, digital literacy, math.

Submissions and Payment: Guidelines and catalogue available on website. Send submissions to authors@capstonepub.com. Include the following in the body of the email, NOT as attachments: sample chapters, résumé, and a list of previous publishing credits (if applicable). Will respond only if submission fits its needs. Publication period and payment policies vary.

> **Capstone Imprints:** Compass Point Books, Heinemann-Raintree, Maupin House, Picture Window Books, Stone Arch Books.

Carson-Dellosa Publishing

P.O. Box 35665, Greensboro, NC 27425-5665. www.carsondellosa.com

Submissions Editor: Julie Killian

Whether on-the-go, in the classroom, or at the kitchen table, Carson-Dellosa provides high-quality and affordable solutions that capture life's many learning moments. It provides parents, teachers, and children with the best possible educational materials including interactive digital resources; supplemental books for math, science, social studies, language arts, and early childhood; classroom decoratives; pocket charts; and games and manipulatives for PreK–grade 8. Its mostly teacher-developed materials are thoughtfully designed to meet children's diverse learning needs. Carson-Dellosa is currently closed to manuscript submissions and book proposals, although its website does include a page listing freelance opportunities for independent contractors.

Freelance Potential: Publishes about 230 titles annually: all are assigned. Receives 10–15 queries each month.

Nonfiction: Publishes supplementary educational material, activity books, resource guides, classroom material, and reproducibles, PreK–grade 8. Topics: reading, language arts, mathematics, science, the arts, social studies, English Language Learners (ELL), early childhood, crafts. Also publishes Christian education titles.

Submissions and Payment: Guidelines and catalogue available on website. It is not currently accepting unsolicited manuscripts or book proposals.

Cavendish Square

243 5th Ave., Suite 136, New York, NY 10016. www.cavendishsq.com

Editor

Cavendish Square publishes highly acclaimed readers that are perfect for emergent through fluent grade 2 readers. Leveraging the magnificent print and digital assets of Marshall Cavendish's US Library Programs, Cavendish Square is proud to announce a robust and diverse list of library-bound circulating nonfiction series and early readers that range in grade level from kindergarten to college. Its circulating reference and nonfiction series support the science, social studies, and health curricula. Books are published in print, as e-books, and many also have digital platforms and databases.

Freelance Potential: Publishes 50 annually.

Nonfiction: Reference books, series, early readers. Topics: science, health, social studies.

Submissions and Payment: Catalogue available on website. For submission information, email csqedit@csqpub.com. Response time, publication period, and payment policies vary.

Cengage Learning

10650 Toebben Drive, Independence, KY 41051. www.cengage.com

Editor

Cengage creates a world where learners have the opportunity to reach their goals and dreams. It creates learning experiences that build confidence and momentum toward the future students want. Serving the higher education, K–12, professional, library, and workforce training markets worldwide, they welcome every student and design tools that make learning accessible to all. Cengage Learning believes that engagement is the foundation of learning. An engaged learner is a successful one, and this leading publisher offers titles to support reading teachers and library professionals.

Freelance Potential: Publishes hundreds of titles over several imprints yearly.

Nonfiction: Middle-grade, YA. Topics: history, social studies, sports, business, politics, health and medicine, law, media, teen issues, culture and society, education, social issues, the arts, literature, the environment, reference.

Submissions and Payment: Check website for submission and payment policy information.

Chelsea House

132 West 31st Street, 16th Floor, New York, NY 10001. www.infobasepublishing.com

Managing Editor: Justine Ciovacco

Chelsea House publishes timely and engaging sets and series spanning historical and contemporary biographies, social studies, geography, science, health, high-interest titles, and more. It has published curriculum-based nonfiction books for middle school and high school students for more than 30 years. It provides colorful, engaging books and e-books that can be used as supplemental reading for the school curriculum and as solid resources for research projects.

Freelance Potential: Publishes 300+ titles annually: less than 10% developed from unsolicited submissions; 10–25% by agented authors; 10–25% by authors who are new to the publishing house. Receives 50–75 queries, 100–150 unsolicited manuscripts monthly.

Nonfiction: Middle-grade, YA, reference. Topics: careers/college, geography, biography, government and law, health/fitness, the arts, history, math, religion, nature, science, social studies, technology.

Submissions and Payment: Guidelines and catalogue available on website. Query with subject overview, intended audience, brief description of contents, sample chapter, competition and market analysis, and author bio. Accepts hard copy and email to editorial@factsonfile.com. Responds in 4 weeks. Publication period, 9 months–2 years. Payment policy varies.

Children's Press

Scholastic Library Publishing, P.O. Box 3765, Jefferson City, MO 65102-3765. www.scholastic.com

Editor-in-Chief

Children's Press, an imprint of Scholastic Library Publishing, publishes engaging, colorfully illustrated stories, each one involving a young child learning a new concept or solving a problem on his or her own, that are sure to hold young readers' interest and build reading confidence. It guides children through the stages of independent reading. It is well-known for its popular book series and biographies for children in grades K–8. It accepts submissions from agents and manuscripts from educators only.

Freelance Potential: Publishes 250 titles annually. Receives 150–200 queries monthly.

Nonfiction: Concept books, early readers, story picture books, chapter books, middle-grade. Topics: animals, arts, culture, biography, economics, geography, history, the human body, military, science, social studies, sports, transportation.

Submissions and Payment: Agented authors only. If you are a professional educator, send a brief description of the idea, targeted grade range, table of contents, sample chapter or activities, and author biography. Responds in 10–12 weeks. Publication in 1–2 years. Flat fee.

Collins

Collins Education, HarperCollins Publishers, Westerhill Road, Bishopbriggs, Glasgow G64 2QT, UK. www.collins.co.uk

Collins Education continues to deliver up-to-date and engaging student resources and exceptional teacher support to help schools tackle new initiatives and utilize the latest technology. It has been publishing educational and informative books for almost 200 years. Collins has a rich heritage of supporting schools through high-quality resources for English, math, science and more. It is launching a new digital learning platform, Collins Connect.

Freelance Potential: Publishes many titles annually.

Nonfiction: Early readers, middle-grade, YA. Topics include history, language arts, math, science, homeschooling.

Submissions and Payment: Guidelines and catalogue available on website. Query via email to editorial@collinseducation.com. Include your full name and relevant experience, along with an outline of your project. Publication in 18–36 months. Royalty; advance.

Compass Point Books

Capstone, 1710 Roe Crest Drive, North Mankato, MN 56003. www.capstonepub.com

Editorial Director: Nick Healy

Compass Point Books is Capstone's middle school nonfiction imprint. With a focus on curriculum support and high-interest topics, Compass Point aims to bring interesting and unique approaches to tried and true subject areas.

Freelance Potential: Parent company Capstone publishes 700+ titles annually.

Nonfiction: Middle-grade, YA. Topics: science, social studies, geography, history, biography, careers, health, the environment, cooking.

Submissions and Payment: Guidelines and catalogue available on website. Query with cover letter, résumé, and 3 writing samples. Accepts hard copy only. Responds in 6 months if interested. Publication period and payment policies vary.

Continental Press

520 East Bainbridge Street, Elizabethtown, PA 17022. www.continentalpress.com

Managing Editor

Continental Press is a K–12 educational publisher serving schools across the United States and around the world. It believes that the addition of supplemental material can positively impact students' performance. It specializes in educational materials that are high quality and affordable for the K–12 reader. It specializes in reading, mathematics, and test preparation. Continental has expanded its print and digital offerings to support special needs, differentiated instruction, intervention, and general classroom learning. It publishes leveled readers for PreK–grade 2 with its Seedling books. It seeks materials that have been classroom-tested and fit specific educational purposes.

Freelance Potential: Publishes 50+ titles (40 juvenile) annually: 10% developed from unsolicited submissions. Receives 20 queries, 20 unsolicited manuscripts monthly.

Fiction: Early readers, middle-grade, YA. Genres: animals, fantasy, adventure, social issues, education, counting, colors.

Nonfiction: Early readers, middle-grade, YA. Topics: math, science, social studies, language arts, ESL, Spanish, technology, test prep. Also publishes teacher resources.

Submissions and Payment: Guidelines and catalogue available on website. For instructional manuscripts, send manuscript with program rationale, author biography, outline, and sample lesson, chapter, or unit. For Seedling fiction submissions, send complete manuscript. No queries. Accepts hard copy only. SASE. Responds in 6 months. Publication period and payment policies vary.

Course Crafters

P.O. Box 100, Amesbury, MA 01913. www.coursecrafters.com

CEO & Publisher: Lise Ragan

Since 1993, Course Crafters has been committed to developing effective educational materials for English language learners (ELLs) and their teachers, Pre-K to grade 12. Course Crafters has conceptualized, written, designed, and produced hundreds of English as a second language (ESL) and bilingual core programs, supplementary materials, and educational technology products, as well as ELL ancillaries, teacher materials, and Spanish-language versions of reading, math, social studies, and science textbook programs, for scores of educational organizations. It works with school districts and educational publishers to provide custom education solutions—professional development, curriculum, and materials—for addressing the needs and challenges of English language learners, particularly students in grades 3–12.

Freelance Potential: Publishes 10–12 titles annually. Receives 1–2 queries monthly.

Nonfiction: Educational materials for English language teachers of grades K–12.

Submissions and Payment: Guidelines available on website. Send résumé and cover letter summarizing ELL experience. Accepts hard copy and email to jobs@coursecrafters.com. SASE. Responds in 1 month. Publication in 1–2 years. Flat fee.

The Creative Company

P.O. Box 227, Mankato, MN 56002. www.thecreativecompany.us

Editor: Kate Riggs

The Creative Company publishes primarily nonfiction children's book series on a wide variety of subjects that are magnificently illustrated. It looks for 4, 6, or 8 titles per series, written at a grade 2 reading level (or below) for 24-page books and a grade 4 and up level for 32- or 48-page books. It also publishes a small number of fiction picture books and nonfiction, illustrated board books. Its imprints are Creative Editions, Creative Education, Creative Paperbacks, and Creative Digital.

Freelance Potential: Publishes 140 titles annually: 1–10% developed from unsolicited submissions; 50–75% assigned. Receives 10–25 queries, 10–25 unsolicited manuscripts monthly.

Fiction: Early picture books, story picture books, early readers. Genres: adventure, fairy tales, poetry.

Nonfiction: Early picture books, story picture books, early readers, middle-grade. Topics: animals, nature, biography, computers, current events, politics, education, regional, social studies, sports, science, history, architecture, geography, the arts.

Submissions and Payment: Guidelines available. Catalogue available on website. Query with proposal for nonfiction series, including an outline of the whole series (4–8 titles) and sample pages. Send complete manuscript for picture books. Accepts hard copy. Accepts simultaneous submissions. SASE. Responds in 2–3 months. Publication period and payment policies vary.

Creative Teaching Press

6262 Katella Avenue, Cypress, CA 90630. www.creativeteaching.com

Idea Submissions

Creative Teaching Press publishes a wide variety of products for grades PreK–8, including teacher resource books, bulletin boards, borders, emergent readers, and charts. It is a family-owned and teacher-managed supplemental educational publisher for children ages 3–14. It has developed a long tradition of producing high-quality, successful, innovative, and educationally sound products that have a proven track record in the classroom and at home. Its subject areas include phonics, reading, writing, math, science, and social studies.

Freelance Potential: Publishes 84 titles (48 juvenile) annually: 15% developed from unsolicited submissions; 5% by authors who are new to the publishing house; 5% by previously unpublished writers. Receives 20–25 queries, 10–20 unsolicited manuscripts monthly.

Fiction: Early readers. Genres: ethnic, multicultural, social issues, ethics and responsibility, fantasy.

Nonfiction: Early readers, chapter books. Topics: history, social issues, science, mathematics, writing. Also publishes supplemental resource books for teachers.

Submissions and Payment: Guidelines and catalogue available on website. Prefers ideas from teachers that have been successfully used in classrooms. Send proposal or complete manuscript along with submission form on website, and a cover letter including: brief description of material (including grade level), synopsis of your background as an educator, audience and competition analysis, summary of material with table of contents, and at least 1 sample chapter. Accepts hard copy. Accepts simultaneous submissions. SASE. Response time varies. Publication period and payment policies vary.

The Critical Thinking Company

1991 Sherman Avenue, Suite 200, North Bend, OR 97459. www.criticalthinking.com

President: Michael Baker

The Critical Thinking Company designs critical thinking into its reading, writing, math, science, and history lessons so students carefully analyze what they are learning. It helps students of all abilities achieve better academic results by developing students' critical thinking skills. Since 1958, its award-winning products have included highly effective lessons that sharpen the mind as they teach standards-based reading, writing, mathematics, science, and history. It is a publisher of educational products for parents, homeschoolers, and teachers. It publishes material for students in preschool through grade 8. It is currently seeking activity-based products in reading, writing, math, science, and social studies that teach and develop critical thinking skills.

Freelance Potential: Publishes 5–30 titles annually: 20% by authors who are new to the publishing house; 30% by previously unpublished writers. Receives 10–20 queries, 20 unsolicited manuscripts yearly.

Fiction: Concept books. Genres: stories that promote development of critical thinking skills.

Nonfiction: Textbooks, concept books, early picture books, early readers, chapter books. Topics: general thinking skills, grammar, spelling, vocabulary, reading, writing, mathematics, science, history. Also publishes activity books.

Submissions and Payment: Guidelines and catalogue available on website. Prefers complete manuscript or software program; accepts query with outline or table of contents and several sample pages. Send cover letter with description of material, target market, and synopsis of your background. Accepts hard copy. SASE. Responds in 6–9 months. Publication in 1–2 years. Royalty.

Didax

395 Main Street, Rowley, MA 01969. www.didax.com

President: Brian Scarlett

For over 44 years Didax has created thousands of original and useful teaching materials. Didax is dedicated to providing innovative and effective learning resources to students, teachers, and parents. It specializes in helping educators address individual learning styles and diverse student needs. Each year they introduce more innovative hands-on, print, and software tools to make teachers more successful. All of its products come directly from teachers, and it is open to considering new ideas, needs, or suggestions.

Freelance Potential: Publishes 25 titles annually: 1% by authors who are new to the publishing house.

Nonfiction: Reproducible activity books and teacher resources for PreK–grade 8. Topics: math fundamentals, fractions, geometry, algebra, probability, problem-solving, the alphabet, pre-reading, phonics, word study, spelling, vocabulary, writing, reading comprehension, social studies, science, art, and character education.

Submissions and Payment: Catalogue available on website. Query with résumé and outline. Accepts hard copy and email queries to brian@didax.com. Accepts simultaneous submissions if identified. SASE. Responds in 2 weeks. Publication in 1 year. Royalty; advance.

Edcon Publishing Group

30 Montauk Boulevard, Oakdale, NY 11769–1399. www.edconpublishing.com

Editor-in-Chief

Edcon has been producing print and digital learning materials for grades K–12 for over 40 years. It specializes in adult/special education, homeschooling, English as a Second Language, and English language learners. Education professionals use these high-interest products to improve basic skills.

Freelance Potential: Publishes 10 titles annually: 20% developed from unsolicited submissions; 10% by authors who are new to the publishing house; 20% by previously unpublished writers. Receives 10 unsolicited manuscripts monthly.

Fiction: Early readers, chapter books, middle-grade, YA. Genres: science fiction, adventure, multicultural and ethnic, fairy tales. Also publishes high/low fiction, 6–18 years.

Nonfiction: Chapter books, YA. Topics: reading comprehension, mathematics, science, technology, social issues, personal growth. Also publishes educational materials for homeschooling and activity books for ages 6–12.

Submissions and Payment: Guidelines available. Send complete manuscript. Accepts hard copy. Accepts simultaneous submissions if identified. Submissions are not returned. Responds in 1 month. Publication in 6 months. Flat fee, $300–$1,000.

Edupress

12621 Western Ave, Garden Grove, CA 92841. https://www.teachercreated.com/landing/edupress/

Product Development Manager: Liz Bowie

Edupress publishes standards-based language arts, math, science, and social studies materials for PreK–grade 8. Edupress, now part of Teacher Created Resources, has been providing teachers with quality educational materials, from classroom decor to test prep, for the past 30 years. Its mission is to help busy educators bring fun and excitement to the classroom. All of their products are "created by teachers for teachers."

Freelance Potential: Publishes 100+ titles annually: 1–10% by authors who are new to the publishing house. Receives 2+ queries monthly.

Nonfiction: Activity books and resource materials for educators, PreK–grade 8. Topics: social studies, science, curriculum coordination, language arts, early learning, math, holidays, arts and crafts.

Submissions and Payment: Guidelines and catalogue available on website. Send proposal and cover letter with résumé, targeted grade range, outline, sample pages, relevant curriculum information, software and platform you use, potential illustrations, and a "Key Market Statement" describing why you wrote/designed the product and competitive products currently in the market. Accepts hard copy and email queries to lbowie@highsmith.com (with "Manuscript Submission" in subject line). SASE. Responds in 2–4 months. Publication in 1 year. Flat fee.

Ferguson Publishing

132 West 31st Street, 16th Floor, New York, NY 10001. www.infobasepublishing.com

Editor-in-Chief: James Chambers

Ferguson continues a more-than-70-year tradition of producing high-quality career education books and e-books for the middle school, high school, and public library markets. Ferguson Publishing is known among librarians and guidance counselors as the premier publisher in the career education field. Their acclaimed references provide comprehensive, up-to-date information on a wide variety of career fields, as well as guidance on essential career skills and professional resources.

Freelance Potential: Publishes 10–20 books annually: less than 10% developed from unsolicited submissions; 10–25% by agented authors; 10–25% by authors who are new to the publishing house. Receives 10–20 queries, 5–10 unsolicited manuscripts monthly.

Nonfiction: Middle-grade, YA. Topics: college planning, career advice, career exploration and guidance, changing careers, job training.

Submissions and Payment: Guidelines and catalogue available online. Majority of books are assigned. Query or send manuscript proposal with an overview of the subject, intended audience, brief description of contents, sample chapter, competition analysis, brief author bio, completion timetable, and relevant experience. To be considered for assignments, send résumé. Accepts hard copy and email to editorial@factsonfile.com. SASE. Responds in 4 weeks. Publication in 12 months. Payment policy varies.

Garlic Press

9316 East Raintree Drive, Suite 120, Scottsdale, AZ 85260. www.garlicpress.com

Publisher: Douglas Rife

Garlic Press has recently been acquired by Remedia Publications. Their titles are targeted for on-level students, homeschoolers, older learners needing to refresh skills, or progressive self-learners. Their mission is to provide materials to teachers, speech pathologists, curriculum specialists, and even parents who educate students with special needs and learning differences, as well as students struggling in regular education and intervention settings. It publishes educational materials in sign language, math, English, and literature for students and educators. Its mission is to provide the best materials available to aid in the education of learners of all ages.

Freelance Potential: Publishes about 1,400 titles annually: many by agented authors.

Nonfiction: Early readers, middle-grade, YA, educators. Topics: language, science, math, education, reference.

Submissions and Payment: Guidelines and catalogue available on website. Send complete manuscript with author bio. Include the manuscript title and proposed audience. Accepts email submissions to douglas@garlicpress.com. Also accepts hard copy. Response time varies. Publication period varies. Royalty; advance.

Goodheart-Willcox

18604 West Creek Drive, Tinley Park, IL 60477-6243. www.g-w.com

President: John F. Flanagan

Goodheart-Wilcox provides students with the knowledge and skills to succeed in life. Publishing textbooks that train and educate, Goodheart-Willcox publishes in both print and digital formats while also producing online courses and other instructional resources. Goodheart-Willcox focuses exclusively on career and technical education (CTE). This focus allows G-W to direct all of their resources and expertise into career and technical education to provide students with comprehensive products for a complete learning experience. With subject-appropriate titles for middle school, high school, higher education, and professional training, G-W is recognized as a go-to source for career and technical education content. Its books, supplements, and multimedia resources combine authoritative content, case studies, and engaging designs to help students learn important life skills. It also produces teacher resource guides, software, and professional training manuals.

Freelance Potential: Publishes 10 titles annually. Receives 10+ queries monthly.

Nonfiction: YA, adult. Publishes textbooks, instructor's guides, software, professional development books, and how-to titles. Topics: life management, personal development, family living, child care, child development, parenting, nutrition, housing and interiors, technical trades, fashion, career education, business, marketing, computers, technology, visual arts.

Submissions and Payment: Guidelines and catalogue available on website. Submit proposal with introductory letter, including targeted audience, résumé, book outline, and sample chapter. Accepts hard copy. SASE. Responds in 2 months. Publication in 2 years. Royalty.

Great Potential Press

1650 North Kolb Road, #200, Tucson, AZ 85715. www.greatpotentialpress.com

Acquisitions Editor: Janet L. Gore

Great Potential Press believes the relationship between publisher and author is a partnership wherein each party contributes their respective expertise to make the highest quality content readily available to the reader. It is an award-winning publishing company devoted to informational resources for gifted adults and for parents, educators, and counselors of gifted children. Great Potential Press is interested in proposals for nonfiction books that support the academic, social, or emotional needs of gifted children and adults.

Freelance Potential: Publishes 4–8 titles (1–2 juvenile) annually: 75–100% developed from unsolicited submissions; 25–50% by authors who are new to the publishing house; 25–50% by previously unpublished writers. Receives 2+ queries monthly.

Nonfiction: Books and videos for gifted children of all ages, resources for parents and educators. Topics: gifted students, gifted education, academic, social, and emotional needs of gifted children and adults.

Submissions and Payment: Guidelines and catalogue available on website. Query with introduction, market analysis, market statement, competitive titles, estimated length, table of contents, 2 sample chapters, and author biography. Accepts queries through form on website. Responds in 2 months. Publication period varies. Royalty.

Greenhaven Press

27500 Drake Road, Farmington Hills, MI 48331-3535. https://www.gale.com/ebooks

Publisher

Greenhaven Press has fostered understanding for more than four decades. It presents diverse sources that encourage students to analyze, evaluate, and explore ideas. Greenhaven titles encourage critical thinking by showcasing widely varied perspectives on controversial social, political, and economic issues. Greenhaven Press publishes under the Gale banner.

Freelance Potential: Publishes about 190 titles annually: 5–10% by authors who are new to the publishing house; few by previously unpublished writers. Receives 25–50 queries monthly.

Nonfiction: YA. Topics: contemporary social issues, biography, American and world history, geography, literature, multicultural, explorations of mysteries, religion, science, medicine and health, global issues.

Submissions and Payment: Catalogue available on website. Submit ideas for new publications via form on website. Qualifying submissions that result in a Gale publication are eligible for a $1,000 award. Response time and publication period vary.

Gryphon House

P.O. Box 10, 6848 Leon's Way, Lewisville, NC 27023. www.gryphonhouse.com

Editor: Stephanie Roselli

Gryphon House strives to publish and distribute the highest-quality books for educators, parents, and caregivers. The goal at Gryphon House is to publish books that help teachers and parents enrich the lives of their children. Each year, Gryphon House offers several new titles to help educators, caregivers, and parents give children the confidence to develop the skills necessary to navigate through life successfully. It is always interested in hearing about popular topics in early childhood.

Freelance Potential: Publishes 20 titles annually: 2 developed from unsolicited submissions; 6 reprint/licensed properties. Receives 20 queries monthly.

Nonfiction: Publishes books for parents and teachers working with children up to age 8. Topics: art, mathematics, science, literacy, language development, teaching strategies, conflict resolution, program development, games, lesson plans.

Submissions and Payment: Guidelines and catalogue available on website. Query with proposed title, purpose of the book, table of contents, introductory material, 20–40 sample pages, market and competition analysis, intended audience, author qualifications, and writing sample. Accepts hard copy. SASE. Responds in 3–4 months. Publication in 1–2 years. Payment policy varies.

Hayes School Publishing

7624 Reinhold Drive, Cincinnati, OH 45237. www.hayespub.com

President: Clair Hayes

Hayes School publishing has a passion for manufacturing and distributing quality educational, office, arts and crafts supplies at affordable prices for use in schools, business, and homes. With a focus on teacher supplements, this catalogue from Hayes School Publishing features educational books and resources for preschool through grade 12. They believe in recognizing one's achievements through awards, certificates, and diplomas. This company seeks reproducibles, workbooks, teacher planning guides, and support materials for all subjects and curricula. It is always seeking new material in all academic subject areas, especially testing and Spanish.

Freelance Potential: Publishes 20–30 titles annually: 8% by authors who are new to the publishing house; 15–20% by previously unpublished writers. Receives 30–45 queries monthly.

Nonfiction: Publishes educational resource materials, grades K–12. Topics: language arts, multicultural studies, math, computer literacy, foreign language, social studies, science, health, creative thinking, handwriting, geography, standardized testing.

Submissions and Payment: Catalogue available on website. Guidelines available via email to chayes@hayespub.com, or send SASE for hard copy. Responds in 2–3 weeks. Publication period varies. Flat fee.

Hazelden Publishing

Editorial Department, RW 15, P.O. Box 176, Center City, MN 55012-0176. www.hazelden.org

Manuscript Coordinator

The mission of Hazelden Publishing is to be a force of healing and hope for individuals, families, and communities affected by addiction to alcohol and other drugs, by providing products and services to help people recognize, understand, and overcome addiction and closely related problems. Part of the Hazelden Betty Ford Foundation, the nation's largest nonprofit treatment provider, Hazelden Publishing is the leading publisher of addiction recovery and self-help resources. It offers a variety of accessible and life-changing materials—from daily meditations to evidence-based programs. Many of its titles target preteens and teens, but it is not interested in receiving submissions of children's books. Hazelden discourages submissions of poetry, fiction, personal stories, children's books, and art.

Freelance Potential: Publishes 50 titles annually. Receives 26 queries monthly.

Nonfiction: Books for young adults with alcohol and drug addictions, and for parents, teachers, and professionals who work with people suffering from addiction problems. Also publishes e-books, multimedia products, training materials, and webinars. Topics: alcohol and substance abuse, health, fitness, social issues, mental health, family and relationships, spirituality.

Submissions and Payment: Guidelines and catalogue available on website. Send proposal with overview and objective of your project, target audience, proposed market, competitive titles, table of contents, an introduction, detailed chapter outline, 2–3 sample chapters, and author biography. Accepts hard copy. SASE. Responds in 3 months. Publication in 12–18 months. Royalty. Flat fee.

Heinemann

361 Hanover Street, Portsmouth, NH 03801-3912. www.heinemann.com

Acquisitions Editor

Heinemann's authors are exemplary educators eager to support the practice of other teachers through books, videos, workshops, online courses, and most recently through explicit teaching materials. It runs on the belief that everyone deserves a great education no matter their background. They believe it is vitally important that the teaching profession enjoy a healthy diversity so that every child can benefit by learning from people with varied backgrounds and perspectives. It strives to give voice to those who share a respect for the professionalism and compassion of teachers. It supports those who support teachers' efforts to help children become literate, empathetic, knowledgeable citizens. Heinemann's commitment to its work and customers' enthusiastic response to its offerings have made it a leading publisher in this area.

Freelance Potential: Publishes 100 titles annually: 10% by agented authors; 10% by previously unpublished writers. Receives 100+ queries monthly.

Nonfiction: Educational resources and multimedia material for teachers and school administrators. Topics: math, science, social studies, art education, reading, writing, ESL, bilingual education, special and gifted education, early childhood development, school reform, curriculum development, creative arts.

Submissions and Payment: Guidelines and catalogue available on website. Send a proposal with cover letter, a statement describing your objectives and reasons for writing the book, table of contents with chapter summaries, sample chapters, and résumé. Accepts email to proposals@heinemann.com and hard copy. SASE. Discourages simultaneous submissions. Response time varies. Publication in 10–12 months. Payment policy varies.

Heinemann Raintree

1710 Roe Crest Drive, North Mankato, MN 56003. www.capstonepub.com
http://www.heinemannraintree.com/

Editorial Director

This imprint of Capstone publishes curriculum-driven nonfiction that encourages inquiry. They publish comprehensive text and captivating images that combine to create a reading experience rich in content and diverse points of view. Heinemann-Raintree publishes thousands of high-quality nonfiction books to meet PreK–Secondary needs in the library and in the classroom. Among its most recognized brands are Acorn, Heinemann Library First, and Raintree Perspectives.

Freelance Potential: Publishes 600+ titles annually: 1–10% developed from unsolicited submissions; 75–100% assigned; 1–10% by agented authors; 10–25% by authors who are new to the publishing house; 1–10% by previously unpublished writers. Receives 10–25 queries monthly.

Fiction: Early picture books, early readers, story picture books, chapter books, middle-grade, graphic novels. Genres: adventure, bilingual, fairy tales, historical, humor, multicultural, realistic, sports.

Nonfiction: Concept books, early picture books, early readers, chapter books, graphic nonfiction, middle-grade. Topics: animals, arts, activities, games, crafts, biography, bilingual, education and career, current events, entertainment, social studies, history, geography, health, science, math.

Submissions and Payment: Guidelines and catalogue available on website. For nonfiction, query with cover letter, résumé, and 3 writing samples. Accepts hard copy only. Responds in 6 months if interested. Publication period and payment policies vary.

High Noon Books

20 Leveroni Court, Novato, CA 94949. www.highnoonbooks.com

Acquisitions Editor

High Noon Books cares about the needs of the struggling reader. It publishes titles that serve individuals who are beginning to read English, are reading below reading level, or just need motivating topics to inspire them to read more. High Noon Books provides a means to expose and reinforce the most common words in English for the purpose of getting students reading on grade level. High Noon Books can serve as a bridge between beginning reading material (picture books and stories with only a few words per page) and standard text (as in a magazine, schoolbook, or trade book).

Freelance Potential: Publishes 20 titles annually.

Fiction: Early readers, phonics-based chapter books. Genres: adventure, historical, mystery, science fiction, graphic.

Nonfiction: Early readers, phonics-based chapter books. Topics: high-interest biography, history, social studies, math, science, sports, travel.

Submissions and Payment: Catalogue available on website. Accepts hard copy or email ideas for new products to sales@academictherapy.com. Response time and publication period vary. Flat fee.

History Compass

25 Leslie Road, Auburndale, MA 02466. www.historycompass.com

CEO: Lisa Gianelly

History Compass aims to publish carefully selected, well-researched books that help us better understand our past, give us context for the present, and shed light on our future. It has a goal to provide stories, compelling and true, that give insight into our nation's history. History Compass is known for its primary source–based US history books, guides, and historical fiction for elementary and secondary school students.

Freelance Potential: Publishes about 8 titles annually: 35% by authors who are new to the publishing house; 12% by previously unpublished writers. Receives 4–5 queries monthly.

Fiction: Middle-grade, YA. Genre: historical.

Nonfiction: Early readers, chapter books, middle-grade, YA. Topic: American history. Also publishes biographies and guidebooks for adults.

Submissions and Payment: Catalogue available on website. Guidelines available. Query with cover letter containing description of content, source material, intended audience, author biography, competition analysis, marketing plan, table of contents or outline, and sample chapter. Accepts hard copy. Accepts simultaneous submissions if identified. SASE. Responds in 1 month. Publication in 2–8 months. Royalty.

Incentive Publications

233 North Michigan Avenue, Suite 2000, Chicago, IL 60601. www.incentivepublications.com

Director of Development & Production: Jill Norris

Incentive Publications by World Book has built a reputation for award-winning reference and other educational materials that are both reliable and readable. It produces supplemental resources for student use and instruction and classroom management improvement materials for teachers. This company specializes in resources for middle-grade students, as well as teaching strategies for grades K–12. Many Incentive Publications products are designed specifically to enhance teachers' ability to successfully implement the Common Core State Standards in today's classrooms.

Freelance Potential: Publishes 30 titles annually. Receives 20+ queries monthly.

Nonfiction: Teaching strategy books for all grade levels, and reproducible student materials for grades 5–9. Topics: core curriculum subjects, art, study skills.

Submissions and Payment: Guidelines and catalogue available on website. Query with cover letter, table of contents, and a sample chapter. Accepts hard copy or email to incentive@worldbook.com. SASE. Responds in 6–8 weeks. Publication period varies. Royalty. Flat fee.

ISTE

International Society for Technology in Education, 621 SW Morrison St., Suite 800, Portland, OR 97205. www.iste.org

Acquisitions Editor

The books from ISTE help teachers from around the world use technology to solve tough problems in education. ISTE inspires the creation of solutions and connections that improve opportunities for all learners by delivering practical guidance, evidence-based professional learning, virtual networks, thought-provoking events, and the ISTE Standards. Its titles offer in-depth coverage of the state of digital-age learning and the latest edtech research.

Freelance Potential: Publishes 30 titles annually.

Nonfiction: Educational resources and multimedia material for teachers and school administrators. Topics: math, science, social studies, art education, reading, writing, ESL, bilingual education, special and gifted education, early childhood development, school reform, curriculum development, creative arts.

Submissions and Payment: Guidelines and catalogue available on website. Send a proposal with audience and market information, sample chapters, table of contents, tentative title, and educational topics addressed. Accepts email submissions to books@iste.org. Also accepts hard copy. Responds in 1 month. Publication in 1 year. Payment policy varies.

JIST Publishing

875 Montreal Way, St. Paul, MN 55102. www.jist.com

Product Manager: Rebecca Wagner

How people learn is changing, so JIST offers a wide variety of print and digital learning solutions, including assessments, e-books, workbooks, videos, software, and more. JIST keeps up with the changing trends in learning. They are a leading provider of materials and technology that help hard-to-employ populations build essential skills for career, academic, and life success. Their solutions will help students become proactive, prepare for their futures, and master techniques to achieve their goals as quickly as possible. While most of its titles are directed toward adults, many are geared toward students in middle school or high school.

Freelance Potential: Publishes 20 titles annually. Receives 5–10 queries monthly.

Nonfiction: Middle-grade, YA. Topics: career exploration and assessment, occupations, job retention, job searching, character education, career development.

Submissions and Payment: Guidelines and catalogue available on website. Query with 3- to 7-page proposal that includes working title, summary of book, target audience, target market, competition analysis, sales and marketing analysis, outline, sample chapters, résumé, and project status. Prefers email to rwagner@jist.com. Responds in 14–16 weeks. Publication in 6–9 months. Royalty, 8–10%.

Jossey-Bass

111 River Street, Hoboken, NJ 07030. www.josseybass.com/WileyCDA

Editorial Assistant

Jossey-Bass draws its strength from the collaborative efforts of its authors, a group made up of diverse, knowledgeable, creative people bound together by talent and integrity. Jossey-Bass publishes products and services to inform and inspire those interested in developing themselves, their organizations, and communities. Its catalogue, offering both print and digital books, includes subscription content, webinars, and online courses. All are designed to help customers become more effective in the workplace and to achieve career success by bringing to life the ideas and best practices of thought leaders around the world. Jossey-Bass is a part of John Wiley & Sons, Inc.

Freelance Potential: Publishes 250 titles annually.

Nonfiction: Adults. Topics: K–12 education, school counseling and psychology, curriculum tools, culture and gender, leadership and administration, assessment and research, teaching strategies, professional development, special education, and technology.

Submissions and Payment: Accepts project proposals that include the purpose in developing the project, the audience, why the topic is important, what new information will be included, research background, author bio with your relevant experience, outline, chapter descriptions, sample chapters, format, estimated length, completion timetable, and competition information. Accepts hard copy to appropriate editor (see website). Accepts simultaneous submissions but wants the names of the publishers it's been submitted to. Response time, publication period, and payment policies vary.

Kaeden Books

P.O. Box 16190, Rocky River, OH 44116. www.kaeden.com

Editor: Lisa Stenger

Kaeden Books helps children develop a lifelong love of reading by providing quality materials. For 26 years, Kaeden has worked with educators to improve the quality of the content used to instruct the student in the reading process and encourage confidence while teaching students 21st-century skills for success. It is an ideal complement to any quality reading program. Its books are written for early, emergent, and fluent readers in pre-kindergarten through second grade. It specializes in leveled fiction and nonfiction early literacy books and beginning chapter books that are designed to help teachers guide children through their first years of the reading experience. Its fun stories help children develop confidence in the reading process through the use of predictability and patterned text. It is currently seeking beginning chapter books, unique nonfiction manuscripts, and manuscripts with strong characters that have series potential.

Freelance Potential: Publishes 12–20 titles annually: all developed from unsolicited submissions. Receives 100+ unsolicited manuscripts monthly.

Fiction: Early readers, story picture books, chapter books. Genres: contemporary, animals, humor, life skills.

Nonfiction: Early readers, story picture books, chapter books. Topics: animals, science, nature, nutrition, biography, careers, recreation, social studies.

Submissions and Payment: Guidelines and catalogue available on website. Send complete manuscript with cover letter that includes author bio and manuscript title. Accepts hard copy only. Accepts simultaneous submissions. Responds only if interested. Response time, publication period, and payment policies vary.

Kingfisher

Macmillan, 175 Fifth Avenue, New York, NY 10010. https://us.macmillan.com/publishers/kingfisher

Submissions Editor

With a first-class reputation for creating authoritative yet accessible educational series alongside innovative stand-alone titles, Kingfisher truly has a global reach. Kingfisher is a leading international publisher of illustrated information books, with a readership ranging from preschoolers to older students who find their encyclopedias to be an essential support to their research. Among the topics Kingfisher covers are natural history, science, geography, history, art, and philosophy. Kingfisher is part of Macmillan Publishers.

Freelance Potential: Publishes 10+ titles annually.

Nonfiction: Pre-K, early readers, middle-grade, YA. Topics: natural history, science, geography, history, art, philosophy.

Submissions and Payment: Catalogue available on website. Guidelines available. Response time, publication period, and payment policies vary.

Lerner Publications

1251 Washington Ave N, Minneapolis, MN 55401. www.lernerbooks.com

Editorial Director: Ashley Kuehl

This flagship imprint of Lerner Publishing Group offers unique, engaging books for PreK–grade 12 to help librarians, educators, and parents develop a love of reading and learning in children. It creates nonfiction and fiction books that support national and state curriculum standards that educate, empower, and entertain readers. The books from Lerner Publications are thoroughly researched and exceptionally written with amazing illustrations and captivating photography that hold readers' attention. Its educational titles offer photo-driven designs and features that help young readers understand, enjoy, and share information. This company does not accept unsolicited submissions but does put out calls for specific submissions via its website or in writers' newsletters.

Freelance Potential: Publishes 250 titles annually: most are developed in-house; 1–10% developed from unsolicited submissions; 20% by agented authors; 1–10% by authors who are new to the publishing house.

Nonfiction: Early readers, chapter books. Topics: ethnic and multicultural issues, nature, the environment, science, sports, history, biography.

Submissions and Payment: Guidelines and catalogue available on website. No unsolicited submissions. Does seek targeted submissions for specific reading levels and subject areas. Check website for current needs. Response time, publication period, and payment policies vary.

Libraries Unlimited

ABC-CLIO, 147 Castilian Drive, Santa Barbara, CA 93117. www.abc-clio.com

Acquisitions Editor

Libraries Unlimited serves the needs of the library profession through high-quality publications for library and information science students and faculty; public, academic, and school librarians; media and technology specialists; and teachers. As part of the ABC-CLIO, LLC, umbrella since 2008, Libraries Unlimited remains committed to serving academic, public, school, and special libraries by producing library science textbooks, reference works, practical handbooks, and professional guides of unparalleled quality.

Freelance Potential: Publishes 100 titles annually: 5–10% developed from unsolicited submissions; 50% by authors who are new to the publisher. Receives 35 queries monthly.

Nonfiction: Bibliographies, professional reference titles and materials, textbooks, handbooks, and manuals. Topics: library science, information science, professional development.

Submissions and Payment: Catalogue available on website. Query with author qualifications. Accepts email (see website for appropriate acquisitions editor) and hard copy. SASE. If interested, publisher will ask for proposal with working title, scope and purpose of book, an outline, methodology and presentation, and competitive titles. Responds in 8–10 weeks. Publication in 10–12 months. Royalty.

Lorenz Educational Press

P.O. Box 802, Dayton, OH 45401-0802. www.lorenzeducationalpress.com

Submissions

Every product created at Lorenz Educational Press is based on a commitment to helping teachers provide a positive educational experience for students. Lorenz Educational Press embraces that mission, defining learning areas vital to developing well-rounded students and empowering our future leaders.

Freelance Potential: Publishes 35 titles annually: 85% developed from unsolicited submissions; 17% by authors who are new to the publishing house; 8% by previously unpublished writers. Receives 100 unsolicited manuscripts monthly.

Nonfiction: Educational teacher resource materials and supplementary classroom materials for PreK–grade 12, in print and electronic formats. Topics: arts and crafts, current events, language arts, mathematics, multicultural issues, science, social studies.

Submissions and Payment: Guidelines and catalogue available on website. Send complete manuscript with cover letter describing targeted grade level, page count, and content areas covered. Accepts hard copy. SASE. Response time varies. Publication in 1–3 years. Flat fee.

Lucent Books

27500 Drake Road, Farmington Hills, MI 48331-3535. www.gale.cengage.com/greenhaven/lucent

Administrative Assistant: Kristine Burns

Lucent Books publishes engaging nonfiction titles that foster the cognitive skills of students in middle school and early high school. Supporting a range of grades and reading levels, the goal of Lucent Books is to provide multiple points of view on controversial topics and to present complex ideas and events in a way that middle-school students will understand. Lucent Books publishes under the Gale banner.

Freelance Potential: Publishes 110 titles annually: 10% by authors who are new to the publishing house; 3% by previously unpublished writers. Receives 8–10 queries monthly.

Nonfiction: Middle-grade, YA. Topics: contemporary social issues, biography, history, geography, health, science, sports.

Submissions and Payment: Catalogue available on website. Submit ideas for new publications via form on website. Qualifying submissions that result in a Gale publication are eligible for a $1,000 award. Response time and publication period vary.

Magic Wagon

P.O. Box 398166, Minneapolis, MN 55439. www.abdobooks.com

Editor-in-Chief: Paul Abdo

Blending imagination and information with original illustrations and story lines is the goal of this imprint from Abdo publishing. Magic Wagon offers titles in both English and Spanish for kids in PreK–grade 8. Its focus is on picture books, illustrated chapter books and leveled readers, and graphic novels for students in PreK–grade 8.

Freelance Potential: Parent company publishes 600 titles annually. All writing is done on assignment or a work-for-hire basis.

Fiction: Early picture books, early readers, story picture books, leveled readers, chapter books, middle-grade. Genres: humor, retold classics, graphic novels, animals.

Nonfiction: Early picture books, early readers, story picture books, chapter books, middle-grade. Topics: animals, nature, travel, geography, sciences, social studies, sports, history, biography, leisure, language arts, multicultural.

Submissions and Payment: Catalogue available on website. Guidelines provided to writers under contract only. To be considered for future writing assignments, send résumé with cover letter, area of expertise, and publishing credits. It is currently accepting submissions for picture book, beginning reader, and chapter book manuscripts with the potential to become a series (4–6 titles). Send a detailed outline of the manuscript and series, an introduction, and two sample chapters. Accepts email to submissions@abdopublishing.com. Responds in 6 months. Publication period varies. Flat fee.

Maupin House

125 S Clark Street, 17th Floor, Chicago, IL 60603.
http://www.capstonepub.com/classroom/professional-development/

Acquisitions Editor

The Maupin House imprint is part of Capstone Professional. Its authors are classroom practitioners with vast experiences in helping children of all levels and ability succeed academically. It provides a wide range of print and e-books written by today's leading authors who have a desire to help other teaching professionals succeed in today's high-stakes classroom. Maupin House continues to look for professional development resources that support grades K–8 classroom teachers.

Freelance Potential: Publishes 9 titles annually: 30% by authors who are new to the publishing house. Receives 25 manuscripts monthly.

Nonfiction: Professional educational resources for grades K–12. Topics: literacy, writing, reading comprehension.

Submissions and Payment: Guidelines and catalogue available on website. Send proposal with résumé, publishing credits, book overview, intended audience, research base, intended length, complete table of contents, detailed outline, summary of each chapter, 2 sample chapters, or complete manuscript. Accepts email submissions to proposals@capstonepd.com or hard copy with SASE. Response time varies. Publication in 12–18 months. Standard royalty rates.

Millbrook Press

Lerner Publishing, 241 First Avenue North, Minneapolis, MN 55401. www.lernerbooks.com

Editorial Director: Carol Hinz

This imprint of Lerner Publishing focuses on titles that encourage play, experimentation, and innovation. It approaches curricular topics with a fresh perspective and publishes informative picture books, illustrated nonfiction series, and inspiring photo-driven titles for grades K–5. Millbrook Press believes nonfiction should be distinctive and memorable, both inside and out.

Freelance Potential: Publishes 40 titles annually.

Fiction: Picture books, chapter books, middle-grade. Genres: historical, sports, math, language arts, mystery, adventure.

Nonfiction: Picture books, middle-grade. Topics: the arts, sports, social studies, history, language arts, math, science, biography, nature, the environment, crafts.

Submissions and Payment: Guidelines and catalogue available on website. Does not accept unsolicited submissions. It does seek targeted submissions for specific reading levels and subject areas. Check website for current needs. Response time, publication period, and payment policies vary.

Mitchell Lane Publishers

2001 SW 31st Avenue, Hallandale, FL 33009. www.mitchelllane.com

Publisher: Phil Comer

To capture the attention of readers, Mitchell Lane publishes engaging nonfiction on high-interest topics. All Mitchell Lane books are dedicated to developing educational content for the less-than-enthusiastic reader. Material is developed to the highest standards by experienced youth nonfiction authors and editors. It works with established authors on a work-for-hire basis.

Freelance Potential: Publishes 75 titles annually: very few by authors who are new to the publishing house. Receives 30 queries monthly.

Nonfiction: Early readers, chapter books, middle-grade, YA. Topics: animals, natural disasters, biography, sports, mythology, art, history, poets, playwrights, science, music, health, multicultural, pop culture, science, community service, environmental topics, genealogy, and the Middle East.

Submissions and Payment: Guidelines and catalogue available on website. Work-for-hire only. Query with cover letter, unedited writing sample, comprehensive résumé, and publishing credits. Accepts hard copy. Material is not returned. Responds if interested and when a suitable assignment becomes available. Publication period varies. Flat fee.

Mondo Publishing

980 Avenue of the Americas, New York, NY 10018. www.mondopub.com

Editorial Director

The mission of Mondo is to provide elementary classrooms with high-quality literacy resources and ongoing professional learning that supports more effective teaching and improved student learning. Mondo Education, part of Carnegie Learning, helps teachers differentiate literacy instruction and empowers students to develop into literate learners who can comprehend, communicate, and contribute to their world.

Freelance Potential: Publishes 30 titles annually.

Fiction: Easy-to-read books, story picture books, chapter books, middle-grade. Genres: contemporary and historical fiction, science fiction, fantasy, mystery, folktales, adventure, humor.

Nonfiction: Early picture books, story picture books, YA. Topics: science, nature, animals, the environment, history, music, crafts, hobbies, language arts.

Submissions and Payment: Catalogue available on website. Query. Accepts hard copy. SASE. Response time varies. Publication in 1–3 years. Royalty.

Morgan Reynolds

620 South Elm Street, Suite 223, Greensboro, NC 27406. www.morganreynolds.com

Associate Editor

Morgan Reynolds began with one very simple goal: to publish high-quality nonfiction for young adult readers. That goal remains the same today. Publishing insightful, well-documented, high-quality nonfiction for young adult readers is the only goal of this publisher. Each title captures the life story and details of a historical figure or event that impacted the world. Full-color illustrations and lively, factual text bring each subject in its books to vivid life.

Freelance Potential: Publishes 30 titles (10 juvenile) annually: 6–10% developed from unsolicited submissions; 10–15% by authors who are new to the publishing house; 10% by previously unpublished writers. Receives 10 queries, 5 unsolicited manuscripts monthly.

Nonfiction: YA. Topics: history, music, science, business, feminism, world events, biography, social studies, literature, music.

Submissions and Payment: Catalogue available on website. Published authors, query with outline and sample chapter; unpublished authors, send complete manuscript. Accepts hard copy. SASE. Accepts simultaneous submissions if identified. Responds to queries in 1 month, to manuscripts in 1–3 months. Publication in 12–18 months. Submit through www.editorialmanager.com/nctebp/. Payment policy varies.

National Council of Teachers of English

The Books Program, 1111 West Kenyon Road, Urbana, IL 61801-1096. www.ncte.org

Director of Publications: Kurt Austin; Publisher-in-Residence: Robb Clouse;
Senior Editor: Bonny Graham

This publisher offers professional development books and resources for teachers of pre-kindergarten through post-college. Its books focus on current issues and challenges in teaching, research findings and their applications to classrooms, and ideas for teaching all aspects of English and literacy more broadly. NCTE is always interested in new approaches to teaching reading, writing, literature, poetry, etc. They are especially looking to expand their elementary level list on literacy-related topics. Some potential topics include phonological and phonemic awareness, grammar, teaching with picture books, reading conferences, teaching informational/nonfiction texts, as well as undergraduate research, de-colonialism and equity, disruption, multi-modality, the maker movement, digital rhetoric, etc.

Freelance Potential: Publishes 12–15 titles annually: less than 10% developed from unsolicited submissions.

Nonfiction: Books for English and language arts teachers. Topics: reading, writing, grammar, literature, poetry, rhetoric, censorship, media studies, technology, research, classroom practices, student assessment, professional issues

Submissions and Payment: Catalogue available on website. Accepts electronic submissions through www.editorialmanager.com/nctebp/. Payment policy varies.

National Science Teachers Association Press

1840 Wilson Boulevard, Arlington, VA 22201. www.nsta.org/publications

Submissions

NSTA Press publishes classroom-ready activities, hands-on approaches to inquiry, relevant professional development, the latest scientific education news and research, assessment, and standards-based instruction. It produces titles that are of interest to science teachers of students in grades K–12 and at the undergraduate college level and develops and produces the high-quality resources that science educators need in all disciplines. It accepts submissions that deal with science content, best teaching methods, and classroom activities; it is especially interested in works that link science with reading or math.

Freelance Potential: Publishes 15–20 titles annually.

Nonfiction: Textbooks, teacher manuals, activity books. Topics: science, teaching techniques.

Submissions and Payment: Guidelines and catalogue available on website. Send completed Book Proposal Form (on website), detailed outline or table of contents, curriculum vitae, introduction or preface, and 1 or 2 sample chapters. Accepts electronic submissions through website. For questions, email nstapresseditorialof@nsta.org. Publication in 6 months. Royalty.

Neal-Schuman Publishers

ALA Editions, 50 Huron Street, Chicago, IL 60611. www.alastore.ala.org/

Marketing Assistant: Brett Beasley

Authors and developers are leaders in their fields, and their content is published in a growing range of print and electronic formats. Part of the American Library Association, Neal Schuman publishes books for school and public librarians. It focuses on curriculum, literacy, and informational science titles. The imprint publishes professional books intended for archivists, knowledge managers, and librarians.

Freelance Potential: Publishes 40 titles annually: 25% developed from unsolicited submissions; 30% by authors who are new to the publishing house; 80% by previously unpublished writers. Receives 20 queries monthly.

Nonfiction: Publishes resource materials for school media specialists and librarians. Topics: curriculum support, the Internet, technology, literacy skills, reading programs, collection development, reference needs, staff development, management, communication.

Submissions and Payment: Guidelines and catalogue available on website. Query with proposal that includes general description of book including audience and market; competition analysis; table of contents; detailed outline; sample chapter or 6–10 sample pages; draft preface addressing topic, reasons for writing, how book is compiled and organized; projected completion date; software used; special considerations (e.g. illustrations, permissions, etc.); and résumé. Accepts hard copy and email queries with Word attachments to editionsmarketing@ala.org. Responds in 6–8 weeks. Publication in 10–12 months. Royalty.

Nelson Education

1120 Birchmount Road, Scarborough, Ontario M1K 5G4 Canada. www.nelson.com

Nelson is Canada's leading educational publisher, providing innovative products and solutions for learners of all ages. Nelson values and respects the lifelong learning continuum and works together with educators to make a positive difference. It dedicates its business efforts to the diverse learning needs of both students and educators. Nelson Education Ltd. is active in Canada's K–12, higher education, professional learning, business, industry, and government markets.

Freelance Potential: Publishes 60 titles annually. Receives 8–10 queries monthly.

Fiction: Early readers, chapter books. Genres: social skills, sports, activities, relationships, adventure, language arts, graphic novels.

Nonfiction: Early readers, middle-grade, YA. Topics: writing, literacy, science, the arts, math, technology, business, social studies, French.

Submissions and Payment: Guidelines and catalogue available on website. Query with proposal that includes statement of purpose and intended market, market analysis, project description, detailed table of contents, project timeline, competition review, and 1–2 sample chapters. Accepts hard copy and email to nelson.hededitorial@nelson.com. Responds in 6–12 months. Publication period and payment policies vary.

Nomad Press

2456 Christian Street, White River Junction, VT 05001. www.nomadpress.net

Acquisitions Editor

Publishing books that inspire learning, Nomad Press is passionate about sparking the interest of young readers. Nomad Press books fit perfectly into classrooms and homeschools. It takes kids far beyond the words on a page, into a world of exploration and experiential education. Biographies, project-based narratives, nonfiction picture books, and historical mysteries make up its title list, and every book includes unique illustrations, links to primary sources, fascinating fun facts, and much more. As kids use their books to explore the history and science behind a wide variety of topics they become curious and engaged lifelong learners.

Freelance Potential: Publishes 10–12 titles annually: 60% by authors who are new to the publishing house; 25% by previously unpublished writers. Receives 2–3 queries monthly.

Nonfiction: Early readers, middle-grade. Topics: science, geology, the environment, energy, social studies, history, foreign countries, biography, math, astronomy, food.

Submissions and Payment: Guidelines and catalogue available on website. Does not accept unsolicited manuscripts. For work-for-hire, query with résumé and publishing credits. Prefers email to info@nomadpress.net. Accepts hard copy. Responds in 3–4 weeks. Publication in 6–18 months. Royalty. Flat fee.

W. W. Norton & Company, Inc.

500 Fifth Avenue, New York, NY 10110. http://books.wwnorton.com/books/index.aspx

This publisher publishes books that educate, inspire, and endure. Printing books that reflect their social moment and resonating beyond, W. W. Norton publishes the work of some of the world's most influential voices. W. W. Norton is a global company offering textbooks of high editorial quality for high school and college level courses. Its earliest titles stem from music and literature, but its current textbook list has expanded across liberal arts. It consistently publishes books that reflect their social moment and resonate well beyond it.

Freelance Potential: Publishes 30+ titles each year.

Nonfiction: YA, adult. Topics: history, education, language, social studies.

Submissions and Payment: Catalogue available on website. Accepts submissions through literary agents only. Responds in 3–6 months. Publication period, payment rates, and policies vary.

Okapi Educational Publishing

42381 Rio Nedo, Temecula, CA 92590. www.myokapi.com

Editor

Okapi believes that children construct their own learning, and its resources promote creativity and innovation. Okapi Educational Publishing was founded in 2008 with the goal of supporting educators as they help children become active participants in their own learning and become productive, literate members of society. With materials closely correlated to the new College and Career Readiness Standards, Okapi fulfills its mission of creating real-world literacy for real-world kids with real-world results.

Freelance Potential: Publishes about 100 titles annually: many by agented authors.

Fiction: Early readers, middle-grade, YA. Genres: adventure, mystery, real-life, and historical fiction.

Nonfiction: Educators. Topics: science, literature, reading, math, literacy, education.

Submissions and Payment: Catalogue available on website. Query with author bio and relevant publishing credits. Accepts hard copy.

Pembroke Publishers

538 Hood Road, Markham, Ontario L3R 3K9 Canada. www.pembrokepublishers.com

President: Mary Macchiusi

Exploring a wide range of topics, from reading and writing, to drama and speaking, to critical thinking and technology in the classroom, Pembroke Publisher's books celebrate the joy of learning. Pembroke books are all ready to be taken directly into the classroom by offering the perfect blend of new ideas, best practice, and practical strategies and tools.

Freelance Potential: Publishes 20 titles annually: 5% by authors who are new to the publishing house. Receives 4+ queries monthly.

Nonfiction: Chapter books, middle-grade. Topics: history, science, writing, notable Canadians. Also publishes titles for educators about reading, writing, literacy learning, drama, the arts, school leadership, discipline, and working with parents.

Submissions and Payment: Guidelines available. Catalogue available on website. Query with résumé, outline, and sample chapter. Accepts hard copy. SAE/IRC. Accepts simultaneous submissions if identified. Responds in 1 month. Publication in 6–24 months. Royalty.

Perfection Learning

1000 North Second Avenue, P.O. Box 500, Logan, IA 51546-0500. www.perfectionlearning.com

Editorial Department

For more than 90 years, Perfection Learning has been a leader in the literature and language arts programs for grades 6–12. Perfection Learning is also one of the leading providers of trade books to classrooms across the country and delivers an unsurpassed selection of novels, nonfiction books, classroom collections, and literature-based teaching support. Its titles target educators and cover a wide range of education topics including teaching critical thinking skills, Common Core Standards, nonfiction reading, intervention programs, and math. It also offers material on homeschooling.

Freelance Potential: Publishes 25+ titles each year.

Submissions and Payment: Catalogue available on website. Query with author biography and publishing credits. Accepts hard copy. Responds if interested. Publication in 18–24 months. Payment policy varies.

Phoenix Learning Resources

P.O. Box 510, Honesdale, PA 18431. www.phoenixlearningresources.com

Editor

Phoenix Learning Resources is committed to bringing you the best products possible. It is an educational publisher of resources in all curriculum areas. The mission of Phoenix Learning Resources, is to produce quality skill-based basal and supplemental educational materials for primary grade students through adults. A strong focus on language arts and math literacy make it a leader in providing materials for ESL, ELL, and special needs students.

Freelance Potential: Publishes 45 titles annually. Receives 2–3 queries monthly.

Nonfiction: Publishes textbooks and educational materials for PreK–grade 12 and beyond. Also publishes books for special education and for gifted students, materials for use with ESL students, and reference books. Topics: biography, language skills, integrated language arts, reading comprehension, social studies, math, study skills, social skills.

Submissions and Payment: Catalogue available on website. Query with résumé. Accepts hard copy. SASE. Accepts simultaneous submissions if identified. Responds in 1–4 weeks. Publication in 1–15 months. Royalty. Flat fee.

Picture Window Books

Capstone, 1710 Roe Crest Drive, North Mankato, MN 56003. www.capstonepub.com

Editorial Director: Nick Healy

Picture Window books are approachable, appropriate, and diverse. This publisher focuses on early childhood themes, social and emotional development, early literacy, and curriculum support topics. Creating bright, wholesome books that educate and delight young readers, Picture Window Books was founded in 2001.

Freelance Potential: Publishes 40 titles annually: 2% by agented authors; 20% by authors new to the publishing house; 5% by previously unpublished writers. Receives 30 queries monthly.

Fiction: Concept books, early picture books, story picture books, early readers, chapter books. Genres: realistic, adventure, humor, folklore, fantasy, mystery, life skills, contemporary.

Nonfiction: Picture books, early readers, chapter books. Topics: science, geography, history, social sciences, language, folklore, mythology, the environment, arts and recreation.

Submissions and Payment: Guidelines and catalogue available on website. For nonfiction, query with cover letter, résumé, and 3 writing samples. Accepts hard copy only. For fiction, query with sample chapters, résumé, and list of publishing credits. Responds in 6 months if interested. Publication period and payment policies vary.

PowerKids Press

Rosen Publishing, 29 East 21st Street, New York, NY 10010. www.rosenpublishing.com

Editorial Director: Rachel O'Connor

An imprint of Rosen Publishing, PowerKids Press books provide the foundational learning experience that is related to language growth, emergent literacy, and reading achievement. It has set the pace for providing rich and diverse material to support the needs of primary, emergent, and elementary students.

Freelance Potential: Publishes 200 titles annually: 8% by authors who are new to the publishing house, 8% by previously unpublished writers. Receives 40–45 queries monthly.

Nonfiction: Story picture books, early readers, middle-grade. Topics: art, social studies, science, geography, health, fitness, sports, math, Native American, ancient history, natural history, politics and government, multicultural and ethnic issues, biography. Also titles for special education and bilingual programs.

Submissions and Payment: Catalogue available on website. Contact Customer Service team via website for information about submissions. Responds in 3 months. Publication in 9–18 months. Flat fee.

Prometheus Books

59 John Glenn Drive, Amherst, NY 14228-2197. www.prometheusbooks.com

Editor-in-Chief: Steven L. Mitchell

Prometheus Books is committed to testing the boundaries of established thought and providing readers with thoughtful and authoritative books in a wide variety of categories. Publishing intelligent nonfiction for the thoughtful lay reader, Prometheus Books is a leading publisher of the areas of popular science, philosophy, atheism, humanism, and critical thinking. Its children's titles focus on sciences, sexual education, and contemporary issues. Prometheus publishes science fiction under its Pyr imprint and mystery/thriller fiction under its Seventh Street Books.

Freelance Potential: Publishes 110 titles annually.

Nonfiction: Early readers, middle-grade, YA. Topics: social issues, health, sexuality, religion, politics, critical thinking, science, moral issues, emotional issues, decision-making.

Submissions and Payment: Guidelines and catalogue available on website. Query with topic, brief outline, competition analysis, potential market, completion schedule of the manuscript, tentative length, and résumé that includes publishing history. Accepts hard copy. Accepts simultaneous submissions if identified. SASE. Responds in 1–2 months. Publication in 12–18 months. Payment policy varies.

Prufrock Press

P.O. Box 8813, Waco, TX 76714. www.prufrock.com

Submissions Editor: Stephanie McCauley

Prufrock Press is the nation's leading publisher supporting the education of gifted and advanced learners. Its line of more than 500 titles offers teachers and parents exciting research-based ideas for gifted, advanced, twice-exceptional, and special needs learners. It is actively seeking teaching resources or curriculum that support higher order critical thinking and questioning skills, differentiation strategies and resources, resources that support the facilitation of project-based learning and other authentic learning experiences, social-emotional learning tools and curriculum, advanced reading strategies, resources for teaching growth mindset and resilience, and advanced STEM activities or lessons.

Freelance Potential: Publishes 30–40 titles annually: 30% by authors who are new to the publishing house.

Nonfiction: Supplemental classroom materials and talent development resources for gifted and advanced learners in grades K–12, professional learning and development books for teachers, resources for children with special needs, primary and supplementary college textbooks, trade books, general education, parenting resources, children's and teens' nonfiction. Topics: authentic learning; project-based learning; inquiry-based learning; growth mindset; grit and resilience; social-emotional skills; math; science; STEM; social studies; language arts; thinking skills; problem solving; research; differentiated instruction; teaching strategies; independent study; identifying, parenting, and counseling gifted children; enrichment.

Submissions and Payment: Guidelines and catalogue available on website. Send prospectus with working title, general book description, target market, annotated table of contents, competitive titles, your book's unique qualities, length, anticipated completion date, marketing suggestions, and résumé. Accepts submissions via Submittable (https://prufrockpress.submittable.com/submit). No simultaneous submissions. Responds in 10–12 weeks. Publication period varies. Royalty; advance. To be considered for freelance projects, send résumé to editorial@prufrock.com.

Redleaf Press

10 Yorkton Court, St. Paul, MN 55117–1065. www.redleafpress.org

Acquisitions and Development Editor: Kyra Ostendorf

Redleaf Press titles represent a broad range of topics designed to assist teachers in providing a stimulating, child-centered curriculum based on sound and accepted theory. It is a leading nonprofit publisher of exceptional curriculum, management, and business resources for early childhood professionals. It is currently seeking proposals for nonfiction books focusing on some aspect of early childhood education. Redleaf Press is a division of Think Small, a nonprofit organization dedicated to the advancement of early childhood professionals.

Freelance Potential: Publishes 20–30 titles annually: 10–25% developed from unsolicited submissions; 1–10% assigned; 10–25% by authors who are new to the publishing house; 50–75% by previously unpublished writers. Receives 1–10 queries monthly.

Nonfiction: Books for educators on social/emotional issues; curriculum, management, and business resources for early child care professionals. Topics: math, science, language, literacy, cultural diversity, music, movement, health, safety, nutrition, child development, special needs, and teacher training and assessment.

Submissions and Payment: Guidelines and catalogue available on website. Does not accept proposals for children's picture books. Query with cover letter that describes book idea, intended audience, competition analysis, and author's expertise; résumé or CV; outline; table of contents; and sample chapters. Accepts email queries to acquisitions@redleafpress.org with Word attachments, and hard copy. Responds in 6 weeks. Publication in 24 months. Authors earn royalties on the sales of their books. Freelance writers are paid on work-for-hire basis.

Renaissance House

465 Westview Avenue, Englewood, NJ 07631. www.renaissancehouse.net

Editorial Director: Raquel Benatar

Renaissance House is a book packager that provides editorial, translation, creative, and production services to publishers. It specializes in the development, translation, and illustration of educational materials in English and Spanish. Its focus on educational titles specifically includes bilingual children's books, multicultural books, legends, and biographies. The packager/editorial service company is "looking for opportunities in partnering with illustrators and authors [who] want to co-publish their book projects." The company also represents more than 60 illustrators.

Freelance Potential: Publishes 15 titles annually: 90% by authors who are new to the company; 75% by previously unpublished writers. Receives 10–25 queries, 75–100 manuscripts monthly.

Fiction: Middle-grade, YA. Genres: bilingual, multicultural, biography, folktales.

Nonfiction: Middle-grade, YA. Topics: biography, multicultural.

Submissions and Payment: Catalogue available on website. Send complete manuscript for fiction. Query with outline for nonfiction. Accepts email submissions to raquel@renaissancehouse.net (Word or PDF attachments). Responds in 2–3 weeks. Publication in 1 year. Flat fee.

Rosen Central

Rosen Publishing, 29 East 21st Street, New York, NY 10010. www.rosenpublishing.com

Editorial Director

Rosen Central gives a comprehensive, thoughtful voice to the middle-school experience by providing insight into the self and the events of the world. It has an understanding that students in grades 5–8 have vastly diverse abilities in reading and comprehension as well as wide-ranging interests.

Freelance Potential: Parent company Rosen Publishing publishes 700+ titles annually.

Nonfiction: Chapter books, middle-grade. Topics: health, technology, study skills and research, sports, recreation, history, careers, contemporary issues, geography, science, ethics.

Submissions and Payment: Catalogue available on website. Contact Customer Service team via website for information about submissions. Responds in 3 months. Publication in 9–18 months. Flat fee.

Rosen Publishing

29 East 21st Street, New York, NY 10010. www.rosenpublishing.com

Editorial Director, YA Division: Iris Rosoff

Rosen Publishing has an enduring tradition of addressing topics such as this and ensuring dissemination of information through library-bound editions of our books, which have made their way into the circulating reference collections of libraries across North America and many other English-speaking countries around the world. It is an independent educational publishing house that sets out to combine a commitment to social justice, technological innovation, and a publishing ethos. It serves the needs of students in PreK–grade 12 with high interest, curriculum-correlated materials and believes there is no taboo information; there is only information.

Freelance Potential: Publishes 700+ titles annually: very few by authors who are new to the publishing house. Receives 5–7 queries monthly.

Nonfiction: Concept books, board books, early readers, chapter books, middle-grade, YA. Topics: digital and information technology, health, reference, history, geography, science, life skills, guidance, careers, contemporary social issues.

Submissions and Payment: Catalogue available on website. Contact Customer Service team via website for information about submissions. Responds in 3 months. Publication in 9–18 months. Flat fee.

Rosen Young Adult

Rosen Publishing, 29 East 21st Street, New York, NY 10010. www.rosenpublishing.com

Editorial Director

Speaking exclusively to the teen experience, Rosen Young Adult tackles challenging and intriguing topics. Rosen Young Adult has been a trusted go-to resource for teens, parents, librarians, counselors, and teachers seeking books that explore these situations. Its books present high-interest topics with unbiased narratives that are often supported with thought-provoking analytical activities and next-step guidelines.

Freelance Potential: Parent company Rosen Publishing publishes 700+ titles annually.

Nonfiction: Middle-grade, YA. Topics: health, technology, ethics, philosophy, economics, current events, history, careers, contemporary issues, geography, science.

Submissions and Payment: Catalogue available on website. Contact Customer Service team via website for information about submissions. Responds in 3 months. Publication in 9–18 months. Flat fee.

Rourke Educational Media

P.O. Box 643328, Vero Beach, FL 32964. www.rourkeeducationalmedia.com

Editor-in-Chief: Luana Mitten

Rourke Educational Media's expansive offerings include literacy-rich, cross-curricular, print and digital formats and programs with diverse characters, storylines, images, and global perspectives. Eye-catching, engaging nonfiction is the mainstay of Rourke Educational Media. It publishes children's books that comply with national curriculum standards. Rourke understands the importance placed on educators to follow state and federal standards guidelines and offers cutting-edge software for science, social studies, and other classroom programs. Most books available in digital format as well.

Freelance Potential: Publishes 150–200 titles annually: many by freelance or contract writers and previously unpublished writers.

Nonfiction: Early readers, chapter books, middle-grade. Topics: science, social studies, reading adventures, sports, biography, reference.

Submissions and Payment: Catalogue available on website. Query with résumé, indicating the topic and age you are interested in writing for. Accepts hard copy and email queries to luana@rourkepublishing.com. Guidelines are sent to writers with their contracts. Work-for-hire agreements, with a choice of 20% of payment when the book is commissioned.

Rubicon Publishing

2040 Speers Rd, Oakville, Ontario L6L 2X8 Canada. www.rubiconpublishing.com

Associate Publisher: Amy Land

Rubicon Publishing works hard to create learning resources that combine effective instructional design with edgy and engaging content. It is an award-winning publisher of K–12 educational resources for students and educators. Creating the best learning situations in the world, the titles from this publisher combine innovative ideas with a strong foundation in education to create original and high-quality titles. All of its educational resource books are assigned.

Freelance Potential: Publishes 30+ titles annually: 100% are assigned; 2% by authors new to the publishing company; 5% by previously unpublished writers. Receives 5 queries monthly.

Fiction: Early picture books, early readers, story picture books, chapter books, middle-grade, YA. Genres: poetry, drama, graphic novels, fairy tales, fantasy, historical, multicultural, romance, science fiction, social issues, sports, Westerns.

Nonfiction: Early picture books, early readers, story picture books, chapter books, middle-grade, YA, books for educators. Topics: current events, math, language arts, social studies, science, entertainment, humor, social issues, sports, multicultural and ethnic issues, technology. Also publishes teacher resources.

Submissions and Payment: Catalogue available on website. All work is assigned. Query with clips. Accepts hard copy and email to submissions@rubiconpublishing.com. SASE. Response time varies. Publication in 1 year. Royalty or flat fee depending on project.

Ruckus Media Group

55 Tory Hill Lane, Norwalk, CT 06853. www.ruckuslearning.com

President: Rick Richter

Ruckus is a learning platform that harnesses the brands kids love and motivates students to become better, more active learners. Ruckus is a mobile learning platform that helps families solve the problem of reluctant readers. It creates interactive applications for mobile devices designed to entertain and educate children. It transforms some of the biggest entertainment brands into personalized educational content that engages children and ignites their interest in learning.

Freelance Potential: Publishes 40 digital titles annually. Actively looking for new content.

Fiction: Early picture books, story picture books, early readers. Genres: adventure, fantasy, contemporary, licensed characters.

Nonfiction: Story picture books, early readers. Topics: animals, biography.

Submissions and Payment: Guidelines and catalogue available on website. Submissions accepted via form on website. Response time, publication period, and payment policies vary.

Saddleback Educational Publishing

151 Kalmus Drive, Suite J-1, Costa Mesa, CA 92626. www.sdlback.com

Editorial Director: Carol Pizer

Saddleback is always looking for fresh, new talent. It publishes curriculum-based and reference books across all major disciplines, including math, science, language arts, social studies, special education, and life skills/careers. Saddleback creates engaging, age-respectful content for grades 4–12 at accessible reading levels in a variety of styles. Most of its titles are geared toward middle and high school students, although it does offer a few elementary level reference books. Saddleback is currently seeking high/low nonfiction written at reading levels 0.5–2.0 for interest levels 4–12.

Freelance Potential: Publishes 10–20 titles yearly.

Fiction: Middle-grade, YA. Genres: the classics, contemporary, real life, high/low, reluctant reader.

Nonfiction: Elementary, middle-grade, YA. Topics: science, language arts, math, social studies, career, lifestyle, technology, reference, teacher references.

Submissions and Payment: Catalogue available on website. Query with manuscript. Not currently seeking curriculum material but is always looking for fiction and urban fiction appropriate for grades 6–12. Email submissions to contact@sdlback.com. Response time, publication period, and payment policies vary.

SAGE Publishing

2455 Teller Road, Thousand Oaks, CA 91320. https://us.sagepub.com/en-us/nam/home

SAGE is an independent international publisher of journals, books, and electronic media. Known for their commitment to quality and innovation, SAGE has helped inform and educate a global community of scholars, practitioners, researchers, and students across a broad range of subject areas. Its Corwin Press imprint publishes leading-edge books for practicing elementary and secondary educators.

Freelance Potential: Publishes 10+ titles each year.

Nonfiction: Resource books and manuals for educators, grades K–12. Topics: administration, assessment, evaluation, professional development, curriculum development, classroom practice and management, gifted and special education, bilingual learning, counseling, school health, educational technology.

Submissions and Payment: Guidelines and catalogue available on website. Send prospectus with rationale, outline, target audience, competitive titles, length and completion schedule, sample chapters, and résumé. Accepts email (see website for appropriate editor). Response time varies. Publication in 7 months. Royalty.

School Zone Publishing

1819 Industrial Drive, P.O. Box 777, Grand Haven, MI 49417. www.schoolzone.com

Editor

School Zone Publishing is a market leader in workbooks and flash cards for preschoolers through sixth graders. School Zone is family-owned, focused on excellence, responsive to customers, alert to emerging technology, and committed to community. Almost 40 years ago, School Zone Publishing identified a need for at-home learning materials to help parents support and supplement their children's classroom instruction. With research-based content, designed by educators and delivered across multiple learning platforms, School Zone connects with kids "where they are." It continually updates its products with new features and content, reflective of changing standards, evolving teaching methods, and overall best practices.

Freelance Potential: Publishes 5–6 titles annually. Receives 8–10 queries monthly.

Fiction: Story picture books, early readers. Themes: phonetics, animals, life skills, contemporary, jobs, social and character issues.

Nonfiction: Publishes workbooks, software, and flashcards for PreK–grade 6. Topics: reading, spelling, writing, mathematics, bilingual studies, music, arts, language arts, geography.

Submissions and Payment: Catalogue available on website. Query with résumé and writing samples. Response time and publication period vary. Flat fee.

Scobre Press

2255 Calle Clara, La Jolla, CA 92037. www.scobre.com

Editor: Scott Blumenthal

Created by two 21-year-old college students that have hooked up with respected educators from around the country who have embraced their concept and passion, Scobre Press offers elementary, middle-grade, and young adult books. The mainstay of Scobre Press Books are books that are fun, interesting to read, multicultural, and socially relevant. Inspired by the idea of producing relevant and engaging young adult books that would have appealed to themselves as readers, Scobre has created a successful line of educational books designed to truly interest young people. Its titles are available on two different reading levels.

Freelance Potential: Publishes about 6 titles annually: 65% by authors who are new to the publishing house; 35% by previously unpublished writers. Receives 1–2 queries monthly.

Fiction: Middle-grade, YA. Genres: sports, dance, music, popular culture, character issues, contemporary, real life/problems.

Nonfiction: Middle-grade, YA. Topics: sports, technology, music, popular culture, real life/problems, contemporary. Also publishes teacher resources.

Submissions and Payment: Catalogue available on website. Guidelines available via email to info@scobre.com. Query. Accepts hard copy and email to info@scobre.com. SASE. Responds in 1 week. Publication in 6 months. Royalty, 12%.

Seedling Publications

520 East Bainbridge Street, Elizabethtown, PA 17022. www.continentalpress.com

Managing Editor: Megan Bergonzi

Seedling fills the latest teaching and curriculum needs in schools. The goal of this publisher is to help students in the earliest stages become successful in the reading process. Part of Continental Press, Seedling offers a line of early literacy resources and parent involvement tools for grades K–2, specializing in reading, mathematics, and test preparation materials. It is not currently accepting submissions for Seedling leveled readers or instructional materials.

Freelance Potential: Publishes 50+ titles (40 juvenile) annually: 10% developed from unsolicited submissions. Receives 20 unsolicited manuscripts monthly.

Fiction: Early readers. Genres: fairy tales, adventure, humor, sports, nature, real life.

Nonfiction: Early readers. Topics: nature, science, technology, mathematics, animals, multicultural. Also publishes workbooks and test prep materials, as well as resources for parents and teachers.

Submissions and Payment: Guidelines and catalogue available on website. Send complete manuscript. Manuscript should be an 8-, 12-, or 16-page format (including title page); 25–300 words. Does not accept poetry, full-length picture books, rhyming manuscripts, or religious books. Accepts hard copy only. Accepts simultaneous submissions if identified. SASE. Responds in 6 months. Publication in 1 year. Payment policy varies.

Smith & Kraus

P.O. Box 127, Lyme, NH 03768. www.smithandkraus.com

Editor: Carol Boynton

Smith & Kraus welcomes manuscript proposals for books of interest to the greater theatrical community. Smith and Kraus publishes books that enrich the theater experience for theater students, theater professionals, and theater audiences. It is the premier US publisher of contemporary trade theater books and associated digital resources. If you are a playwright you can have your play published and available for sale during your production or have copies made after the production to use for promotional and marketing purposes.

Freelance Potential: Publishes 12–24 titles annually: 45–50% by authors new to the publishing house. Receives 8+ queries monthly.

Fiction: Collections of plays, scenes, and monologues, grades K–12. Also publishes anthologies, translations, and collections of works by contemporary playwrights.

Nonfiction: Instructional books for teachers, grades K–12. Topics: theater history, stage production, Shakespeare, movement, dramatizing literature.

Submissions and Payment: Guidelines and catalogue available on website. Query with synopsis and writing sample; include reviews/production information if querying about a play. Accepts hard copy and email queries to editor@smithandkraus.com. SASE. Accepts simultaneous submissions if identified. Responds in 1–2 months. Publication in 1 year. Royalty; advance. Flat fee.

Spotlight

P.O. Box 398166, Minneapolis, MN 55439. www.abdobooks.com

Editor-in-Chief: Paul Abdo

This division of Abdo Publishing offers licensed character titles, graphic novels, and more. Spotlight makes fiction come to life in their offerings for PreK–grade 8.

Freelance Potential: Parent company publishes 600 titles annually. All writing is done on assignment or a work-for-hire basis.

Fiction: Early picture books, early readers, story picture books, chapter books, graphic novels, middle-grade. Genres: stories about licensed and popular characters.

Submissions and Payment: Catalogue available on website. Guidelines provided to writers under contract only. To be considered for future writing assignments, send résumé with cover letter, area of expertise, and publishing credits. Accepts email to submissions@abdopublishing.com. Response time varies. Publication period varies. Flat fee.

State Standards Publishing

P.O. Box 68, Athens, GA 30603. www.statestandardspublishing.com

President: Jill Ward

While other publishers may provide state studies books, they may not fully cover the topics required in that state's standards, or be written at grade level. State Standards Publishing was started in response to the need for books to supplement curriculum for specific state studies. It offers leveled information text at grade level. Titles are produced to meet state education requirements at specific grade levels and are determined by the publisher. The publisher prefers to hire writers from the state that each book is about.

Freelance Potential: Publishes 6–10 titles annually.

Nonfiction: Early readers, middle-grade, YA. Topics: state history, geography, regional, biographies, natural history and resources.

Submissions and Payment: Catalogue available on website. Does not accept unsolicited manuscripts or queries. To be considered for work-for-hire, send résumé and nonfiction writing sample. Prefers authors living in title's state. Accepts hard copy and email to jward@statestandardspublishing.com and mchandler@statestandardspublishing.com. Response time, publication period, and payment policies vary.

Stone Arch Books

Capstone, 1710 Roe Crest Drive, North Mankato, MN 56003. www.capstonepub.com

Editorial Director: Michael Dahl

Whether graphic novels or chapter books, on-level or hi/low, Stone Arch books are designed to meet kids where they are. Stone Arch Books creates series fiction that is exciting, fun, and easy to accomplish. The stories are fast-paced and cool, yet appropriate for middle-grade readers. Short chapters and lower page counts build reading confidence while modern themes and original, exciting characters keep readers coming back for more. Each book is leveled with controlled vocabulary and word counts and extends the reading experience with full back matter.

Freelance Potential: Publishes 161 titles annually: 5–10% by agented authors; 15–20% reprint/licensed properties; 20% by authors who are new to the publishing house; 5% by previously unpublished writers. Receives 50 queries monthly.

Fiction: Early readers, chapter books, middle-grade, graphic novels. Genres: realistic, war stories, adventure, fantasy, horror, science fiction, mystery, sports, humor, fairy tales, folklore.

Submissions and Payment: Guidelines and catalogue available on website. For nonfiction, query with cover letter, résumé, and 3 writing samples. Accepts hard copy only. For fiction, query with sample chapters, résumé, and list of publishing credits. Prefers email to author.sub@stonearchbooks.com. Responds in 6 months if interested. Publication period and payment policies vary.

Teacher Created Materials

P.O. Box 1040, Huntington Beach, CA 92647. www.teachercreatedmaterials.com

Editor-in-Chief: Donna Rice

Teacher Created Materials is a leading educational publisher with products that are used in classrooms in all 50 states and in 89 countries. For over 40 years, Teacher Created Materials has published innovative, imaginative, and award-winning resources for teachers and students in all subjects for grades K–12. Everything they publish is still created by teachers for teachers and students because they still believe that no one knows what teachers need more than other teachers and they know that all students can become lifelong learners.

Freelance Potential: Publishes 25 titles annually.

Nonfiction: Publishes workbooks, activity books, teacher resources, and classroom aids, aimed at PreK–grade 8. Topics include writing, reading, science, geography, history, technology. Also publishes teacher materials on student testing, multiple intelligences, assessment, and classroom management.

Submissions and Payment: Guidelines and catalogue available on website. Send complete manuscript through the website in .doc or .docx format. Responds in 6 months. Publication in 3–12 months. Work-for-hire, flat fee.

Teacher Created Resources

12621 Western Ave, Garden Grove, CA 92841. www.teachercreated.com

Editor-in-Chief: Karen Goldfluss

Teacher Created Resources' products are created by teachers for teachers and parents. This educational publisher publishes books that cover all aspects of the curriculum. It has an extensive inventory of quality and affordable materials, school supplies, lessons, and more. It is proud to publish materials that have been written by credentialed professionals and successfully used in the classroom. They believe that the main reason for their successes is that they know—first-hand—about teaching. Teacher Created Resources is currently interested in acquiring ELL titles for PreK–grade 8 and books in the areas of language arts, reading, math, science, and social studies. Books should be based on successful classroom lessons and should be able to be correlated to national and/or state standards.

Freelance Potential: Publishes 50–75 titles annually: 10–25% developed from unsolicited submissions; 50–75% assigned; 5% by authors who are new to the publishing house; 5% by unpublished writers.

Nonfiction: Publishes workbooks, activity books, teacher resources, and classroom aids, aimed at PreK–grade 8. Topics include writing, reading, science, geography, history, technology, Christian education. Also publishes teacher materials on student testing, multiple intelligences, assessment, and classroom management.

Submissions and Payment: Guidelines and catalogue available on website. Query with résumé, summary, intended audience, table of contents, and 10–12 manuscript pages. Accepts hard copy. SASE. Responds in 6 months. Publication in 3–12 months. Work-for-hire, flat fee.

Charles C. Thomas Publisher

2600 South First Street, Springfield, IL 62704. www.ccthomas.com

Editor: Michael P. Thomas

This publisher's goal has been and is to publish original, significant titles that will accommodate current needs for information and that often will become standard texts and classics in their respective fields. Charles C. Thomas has been producing a strong list of specialty titles and textbooks in biomedical science since 1927. In addition, they also have an active program in producing books for the behavioral sciences, education and special education, speech-language and hearing, as well as rehabilitation and long-term care. Thomas is also one of the largest producers of books in all areas of criminal justice and law enforcement.

Freelance Potential: Publishes 60 titles annually: all developed from unsolicited submissions. Receives 50 queries and unsolicited manuscripts monthly.

Nonfiction: Titles for educators, PreK–grade 12. Topics: early childhood, elementary, and higher education; reading; research and statistics; physical education and sports; special education; the learning disabled; teaching the blind and visually impaired; gifted and talented education; speech-language pathology. Also publishes parenting titles and professional development books for the science and criminal justice fields.

Submissions and Payment: Guidelines and catalogue available on website. Query with preface outlining scope, plan, and purpose of your manuscript (300 words or more); possible illustrations; tentative outline and contents; estimated size and completion schedule; curriculum vitae; and authors/editors marketing questionnaire (on website). Or send complete manuscript with accompanying disk (Word format). Each section of the manuscript should be saved as a separate file, i.e. title page, preface, table of contents, list of figures or tables, etc. Accepts hard copy with flash drive or disk. SASE. Response time varies. Publication in 6+ months. Payment policy, unknown.

Tilbury House

12 Starr Street, Thomaston, ME 04861. www.tilburyhouse.com

Children's Book Editor: Jonathan Eaton

Tilbury House's primary emphasis is on nonfiction picture books that appeal to children ages 2–12 and their parents. It publishes award-winning children's picture books about cultural diversity, social justice, nature, and the environment. The aim of Tilbury House is to publish picture books that nourish and cultivate a child's imagination. Picture books must be beautiful, of course, or they will not be opened. And they must be accurate, even when exploring a concept as complex as the Big Bang or as fraught as race, family, or death. But sparking the imagination is the most important thing, and the hardest. In response to the increasing classroom use of its books, Tilbury House also began developing teacher guides for many of its titles.

Freelance Potential: Publishes 22 titles annually: 25–50% developed from unsolicited submissions; 25–50% by authors who are new to the publishing house; 25–50% by previously unpublished writers. Receives 75–100 unsolicited manuscripts monthly.

Fiction: Picture books, story picture books. Genres: realistic, contemporary, multicultural, nature, the environment.

Nonfiction: Picture books, story picture books. Topics: nature, the environment, real-life issues, social issues, social skills.

Submissions and Payment: Guidelines and catalogue available on website. Send complete manuscript. Accepts hard copy and email submissions to info@tilburyhouse.com. Accepts simultaneous submissions if identified. SASE. Responds in 6 months. Publication in 2 years. Royalty.

Twenty-First Century Books

241 First Avenue North, Minneapolis, MN 55401. www.lernerbooks.com

Editorial Director: Domenica Di Piazza

Twenty-First Century Books is a trusted source for engaging young adult nonfiction focusing on topical, high-interest subjects across a diverse spectrum of disciplines and points of view. With authoritative writing and captivating photography, TFCB titles are excellent launching pads for stimulating in-depth research, supporting evidence-based coursework, and fostering an awareness of the rewards of nonfiction reading.

Freelance Potential: Publishes around 20 titles annually. Receives 8–10 queries monthly.

Nonfiction: Middle-grade, YA. Topics: human interest, history, social studies, contemporary issues, language arts, biography, sports, multicultural, current events, science, technology, health, medicine, government, politics.

Submissions and Payment: Guidelines and catalogue available on website. Does not accept unsolicited submissions. Does seek targeted submissions for specific reading levels and subject areas on an as-needed basis. Check website for current needs. Response time, publication period, and payment policies vary.

U-X-L

27500 Drake Road, Farmington Hills, MI 48331-3535. www.gale.cengage.com/uxl

Publisher

U-X-L titles are mostly written at a seventh-grade reading level and most are published in both print and e-book format. Part of Cengage Learning, this publisher offers an extensive line of reference books for students in upper elementary through high school. Their catalogue covers a broad range of academic subject areas such as primary source volumes, encyclopedias, almanacs, chronologies, and biographies.

Freelance Potential: Publishes 20 titles annually.

Nonfiction: Middle-grade, YA. Topics: science, medicine, history, social studies, current events, biographies, multicultural issues, the arts, sports, careers. Also publishes curriculum-based reference titles, encyclopedias.

Submissions and Payment: Catalogue available on website. Accepts some unsolicited material; most work is assigned on a work-for-hire basis. Query with résumé and writing samples. Accepts hard copy. Accepts simultaneous submissions if identified. SASE. Response time and publication period vary. Flat fee.

Walch Education

40 Walch Drive, Portland, ME 04103–1286. http://walch.com

Submissions: Jill Rosenblum

Walch Education works with educators to develop, produce, and implement materials that meet state and national standards. It also offers a variety of supplemental middle school, high school, and adult educational materials. It celebrates the progress of students of all levels of ability and interest, who are most successful and happiest if given the individually appropriate materials from which to learn. The company has a large, in-house team of educators that creates most of its materials, but it does employ freelance writers on large projects and commissioned titles, and considers unsolicited manuscripts.

Freelance Potential: Publishes 50 titles annually: 2% developed from unsolicited submissions. Receives 2 queries monthly.

Nonfiction: Middle-grade, YA. Topics: reading, writing, vocabulary, grammar, geometry, algebra, critical thinking, world history, social studies, math, science, chemistry, physics, money management, careers, life skills, art, special education. Also publishes resource materials for teachers.

Submissions and Payment: Guidelines and catalogue available on website. Query with detailed proposal that includes author introduction; why you are writing this book; target audience, including subject area, teacher skill level, student grade level and ability; learning objectives, including No Child Left Behind requirements and state standards; marketing potential; table of contents; a sample chapter and supporting materials; and manuscript development timeline. Prefers email to ideas@walch.com (Word or PDF attachments). Accepts hard copy. SASE. Responds in 4–6 months. Publication period varies. Royalty. Flat fee.

Wiley

111 River Street, Hoboken, NJ 07030-5774. www.wiley.com/en-us

Editor

Wiley is bridging the higher education gap by delivering content solutions in new and innovative ways to enrich the learning experience. Wiley is a large reference and educational publisher that includes nonfiction for children and teens in its mix. Among its imprints and brands are CliffsNotes, the Dummies books, and Jossey-Bass. In addition to educational books for students, the company publishes books on parenting, reference, self-help, and technology, as well as books for educators and counselors of children and teens. It also offers products and services on the Internet, along with a platform for scientific, technical, medical, and professional content, now called Wiley Online Library.

Freelance Potential: Publishes hundreds of titles annually.

Nonfiction: Middle-grade, YA, adult. Topics: accounting, agriculture, arts, business, computers, culinary, economics, education, engineering, environment, languages, lifestyle, math, medicine, psychology, reference, science, social sciences.

Submissions and Payment: Guidelines and catalogue available on website. See website for specific guidelines for each division. Response time, publication period, and payment policies vary.

Windmill Books

Rosen Publishing, 29 East 21st Street, New York, NY 10010. www.rosenpublishing.com

Editorial Director

Books that are fun to read and provide information and knowledge make up this publisher's catalogue. Working together with reading experts and educators, Windmill has developed fiction and nonfiction books. From captivating concept books to thrilling historical fiction to photo-driven nonfiction, each book from Windmill is a celebration of its core tenet—to inspire a love of learning through reading.

Freelance Potential: Parent company Rosen Publishing publishes 700+ titles annually.

Fiction: Concept books, board books, story picture books, early readers, chapter books, middle-grade. Genres: real life/problem, multicultural, adventure, classics, historical, mystery, contemporary issues.

Nonfiction: Concept books, board books, story picture books, early readers, chapter books, middle-grade. Topics: math, history, biography, life skills, science, contemporary issues, real life problems, leisure.

Submissions and Payment: Catalogue available on website. Contact Customer Service team via website for information about submissions. Responds in 3 months. Publication in 9–18 months. Flat fee.

World Book

180 North LaSalle Street, Suite 900, Chicago, IL 60601. www.worldbook.com

Editor-in-Chief: Paul A. Kobasa

Education is World Book's commitment and its editorial team is World Book's strength. The mission of World Book is to enhance learning and reading for children around the world by developing trustworthy, engaging content to create products that will engage children of all ages at home, on the go, in the classroom, or in libraries worldwide. It prides itself on accurate, objective, and reliable research materials in the form of encyclopedias, reference sources, and digital products for home and school use. World Book builds bridges connecting users to greater learning through proven content creation methods, cutting-edge delivery systems, and an inextinguishable passion for knowledge.

Freelance Potential: Publishes numerous titles each year.

Nonfiction: Early readers, middle-grade, YA, adult. Topics: animals, careers, concepts, geography, health, history, how-to, languages, multicultural, reference, science.

Submissions and Payment: Catalogue available on website. Query with outline/synopsis. Do not send manuscript. Accepts simultaneous submissions. Responds in 2 months. Publication in 18 months. Payment policy varies by product.

YouthLight

P.O. Box 115, Chapin, SC 29036. https://youthlight.com/

Submission Editor

Since 1995, YouthLight has been addressing the current issues facing counselors and other care-giving professionals. They continually work to develop and promote best-practice, preventive, strengths-based approaches to helping young people. YouthLight is an educational support company that develops and markets resources primarily for professional educators. Its wide array of titles deals with everything from bullying and anger management to self-esteem and conflict resolution. It always strives to provide a preventive, strengths-based approach to helping students become the facilitators of change.

Freelance Potential: Publishes 15–20 titles annually: 40% developed from unsolicited submissions; 10% by authors who are new to the publishing house; 5% by previously unpublished writers. Receives 4 queries monthly.

Fiction: Easy-to-read books, story picture books, middle-grade, YA. Themes: multicultural fiction and stories about children dealing with social pressures.

Nonfiction: Easy-to-read books, story picture books, middle-grade, YA. Topics: self-help, social issues. Also publishes titles for adults.

Submissions and Payment: Guidelines and catalogue available on website. Query with type of work (book, CD, kit), title, outline, and sample pages, or send complete manuscript. Include résumé, target audience, and marketing plan with all submissions. Prefers online submissions through website. Accepts hard copy. Responds in 1–3 months. Publication in 6 months. Royalty, 10%.

Zaner-Bloser Educational

1400 Goodale Blvd., Suite 200, Grandview Heights, OH 43212. www.zaner-bloser.com

Senior Vice President of Editorial: Marytherese Croarkin

Zaner-Bloser believes true literacy is grounded in a set of complementary skills that empower us to do amazing things. It provides the most current resources based on the latest scientific evidence. It is driven by a singular mission: to support teachers with effective educational resources that make learning successful and joyful. It aims to create dynamic, appealing, and effective educational programs and services. Its focus is on distinctive programs that inspire all students to become engaged, literate participants in the global society.

Freelance Potential: Publishes 200+ titles annually.

Fiction: Early readers, story picture books, middle-grade, YA. Genres: contemporary, life skills, animals, language arts, fantasy, historical, adventure.

Nonfiction: Early readers, story picture books, middle-grade, YA. Topics: language arts, phonics, vocabulary, reading, spelling, handwriting, math, science, social studies.

Submissions and Payment: Catalogue available on website. Query with résumé and clips. Accepts hard copy. SASE. Response time and publication period vary. Flat fee.

Parenting Publishing

Personal experience may be the motivating factor in writing books directed at parents, as there are many struggles that need to find an answer. The combination of writing books for children and teens with writing books about young people can offer additional opportunities for those passionate about raising and supporting kids.

The publishing companies in this section devote some or all of their focus to parenting books. Some have an even more defined niche: adoption, autism and other disorders, military families, healthy pregnancy and child development, family travel, emotional health, family nutrition, relationships, dealing with life struggles, and, on the other end of the spectrum, books about creating a home, parties, and activities for children.

Some of these publishers offer titles that target parents primarily, and some have books for adults and books for children. They represent another potential realm of writing for those looking to expand their careers.

AMACOM Books

1601 Broadway, New York, NY 10019-7420. https://www.harpercollinsleadership.com/amacombooks/

Editor

Now a division of HarperCollins Leadership, AMACOM specializes in books that drive professional and personal growth. It also publishes a large number of parenting, health and fitness, and popular psychology titles. Its mission is to help its readers lead a more satisfying and successful life through books.

Freelance Potential: Publishes 15+ titles each year.

Nonfiction: Adult. Topics: parenting, children with special needs, psychology, pregnancy, performing arts, health and fitness.

Submissions and Payment: Guidelines and catalogue available on website. Query with working title, overview, target audience, table of contents, competitive comparison, author credentials, and 1–3 sample chapters. Accepts hard copy. Responds in 3 months. Publication period varies. Payment rates and policies vary.

Autism Asperger Publishing Company

6448 Vista Drive, Shawnee, KS 66218. www.aapcpublishing.net

Submissions: Ashley Nichols

AAPC Publishing provides parents, professionals, and individuals with autism spectrum disorders and other mental health disorders with practical solutions covering the lifespan, focusing on evidence-based practices, and aligned with current standards in the field. It accepts proposals for books on autism and Asperger Syndrome, as well as effective strategies and techniques that can be easily implemented in school, clinic, and home settings.

Freelance Potential: Publishes about 30 titles (15% juvenile) annually: 15% developed from unsolicited submissions; 85% by authors who are new to the publishing house; 85% by previously unpublished writers. Receives 20 queries monthly.

Fiction: Story picture books, early readers, chapter books, middle-grade, YA. Genres: mystery, fantasy, education, real life/problems.

Nonfiction: YA, Adult. Topics: education, social skills, health, real life/problems.

Submissions and Payment: Guidelines available. Query with cover letter including concept statement, intended audience, and what makes your book unique; table of contents/outline; synopsis and approximate length of each chapter; 1–2 sample chapters; suggested illustrations; author profile establishing your credibility; and promotion suggestions. Submit your proposal electronically to ashley.nichols@aapcpublishing.net. Also accepts hard copy. SASE. Responds in 3–6 months. Publication in 8 months. Royalty, 10%.

Da Capo Press

Market Place Center, 53 State Street, Boston, MA 200109. www.dacapopress.com

Executive Editor: Robert Pigeon

Da Capo Press, part of the Perseus Group, believes that learning is lifelong. It has been offering a wide-ranging list of mostly nonfiction titles in both hardcover and paperback since 1964. Its books focus on history, music, performing arts, sports, and popular culture. It also includes books on parenting and child rearing.

Freelance Potential: Publishes about 70 titles annually: all by agented authors. Receives 12–15 queries monthly.

Fiction: Adult. Genres: historical, short stories, fantasy, social issues, contemporary, mystery.

Nonfiction: Adult. Topics: history, health, nature, current events, entertainment, parenting, pregnancy, science, social issues, multicultural issues, religion, sports, self-help, humor, biography, cooking, crafts, arts, animals.

Submissions and Payment: Catalogue available on website. Does not accept unsolicited proposals or manuscripts. Only accepts agented submissions. Publication in 1 year. Royalty; advance.

Elva Resa

8362 Tamarack Village, Suite 119-106, St. Paul, MN 55125. www.elvaresa.com

Senior Editor: Terri Barnes

Elva Resa works with military and community organizations, family support groups, nonprofits, schools, health care companies, legislators, and many other groups to produce quality resources that support military family members of all ages and for all service branches. It has a mission to make a positive difference in people's lives. This small independent publisher publishes books, newsletters, and workshop materials for and about military families. The children's imprint, Alma Little, publishes general interest picture books and novels for children up to age 10. Elva Resa also features books that cover military life topics for teens.

Freelance Potential: Publishes about 5 titles annually: 10–25% developed from unsolicited submissions; 75–100% assigned; 25–50% by authors who are new to the publishing house; 10–25% by previously unpublished writers. Receives 100–150 queries, 15+ manuscripts monthly.

Nonfiction: Families. Topics: self-help, current events/politics, how-to, activities, biography, inspirational, real life/problems, religious, reference, parenting, military resources.

Submissions and Payment: Guidelines and catalogue available on website. Not currently accepting submissions. Accepts submissions during their annual open call only. Check website for more information. Email queries only (Word or PDF attachments), including target audience, market opportunity, how your book compares with others on the market, and a book outline to submissions@elvaresa.com. Also accepts queries and résumés for work-for-hire assignments. Responds in 3 weeks if interested. Publication in 12–24 months. Royalty; advance. Flat fee.

EMK Press

16 Mt. Bethel Road #219, Warren, NJ C7059. www.emkpress.com

Submissions

EMK Press believes that information has power when it is shared and they work hard to get information to those need it. It is a publisher of books for families whose lives have been touched by adoption, domestic or international, are fostering children or work with foster children, are adoptees, or are former foster youth. Its mission is education for anyone involved with adoption, kinship, or fostering. It has books to help parents do a better job of parenting the children who have come to them, books for children that allow them to voice their thoughts and feelings, and books for teens to help them understand they aren't alone. It is particularly interested in books for tweens and teens at this time.

Freelance Potential: Publishes 15+ titles each year.

Nonfiction: Middle-grade, YA. Topics: Social issues, real life issues, family, education.

Submissions and Payment: Guidelines and catalogue available on website. Send hard copy of complete manuscript with competitive analysis and SASE. Potential writers should familiarize themselves with our titles before submitting material. Accepts hard copy. Responds if interested. Publication in 18–24 months. Payment policy varies.

Familius

1254 Commerce Way, Sanger, CA 93657. www.familius.com

Acquisitions Editor: Michele Lynne Robbins

Familius is all about strengthening families. Collectively, its authors and staff have experienced a wide piece of the family-life spectrum. It is currently seeking children's fiction, titles on parenting, pregnancy, family relationships, health and wellness, and education.

Freelance Potential: Publishes about 65 titles annually digitally and approximately 30 in print. Plans to increase these numbers. Receives 20 queries monthly.

Fiction: Story picture books, early readers, chapter books. Genres: social skills, social issues, contemporary, historical.

Nonfiction: All ages. Topics: parenting, marriage, family fun, health and wellness, education, children.

Submissions and Payment: Guidelines and catalogue available on website. Submit 1-page cover letter with brief description of project, outline, marketing platforms, writing sample, and author bio. Accepts email submissions to bookideas@familius.com. Tell us why you think Familius is the right fit for your project. Response time varies. Publication period varies. Royalty, 30% on digital, 10–20% on print versions, and 50% subsidiary rights, paid monthly.

Globe Pequot Press

246 Goose Lane, 2nd Floor, P.O. Box 480, Guilford, CT 06437. www.globepequot.com

Submissions Editor

For more than 60 years, Globe Pequot Press has been publishing books about iconic brands and people, regional interest, history, lifestyle, cooking and food culture, and folklore—books that hit the intersection of a reader's interest in a specific place and their passion for a specific topic. Its books tell untold or little known stories from history, celebrate the unique or iconic characteristics of specific places, and tap into local pride.

Freelance Potential: Publishes 400+ titles annually: many developed from unsolicited submissions; some reprint/licensed properties; about 20% by authors who are new to the publishing house. Receives 20–30 queries monthly.

Fiction: Adult. Genres: regional, mystery, adventure, outdoors, history.

Nonfiction: Adult. Topics: outdoor life, camping, hiking, nature, animals, travel, recreation, sports, regional, pets, biography, cooking, current events, home and garden, self-help, inspirational.

Submissions and Payment: Guidelines and catalogue available on website. Globe is currently closed to unsolicited manuscript and proposal submissions but is still offering freelance work. To be considered, send résumé, writing credits, and 3 brief writing samples. Accepts hard copy. Prefers email submission to GPSubmissions@rowman.com. Responds in 3 months. Publication in 18 months. Royalty, 8–12%; advance, $500–$1,500.

Hunter House

www.hunterhouse.com

Acquisitions

Hunter house focuses on nonfiction for families and communities on health and fitness, family/partner relationships, sexuality, personal growth, violence intervention/prevention, activity books for teachers, and counseling resources. Part of the Turner Publishing group, it aims to present comprehensive books that provide balanced information, often for a neglected audience. It looks for authors with credentials in their subject area.

Freelance Potential: Publishes about 12 titles annually: most are developed from unsolicited submissions. Receives 15–25 queries monthly.

Nonfiction: Workbooks for children, YA, adults. Topics: health, fitness, family, personal growth, relationships, sexuality, violence prevention and intervention, teaching and counseling materials, lesser-known illnesses.

Submissions and Payment: Guidelines and catalogue available on website. Query with proposal containing an overview, chapter-by-chapter outline, approximate length, illustrations and other features, author biography, and market analysis. Accepts hard copy or email to submissions@turnerpublishing.com. Accepts simultaneous submissions if identified. SASE. Responds in 3–4 months. Publication in 1–2 years.

Impact Publishers

5674 Shattuck Avenue, Oakland, CA 94609
https://www.newharbinger.com/imprint/impact-publishers

Acquisitions Editor: Freeman Porter

Impact Publishers, an imprint of New Harbinger Publications, believes in their motto "psychology you can use from professionals you can trust." Libraries are not complete without Impact Publishers titles. It produces a select list of psychology and self-improvement books and audio and video recordings for adults, children, families, professionals, organizations, and communities by highly respected psychologists and other human service professionals.

Freelance Potential: Publishes 5–10 titles annually. Receives 60–70 queries monthly.

Nonfiction: Middle-grade, YA, adult. Topics: emotional development, self-esteem, self-expression, marriage, divorce, careers, social issues, parenting, child development and behavior, health and wellness, practical therapy on parenting, divorce recovery, stress, personal growth, and mental health.

Submissions and Payment: Guidelines and catalogue available on website. Writers must be licensed professionals. Query with letter of introduction, prospectus, table of contents, 2–3 sample paragraphs, and the author's background. Accepts hard copy or email queries to proposals@newharbinger.com. Responds in 2–3 months. Royalty.

Love and Logic Press

2207 Jackson Street, Golden, CO 80401-2300. www.loveandlogic.com

Acquisitions

Loving yet powerful tools for parenting children of all ages are what Love and Logic Press provides. It has been dedicated to making parenting and teaching fun and rewarding, instead of stressful and chaotic. It helps parents raise self-confident children who are ready for the real world. It is the approach of choice among leading educators, parents, and other professionals worldwide. Love and Logic Press provides practical tools and techniques that help adults achieve respectful, healthy relationships with their children.

Freelance Potential: Publishes 8–10 titles annually: all are assigned.

Nonfiction: Adults. Topics: parenting, family, discipline, education, social issues.

Submissions and Payment: Catalogue available on website. All work is assigned. Send résumé only. No queries or unsolicited manuscripts.

Magination Press

750 First Street NE, Washington, DC 20002-4242. https://www.apa.org/pubs/magination/

Director: Kristine Enderle
Managing Editor: Darcie Conner Johnston

Magination Press publishes psychology-based books covering a broad range of topics of concern to children and teens. It is an imprint of the American Psychological Association. Magination Press was created out of a desire to publish innovative books that would help children deal with the many challenges and problems they face as they grow up. Written for ages 4–18, these books deal with topics ranging from the everyday—starting school, shyness, normal fears, and a new baby in the house—to more serious problems such as divorce, attention deficit disorder, depression, serious injury or illness, autism, trauma, death, and much more. This publisher encourages potential authors to include a "genuine, warm, and personal cover letter" so they can get a feel for who the author is.

Freelance Potential: Publishes 18–20 titles annually: 1–10% developed from unsolicited submissions; 90% assigned; 10% by authors who are new to the publishing house; 1–10% by previously unpublished writers. Receives 75–100 unsolicited manuscripts monthly.

Fiction: Story picture books. Topics: real life, social issues, family issues, social skills, mental health.

Nonfiction: Middle-grade, YA. Topics: divorce, ADHD/ADD, learning disabilities, depression, death, anxieties, self-esteem, family matters, real life/problems, self-help, social issues, social skills, mental health, workbooks.

Submissions and Payment: Guidelines and catalogue available on website. Send complete manuscript with résumé, synopsis, market analysis, author credentials, and intended audience. Accepts email submissions to kenderle@apa.org. Responds if interested. Publication in 18–24 months. Royalty.

New Harbinger Publications

5674 Shattuck Avenue, Oakland, CA 94609. www.newharbinger.com

Acquisitions Director: Catharine Meyers

New Harbinger Publications is an independent publisher of books on psychology, health, spirituality, and personal growth. New Harbinger's self-help books and workbooks are grounded in science, careful research, and a tradition of empirically validated clinical practice. It has brought readers effective, scientifically sound self-help books that deal with a range of topics in psychology, health, and personal growth for more than 40 years. Its self-help books teach skills to use to significantly improve the quality of one's life.

Freelance Potential: Publishes 60 titles (7 juvenile) annually: about 60% developed from unsolicited submissions; 40% by agented authors; 10% reprint/licensed properties; 60% by authors who are new to the publishing house; 75% by previously unpublished writers. Receives 50 queries, 50 manuscripts each month.

Nonfiction: Step-by-step, evidence-based self-help and therapeutic workbooks for children, young adults, and adults. Topics: communication, divorce, adoption, pregnancy, ADHD, autism, sensory processing disorder, depression, social anxiety, eating disorders, self-injury, self-control. Also publishes parenting titles.

Submissions and Payment: Guidelines and catalogue available on website. Send 2- to 3-page prospectus only (no manuscripts) explaining your primary and secondary audiences, the precise problem the book addresses, new or breakthrough techniques it covers, and 3 key selling points, along with a table of contents, 1–3 chapters, analysis of the competition, estimated completion date, and résumé. Accepts hard copy (to the attention of the acquisitions department) and email to proposals@newharbinger.com. SASE. Responds in 2–3 months. Publication in 9 months. Royalty; advance. Flat fee.

New Horizon Press

P.O. Box 669, Far Hills, NJ 07931. www.newhorizonpressbooks.com

Submissions: Ms. P. Patty

New Horizon Press is focused on true crime as well as psychological and social problems, women's and men's issues, and parenting advice written by experts with credentials in their fields. The catalogue from New Horizon Press features self-help titles for children on contemporary social and emotional issues, and books for parents on family relationships. It publishes books for general and specialized audiences. It looks for submissions that fit its 60 Second series as well as targeted self-help topics and hard-hitting issues with news impact and publicity value.

Freelance Potential: Publishes 12 titles (1 juvenile) annually: about 40% developed from unsolicited submissions; 100% by authors who are new to the publishing house; 90% by previously unpublished writers. Receives 141 queries, 125 unsolicited manuscripts monthly.

Nonfiction: Publishes self-help titles for children and adults on family, parenting, and relationship issues.

Submissions and Payment: Guidelines and catalogue available on website. Query or send manuscript (partial manuscript acceptable for previously published nonfiction authors) with cover letter, title page, table of contents, overview, chapter-by-chapter outline, author photograph, author bio, marketing outlook, competitive titles, and promotion outlets. Accepts email for queries only to nhp@newhorizonpressbooks.com; include "Attn: Ms. P. Patty" in the subject line and hard copy. SASE. Response time, publication period, and payment policy vary.

New Society Publishers

P.O. Box 189, Gabriola Island, British Columbia V0R 1X0 Canada. www.newsociety.com

Editor: Ingrid Witvoet

New Society Publishers is driven by the ideal of a healthy, just, and diverse world of ecological integrity, where everyone has the opportunity to thrive. It has been publishing books to build a new society for over 30 years. They help you to know the talk, and walk the talk. It looks for cutting edge ideas, analyses that are hard to find, and books that offer inspiration for daily struggles.

Freelance Potential: Publishes 25 titles annually: 60% by authors who are new to the publishing house; 25% by previously unpublished writers. Receives 25 queries monthly.

Nonfiction: YA. Topics: the environment, conflict resolution, social responsibility, democratic behavior in young people. Also publishes parenting titles.

Submissions and Payment: Guidelines and catalogue available on website. Query with an annotated table of contents; sample chapter; and a proposal detailing what the book is about, author credentials, competitive titles, unique qualities of your book, why you are choosing New Society Publishers, target audience, your plans for promotion, number of copies you plan to purchase, book length, and target completion date. Accepts email to editor@newsociety.com (Word or PDF attachments) and hard copy. SAE/IRC. Responds in 6–8 weeks. Publication in 1 year. Payment policy varies.

New World Library

14 Pamaron Way, Novato, CA 94949. www.newworldlibrary.com

Submissions Editor: Jonathan Wichmann

New World Library has published books and audios that inspire and challenge us to improve the quality of our lives and our world for over 35 years. The ultimate goal of the company is a sweeping one: personal and planetary transformation—awakening both individual consciousness and global social potential by publishing inspirational and practical materials in spirituality, personal growth, and other related areas. Many of its books are categorized as New Age. At this time it is not accepting manuscripts for children.

Freelance Potential: Publishes 35 titles annually. Receives many queries monthly.

Nonfiction: Adult. Topics: spirituality, personal growth, women's issues, sustainable business, human-animal relationships, Native American interests, the environment, parenting.

Submissions and Payment: Guidelines and catalogue available on website. Send a brief synopsis; an outline or table of contents; at least 2–3 sample chapters including any introduction or preface; a market assessment (a list of competing books and how your book is different); and a detailed statement of author credentials and biographical information. Please do not send original artwork, as publisher cannot be responsible for it. Instead, recommended you send only copies of artwork, when appropriate. Not accepting children's book manuscripts. Also, not accepting audio projects. Prefers email to submit@newworldlibrary.com (Word or PDF attachments). Accepts simultaneous submissions. Responds only if interested. Publication in 12–18 months. Payment policy varies; contracts negotiated on a case-by-case basis.

Pinter and Martin 🌐

6 Effra Parade, London, SW2 1PS, United Kingdom. www.pinterandmartin.com

Publishing Manager: Zoe Hutton

Pinter and Martin publish authors who challenge the status quo. They feature titles on parenting, breastfeeding, health, and nutrition. Specializing in psychology, pregnancy, birth and parenting, and yoga, it also publishes a limited number of titles for children, as well as general nonfiction for adults.

Freelance Potential: Publishes about 15–20 titles annually.

Nonfiction: Publishes parenting titles on pregnancy, childbirth, health, and yoga.

Submissions and Payment: Guidelines and catalogue available on website. Query with sample chapters, author credentials, and target audience. Only accepts children's books from a writer/illustrator team. Accepts email queries to submissions@pinterandmain.com. Responds in 4 weeks. Payment policy and rates vary.

Rainbow Books, Inc.

P.O. Box 430, Highland City, FL 33846-0430. www.rainbowbooksinc.com

Acquisitions Editor

Rainbow Books has published hundreds of books, mostly in the self-help and how-to nonfiction categories. Nonfiction titles that build self-esteem and improve coping mechanisms in school-age kids, improve parenting skills and help build family relationships, how-to and self-help nonfiction by credentialed authors, travel books (especially hiking memoir with a how-to component), and a limited line of fiction (mostly metaphysical mysteries, medical mysteries, cozy mysteries, and YA mysteries) make up this publisher's catalogue. All titles are also produced as e-books.

Freelance Potential: Publishes about 10 titles (2 juvenile) annually: 50% developed from unsolicited submissions; 1–10% by agented authors; about 50% by authors who are new to the company; about 25% by previously unpublished writers. Receives 25–35 queries monthly.

Fiction: YA, adults. Topics: Cozy mysteries, medical mysteries, historical fiction.

Nonfiction: YA, adults. Topics: how-to, parenting, family, relationships, self-esteem, self-help, travel.

Submissions and Payment: Query with cover letter, 1-page synopsis, up to 3 sample chapters, description of photos or illustrations, author bio to include any publishing credits, and approximate word count of final work. Accepts hard copy or email to submissions@rainbowbooksinc.com; will not open any attached files. Completed works only. Include SASE if material is to be returned. Responds in 6 weeks. Publication in 1 year. Royalty: 15% percent on the net on physical copies, 25% on actual cash received for e-books. Payment January and July.

Square One Publishers

115 Herricks Road, Garden City, NY 11040. www.squareonepublishers.com

Acquisitions Editor

Titles from Square One Publishers aim to be accessible, accurate, interesting, and smartly written with a strong point of view by authors who know their subjects well. Its goal is to provide an accessible starting point for people who want to know more. Square One specializes in adult nonfiction books providing information that is designed to meet the needs of specific audiences including parents.

Freelance Potential: Publishes 15 titles annually: 65% developed from unsolicited submissions; 35% by authors who are new to the publishing house; 55% by previously unpublished writers. Receives 100 queries monthly.

Nonfiction: Self-help and how-to books for adults. Topics: pregnancy, childbirth, infant care, food and nutrition, history, parenting, social issues, health and fitness, religious.

Submissions and Payment: Guidelines and catalogue available on website. Query with a cover letter explaining the concept of your book, why you wrote it, and its intended audience; detailed table of contents; brief overview of the book; and author bio. Accepts hard copy. SASE. Responds in 4–6 weeks. Publication period varies. Royalty.

Woodbine House

6510 Bells Mill Road, Bethesda, MD 20817. www.woodbinehouse.com

Acquisitions Editor

Woodbine House specializes in books that are created by parents and professionals who have dedicated their lives to making the world a better place for people with disabilities. The books from Woodbine House target parents, children, therapists, health care providers, and teachers. Prefers authors to have experience with children with special needs. It is currently looking for parents' guides to disabilities, reference books on disability topics, and memoirs. They are not looking for fiction with the exception of children's picture books.

Freelance Potential: Publishes 4–8 titles annually.

Fiction: Concept books for preschoolers, story picture books for ages 3–8. No chapter books. Topics: developmental and intellectual disabilities. Please do not try to adapt a book you have written for a general audience by merely putting a character in a wheelchair.

Nonfiction: Guides and reference books for parents and professionals and an occasional memoir. Topics: autism spectrum disorders, Down syndrome, Tourette syndrome, executive dysfunction, and other developmental disabilities.

Submissions and Payment: Guidelines and catalogue available on website. For nonfiction, query with table of contents, 2–3 sample chapters, an annotated list of competitive titles with an explanation of how your book differs, potential markets, author qualifications, published or unpublished writing samples, and estimated length and completion date. For children's fiction, send complete manuscript, including a few representative illustrations. Accepts hard copy only. Accepts simultaneous submissions if identified. SASE. Responds in 3 months. Publication in 18 months. Payment policy varies.

Wyatt-MacKenzie Publishing

15115 Highway 36, Deadwood, OR 97430. www.wymacpublishing.com

Publisher: Nancy Cleary

Wyatt-MacKenzie has published hundreds of products over the last 23 years with a special focus on women writers. It has been an award-winning independent press. Along with traditional publishing, Wyatt-MacKenzie also has self-publishing, imprint, and editorial consulting services available.

Freelance Potential: Publishes 5–8 titles annually.

Fiction: Adult. Genres: contemporary, mystery, realistic.

Nonfiction: Adult. Topics: parenting, child development, social issues, business, careers, multicultural, health, relationships, biography.

Submissions and Payment: Guidelines and catalogue available on website. Accepts proposals from agented writers as well as unsolicited submissions. Accepts hard copy and email to nancy@wyattmackenzie.com (put "Major Release" in subject line). Response time, publication period, and payment policies vary.

Religious Publishing for Children & Families

Religious publishing embraces books of almost every kind, from the earliest board books to young adult fiction, from biblical education to inspiring adolescents in faith or spirituality. In the last few decades, religious publishing has expanded mightily. It has also moved well beyond a reputation for rather narrow and, truth be told, often second-rate books.

Today, religious publishing is like any other segment of the industry. Much of it is very high quality, and some companies cover many, many subjects. Other companies take a tight focus on particular religious topics and genres, and require that their books reflect specific tenets.

Look here for what interests you: mainstream companies open-ended in their need for religious, spiritual, or inspirational books for children and adults, or more denominational publishers with beliefs and goals that match your own beliefs and writing interests.

Abingdon Press

2222 Rosa L. Park Blvd., Nashville, TN 37202. www.abingdonpress.com

Manuscript Submissions

Abingdon Press is the place for readers to go for every conversation on faith. It publishes a wide array of high-caliber, academic, professional, inspirational, and life-affirming religious literature to enrich church communities around the globe. As an imprint of The United Methodist Publishing House, Abingdon Press continues to bring its readers thought-provoking and enjoyable books, while committing to providing the best, most effective religious publications available.

Freelance Potential: Publishes about 10 titles annually. Receives 50 queries monthly.

Nonfiction: Board books, middle-grade, YA. Topics: religion, holidays, education, theology, activities, puzzles.

Submissions and Payment: Guidelines and catalogue available on website. Fiction submissions only accepted from agents and writers met at writers conferences. For nonfiction, query with outline and 1–2 sample chapters (30 pages maximum). All curriculum writing is done on assignment by active members of the United Methodist Church. Accepts email to umpublishing.submittable.com. No simultaneous submissions. Responds in 2 months. Publication in 2 years. Royalty.

ACTA Publications

4848 North Clark Street, Chicago, IL 60640. www.actapublications.com

Acquisitions Editor

Most of ACTA's titles are meant to be given as gifts, both on special occasions or to people who are going through specific life situations or stages. ACTA Publications is a publisher of books and audio/video resources for religious education and spiritual development. While ACTA Publications publishes many books that are strictly of Catholic nature, it has broadened its scope to include an ecumenical audience. It has also broadened its editorial scope to include sports; social justice and community organizing; caregiving, grief, and mourning; storytelling and novels; and children's books, all with a Christian theme. ACTA Publications also offers books and video resources for Catholic religious education and marriage preparation.

Freelance Potential: Publishes about 8-10 titles annually: most developed from unsolicited submissions and by agented authors. Receives 12 queries monthly.

Nonfiction: Story picture books, YA. Topics: sports, religion, parenting, education, divorce, grief, self-help, contemporary social issues, theology, history—all with a Christian theme.

Submissions and Payment: Guidelines and catalogue available on website. Query with table of contents, sample chapter, author credentials, and cover letter that describes the audience for your book. Accepts simultaneous submissions if identified. SASE. Responds in 8–12 weeks. Publication time varies. Royalty, 10%.

AMG Publishers

6815 Shallowford Road, Chattanooga, TN 37421. www.amgpublishers.com

Acquisitions: Amanda Jenkins

AMG Publishers looks for books that give a hunger to studying and understanding scripture. Since its inception, AMG Publishers has become a leader in Christian publishing with the Hebrew-Greek Key Word Study Bible, award-winning youth fiction, exhaustive reference, multiple Bible studies, and patriotic literature. It publishes under the imprints AMG Publishers, Living Ink Books, and God and Country Press. AMG Publishers' focus is to help the reader get into the Bible, directly or indirectly, encourage personal growth and change through the Scriptures, and develop a hunger for studying, understanding, and applying scripture.

Freelance Potential: Publishes about 30 titles (12 juvenile) annually: 50% by agented authors; 20% reprint/licensed properties; about 30% by authors who are new to the publishing house; about 30% by previously unpublished writers. Receives 100 queries monthly.

Fiction: Chapter books, middle-grade, YA. Genres: fantasy, contemporary with Christian themes.

Nonfiction: Middle-grade, YA, adult. Topics: Bible study materials, devotionals, inspirational, history, real life, parenting, family life.

Submissions and Payment: Guidelines and catalogue available on website. Query with brief book description including proposed page count, target audience, and author credentials. Accepts email queries to sales@amgpublishers.com. Response time and publication period vary. Royalty; advance.

Ancient Faith Publishing

P.O. Box 748, Chesterton, IN 46304. http://ancientfaith.com

Children's Acquisitions Editor: Jane Meyer

Ancient Faith Publishing is one of the largest, most valued resources for Orthodox books and other materials in the English-speaking world. It exists to carry out the Great Commission of Jesus Christ through accessible and excellently crafted publications and creative media that educate, edify, and evangelize, leading to a living experience of God through His Holy Orthodox Church. It offers books for children and adults. Its mission is to embrace the fullness of the Orthodox faith, encourage discipleship of believers, equip the faithful for ministry, and evangelize the unchurched. Its editors look for accessible, well-crafted books. This publisher's middle-grade/YA fiction reflects an Orthodox Christian worldview and lifestyle but is not moralistic or pedantic. It only considers submissions by Eastern Orthodox Christians with specifically Orthodox subject matter.

Freelance Potential: Publishes 1–4 titles annually: 50–75% developed from unsolicited submissions; 25–50% by authors who are new to the publishing house; 25–50% by previously unpublished writers. Receives 1–10 queries, 1–10 unsolicited manuscripts monthly.

Fiction: Toddler books, picture books, early picture books, story picture books, middle-grade, YA. Genres: coming-of-age, historical fiction, multicultural, real life/problems. All fiction must have strong Orthodox content, showing God at work in children's lives, or the Orthodox Christian worldview and lifestyle.

Nonfiction: Toddler books, early picture books, story picture books, middle-grade, YA. Genres: church life or history, lives of saints, Bible stories, biographies, holidays, practical theology about living out the Orthodox faith in contemporary life.

Submissions and Payment: Guidelines and catalogue available on website, http://www.ancientfaith.com/publishing#af-resources. Query with brief description of the book, intended audience, author qualifications, projected word count, and completion date. Accepts email queries only with "AFP Submission" and your surname in the subject line (Word or RTF attachments) to jmeyer@ancientfaith.com. Accepts simultaneous submissions. Responds to queries in 1 month, requested manuscripts in 6 months. Publication period, 12–24 months. Royalty.

Augsburg Fortress

P.O. Box 1209, Minneapolis, MN 55440. www.augsburgfortress.org

Acquisitions Editor

Augsburg Fortress develops engaging resources for Lutheran congregations. Augsburg Fortress is committed to the development and publication of resources to support the ministry of congregations in the areas of worship and music, adult education and leadership, and resources for children.

Freelance Potential: Publishes 20 titles annually.

Fiction: Toddler books, early picture books, early readers, story picture books. Genres: religious, real life/problems, inspirational.

Nonfiction: Concept books, early readers, story picture books. Topics: devotionals, Bible storybooks, religious holidays.

Submissions and Payment: Catalogue available on website. Query with outline or send complete manuscript. Accepts email submissions to afsubmissions@augsburgfortress.org (MS Word or PDF). Response time and publication period vary. Royalty; advance.

Ave Maria Press

P.O. Box 428, Notre Dame, IN 46556. www.avemariapress.com

Acquisitions Department

This Catholic book publisher is owned by the United States Province of the Congregation of Holy Cross. It serves the spiritual and educational needs of individuals, groups, and the church as a whole. It perpetuates the vision to honor Mary and provides an important outlet for good Catholic writing. While many of its books address a wide ecumenical readership, its primary interest is in books for Catholics and Catholic institutions. Ave Maria is also recognized as a leader in publishing Catholic high school religion textbooks, parish resources, and books on prayer and spirituality. Familiar topics with a fresh twist will catch this publisher's eye.

Freelance Potential: Publishes about 40 titles annually: a very few developed from unsolicited submissions; some by agented authors; a very few by authors who are new to the publishing house. Receives 15 queries, 25+ manuscripts monthly.

Nonfiction: Adult. Topics: catechism, Christian living, prayer, relationships, religion, sacraments, spirituality, education, youth ministry.

Submissions and Payment: A single document that offers a working title and subtitle, a single paragraph describing the work, your reflections on why and how your book is unique, a short author biography (not your complete CV), an annotated table of contents, and a sample of the writing (not the entire manuscript) — preferably the introduction and/or chapter one. There are a number of areas in which it does not accept unsolicited manuscripts: fiction (for adults or teens), children's books (fiction or nonfiction), poetry, and accounts of personal conversion or private revelation. Paper submissions not returned. You must provide a valid email address for contact. Accepts simultaneous submissions if identified. Does not return unsolicited materials. Responds in 6–8 weeks.

Baker Publishing Group

Baker Publishing Group, 6030 East Fulton Road, Ada, MI 49301. www.bakerpublishinggroup.com

Editor

Baker Publishing Group has a vision for building up the body of Christ through books that are relevant, intelligent, and engaging. It publishes high-quality writings that represent historic Christianity and serve the diverse interests and concerns of evangelical readers. This Christian publisher is made up of several divisions, including Baker Books, Bethany House, Revell Books, and other academic and theological divisions. Bethany House publishes Christian fiction, children's fiction and nonfiction, and books on family, health, theology, and devotionals. It is currently not accepting unsolicited submissions; check website for changes to this policy.

Freelance Potential: Publishes hundreds of books annually.

Fiction: Middle-grade, YA, adult. Genres: animals, religious, holidays, girls, people and places, sports. For adults: Christian, romance, historical, contemporary, fantasy, men's, women's, psychological, suspense, humor, mysteries.

Nonfiction: Middle-grade, YA, adult. Topics: religion, Bible stories, biography, history, family, home, health, crafts, cooking, current events, education, parenting, pets, relationships, self-help, sports.

Submissions and Payment: Baker Publishing accepts unsolicited manuscripts only through agents; at conferences where Baker staff participates; or through the manuscript services Authonomy.com, Writer's Edge (www.writersedgeservice.com), or Christian Manuscript Submissions, an online service of the Evangelical Christian Publishers Association (www.christian-manuscriptsubmissions.com). Response time and publication period vary. Royalty, 15% of net.

B&H Kids

One Life Way Plaza, Nashville, TN 37234. www.bhpublishinggroup.com

Submissions

B&H Kids creates Bible-centered, age-appropriate, engaging content for kids. From board books to Bibles, our resources are designed to help kids develop a lifelong relationship with Jesus and to empower parents to guide their child's spiritual growth.

Freelance Potential: Publishes 20 books annually.

Fiction: Story picture books, early readers, YA. Genres: Bible stories, inspirational, romance.

Nonfiction: YA. Topics: theology, the Bible, prayer, contemporary issues, history, current events, devotionals, real life/problems, evangelizing, missions.

Submissions and Payment: Agented authors only. Must go through an agent and agent will submit proposal.

B&H Publishing

One LifeWay Plaza, Nashville, TN 37234-0188. www.bhpublishinggroup.com

Submissions

B&H Publishing is always working with a broad range of new and veteran writers alike. B&H Publishing Group is an imprint of LifeWay Christian Resources. B&H seeks to provide intentional, biblical content that positively impacts the hearts and minds of people, inspiring them to build a lifelong relationship with Jesus Christ. Key imprints are Holman Bibles, B&H Español, B&H Kids and B&H Academic.

Freelance Potential: Publishes 100 books annually. Receives 30 unsolicited manuscripts monthly.

Fiction: Story picture books, early readers, YA. Genres: Bible stories, inspirational, romance.

Nonfiction: YA. Topics: theology, the Bible, prayer, contemporary issues, history, current events, devotionals, real life/problems, evangelizing, missions, family.

Submissions and Payment: Agented authors only. Must go through an agent and agent will submit proposal.

Barbour Publishing

1810 Barbour Drive, Uhrichsville, OH 44683. www.barbourbooks.com

Submissions Editor

Inspiring the world with the life-changing message of the Bible is the mission of Barbour Publishing. Faithfulness to the Bible and Jesus Christ are the bedrock values behind every book Barbour's staff produces. This conservative, evangelical Christian publisher offers religious and inspirational fiction and nonfiction for toddlers through teens. It also publishes biblical reference books for a variety of ages and general titles for adults. Submissions must come via an agent.

Freelance Potential: Publishes about 150 titles (30 juvenile) annually.

Fiction: Toddler books, story picture books, early readers, middle-grade, YA. Genres: historical, adventure, mystery, contemporary, Bible stories.

Nonfiction: Story picture books, middle-grade, YA. Topics: holidays, biography, the Bible, inspiration, prayer, self-help, real life, sports, puzzles, activities, devotionals.

Submissions and Payment: Guidelines and catalogue available on website. Does not accept unsolicited proposals, must go through an agent. Query with cover letter, synopsis, and part of manuscript to show writing ability. Accepts email queries only to submissions@barbourbooks.com. Accepts simultaneous submissions, if identified. Responds in 4–6 months. Publication period varies. Royalty; advance.

Behrman House

241B Millburn Avenue, Millburn, NJ 07041. www.behrmanhouse.com

Editorial Committee

Behrman House family has served the educational needs of the Jewish community for almost a century. It publishes materials, books, apps, and lesson plans for preschool through high school students. Resources are geared to different instructional methods of educators and the varied needs and learning styles of students. Behrman also produces books about Jewish life, holidays, history, and traditions.

Freelance Potential: Publishes about 10 titles annually. Receives 4 queries, 4 unsolicited manuscripts each month.

Nonfiction: Early picture books, chapter books, middle-grade, YA. Topics: Judaism, religion, theology, prayer, holidays, the Bible, the Holocaust, history, liturgy, Hebrew, Israel, social issues, ethics.

Submissions and Payment: Catalogue available on website. Query with cover letter, intended audience, table of contents and sample chapters. Prefers email to customersupport@behrmanhouse.com (Word documents). Accepts hard copy. Accepts simultaneous submissions if identified. Responds in 1 month. Publication in 18 months. Royalty, 3–10%; advance, $1,500. Flat fee.

Bethany House Publishers

Baker Publishing Group, 6030 East Fulton Road, Ada, MI 49301. www.bethanyhouse.com

Submissions Editor

Bethany House publishes nonfiction books to help evangelical readers deepen their relationships with God and other people. For the past 40 years, Bethany has also been a leading publisher of Christian fiction. Bethany House is part of the Baker Publishing Group, whose other divisions include Baker Books, Baker Academic, Brazos Press, Chosen Books, and Revell.

Freelance Potential: Publishes approximately 85 titles annually: 100% by agented authors or authors using Christian submission services; 20% by authors who are new to the publishing house.

Fiction: Adult. Genres: historical, Amish, contemporary, romance, suspense, fantasy, inspirational.

Nonfiction: Adult. Topics: devotionals, the Bible, history, biography, personal growth, Christian living, theology, leadership.

Submissions and Payment: Accepts manuscripts only through agents, conferences where Baker staff participates, or the manuscript services Writer's Edge (www.writersedgeservice.com) or Christian Manuscript Submissions, an online service of the Evangelical Christian Publishers Association (www.christianmanuscriptsubmissions.com). Response time, publication period, and payment policy vary.

Bridge Logos Foundation

14260W Newberry Road, Newberry, FL 32669. www.bridgelogos.com

Acquisitions Editor: Suzi Woolridge

For over 50 years Bridge Logos has been providing inspirational fiction and nonfiction titles for children, teens, and adults. Its mission is to publish titles that honor and glorify God. Its titles cover Christian living, social issues, evangelism, and theology. While Bridge Logos is not a vanity publisher, it may require new authors without an established marketing platform to pre-purchase books. It is not currently accepting children's submissions.

Freelance Potential: Publishes 20–24 titles annually: 15% by agented authors, 40% by authors new to the publishing house, 40% by previously unpublished writers. Receives 75 queries, 50 mss yearly.

Fiction: Picture books, chapter books, YA. Genres: fantasy, contemporary, historical, inspirational, multicultural, religious, romance, science fiction, Westerns.

Nonfiction: Picture books, early readers, YA. Topics: creation, theology, biography, religious, inspirational, real life/problems, self-help.

Submissions and Payment: Guidelines and catalogue available on website. Query or send complete manuscript with proposal letter that includes summary and approximate word count, market analysis, and author biography, including professional background and previously published works. Prefers email queries with Word attachments to swooldridge@bridgelogos.com; payment must be mailed ahead. Responds in 12 weeks. Publication in 1 year. Payment policy varies.

Cedar Fort

2373 West 700 South, Springville, UT 84663. www.cedarfort.com

Acquisitions Manager: Angela Johnson

The mission at Cedar Fort is to gather and develop books as products that are uplifting and life-enhancing. For over 30 years, Cedar Fort has been publishing a solid catalog of LDS fiction and nonfiction, general release titles, including cookbooks, clean romance, and young adult adventures, and an LDS-oriented product line. Imprints include Council Press (historical Western fiction and nonfiction); Front Table Books (cookbooks), Hobble Creek Press (Dutch oven/outdoor cooking); Sweetwater Books (fiction); Bonneville Book (LDS fiction all ages), King Dragon Press (martial arts) and Plain Sight Publishing (nonfiction). It is currently looking for young adult LDS fiction.

Freelance Potential: Publishes 158 titles annually: 50–75% developed from unsolicited submissions; approximately 6% by agented authors; 66% by authors who are new to the publishing house; 57% by previously unpublished writers. Receives 75+ manuscripts monthly.

Fiction: Chapter books, middle-grade, YA. Genres: adventure, fantasy, contemporary, coming of age, historical, humor, realistic, multicultural, romance, sports, political thrillers.

Nonfiction: YA. Topics: history, religion, self-help, biography, crafts, games/puzzles, health, holidays, nature, cookbooks, gardening, LDS doctrine. Also publishes books for adults.

Submissions and Payment: Guidelines and catalogue available on website. Query with synopsis, table of contents, manuscript submissions form from website, and first 3 chapters; or send complete manuscript with résumé, author bio, and manuscript submission form from website. Currently only accepting electronic submissions through submittable.com at https://cedarfort.submittable.com/submit. Accepts simultaneous submissions. Response time, 4-6 months. Royalty, escalated scale.

Christian Focus Publications 🌐

Geanies House, Fearn, Tain, Ross-shire IV20 ITW Scotland, United Kingdom. www.christianfocus.com

Children's Editor: Catherine Mackenzie

Christian Focus Publications (CFP) seeks to impact the world through literature faithful to God's infallible word. It is all about the message of the Gospel. Although CFP is distinctively evangelical and conservative in nature, CFP is not a denominational publisher. Christian Focus Publications focuses on the message of God's word communicated in the Bible. Christian Focus Publications has four imprints: Christian Focus (adult), CF4K (children), Christian Heritage (classic books) and Mentor (thought-provoking).

Freelance Potential: Publishes about 80 titles (40 juvenile) annually: 1–10% developed from unsolicited submissions; 1–10% by agented authors; 1–10% reprint/licensed properties; 1–10% by authors who are new to the publishing house; 1–10% by previously unpublished writers. Receives 20 queries, 20 unsolicited manuscripts monthly.

Fiction: Toddler books, early picture books, story picture books, early readers, chapter books, middle-grade, YA. Genres: contemporary, religious, real life/problems, historical.

Nonfiction: Toddler books, early readers, story picture books, chapter books, middle-grade, YA. Topics: the Bible, biographies, devotionals, puzzles, activities.

Submissions and Payment: Guidelines and catalogue available on website. Query with author information sheet (available on website), synopsis, and 3 sample chapters. Send complete manuscript for works under 10 chapters. Prefers email to catherine.mackenzie@christianfocus.com (children's editor). For adult submissons may send via email to submission@christianfocus.com. Accepts hard copy. Only will return submissions if postage is included. Responds in 3–6 months. Publication period and payment policies vary.

Concordia Publishing House

3558 South Jefferson Avenue, St. Louis, MO 63118. www.cph.org

Managing Editor for Books: Laura Lane

Concordia Publishing House is the publishing arm of the Lutheran church. It aims to reach the world with God's word. Its mission is to provide doctrinally sound materials for churches and individuals. Concordia offers books and other resources that are faithful to the Scriptures and the Lutheran Confessions to families, congregations, and church school teachers.

Freelance Potential: Publishes 50–75 titles annually: all on assignment. Receives 120 queries monthly.

Fiction: Middle-grade, YA. Genres: contemporary, coming of age, religious, real life.

Nonfiction: Early picture books, early readers, story picture books, middle-grade, YA. Topics: faith, religious holidays, prayer, spirituality, Bible studies, social issues, biography. Also publishes religious education resources and devotionals.

Submissions and Payment: Guidelines and catalogue available on website. Submit a proposal package that includes peer review proposal form, résumé, summary, outline or table of contents, sample chapter. Accepts email to laura.lare@cph.org (Word or PDF attachments only). Response time, publication period, and payment policies vary.

David C. Cook

4050 Lee Vance Drive, Colorado Springs, CO 80919. www.davidccook.org

Acquisitions Editor

David C. Cook has been empowering the church since 1875. It served the Global Church with life transforming materials from best-selling books and curriculum, to toys and games, and small group resources. Its titles are published in more than 150 languages and distributed in more than 170 countries. David C. Cook accepts submissions from literary agents only.

Freelance Potential: Publishes hundreds of titles annually: most by agented authors.

Fiction: Early picture books, early readers, story picture books, middle-grade. Genres: religious, real life/problems, inspirational, action/adventure, fantasy, social issues.

Nonfiction: Concept books, early readers, story picture books, middle-grade, YA, devotionals, Bible storybooks. Topics: the Bible, Christianity, Christian living, inspirational, biography.

Submissions and Payment: Catalogue available on website. Accepts submissions from literary agents only. Will consider proposals submitted in response to select invitations extended at writers' conferences. Response time and publication period vary. Royalty; advance.

Covenant Communications

1226 South 630 East, Suite #4, American Fork, UT 84003. www.covenant-lds.com

Submissions Editor: Ashley Gebert

This division of Deseret Book Corporation was founded more than fifty years ago. It features many kinds of books including adult fiction and nonfiction, children's books, and holiday books, all representing the values espoused by The Church of Jesus Christ of Latter-day Saints. At this time it is particularly interested in historical and contemporary romance, romantic suspense, and inspirational nonfiction.

Freelance Potential: Publishes 50 titles (6 juvenile) annually: 100% developed from unsolicited submissions.

Fiction: Concept books, toddler books, early picture books, adult. Genres: adventure, suspense, historical, romance.

Nonfiction: Concept books, toddler books, story picture books. Topics: Bible stories, history, religion, regional, biography, activity, reference books.

Submissions and Payment: Guidelines and catalogue available on website. Send complete manuscript; cover letter indicating fiction or nonfiction, the intended audience, what makes the proposed book distinct, and the LDS elements of your work; author biography, especially in relation to the book topic; and author questionnaire (downloadable from the website). Prefers email submissions with Word attachments to submissionsdesk@covenant-lds.com. Responds in 4–6 months. Publication in 6–12 months. Royalties vary by contract.

Crossroad Publishing

831 Chestnut Ridge Road, Chestnut Ridge, NY 10977. www.crossroadpublishing.com

Editor

Crossroad Publishing is always seeking new projects that use the power of words to awaken wisdom in readers. Its expertise and passion are to provide healthy spiritual nourishment through the written word. The books from Crossroad Publishing Company are consistent with basic Judeo-Christian values, advocate dignity of life, and aim to share the rich experience of the Catholic people.

Freelance Potential: Publishes about 50+ titles annually: many by agented authors.

Nonfiction: Parents. Topics: religion, parenting, family.

Submissions and Payment: Guidelines and catalogue available on website. Query with proposed title, a 40-word sales pitch, 2- to 3-paragraph description of the project, approximate length and author bio, endorsements, intended audience, finished manuscript. Accepts proposals by email only to submissions@crossroadpublishing.com. Response 6–8 weeks. Publication period varies. Royalty; advance.

Crossway

1300 Crescent Street, Wheaton, IL 60187. www.crossway.org

Editorial Administrator: Jill Carter

The mission of Crossway is to remain faithful to the "gospel-centered" vision that the Lord has entrusted them. The books from Crossway are thoroughly evangelical in perspective. Its titles bear witness to God's truth, beauty, and holiness, as well as to the Lordship of Christ in every area of life. It publishes titles for all ages to help people understand the massive implications of the gospel and the truth of God's Word.

Freelance Potential: Publishes 80 titles (2 juvenile) annually: 1–5% reprint or licensed properties; 1% by authors who are new to the publishing house. Receives about 5 queries and unsolicited manuscripts each month.

Nonfiction: YA. Topics: religion, church history, contemporary Christian issues, Christian living, biblical studies, parenting.

Submissions and Payment: Guidelines and catalogue available on website. Email queries to submissions@crossway.org. Do not send manuscripts. Responds within a month to request a proposal, if interested. Publication period and payment policies vary.

CSS Publishing

5450 North Dixie Highway, Lima, OH 45807. www.csspub.com

Acquisitions Editor

CSS focuses on "ready-to-use" ministry needs of congregations. It is proud to be one of the first publishers in the United States to produce preaching and worship resources that actively utilize the Revised Common Lectionary. The company has grown today into a nationally known publisher of Christian preaching and worship books, as well as other resources. It publishes resources for working with youth, children's object lessons and sermons, Lectionary-based resources for worship, preaching, group study, and drama. It does not publish books for children, but does publish children's object lessons and sermons.

Freelance Potential: Publishes 20–25 titles annually: most developed from unsolicited submissions; 1–10% by authors who are new to the publishing house; 1–10% by previously unpublished writers. Receives 10–20 queries, 10 unsolicited manuscripts monthly.

Nonfiction: Christian education materials, program planners, children's sermons, children's object lessons, pastoral aids. Topics: religious education, the Bible, prayer, worship, parenting, family life.

Submissions and Payment: Guidelines and catalogue available on website. Mail query with 1- to 2-page summary, author bio, marketing information about the proposed audience and how it may be reached, and 1–2 sample chapters. Also accepts email queries to editor@csspub.com, with no attachments; will respond if interested. Publication in 1 year. Payment policy varies.

Eerdmans Books for Young Readers

4035 Park East Court SE, Grand Rapids, MI 49546. www.eerdmans.com/youngreaders

Acquisitions Editor

Eerdmans Books for Young Readers is an imprint of Wm. B. Eerdmans Publishing Company. The company has developed a reputation for publishing excellent literary and intellectual works from across the religious spectrum. Offering board books, picture books, middle readers, novels, nonfiction, and religious titles for children and young adults, Eerdmans Books for Young Readers seeks to engage young minds with books—books that are honest, wise, and hopeful; books that delight us with their storyline, characters, or good humor; books that inform, inspire, and entertain. At this time, it is especially interested in stories that celebrate diversity, stories of historical significance, and stories that relate to contemporary social issues.

Freelance Potential: Publishes 12–18 titles annually: 1–10% developed from unsolicited submissions; 25–50% by agented authors; 50–75% by authors who are new to the publishing house; 10–25% by previously unpublished writers. Receives 1–25 queries, 75–100 unsolicited manuscripts monthly.

Fiction: Toddler books, early picture books, early readers, story picture books, chapter books, middle-grade, YA. Genres: adventure, multicultural, historical, folktales, coming-of-age, animals, nature, sports, real life.

Nonfiction: Picture books, middle-grade, YA. Topics: history, religion, social issues, biography.

Submissions and Payment: Guidelines and catalogue available on website. Only accepting proposals via email in PDF, MS Word, or RTF format to submissions@eerdmans.com. Include description, table of contents, résumé, and 1–2 sample chapters or completed manuscript. Accepts simultaneous submissions if identified. Responds in 2 months if interested; publication period varies. Royalty; advance.

Feldheim Publishers

208 Airport Executive Park, Nanuet, NY 10954. www.feldheim.com

Submissions Editor

Feldheim Publishers has been family owned and operated publisher since 1939. Their readers are Torah-observant Jews, and their books take their interests and sensitivities to heart. Publishes high-quality Jewish texts, as well as English translations of Hebrew texts. Accepts only quality literature that is true to the Torah. Along with texts of Jewish law, thoughts, and philosophies, Feldheim Publishers also publishes books with Jewish themes for young readers and novels for young adults.

Freelance Potential: Publishes about 40–50 titles annually.

Fiction: Early readers, middle-grade, YA. Genres: adventure, religious fiction, mystery.

Nonfiction: Early readers, middle-grade, YA. Topics: religion, memoir, biography, reference.

Submissions and Payment: Guidelines and catalog on website. Send complete manuscript. Accepts hard copy and email submissions to submissions@feldheim.com (Word documents). Responds in 3 months. Publication period and payment policies vary.

Focus on the Family Book Publishing

8605 Explorer Drive, Colorado Springs, CO 80920. www.focusonthefamily.com

Director: Larry Weeden

Focus on the Family is a global Christian ministry that believes that the purpose of life is to know and glorify God through an authentic relationship with His Son, Jesus Christ. It's dedicated to helping families thrive. It provides help and resources for couples to build healthy marriages that reflect God's design, and for parents to raise their children according to morals and values grounded in biblical principles. No matter who you are, what you're going through, or what challenges your family may be facing, Focus on the Family is here to help. Its book development division publishes books for families and a children's fiction series called Imagination Station, a spin-off of Focus on the Family Adventures in Odyssey radio dramas. In nonfiction, Focus on the Family is currently publishing books of advice on parenting, marriage, and topics for women and seniors. In fiction, it is looking for books on family issues that promote traditional values. Fiction must be set in the years between 1900 and the present day.

Freelance Potential: Publishes 15 titles (about 3 juvenile) annually: all by agented authors or from writers' conference requests; very few are by new or previously unpublished writers. Receives about 15 queries monthly.

Fiction: Chapter books. Genres: religious, social skills.

Nonfiction: Middle-grade, YA, adult. Topics: family advice, marriage, parenting, relationships, encouragement for women, life challenges.

Submissions and Payment: Agented queries only or by request from a Focus on the Family editor at a writers' conference. Guidelines available. Response time varies. Publication in 18 months. Payment policy varies.

Forward Movement

412 Sycamore Street, Cincinnati, OH 45202–4011. www.forwardmovement.org

Managing Editor

Inspiring disciples and empowering evangelists around the globe every day, Forward Movement is an official agency of The Episcopal Church. Forward Movement's flagship publication is *Forward Day by Day*, a devotional as part of the spiritual practices. In addition to *Forward Day by Day*, they publish books, pamphlets, and other materials with a focus on discipleship. Forward Movement strives to provide insightful, engaging, and accessible content on a range of topics, including prayer, spiritual practices, stewardship, church traditions, emerging trends, and Bible study. Their materials are published in a variety of manners, including print, electronic books, PDF downloads, and smartphone applications.

Freelance Potential: Publishes about 10 titles annually: about 15% developed from unsolicited submissions; 15% by authors who are new to the publishing house; 30% by previously unpublished writers. Receives 5 unsolicited manuscripts monthly.

Nonfiction: Early readers, middle-grade, YA, adult. Topics: religion, the Bible, devotionals, parenting, church, prayer, holidays, healing.

Submissions and Payment: Guidelines and catalogue available on website. Send table of contents, introduction and 1–2 sample chapters with cover letter or proposal including author bio, intended audience, and scope of the work. Accepts email to editorial@forwardmovement.org. Responds in 1–2 months. Publication period varies. Flat fee; Royalty.

Foundry Publishing

The Foundry Publishing Company, PO Box 419527, Kansas City, MO 64141. www.thefoundrypublishing.com

Product Development

The good work of The Foundry Publishing is to empower people with life-changing ways to engage in the mission of God. Foundry Publishing, the book publishing arm of Nazarene Publishing House, is a leading provider of Wesleyan Christian books, Bible studies, and Bible commentaries. The church lives in a new day and a changing time. Through encouraging literature, personal devotion, and small group resources, it equips Christ-followers with engaging books. It specializes in three genres of books: Ministerial Resources, Spiritual Formation, and Christian Care. Its mission is to provide inspiration and support with biblically sound materials that are relevant to the church's changing needs.

Freelance Potential: Publishes about 40 titles annually: about 20% developed from unsolicited submissions; 25% by authors who are new to the publishing house; 25% by previously unpublished writers. Receives many queries and unsolicited manuscripts monthly.

Nonfiction: YA, books for parents and teachers. Topics: Church of the Nazarene theology, the Bible, church history, self-help, parenting, spiritual growth, Christian living.

Submissions and Payment: For manuscript consideration, send hard copy submission to: Attention Product Development.

Franciscan Media

28 West Liberty Street, Cincinnati, OH 45202–6498. www.franciscanmedia.org

Product Development Director: Mary Carol Kendzia

To spread the Gospel in the spirit of St. Francis is the mission of Franciscan Media. Reaching millions of people around the globe with the liberating message of Jesus Christ, Franciscan Media has sought to inform and inspire Catholics and others across the globe. As a well-established Catholic publisher, it seeks to inspire the discovery, growth, and sharing of God's love. It does not publish children's books but some titles will be of interest to young adults and parents.

Freelance Potential: Publishes 20–30 titles annually: 25–35% by authors who are new to the publishing house; 10–15% by previously unpublished writers. Receives 15–25 queries monthly.

Nonfiction: YA, adult (parents, ministers, religious education teachers). Topics: Christian living, Scripture, prayer, spirituality, the saints, family, parenting, Catholic life and identity, Catholic heroes, contemporary issues, social issues, church history, parish life.

Submissions and Payment: Guidelines and catalogue available on website. Query with cover letter that indicates the topic, working title, approximate length, audience, and competition; table of contents; outline or chapter-by-chapter synopsis; 1–2 sample chapters; author biography; any endorsements; a description of your platform (social media, blog, speaking engagements, etc.); and promotion and marketing ideas. Prefers submissions through online form on website or by email to letters@franciscanmedia.org. Accepts hard copy. SASE. Responds in 2 months. Publication in 1–2 years. Royalty, 10%.

Friends United Press

101 Quaker Hill Drive, Richmond, IN 47374. https://bookstore.friendsunitedmeeting.org/

Editor

Friends United Press, a Quaker publisher, produces books that reflect the denomination's beliefs and heritage including Quaker history, biography, theology, spirituality, and inspirational titles. Friends United Press is the publishing arm of Friends United Meeting, an international association of Friends meetings and churches, whose purpose is to "energize and equip friends through the power of the Holy Spirit to gather into fellowships where Jesus Christ is known, loved, and obeyed as Teacher and Lord." While most of its offerings are designed for adults, the company publishes a number of titles that are appropriate for middle-grade and young adult readers, as well as religious curricula. It is always interested in books on peace and social justice.

Freelance Potential: Publishes 2–5 books annually: some developed from unsolicited submissions. Receives 4–5 queries monthly.

Fiction: Middle-grade, YA. Genres: historical, religious.

Nonfiction: Middle-grade, YA. Topics: Quaker history, theology, the Bible, biography, spirituality, peace, justice, African American culture, the Underground Railroad.

Submissions and Payment: Guidelines and catalogue available on website. Submit cover letter, proposal, and 2–3 sample chapters. Accepts hard copy and electronic submissions to friendspress@fum.org (Word attachments). SASE. Responds in 3 to 6 months. Publication in 1 year. Royalty, 15%.

Gefen Kids ⊕

6 Hatzvi Street, Jerusalem 94386 Israel. www.gefenpublishing.com

Editor: Ilan Greenfield

Gefen Publishing House offers a warm atmosphere of cooperation. It is a leading Israeli publisher, with a line of children's books that includes English-language fiction and nonfiction. It also publishes popular titles in Hebrew. All of its books have subjects of interest to a Jewish readership, and some of its adult books may also appeal to a young adult audience. Gefen Books is the company's US distribution partner.

Freelance Potential: Publishes 20 titles (4–5 juvenile) annually: most developed from unsolicited submissions. Receives 20 queries, 10+ unsolicited manuscripts monthly.

Fiction: Story picture books, chapter books, YA. Genres: religious, Jewish holidays, folktales, historical, social issues.

Nonfiction: Story picture books, early readers, YA. Topics: Jewish holidays, history, religion, Jewish lifestyle, the Holocaust, contemporary issues.

Submissions and Payment: Guidelines and catalog available on website. Send complete manuscript with cover letter, table of contents, 1- to 2-page synopsis, author bio, and audience description. Accepts hard copy or email submissions to info@gefenpublishing.com. Accepts simultaneous submissions. SASE. Responds in 6 months. Publication period and payment policies vary.

Group Publishing

1515 Cascade Ave., Loveland, CO 80539. www.group.com

Manuscript Submissions

Group Publishing has one goal: to help people grow in relationship with Jesus and each other. Its catalogue is filled with titles that represent that the Bible is the inspired, authoritative Word of God.

Freelance Potential: Publishes 20–30 titles annually: 10–25% developed from unsolicited submissions; 50–75% assigned; less than 10% by agented authors; 10–25% by authors who are new to the publishing company; less than 10% by previously unpublished writers. Receives 10–12 manuscripts monthly.

Nonfiction: Christian educational resources for all ages. Topics: children's sermons and worship ideas, Bible lessons and activities, crafts, devotions, games, plays and skits, leadership, volunteer management, spiritual growth, counseling, the media, current events and social issues, messages, music, retreats, parenting, technology, family ministry.

Submissions and Payment: Catalogue available on website. Query with outline, 2–3 sample chapters, and sample activities; or send complete manuscript as a Word attachment to puorgBus@group.com. No hard copy. No simultaneous submissions. Responds in 6–10 weeks. Publication period varies. Royalty, rate varies. Flat fee.

Hachai Publishing

527 Empire Boulevard, Brooklyn, NY 11225. www.hachai.com

Editor: Devorah L. Rosenfeld

This publisher is dedicated to producing high quality children's literature with Jewish themes. Its books promote universal values such as sharing, kindness and charity, and teaching Jewish history and tradition. It seeks books that convey the Jewish experience through engaging and well-crafted stories that impart a love of Hashem and an understanding of Judaism. Its books convey the traditional Jewish experience of both modern times or long ago. It is currently looking for historical fiction adventure novels for beginning readers.

Freelance Potential: Publishes 5–10 titles annually: 50–75% developed from unsolicited submissions; 25–50% assigned; 1–10% by agented authors. Receives 20 queries, 20 unsolicited manuscripts monthly.

Fiction: Early picture books, early readers, story picture books, chapter books. Genres: Jewish historical, folklore, adventure.

Nonfiction: Early picture books, story picture books, early readers, chapter books. Topics: the Torah, holidays, prayer, biography, mitzvos, middos, Jewish history.

Submissions and Payment: Guidelines and catalogue available on website. No animal stories. Query with outline and sample chapter, or send complete manuscript. Accepts hard copy and email to editor@hachai.com (no attachments). SASE. Responds in 2–6 months. Publication in 18–36 months. Flat fee.

HarperCollins Christian Publishing

501 Nelson Place, Nashville, TN 37214. www.harpercollinschristian.com

Acquisitions Editor

With nearly 300 years of experience, HarperCollins Christian Publishing, Inc. is a world-leading Christian and inspirational content provider. With imprints that include Zondervan, Zonderkidz, Tommy Nelson, and more, this division of HarperCollins focuses on publishing material with Christian themes. Representing the works of over 2,000 authors and the world's largest Bible translations, HCCP is the most award-winning inspirational publisher in the industry, publishing best-selling content in every format, connecting words and people together wherever they live, work, or play. The company produces best-selling Bibles, inspirational books, academic resources, and curriculum in both traditional and digital formats. It also recognizes the importance of being at the forefront of innovation and technology, by constantly creating unique experiences for its consumers.

Freelance Potential: Publishes hundreds of titles annually: most by agented authors. Receives 85+ submissions monthly.

Fiction: Toddler books, early picture books, early readers, story picture books, middle-grade. Genres: religious, real life/problems, inspirational, action/adventure, fantasy, social issues.

Nonfiction: Concept books, early readers, story picture books, middle-grade, YA, devotionals, Bible storybooks. Topics: the Bible, Christianity, Christian living, inspirational, biography, books of interest to girls, books of interest to boys.

Submissions and Payment: Guidelines and catalogue available on website. Only accepting submissions for Zondervan Reflective and Academic imprints. Self-publishing guidelines available. Response time and publication period vary. Royalty; advance.

Horizon Publishers

191 North 650 East, Bountiful, UT 84010-3628. www.ldshorizonpublishers.com

Manuscript Acquisition Editors: Duane Crowther, Jean Crowther

Wholesome media can be difficult to come across in today's world, but Horizon Publishers is here to provide top-notch Latter-day Saint entertainment. Horizon Publishers publish across several subject areas, including outdoor life, family preparedness, family life, crafts, cooking, writing skills, and music, but most of its books are directed toward the Latter-day Saint market. For children and teens, it wants religious education materials and fiction with LDS values.

Freelance Potential: Publishes 20–30 titles annually: most developed from unsolicited submissions and by assignment. Receives 1 unsolicited submission monthly.

Fiction: Early readers, middle-grade, YA. Genres: LDS faith, inspirational, romance, adventure, holidays.

Nonfiction: Chapter books, middle-grade, YA. Topics: Latter-day Saint life, the Mormon faith, church history, spirituality, social issues, activities, holidays, cooking, stitchery, camping, scouting, outdoor life.

Submissions and Payment: Guidelines and catalogue available on website. Currently closed to submissions. Check website for changes to this policy. Publication in 6–12 months. Royalty, 10% of wholesale.

Intervarsity Press

P.O. Box 1400, Downers Grove, IL 60515. www.ivpress.com

Academic Editor, General Editor

InterVarsity Press is the publishing arm of InterVarsity Christian Fellowship. They love the church, respect and feed on its rich heritage, and desire to serve it with grace and truth. The press publishes books that are biblically based and reflect mature understanding. It believes that the lordship of Christ must be extended over every area of life. It considers manuscripts in virtually every area in which the teachings of the Lord are thoughtfully applied. It focuses on general interest books, Bible studies, and study guides for religious education. InterVarsity is an interdenominational publisher and therefore does not publish on strictly denominational issues. It only considers unsolicited submissions if they come from pastors, professors, or previously published authors.

Freelance Potential: Publishes about 110 titles annually; about 60 academic and about 50 trade books; very few developed from unsolicited submissions; about 30% of the trade books are by agented authors; about 30% by authors who are new to the publishing house. Receives 110–120 queries monthly.

Nonfiction: YA, adult (educators, college students, parents). Topics: religion, education, how-to, reference, contemporary issues, Christian lifestyle, the Bible, the church, history, theology, doctrine, prayer, science.

Submissions and Payment: Guidelines and catalog available at website. Query with résumé, chapter-by-chapter summary, and 2 sample chapters to the Academic Editor if you are associated with a college or seminary; to the General Editor if you are a pastor or previously published author. Manuscripts may also be submitted through www.christianwritersubmissions.com or Writer's Edge (www.writersedgeservice.com). Accepts hard copy. Accepts simultaneous submissions, if identified. SASE. Response time, 12 weeks. Publication period and payment policies vary.

Jewish Lights

Sunset Farm Offices, Route 4, P.O. Box 237, Woodstock, VT 05091. www.jewishlights.com

Vice President, Editorial: Emily Wichland

Jewish Lights, an imprint of Turner Publishing, has a goal to stimulate thought and help all people learn about who the Jewish People are, where they come from, and what the future can hold. Jewish Lights seeks out books that reflect the Jewish wisdom tradition, and the search for meaning, for people of all faiths and backgrounds. It seeks materials about the unity and community of the Jewish people and the relevance of Judaism to everyday life. The children's catalogue includes nonfiction titles on Jewish holidays and traditions, spiritual issues, social issues, and guidance.

Freelance Potential: Publishes about 25 titles annually: 60% by authors who are new to the publishing house. Receives 80 queries, 35 unsolicited manuscripts monthly.

Fiction: Story picture books, early readers, chapter books, middle-grade, YA. Genres: graphic novels, religious, multicultural, Bible stories, Jewish customs, holidays, social issues, real life/problems.

Nonfiction: Toddler books, early readers, story picture books, middle-grade, YA. Topics: religion, inspirational, self-help, the Bible, social issues.

Submissions and Payment: Guidelines available on website. Send materials for consideration to submissions@turnerpublishing.com. Publication period varies. Payment policy varies.

Jewish Publication Society

2100 Arch Street, 2nd Floor, Philadelphia, PA 19103. www.jps.org

Editorial Director: Rabbi Barry Schwartz

Jewish Publication Society is committed to its mission to enhance Jewish literacy while embracing creativity. It is the preeminent publisher of Jewish books to the English-reading world. JPS only publishes nonfiction titles.

Freelance Potential: Publishes about 12 titles annually. Receives 40–50 queries monthly.

Nonfiction: Adult. Topics: the Bible, Jewish ethics, scholarship, Midrash, interfaith, history.

Submissions and Payment: Guidelines and catalogue available on website. Send a 1-page query that includes a brief description of the book, target audience, author qualifications, market analysis of other works on the same topic, résumé. Accepts hard copy and email to bschwartz@jps.org. SASE. Response time, publication period, and payment policies vary.

JourneyForth

1430 Wade Hampton Blvd., Greenville, SC 29609-5046. www.journeyforth.com

Acquisitions Editor: Nancy Lohr

This publisher offers fiction and nonfiction books for children from preschool through high school. The books from JourneyForth reflect a worldview based solidly on the Bible. It also publishes Bible studies and Christian living books for teens and adults. Its current needs include engaging first chapter books with a biblical worldview; relevant Bible studies and Christian living for teens or adults. JourneyForth is not currently accepting picture book submissions.

Freelance Potential: Publishes 8–10 titles annually: 1–10% developed from unsolicited submissions; 1–10% by agented authors; 1–10% by authors who are new to the publishing house; 1–10% by previously unpublished writers. Receives 10–25 queries, 10–25 unsolicited manuscripts monthly.

Nonfiction: Chapter books, middle-grade, YA, adult. Topics: spiritual growth, biography, Christian living, Bible study.

Fiction: Chapter books, middle-grade, YA. Genres: historical, biblical, Christian, animal adventure, mystery, contemporary, folktales, Westerns, fantasy.

Submissions and Payment: Guidelines and catalogue available on website. For nonfiction, query. For fiction, query with cover letter including target audience and author bio, and first 5 chapters. Prefers email submissions to journeyforth@bjupress.com. Will accept hard copy. See website for specific guidelines for each genre. Accepts simultaneous submissions if identified, but not multiple submissions. Responds in 12 weeks. Publication in 12–18 months. Royalty, advance.

The Judaica Press

123 Ditmas Avenue, Brooklyn, NY 11218. www.judaicapress.com

Editor

The Judaica Press motto is "Jewish Books that Matter" and represents the standard set by this company. It has been publishing books for fifty years, and during that time has created an extensive line of quality Jewish books. Judaica Press has been publishing impressive titles that hold true to the ideals of authentic Judaism and its traditions. They view it as their mission to publish and disseminate books that truly matter to the Jewish people. It publishes titles for children under its JP Kids imprint.

Freelance Potential: Publishes 20–25 titles annually: about 25% by authors who are new to the publishing house. Receives about 10 queries, 10 unsolicited manuscripts monthly.

Fiction: Board books, early picture books, early readers, story picture books, chapter books, middle- grade, YA. Genres: historical, religious, contemporary, mystery, suspense, folktales, Jewish holidays and heritage.

Nonfiction: Story picture books, early readers, YA. Topics: Jewish traditions, Torah stories, the Hebrew language, crafts, hobbies, holidays.

Submissions and Payment: Guidelines and catalogue available on website. Send complete manuscript with cover letter that summarizes the manuscript and states its intended purpose and audience. Email to submissions@judaicapress.com as a Word, DavkaWriter, RTF, or PDF file attachment. Availability of artwork improves chance of acceptance. Responds in 3 months. Publication in 1 year. Royalty.

Judson Press

1075 First Avenue, King of Prussia, PA 19406. www.judsonpress.com

Acquisition Editor

Judson Press honors its denominational identity, being passionate about contemporary social issues, including gender, racial, and environmental justice. Since 2003, Judson Press has been the publishing ministry of the American Baptist Home Mission Societies. Judson specializes in practical books for church leaders and Christians. Titles for children are mostly non-curriculum educational materials and ministry resources.

Freelance Potential: Publishes 10–12 titles annually: about 60% developed from unsolicited submissions; 10% by agented authors; 5% reprint/licensed properties; 50% by authors who are new to the publishing house; 30% by previously unpublished writers.

Nonfiction: Education and youth ministry titles. Topics: religion, history, social issues, real life/problems, theology, education, devotionals.

Submissions and Payment: Guidelines, including current needs, and catalogue available on website. Query with cover letter that indicates the working title, a summary of 3–5 sentences, and target audience; proposal with annotated table of contents; related/competing titles, market analysis; marketing plan; résumé; and 25 manuscript pages that include the first chapter (send complete manuscript for picture books only). Accepts hard copy and email to acquisitions@judsonpress.com (Word attachments). SASE. Responds in 3–6 months. Publication in 12–18 months. Royalty, 10%.

Kar-Ben Publishing

241 First Avenue North, Minneapolis, MN 55401. www.karben.com

Publisher

This division of Lerner Publishing Group exclusively offers Jewish-themed picture books. Its catalogue is filled with books on Jewish holidays, Bible stories, folktales, and stories reflecting the rich diversity of contemporary Jewish life.

Freelance Potential: Publishes 24 titles annually: 50–75% developed from unsolicited submissions; 10-20% assigned; 1–10% by agented authors; 25–50% by authors who are new to the publishing house; 10–25% by previously unpublished writers. Receives 25–50 unsolicited manuscripts monthly.

Fiction: Jewish-themed concept books, toddler books, early picture books, story picture books, chapter books. Genres: folklore, tales from the Torah, Jewish identity, holiday stories.

Nonfiction: Board books, activity books, early picture books, story picture books, and early reader books with Jewish subjects. Topics: Jewish identity, traditions, Holocaust, holidays, history, doctrine, Israel, the Jewish experience, prayer books.

Submissions and Payment: Guidelines and catalogue available on website. Send complete manuscript. Prefers email with Word attachment to editorial@karben.com. Simultaneous submissions accepted if identified. Responds in 3 months. Publication period varies. Advance, royalty.

Kregel Publications

2450 Oak Industrial Ave NE, Grand Rapids, MI 49505. www.kregel.com

Acquisitions Editor

Kregel Publications mission as an evangelical Christian publisher is to develop and distribute trusted, biblically based resources that lead individuals to know and serve Jesus Christ. Its backlist includes more than 1,000 titles of both trade and academic books, including books on Christian living, theology, contemporary issues, fiction, and Biblical studies.

Freelance Potential: Publishes about 80 titles (1–8 juvenile) annually: 85% by agented authors; 1–2% reprint/licensed properties; 25% by authors who are new to the publishing house; 1–10% by previously unpublished writers.

Fiction: Board books, story picture books, early readers, chapter books, middle-grade, YA. Genres: Bible stories, adventure, prayer, religion, holidays, folktales, activity.

Nonfiction: Board books, story picture books, early readers, middle-grade, YA. Topics: the Bible, religion, holidays, family, Christian parenting, Christian lifestyle.

Submissions and Payment: Catalogue available on website. Accepts queries from agents. No unsolicited manuscripts. Reviews manuscripts through the manuscript screening services Writer's Edge (www.writersedgeservice.com) and Christian Manuscript Submissions (www.christianmanuscriptsubmissions.com). Royalty.

Lighthouse Christian Publishing

754 Roxholly Walk, Buford, GA 30518. www.lighthousebooks.com

Submissions Department: Sylvia Charvet

This publisher offers titles ranging from novels to children's books, to technical manuals and self-help titles. While not all of its titles have a Christian message, Lighthouse Christian Publishing is dedicated to producing work that will positively impact a person's life. Many of its titles promote Christianity or at least do not go contrary to the tenets of the Bible. It uses the New American Standard Bible as a guide to determining content. Titles published are fiction, devotionals, inspirational books, and books for children.

Freelance Potential: Publishes 50–55 titles annually: 95% developed from unsolicited submissions; 10–15% by agented authors; 70% by authors who are new to the publishing house, 30–35% by previously unpublished writers. Receives 200 manuscripts yearly.

Nonfiction: YA, adult. Also publishes church school materials and devotionals. Topics: the Bible, history, religion, evolution, social issues, real life/problems.

Fiction: Story picture books, early readers, chapter books, middle-grade. Genres: fantasy, mystery, social issues, religious, inspirational.

Submissions and Payment: Guidelines and catalogue available on website. Send complete manuscript with a synopsis of the book, a brief outline of each chapter, and résumé. Accepts email submissions only (Word or RTF attachments) to info@lighthouseebooks.com. Responds in 3–6 weeks. Publication in 4–6 months. Royalty, 50% of net.

Lion Children's Books

Wilkinson House, Jordan Hill Business Park, Banbury Road, Oxford 0X2 8DR United Kingdom. www.lionhudson.com

Editorial Administrator

Lion Childrens' Books is committed to publishing quality literature, worldwide, which is true to the Christian faith. It is one of 5 imprints of Lion Hudson. The company publishes fiction and nonfiction titles for adults and children that reflect a Christian worldview, as well as books that support the devotional and spiritual lives of individuals and communities.

Freelance Potential: Publishes 45 titles annually: only a few developed from unsolicited submissions or agented authors; 2% reprint/licensed properties. Receives 80 queries monthly.

Fiction: Early picture books, concept books, toddler books, chapter books, YA. Genres: fairy tales, religious, inspirational, social issues, adventure.

Nonfiction: Toddler books, early picture books, early readers, story picture books, middle-grade, YA. Topics: religion, history, nature, social issues, health and fitness.

Submissions and Payment: Guidelines and catalogue available on website. Query with cover letter, synopsis, and résumé. Send to submissions@lionhudson.com in doc, docx, or PDF file. Responds in 3 months, if interested. Publication period and payment policies vary.

Little Lamb Books

PO Box 211724, Bedford, TX 76095. www.littlelambbooks.com

Submissions

Little Lamb Books is dedicated to publishing titles that share a Christian message, whether explicit or implied, through a variety of different genres, stories, and characters. It offers titles for elementary, middle grade, and young adult readers. This publisher will not accept submissions with any kind of profanity. It will not review horror or paranormal submissions or graphic novels.

Freelance Potential: Publishes 4–6 titles. Receives 125–175 queries yearly.

Fiction: Picture books, middle grade, YA. Genres: contemporary, mystery, inspirational, religious, adventure, historical fiction, fantasy.

Submissions and Payment: Guidelines and catalogue available on website. Accepts submissions during open submission periods only. Submissions are accepted February 1–March 30; June 1–July 31; and November 1–December 31. Send complete manuscript for picture books only. Query with sample chapters for all other submissions. Accepts email submissions to subs@littlelambbooks.com. Responds in 3–4 months. Publication period varies.

Living Ink Books

AMG Publishers, 6815 Shallowford Road, Chattanooga, TN 37421. www.amgpublishers.com

Acquisitions: Amanda Jenkins

For more than 25 years, Living Ink Books, an imprint of AMG Publishers, has been producing exciting, Christian-themed fiction for middle-grade and young adult readers. Living Ink's focus is on books that help the reader get into the Bible, hoping to give every individual at least one experience in which they hear and respond to the Gospel. Its books are inspiring with action and emotion.

Freelance Potential: Publishes about 10 juvenile and 3–5 adult titles annually. Receives 100 queries monthly.

Fiction: Middle-grade, YA adult. Genres: fantasy, dystopian, historical, mystery, adventure—all with Christian themes.

Submissions and Payment: Guidelines and catalogue available on website. Query with brief book description including proposed page count, target audience, and author credentials. Accepts email queries to sales@amgpublishers.com. Response time and publication period vary. Royalty; advance.

Master Books

3142 Highway 103N, Green Forest, AR 72638. www.masterbooks.net

Assistant Editor

Master Books has a special interest in books for the homeschooling community. It is the world's largest publisher of creation-based material for all ages, including apologetics, homeschool resources, reference titles, and quality children's literature. It is one of New Leaf Publishing Group's three imprints. This imprint focuses on Christians needing to understand the times to know what the church would do. Master Books remains a strong voice of truth in defense of the Holy Scripture from the very first verse, continuing the evangelistic tradition and vision at the heart of New Leaf Publishing Group. It is interested in educational materials for grades K–12, homeschooling materials, and inspirational books on faith. It also publishes a small amount of fiction. It is currently seeking nonfiction manuscripts.

Freelance Potential: Publishes 30–35 titles annually: 10–25% developed from unsolicited submissions; 50–75% assigned; 10–25% by agented authors; 25–50% by authors new to the publishing company; 25–50% by previously unpublished writers. Receives 25–50 queries, 50–75 manuscripts monthly.

Fiction: Concept books, chapter books, middle-grade, YA. Genres: religious, inspirational.

Nonfiction: Picture books, middle-grade, YA. Topics: science, biography, education, inspirational, real life/problems, social issues, sports, animals, reference materials.

Submissions and Payment: Catalogue available on website. Email proposal form on website as an attachment to submissions@newle.nlpg.com. Accepts simultaneous submissions if identified. Responds in 3 months and will request complete manuscript if interested. Publication in 9-12 months. Royalty.

Moody Publishers

820 North LaSalle Blvd, Chicago, IL 60610. www.moodypublishers.com

Acquisitions Coordinator

Moody Publishers publishes books on virtually every part of the Christian life. It has distributed millions of books, from Bible commentary and reference to spiritual and relational growth, as well as award-winning fiction. The titles from Moody Publishers are designed to glorify God in content and style. Titles are selected for publication based upon this goal, quality of writing, and potential for market success. This publisher accepts submissions from literary agents only.

Freelance Potential: Publishes about 10–20 titles yearly.

Fiction: YA, adult. Genres: religious, inspirational.

Nonfiction: YA, adult. Topics: Bible study materials, devotionals, inspirational, history, real life, religion, parenting, family life.

Submissions and Payment: Guidelines and catalogue available on website. Accepts submissions from agents or authors who have made a personal contact with one of our the editors at Moody Publishers through a writer's conference. Response time and publication period vary. Royalty; advance.

Thomas Nelson Children's Books and Education

501 Nelson Place, P.O. Box 141000, Nashville, TN 37214. www.thomasnelson.com

Acquisitions Editor

Thomas Nelson's award-winning products are designed to expand children's imaginations and nurture their faith while inspiring them to develop a personal relationship with Jesus. Thomas Nelson is a world-leading publisher and provider of Christian content and has been providing readers with quality inspirational products for nearly 300 years. As part of HarperCollins Christian Publishing, Inc., the publishing group provides multiple formats of award-winning Bibles, books, cookbooks, curriculum, and digital content. Thomas Nelson houses the works of some of the most renowned Christian authors. Its publishing program is guided by two goals—to honor God and to serve people. It offers books for very young children through young adults under its Tommy Nelson imprint. This Christian publisher's mission is to inspire the world with works of fiction and nonfiction on a wide variety of topics. Common to all of its products are biblical themes, Christian values, and quality writing.

Freelance Potential: Publishes about 50 titles annually: 100% by agented authors.

Fiction: Toddler books, early picture books, story picture books, middle-grade. Genres: religious, real life/problems, contemporary, inspirational, action/adventure, fantasy, social issues.

Nonfiction: Concept books, early readers, story picture books, middle-grade, YA, devotionals, Bible storybooks. Topics: the Bible, Christianity, Christian living, inspirational, biography, books of interest to girls, books of interest to boys.

Submissions and Payment: Catalogue available on website. Accepts proposals through literary agents only. Response time and publication period vary. Royalty; advance.

New Hope Publishers

100 Missionary Ridge, Birmingham, AL 35242. www.newhopepublishers.com

Publisher

New Hope Publishers offers books in a variety of areas that challenge and equip Christians to be radically involved in God's mission. Their books address specific topics of contemporary need and interest for women and families; provide believers with the very best Bible studies and teaching resources; and connect believers with social issues and Christian living topics. This company is about helping people in their spiritual journey, specializing in titles for women—their service, families, and community. It offers inspirational, self-help, Bible studies, and spiritual books.

Freelance Potential: Publishes about 20 titles annually: 50% by agented authors.

Fiction: YA, adult. Genres: inspirational, historical, romance, adventure.

Nonfiction: YA, adult. Topics: spiritual growth, religion, contemporary issues, real life/problems, prayer, women's issues, parenting, relationships, mission life, Christian living, Bible study, religious education materials.

Submissions and Payment: Guidelines and catalogue available on website. Send proposal containing details, bio, synopsis, and samples to proposals@newhopepublishers.com. Response time 4 months, publication period vary. Royalty. Flat fee. Occasionally offers advance.

New Leaf Press

P.O. Box 726, Green Forest, AR 72638. www.nlpg.com

Assistant Editor: Craig Froman

Working with accomplished speakers, pastors, and ministry leaders, New Leaf Press is all about inspiring believers in a world struggling to understand God's relevance. New Leaf Press maintains a strong reputation within the industry for unique, faith-building titles for all ages related to Christian living and incomparable gift books with enduring truths. The mission statement for New Leaf Press has always been, "Dedicated to ink on paper to impact eternity, reaching hearts across the world to know Him and make Him known as our Savior." It specializes in nonfiction religious books for children, young adults, parents, and teachers. It offers a broad range of inspirational titles for families and ministries, including books on Christian values and Bible stories, as well as gift books, church leadership resources, and children's Bibles. It is currently seeking homeschool education titles.

Freelance Potential: Publishes 30–35 titles annually: 10–25% developed from unsolicited submissions; 70–80% assigned; 10% by agented authors; 15–20% by authors who are new to the publishing house; 15–20% by previously unpublished writers. Receives 50–75 queries and manuscripts monthly.

Fiction: Currently not accepting children's fiction, memoirs, or poetry.

Nonfiction: Concept books, picture books, middle-grade, YA. Topics: the Bible, Christian living, history, education, current events, animals, sports, biography, career/college, science, real life/problems, social issues.

Submissions and Payment: Guidelines and catalog available on website. Must use submission form on website with query letter. Prefers submissions via email with Word attachments, to submissions@nlpg.com. Accepts simultaneous submissions if identified. Responds only if interested in manuscript. Publication in 9–12 months. Royalty.

O Books

Laurel House, Station Approach, Alresford, Hampshire SO24 9JH United Kingdom
www.o-books.com

Editor

An imprint of John Hunt Publishing, O-Books is a leading publisher of spirituality, personal development, and self-help titles, working in partnership with authors to produce authoritative and innovative books. Taking its name from the symbol of the world, oneness, and unity, O Books aims to inform and help people on this journey through life. O Books is particularly looking for books that cross boundaries and push the envelope, that are in their own way unusual or definitive (or both).

Freelance Potential: Publishes 200 titles annually: 25% developed from unsolicited submissions; 10% by agented authors; 30% by authors who are new to the publishing house; 20% by previously unpublished writers. Receives 500 queries monthly.

Fiction: Early readers, story picture books, chapter books, middle-grade, YA. Genres: religious, spiritual, adventure, fantasy, historical, fairy tales, folktales, contemporary.

Nonfiction: Story picture books, chapter books, middle-grade, YA. Topics: spirituality, religion, meditation, prayer, astrology, social issues, animals.

Submissions and Payment: Guidelines and catalogue available on website. Query with proposal form on website and sample chapters. Response time varies. Publication in 18 months. Royalty. Flat fee.

Orbis Books

Price Bldg, Box 302, Maryknoll, NY 10545. www.orbisbooks.com

Editorial Department

Since 1970, Orbis Books has been a leader in religious publishing. It offers a wide range of titles of interest to young adults and adults. Its titles include books on prayer, spirituality, Catholic life, theology, mission, and current affairs.

Freelance Potential: Publishes about 5 titles annually.

Nonfiction: YA, adult. Topics: religion, spirituality, current events.

Submissions and Payment: Guidelines and catalogue available on website. Send cover letter with working title, intended audience, sample chapter, and table of contents, if available. Include a curriculum vitae or brief summary of qualifications. Accepts hard copy or electronic submission to orbisbooks@maryknoll.org. Material will not be returned. Responds in 6–8 weeks. Publication time varies. Royalty, 10%.

Our Sunday Visitor

200 Noll Plaza, Huntington, IN 46750. www.osv.com

Acquisitions Editor

Our Sunday Visitor's mission is one of simplicity: to serve the Church. It is the country's largest not-for-profit Catholic publishing company. OSV publishes a newsweekly, periodicals, religious education materials, pamphlets, and books. Our Sunday Visitor is about helping people bring their Catholic faith to life, helping them see what is real and important in this life and how it will connect them to the next. OSV is dedicated to publishing books that accompany Catholics on their walk with God, wherever they are in their faith journey. It serves the Church by providing Catholics with materials that will strengthen their relationship with Christ, deepen their commitment to the Church and help them to see the world through the eyes of faith. Responding to peoples' needs, this nonprofit publisher produces trade books, periodicals, and religious education products that reinforce the Roman Catholic perspective. As the largest English-language Catholic publisher in the world, it publishes titles for children, young adults, parents, and church school teachers. Our Sunday Visitor also publishes religious education curricula serving grades K-8, including the materials published by Harcourt Religion, which OSV purchased a few years ago. OSV looks for books and subjects that are engaged with the contemporary world yet are still faithful to what the Catholic Church teaches.

Freelance Potential: Publishes 20 titles annually: 10–15% by authors who are new to the publishing house. Receives 10–12 queries monthly.

Nonfiction: Concept books, story picture books, chapter books, middle-grade, YA. Topics: family issues, parish life, the Bible, sacraments, religion, theology, holidays, prayer, devotionals, real life/problems, social issues, Catholic identity and practices, lives of saints, contemporary issues, educational materials.

Submissions and Payment: Catalogue and guidelines available on website. Query with proposal that includes: cover letter with working title, manuscript length, anticipated completion date, market comparison, and explanation of why your book is unique; 2- to 4-page chapter outline, including projected illustrations or other features; author biography; and 1–2 sample chapters. Email to booksed@osv.com. Also accepts hard copy. Accepts simultaneous submissions, if identified. SASE. Responds in 8 weeks. Publication in 1+ years. Royalty; advance. Flat fee.

Pacific Press Publishing

1350 North Kings Road, Nampa, ID 83687. www.pacificpress.com

Acquisitions Editor

As a spiritual enterprise, Pacific Press Publishing aims to provide information to readers about God's character and ways. Pacific Press Publishing's sole purpose is to uplift Jesus Christ in communicating biblical teachings, health principles, and family values—in many languages—through various types of printed materials, video products, software, electronic products, and recordings of Christian music. Pacific Press publishes a wide variety of Christian books with a Seventh-day Adventist perspective. This perception governs the selection of all materials published. Books are in complete harmony with the Bible and are meant to encourage and uplift readers in the struggles of life as well as prepare them for eternal life with God.

Freelance Potential: Publishes 30–40 titles annually: 10–25% developed from unsolicited submissions; 50–75% assigned; 10–25% by authors who are new to the publishing house; less than 10% by previously unpublished writers.

Fiction: Early readers, chapter books, middle-grade, YA. Topics: real life/problems, adventure, historical.

Nonfiction: Toddler books, chapter books, middle-grade, YA, activity books. Topics: biography, holidays, inspirational, religious nonfiction on Seventh-day Adventist beliefs and key figures.

Submissions and Payment: Guidelines and catalogue available on website. Query with one-sentence thesis of main idea, summary of the book, intended audience, author qualifications, chapter outline, and how far along the manuscript is. Email to booksubmissions@pacificpress.com. Responds in 1–3 weeks. Publication in 12–18 months. Royalty, advance.

P & R Publishing

P.O. Box 817, Phillipsburg, NJ 08865. www.prpbooks.com

Acquisitions Director: Dave Almack

P & R, which stands for "Presbyterian and Reformed," has a mission to serve Christ and his church. It is committed to publishing excellent books that promote biblical understanding and Godly living as summarized in the Westminster Confession of Faith and Catechisms. P & R's list ranges from academic works advancing biblical scholarship to popular books that help readers grow in Christian thought and service. It also publishes religious based titles for young adults. They are always accepting proposals for books that meet these standards.

Freelance Potential: Publishes about 40 titles annually: 30% by authors who are new to the publishing house; 1–20% by previously unpublished authors. Receives 15–25 queries monthly.

Nonfiction: Topics: Christian living, biblical counseling, theology, the Bible, apologetics, Christian issues, ethics, women's issues.

Submissions and Payment: Guidelines and catalogue available on website. Query with submissions form on website by email to editorial@prpbooks.com. Responds in 1–3 months. Publication period varies. Royalties.

Pauline Books & Media

50 St. Paul's Avenue, Boston, MA 02130-3491. www.pauline.org

Children's Editors

Pauline Books & Media is one of the most trusted Catholic publishers of our time. It publishes materials for all ages, from children to adults. Its Pauline Kids and Pauline Teens titles offer wholesome and entertaining reading, help children develop strong Christian values, and inspire hope. The company accepts fiction and nonfiction. It seeks engaging picture book concepts for toddlers and primary readers, as well as manuscripts for beginning, intermediate, preteen, and teen readers. Pauline Books publishes select Spanish and bilingual titles. Also of interest are books for adults on spirituality, Gospel values, family life, faith, Marian themes, the saints, prayer books, and teacher resources.

Freelance Potential: Publishes 20 titles annually: 10% developed from unsolicited submissions; 15% reprint/licensed properties; 20% by authors who are new to the publishing house; 20% by previously unpublished writers. Receives 20–35 queries monthly.

Fiction: Toddler books, early picture books, story picture books, early readers, chapter books, middle-grade, YA. Genres: Bible stories, religion, inspirational, historical fiction, graphic novels, fantasy, fairy tales, science fiction, myths, romance, all with a Catholic perspective.

Nonfiction: Toddler books, chapter books, middle-grade, YA. Topics: religious education, religious coloring/activity books, church holidays, values, prayer, faith, spirituality, saints, sacraments, the Bible, contemporary issues.

Submissions and Payment: Guidelines available on website. Query with cover letter containing synopsis and 2 sample chapters. Send complete manuscript for board books and picture books. Accepts hard copy and email with Word attachments to editorial@paulinemedia.com. Accepts simultaneous submissions, if identified. SASE. Responds within 2 months. Publication in 2–3 years. Royalty, 5–10% of net; advance, $200–$500.

Paulist Press

997 Macarthur Boulevard, Mahwah, NJ 07430. www.paulistpress.com

Submission Editor

Striving to stand at the intersection of faith and culture, Paulist Press is committed to publishing quality materials. Paulist Press publishes quality material that helps bridge the gap between faith and culture by bringing the good news of the Gospel to Catholics and people of other religious traditions; supporting dialogue and welcoming good scholarship and religious wisdom from all sources across denominational boundaries; and fostering religious values and wholeness in society, especially through materials promoting healing, reconciliation, and personal growth. It publishes books for children, young adults, and adults on faith, history, social issues, and personal growth.

Freelance Potential: Publishes 60–75 titles annually: 10% by agented authors; 50–75% assigned; 30% by authors who are new to the publishing house; 1% by previously unpublished writers. Receives 25–50 queries, 25–50 unsolicited manuscripts monthly.

Nonfiction: Early picture books, story picture books, middle-grade, YA. Topics: prayer, saints, modern heroes, Bible stories, Catholic viewpoints on current issues.

Submissions and Payment: Guidelines and catalogue available on website. Send complete manuscript with résumé and cover letter that summarizes the story, states the intended age group and category (see website for list), estimated length and completion date, market analysis, and author promotion ideas. Picture book submissions must include sample illustrations. Prefers email to submissions@paulistpress.com (Word attachments); will accept hard copy. SASE. Responds in 2+ months. Accepts simultaneous submissions if identified. Publication period varies. Royalty.

The Pilgrim Press

700 Prospect Avenue, Cleveland, OH 44115-1100. https://www.thepilgrimpress.com/

Editor: Rachel Hackenberg

The Pilgrim Press bears the testimony that there is "more truth and light yet to break forth." The Pilgrim Press is the publishing division of the United Church of Christ. It holds a 400-year-old legacy of discerning the Spirit's provocation in the world and a 400-year-young commitment to accompanying wayfarers along their faith journeys. The Pilgrim Press especially looks for proposals in the following categories: spiritual health and wellness, congregational innovation, pastoral leadership, worship, justice concerns, and children/youth faith development.

Freelance Potential: Publishes 40 titles annually: about 50% developed from unsolicited submissions; 1–10% by agented authors; about 25% by authors who are new to the publishing house; 1–10% by previously unpublished writers. Receives 20+ queries monthly.

Nonfiction: Middle-grade, YA, adult. Topics: spiritual health and wellness, leadership and congregations, worship, social issues, multicultural, ethnic, religious education.

Submissions and Payment: Detailed guidelines and catalogue available on website. Send an email to proposals@thepilgrimpress.com for a proposal questionnaire. Responds in 9–12 months. Flat fee for work-for-hire projects.

Randall House

114 Bush Road, P.O. Box 17306, Nashville, TN 37217. www.randallhouse.com

Acquisitions Editor: Michelle Orr

As a trusted publisher of Bible-based products for over half a century, Randall House serves people around the world with a specific emphasis on helping church leaders, parents, and grandparents live the principles of Deuteronomy 6. Randall House is a Christian publisher and home of D6 Family Ministries dedicated to promoting the cause of Christ, generational discipleship, and serving both the Church and home through curriculum, books, and events. It publishes Sunday school resources for children of all ages, parenting, family, marriage, theology, Spanish titles, and fiction and nonfiction on Christian themes.

Freelance Potential: Publishes 15 titles annually: 20% developed from unsolicited submissions; 15% by agented authors; 20% by authors who are new to the publishing house; 15% by previously unpublished writers. Receives 80–100 queries monthly.

Nonfiction: Church school curriculum materials for preK–grade 12, story picture books, early readers, middle-grade, YA. Topics: holidays, religion, social issues, theology, parenting, youth ministry, family.

Submissions and Payment: Catalogue available on website. Query with proposal that includes the book's purpose and primary and secondary audience, author biography, market and competition analysis, annotated outline/table of contents, 3–4 sample chapters, estimated manuscript length, suggested illustrations, and experts who will endorse the book. Accepts hard copy, or email queries to michelle.orr@randallhouse.com. Accepts simultaneous submissions, if identified. SASE. Responds in 10–12 weeks. Publication in 12–14 months. Royalty, 10–14%; advance, $1,000–$2,000.

Revell

Baker Publishing Group, 6030 East Fulton Road, Ada, MI 49301. www.revellbooks.com

Editor

Revell saw the need for practical books that would help bring the Christian faith to everyday life. Whether publishing fiction, Christian living, self-help, marriage, family, or youth books, each Revell publication reflects relevance, integrity, and excellence. Revell has been a division of Baker Publishing Group since the 1990s, but it has a history of more than 125 years as a Christian publisher.

Freelance Potential: Publishes hundreds of books annually.

Fiction: Middle-grade, YA, adult. Genres: religious, holidays, people and places, sports, animals. For adults: Christian, romance, historical, contemporary, fantasy, men's, women's, psychological, suspense, humor, mysteries.

Nonfiction: Middle-grade, YA, adult. Topics: religion, Bible stories, biography, history, family, home, health, crafts, cooking, self-help, education, parenting, pets, current events, relationships, sports.

Submissions and Payment: Accepts manuscripts only through agents; conferences where Baker staff participates; or the manuscript services Authonomy.com, Writer's Edge (www.writersedgeservice.com), or Christian Manuscript Submissions (www.christianmanuscriptsubmissions.com). Response time and publication period vary. Royalty, 15% of net.

RoseKidz

P.O. Box 3473, Peabody, MA 01961. www.hendricksonrose.com

Submissions

RoseKidz offers great resources designed to refresh and strengthen kid ministries, family ministries, and more. RoseKidz publishes award-winning and reproducible Bible lesson material for children including Sunday school activities, devotionals, and fiction. The titles from RoseKidz help kids grow closer to God through hands-on activities.

Freelance Potential: Publishes 10 titles each year: 80% developed from unsolicited submissions; 10% by agented authors; 10% reprint/licensed properties; 50% by authors who are new to the publishing house; 50% by previously unpublished writers. Receives 10 queries monthly.

Fiction: Toddler books, story picture books, early readers, chapter books, middle-grade. Genres: adventure, mystery, contemporary, animals, social issues—all with a Christian theme.

Nonfiction: Sunday school activity workbooks, devotionals, chapter books, middle-grade. Topics: the Bible, holidays, cooking, crafts, fashion, social issues, hobbies, sports, real life/problems, activities.

Submissions and Payment: Guidelines and catalogue available on website. Query with table of contents and 2–5 chapters, author bio, and audience analysis. Accepts hard copy only. SASE. Responds in 10–20 weeks. Publication period varies. Royalty; advance, $500+.

Rose Publishing

PO Box 3473, Peabody, MA 01961-3473. www.hendricksonrose.com

Acquisitions Editor

Rose Publishing is an imprint of Hendrickson Publishers. It is passionate about sharing the Good News of Jesus Christ and equipping believers to live out the Great Commandment to love God with all our heart, soul, strength, and mind and to love our neighbors as ourselves. Creating easy-to-understand Christian products that help people grow their faith is what Rose Publishing does best. Helping believers love God by deepening their understanding of who God is, Rose Publishing keeps with the conservative, evangelical Christian perspective, producing easy-to-use Bible study and reference materials, including visual aids such as charts and timelines. Rose Publishing is the only Christian publisher that specializes in graphics-rich products.

Freelance Potential: Publishes about 25 titles annually: 1–10% by authors who are new to the publishing house.

Nonfiction: Church school and Bible reference books, pamphlets, and digital materials for children of all ages, and adults. Topics: the Bible, history, prayer, devotionals, religion, apologetics.

Submissions and Payment: Catalogue available on website. Submit manuscripts through ChristianManuscriptSubmissions.com. Responds in 2–3 months. Publication in 18 months. Flat fee.

Saint Mary's Press

702 Terrace Heights, Winona, MN 55987-1320. www.smp.org

Submissions Editor

Saint Mary's Press is a contemporary expression of the Catholic Church's mission to proclaim the Good News of Jesus Christ and the Lasallian mission to provide a human and Christian education for young people. In schools, parishes, and families, St. Mary's shares the Good News of Jesus Christ with Catholic Christian youth, ages 6 to 19, using all appropriate means and media through publications and services. It publishes materials for schools, parishes, and families, including religious education textbooks, parish curriculum, and youth ministry resources.

Freelance Potential: Publishes 30 titles (15 juvenile) annually: 20% by authors who are new to the publishing house. Receives 20 queries monthly.

Fiction: Middle-grade. Genres: Folktales, drama, religion, inspirational.

Nonfiction: Middle-grade, YA. Topics: spirituality, Christianity, Catholic faith and life, sacraments, the Bible, contemporary issues, social issues, social justice, morality. Also publishes titles for adults who teach or minister to youth; Bibles; and supplemental resources.

Submissions and Payment: Guidelines and catalogue available on website. Query with cover letter that includes author biography and publishing credits; information sheet with product description (and results if it has already been tested), audience, competition, design features, promotion ideas, estimated length, and estimated completion date; and manuscript sample, with title, table of contents, introduction, and sample chapter or activity. Accepts hard copy, or email to submissions@smp.org. Accepts simultaneous submissions, if identified. SASE. Responds in 2 months. Publication in 12–18 months. Royalty or work-for-hire.

Skinner House Books

https://www.uua.org/publications/skinnerhouse

Editorial Director: Mary Benard

Skinner House books are spiritual, practical, and engaging. It offers insightful books for people of all ages. Its titles tackle spiritual challenges ranging from grief and loss, to justice and action, to conscience and belief. It also offers meditations for families and titles on theology, social work, and mentoring.

Freelance Potential: Publishes 10+ titles annually.

Nonfiction: Early reader, middle-grade, YA. Topics: Inspirational, spirituality, social studies, religious.

Submissions and Payment: Guidelines available on website. Query with two sample chapters, table of contents, author bio, and why you feel your manuscript is a good fit for Skinner House. Accepts email submissions to bookproposals@uua.org. Responds if interested. Publication period and payment policies vary.

Standard Publishing 🔒

4050 Lee Vance Drive, Colorado Springs, CO 80918. www.standardpub.com

Editor, Children's Ministry Resources

Bringing the Bible to life is the sole purpose of this publisher. For more than 150 years, Standard Publishing has provided true-to-the-Bible resources that inspire, educate, and motivate people to maintain a growing relationship with Jesus Christ. They believe the Old and New Testaments comprise the infallible, divinely inspired Word of God. Therefore, they consider the entire Bible to be our statement of faith and seek to understand and apply its message. Standard Publishing provides books and other Christian resources that meet church and family needs in the area of children's ministry.

Freelance Potential: Publishes 20–30 titles annually: less than 5% developed from unsolicited submissions; 10–25% assigned; 1–10% by agented authors; 1–10% by previously unpublished writers. Receives 10–15 queries and unsolicited manuscripts monthly.

Fiction: Picture books, middle-grade. Genres: parables, stories that help children understand the meaning behind biblical passages, Christian values, faith in daily life, adventure, mystery, rhyme.

Nonfiction: Board books, activity books, early picture books, early readers, story picture books, middle-grade. Also publishes teacher, parent, and leadership resources, children's classroom resources, devotionals, and materials geared toward smaller churches. Topics: Bible stories, religion, faith, Christianity, Christian values, outreach.

Submissions and Payment: Catalogue and guidelines available on website. Not accepting submissions at this time. Check website for updates. Publication period and payment policies vary.

TAN Books

P.O. Box 410487, Charlotte, NC 28241. www.tanbooks.com

Editor

TAN Books, founded in 1967, is committed to the preservation and promotion of the spiritual, theological and liturgical traditions of the Roman Catholic Church. TAN Books publishes titles on Thomistic theology, traditional devotions, Church doctrine, history, lives of the saints, educational resources, and more. At present TAN books is considering proposals of prayers and devotionals, saints' lives, families and homeschooling, history, miracles, supernatural and current events.

Freelance Potential: Publishes 10+ titles each year.

Nonfiction: YA. Topics: Current events, religion, family.

Submissions and Payment: Guidelines and catalogue available on website. Submit proposal through website. Responds 3 months. Publication period varies. Payment rates and policies vary.

Teach Services

11 Quartermaster Circle, Fort Oglethorpe, GA 30742. www.teachservices.com

Author Advisor: Timothy Hullquist

Since 1984, TEACH Services has helped hundreds of authors publish and market their books. Their mission is to encourage and strengthen individuals around the world through the printing of books that point readers to Christ. It is this vision along with the P.I.L.L.A.R.S. of the Bible that guides everything TEACH publishes. Its secondary mission is to make more Adventist materials available in the areas of health and Christian living.

Freelance Potential: Publishes 60–80 titles annually: 5% by agented authors, 90% by authors who are new to the publishing house, 80% by previously unpublished writers. Receives 10–25 queries, 10–25 unsolicited manuscripts monthly.

Fiction: Early readers, chapter books, middle-grade. Genres: adventure, mystery, historical, religious, Bible stories, values.

Nonfiction: Early readers, chapter books, middle-grade, YA. Topics: Bible study, church doctrine and history, prayer, youth and children's ministry, health, education, spiritual growth, biography.

Submissions and Payment: Guidelines and catalogue available at website. Query with outline, target audience, and author bio; or send complete manuscript with form at website. Prefers email (Word attachments) to publishing@teachservices.com. Accepts simultaneous submissions if identified. Responds in 2 weeks. Publication in 4–6 months. Royalty, 10%. Publisher pays for printing and distribution; author pays for art, editing, and layout.

Tyndale House

351 Executive Drive, Carol Stream, IL 60188. www.tyndale.com

Acquisitions Director, Children & Family: Katara Washington Patton

Tyndale House is one of the largest independently owned Christian publishers in the world. Spreading the good news of Christ around the world is the goal of this publishing house. With a focus on ministering to the spiritual needs of people, primarily through literature consistent with biblical principles, Tyndale publishes Christian fiction, nonfiction, children's books, and other resources, including Bibles. Its children's list includes fiction and nonfiction with a Christian perspective. Tyndale House does not accept unsolicited manuscripts or queries. It only reviews submissions through literary agents or by previous Tyndale authors.

Freelance Potential: Publishes about 15 titles annually: 100% by agented authors. Receives 20 queries each month.

Fiction: Toddler books, story picture books, middle-grade. Genres: mystery, adventure, social issues, holidays, religion.

Nonfiction: Toddler books, story picture books, early readers, middle-grade, YA. Topics: the Bible, religion, spirituality, the Christian faith, real life/problems, devotionals, contemporary issues. Also publishes parenting books and Bibles.

Submissions and Payment: Agented authors only. No unsolicited manuscripts. Publication period varies. Royalty; advance. Flat fee.

Unity Books

Unity Books, 1901 Northwest Blue Parkway, Unity Village, MO 64065-0001. www.unity.org

Editorial Assistant: Sharon Sartin

Unity Books offers literature designed for personal growth, study, and spiritual encouragement. Unity Books is the publishing arm of Unity. Through books and multimedia products, Unity Books provides resources that contribute to Unity's mission of empowering people to realize and express their divine potential for healthy, prosperous, and meaningful lives.

Freelance Potential: Publishes about 2–3 titles annually: most by authors who are new to the publishing house. Receives 35–40 queries monthly.

Nonfiction: YA, adult. Topics: spirituality, parenting, contemporary issues, inspirational, self-help, Unity teachings.

Submissions and Payment: Guidelines and catalogue available on website. Query with an overview of your book including the reason it is unique, description of target audience, competitive titles, author bio with relevant credentials, detailed marketing plan, and sample illustrations, if available. Manuscripts should be professionally edited prior to submission. Accepts hard copies. Email to sartinsm@unityonline.org. Responds in 1–3 months. Royalty.

Warner Press

2902 Enterprise Drive, Anderson, IN 46013. www.warnerpress.org

Kids/Family Ministry Editor: Robin Fogle

Warner Press has a goal to equip the Church for ministry. It produces a wide variety of materials that communicate the message of Jesus Christ, including children's teaching resource books and resources for religious education. It is in need of teaching resources for children's Sunday school or children's church. It is also interested in children's Bible studies, adult Bible studies (personal and small group), and materials geared toward family ministry, Sunday school teachers' leadership and training, and children's ministry. All material needs to be theologically sound and have no denominational bias. It is no longer publishing fiction of any kind.

Freelance Potential: Publishes about 4–6 children's teaching resource books annually: 50–75% developed from unsolicited submissions by authors who are new to the publishing house. Receives 20–25 queries, 5–10 unsolicited manuscripts monthly.

Nonfiction: Early readers, middle-grade, activity books. Topics: the Bible, religious holidays and history, Christianity. Also publishes reference books for parents and teachers.

Submissions and Payment: Guidelines and catalogue available on website. Query with publishing credits. Prefers email to rfogle@warnerpress.org. No simultaneous submissions. Response time varies. Publication in 12 months. Payment policy varies.

WaterBrook Multnomah Publishing Group

10807 New Allegiance Drive, Suite 500, Colorado Springs, CO 80921.
www.waterbrookmultnomah.com

Submissions Editor

As imprints of Penguin Random House, WaterBrook and Multnomah compete with the best publishers in the world while seeking to serve readers and the Church at a personal level. WaterBrook publishes Christian books that seek to intensify and satisfy a reader's elemental thirst for a deeper relationship with God. Multnomah publishes Christian resources that proclaim the Gospel and equip followers of Jesus to make disciples. Both seek timeless messages from trusted Christian voices that challenge readers to approach life from a biblical perspective. It seeks messages that draw on the Bible, experiential learning, story, practical guidance, and inspiration to help readers thrive in their faith.

Freelance Potential: Publishes 60 titles annually. Receives 45–50 queries monthly.

Fiction: Story picture books, YA. Genres: religious, inspirational, romance, adventure, contemporary, fantasy.

Nonfiction: YA. Topics: religion, Christianity, personal faith, social issues, relationships, devotionals. Also publishes parenting titles.

Submissions and Payment: Catalogue and author resources available on website. Accepts queries and proposals through literary agents only. Responds in 6–10 weeks. Publication in 1–2 years. Royalty; advance.

Watershed Books

P.O. Box 1738, Aztec, NM 87410. www.pelicanbookgroup.com

Editor

Watershed publishes Christian books for young adult and the young at heart. Its titles feature teenage protagonists who may or may not be spiritual at the onset, but come to realize through the progression of the plot that faith is a necessity. All of its titles convey life as its lived, or can be lived, by people of faith.

Freelance Potential: Publishes 10–15 titles annually.

Fiction: YA. Genres: action, adventure, mystery, science fiction, inspirational, coming-of-age, Westerns, romance.

Submissions and Payment: Guidelines and catalogue available on website. Manuscripts should be between 25,000 and 65,000 words. Accepts submissions through the website. Response time varies. Publication in 1 year. Royalty.

Weiser Books

65 Parker Street, Suite 7, Newburyport, MA 01950. www.redwheelweiser.com

Publisher Emerita: Jan Johnson

Weiser Books has a long history as one of America's preeminent publishers of esoteric or occult teachings from traditions all around the world and throughout time. Their mission is to publish quality books that will make a difference in people's lives without advocating any one particular path or field of study. It values the integrity, originality, and depth of knowledge of its authors. Weiser Books publishes titles about esoteric or occult teachings from traditions around the world, on topics such as consciousness, new science, Wicca, spirituality, and astrology. Weiser books is the publisher of the bestselling series Random Acts of Kindness. Other books cover self-help and recovery, nutrition and health, and lifestyle. It does not publish children's titles, but some of its books may be of interest to teens.

Freelance Potential: Publishes 30 titles annually: 15% developed from unsolicited submissions; 15% by agented authors. Receives 100+ queries monthly.

Nonfiction: Adult, of interest to YA. Topics: new consciousness, new science, coming Earth changes, magic, Wicca, Western mystery traditions, tarot, yoga, occult, astrology, paranormal, health, lifestyle, spirituality.

Submissions and Payment: Guidelines and catalogue available on website. Query with letter that includes an author biography and brief description of proposed work; proposal with a book overview, table of contents, market/audience analysis, marketing and promotion ideas, author qualifications, and 2–3 sample chapters; and sample photos or art if appropriate. Accepts email to submissions@rwwbooks.com (Word or PDF attachments). Accepts simultaneous submissions if identified. Responds in 3 months. Publication in 18 months. Royalty; advance.

Wisdom Tales

P.O. Box 2682, Bloomington, IN 47402-2682. www.wisdomtalespress.com

Production Director

Wisdom Tales books reflect its commitment to help others appreciate the beauty and sacred ways of diverse cultures and traditions. It strives to produce exceptional books that will spark the imagination and encourage the development of good character. Wisdom Tales' mission is to bring books on Perennial Philosophy to children and young adults. It publishes books on philosophy, religion, and belief systems of many cultures. Its titles are meant to "share the wisdom, beauty, and values of traditional cultures and peoples from around the world with young readers and their families."

Freelance Potential: Publishes 5–10 titles annually.

Fiction: Picture books, middle-grade. Genres: folktales, legends, historical, multicultural.

Nonfiction: Picture books, middle-grade, YA. Genres: religious, inspirational, philosophy, history, culture, multicultural.

Submissions and Payment: Guidelines and catalogue available on website. Send manuscript submission application on website with complete manuscript through webpage. Accepts hard copy. SASE. Responds in 4 months if interested. Publication period and payment policies vary.

Zonderkidz 🔒

3900 Sparks Dr. SE, Grand Rapids, MI 49546. www.zonderkidz.com

Acquisitions

Zonderkidz, the children's division of Zondervan, inspires young lives through imagination and innovation. The mission at Zonderkidz is to be the leader in Biblical, innovative, and imaginative resources that meet the spiritual and developmental needs of kids ages 15 and under. Zonderkidz is a publisher of Christian board books, picture books, storybook Bibles, chapter books, and middle-grade titles. It publishes nonfiction on topics such as nature, sports, religion, and crafts, along with fiction of most genres. It is not currently accepting new children's or YA proposals.

Freelance Potential: Publishes 150 titles (60 juvenile) annually: most by agented authors. Receives 60–72 queries yearly.

Fiction: Board books, picture books, storybook Bibles, early readers, chapter books, middle-grade, YA. Genres: social issues, religion, Christian values, fantasy, adventure, inspirational, real life/problems.

Nonfiction: Board books, picture books, storybook Bibles, early readers, chapter books, middle-grade, YA. Topics: nature, sports, religion, crafts, the Bible, biography, prayer, religion, inspirational.

Submissions and Payment: Catalogue available on website. Currently not accepting proposals for children's and teen books. Check website for updates and current needs. Response time 6–8 weeks. Publication in 2–3 years. Royalty.

Publishing of Interest to Children and Teens

While the prime goal of *Book Markets for Children's Writers 2021* is to provide the best information on publishers of books for children and teens, some authors may be interested in a wider field. This section highlights a number of publishers that offer books that may not directly target children and teens, but that may be of interest. Some of the categories here are study skills and exam preparation, educational or reference books for older readers, crime stories, science fiction for a general audience, fantasy, role-playing games, environmental topics, outdoor recreation, and many others.

The section also includes publishers for adults that offer a limited number of children's or teen titles, and are open to submissions.

Antarctic Press

4700 Timco West, Suite 100, San Antonio, TX 78238. www.antarctic-press.com

Submissions Editor

Antarctic Press, among the top 10 publishers of comics in the United States, was established in 1984 and has produced more than 1500 titles with some as the longest-running independent comic series on the market. Since their inception, their main goal has been to establish a series of titles that are unique, high in both quality and profitability, and entertaining to a range of audiences. It publishes annual books as well as anthologies.

Freelance Potential: Open to submissions from new writers.

Fiction: Anthologies with manga or anime influence.

Submissions and Payment: Guidelines available at website. Send complete manuscript. Accepts hard copy and email to submissions@antarcticpress.com. SASE. Response time varies. Royalty.

Archaia

5670 Wilshire Blvd, Suite 450, Los Angeles, CA 90036. www.archaia.com

Submissions Team

Works that enthrall and excite, that take a unique perspective on a medium, story, character, or genre will gain the attention of this publisher. Archaia has historically looked for work that tests the boundaries of the graphic novel medium. The core mission at Archaia is to publish artful, engaging, and groundbreaking graphical literature from both new and established creators. Most of its graphic novels fall into the genres of adventure, fantasy, horror, pulp noir, and science fiction.

Freelance Potential: Publishes 5–10 titles annually.

Fiction: Adult. Genres: Fantasy, science fiction, adventure, horror.

Submissions and Payment: Catalogue and guidelines available on website. Send complete manuscript with cover letter through the website. Responds in 90 days if interested. Publication period varies. Royalty.

Black Rose Writing

P.O. Box 1540, Castroville, TX 78009. www.blackrosewriting.com

Acquisitions Editor

Established in 2006, Black Rose features an array of fiction, nonfiction, and children's book genres, all having one thing in common—an individual's originality and hardship. It can take endless hours to finish a deserving manuscript, and Black Rose Writing applauds each and every author, giving them a chance at their dream. Because Black Rose Writing takes full advantage of modern printing technology, the company has an infinite print run via print-on-demand services.

Freelance Potential: Publishes 200+ electronic titles annually: 20% by agented authors, 60% by authors who are new to the publishing house, 20% by previously unpublished writers. Receives 250+ queries monthly.

Fiction: Children's picture books, mystery, thriller, suspense, romance, horror, literary, YA, coming-of-age, fantasy, science fiction.

Nonfiction: Bio/memoir, sports, self-help, business, travel.

Submissions and Payment: Catalogue and guidelines available on website. Query with synopsis for proposed book with author bio (no attachments). Children's submissions must include all artwork. Submissions should be sent to creator@blackrosewriting.com. Accepts simultaneous submissions. Responds to queries in 3–6 weeks. Payment rate and policy varies. Net royalties paid biannually.

DAW Books

1745 Hudson, New York, NY 10019. www.dawbooks.com

Submissions Editor: Peter Stampfel

DAW Books was the first publishing company ever devoted exclusively to science fiction and fantasy. Many stars of the science fiction and fantasy world have made their debut with DAW books. While it does not publish stories for children, or even directly target young adults, many of its books appeal to teen readers. It is committed to discovering and nurturing new talent, and to keeping a personal "family" spirit at DAW. It is actively seeking new works of science fiction and fantasy written by and/or featuring people of color, Native people, disabled people, neurodiverse people, LGBTQIA+ people, and those from other underrepresented or marginalized communities.

Freelance Potential: Publishes 35 titles annually. Receives 150 unsolicited mss monthly.

Fiction: Genres: science fiction, fantasy.

Submissions and Payment: Guidelines and catalogue available on website. Currently open to digital submissions. Check the website for changes to this policy. Publication period varies. Royalty; advance.

The Feminist Press

The Graduate Center, 365 Fifth Avenue, Suite 5406, New York, NY 10016. www.feministpress.org

Editor: Lauren Rosemary Hook

The Feminist Press publishes books that ignite movements and social transformation. The Feminist Press is an educational nonprofit organization founded to advance women's rights and amplify feminist perspectives. FP publishes classic and new writing from around the world, creates cutting-edge programs, and elevates silenced and marginalized voices.

Freelance Potential: Publishes 15–20 titles annually: 10% developed from unsolicited submissions; 75% reprint/licensed properties; 60% by authors who are new to the publishing house. Receives 100+ queries monthly.

Fiction: Genres: multicultural, historical.

Nonfiction: Topics: memoirs, essays, biography, historical references about feminist issues.

Submissions and Payment: Guidelines available on website. Send proposal with sample chapters, author biography, and email address to receive a reply. Prefers email queries to editor@feministpress.org (include "Submission" in subject line). Response time and publication period vary. Royalty; advance.

Folklore Publishing

11414 - 119 St NW, Edmonton, AB T5G 2X6, Canada. www.folklorepublishing.com

Publisher: Faye Boer

Founded in 2002, Folklore Publishing is about developing a body of work that will create a library of wonderful stories about Canadian heroes and their glorious but often unsung past. It seeks submissions from people who are knowledgeable about specific aspects of Canadian history and current affairs. Among its current needs are Canadian history, humor, and children's nonfiction.

Freelance Potential: Publishes 4–8 titles annually: 10% developed from unsolicited submissions; 25% by authors who are new to the publishing house; 25% by previously unpublished writers.

Nonfiction: Middle-grade, YA, adult. Topics: Canada-related history, biography, humor.

Submissions and Payment: Guidelines and catalogue available on website. For completed manuscripts, send résumé detailing your interests and passions, an overview of your manuscript and its marketability, a chapter-by-chapter synopsis, and 2–3 sample chapters (up to 75 pages). To be considered for work-for-hire projects, send résumé detailing your interests and passions, and 3 nonfiction writing samples, preferably about a topic of interest to Canadians. Accepts hard copy and email to submissions@folklorepublishing.com (Word or PDF files). Response time varies. Publication in 6–18 months. 10% royalty.

Gollancz

www.orionbooks.co.uk

Editor

Gollancz, part of the Orion publishing group, fosters a culture of openness where all contributions are encouraged and valued. It is the oldest specialist science fiction and fantasy publisher in the UK. It has one of the largest ranges of science fiction and fantasy in the world.

Freelance Potential: Publishes 50+ titles yearly.

Fiction: YA–adult. Genres: science fiction, fantasy.

Submissions and Payment: Guidelines and catalogue available on website. Accepts submissions from agents only. Response time and publication period vary. Royalty.

Loving Healing Press

5145 Pontiac Trail, Ann Arbor, MI 48105-9627. www.LHpress.com

Senior Editor: Victor R. Volkman

Loving Healing Press is dedicated to producing books about innovative and rapid therapies that empower and heal the mind and spirit. Its titles for adults and children focus on life's issues, with a strong focus on children's and parenting subjects, such as developmental disorders and cyberbullying, as well as trauma and healing for all ages. Their advice is to read the book aloud to a friend and see what type of response you get. Loving Healing Press is seeking books on mental and physical disabilities.

Freelance Potential: Publishes 15 titles annually.

Fiction: Middle grade, YA. Genres: multicultural.

Nonfiction: Story picture book, middle-grade, YA, adult. Topics: health, trauma, mental health, family, social issues, self help.

Submissions and Payment: Guidelines and catalogue available on website. Query with outline of book listing all chapters, 1–4 sample chapters, statement of market and marketing plans, and estimates of total length of manuscript and date of completion. Accepts email to victor@LHpress.com (Word files). Response time, publication period, unknown. Royalty.

Orbit Books

Hachette Book Group, 237 Park Avenue, 16th Floor, New York, NY 10017. www.orbitbooks.net

Editorial Department

Orbit Books, an imprint of Hachette Book Group, has quickly established itself as one of the market-leading science fiction and fantasy imprints in the US, and the fastest growing imprint in the field. It publishes the most exciting science fiction and fantasy for the widest possible readership. While most titles are geared toward adult readers, some are suitable for young adults. Orbit Books will consider the work of new writers, but accepts submissions only from writers who are represented by literary agents.

Freelance Potential: Publishes 40 titles annually.

Fiction: YA. Genres: science fiction, fantasy.

Submissions and Payment: Accepts submissions from agented authors only. Responds in 2–6 months. Publication period varies. Royalty; advance.

Twilight Times Books

P.O. Box 3340, Kingsport, TN 37664. www.twilighttimesbooks.com

Publisher: Lida Quillen

Twilight Times Books' mission is to promote excellence in writing and great literature. It is a royalty-paying small press print publisher. Publishing in both print and electronic form, it is dedicated to getting great literary, New Age, and science fiction/fantasy books into the hands of readers. Also publishes in the historical, mystery, romance, and fantasy genres. It is currently interested in acquiring more juvenile titles and also looking for YA fiction and nonfiction.

Freelance Potential: Publishes 15 titles annually: 50% developed from unsolicited submissions; 10% by authors who are new to the publishing house; 10% by previously unpublished writers. Receives 150+ queries monthly.

Fiction: YA. Genres: historical, literary, science fiction, fantasy, mystery, suspense.

Nonfiction: YA. Topics: self-improvement, how-to, humor.

Submissions and Payment: Guidelines and catalogue available on website. See guidelines for latest submission periods. Query with cover letter, synopsis, first chapter, and marketing plan. Accepts email queries to publisher@twilighttimesbooks.com (no attachments). Responds in 3–4 weeks during submission period. Publication period varies. Royalty.

Contests

The Alcott Award for Young Adult Fiction

Hidden River Arts, www.hiddenriverarts.wordpress.com/

Sponsored by Hidden River Arts, the Alcott Award is offered for a YA novel that, in the tradition of *Little Women*, offers at least one central female character. The story may be any form of fiction writing. The winning manuscript will be published by Many Frog Press. This competition is open to all writers, but only accepts submissions in English.

Length: Book-length.

Requirements: Entry fee, $22. Submissions are accepted online through Submittable at the website. Submissions should include a synopsis before the manuscript in one document. Simultaneous submissions are accepted.

Prizes: Winner receives a $1,000 cash prize and publication of their manuscript by Many Frog Press.

Deadline: September.

Arizona Authors Association Literary Contest

1119 East Le Marche, Phoenix, AZ 85022. www.arizonaauthors.com

The Arizona Authors Association places a high value on literature to enrich the lives of those who read it. Since it began in 1978, the *Arizona Literary Magazine* has launched the careers of many authors. Celebrating literary excellence, this annual contest welcomes submissions from worldwide writers; however, special categories are offered to Arizona state residents. Unpublished essays, novels, articles, short stories, new dramas, and poems, along with published fiction, children's literature (board and chapter books), and nonfiction will be considered. Picture books and juvenile fiction have also been recently added as categories.

Length: Varies for each category.

Requirements: Entry fees range from $15–$30, depending on category. Send 3 copies of each unpublished entry or 3 copies of published book with completed entry form, found on the website. Manuscripts are not returned; published books are donated. Visit the website or contact the contest coordinator for complete submission guidelines for each category.

Prizes: For all categories: First prize, $100; second prize, $50; third prize, $25; plus publication or feature in *Arizona Literary Magazine* and additional promotional listings. First and Second Prize Winner in Poetry, Essay, and Short Story will receive a nomination for the Pushcart Prize.

Deadline: Entries must be postmarked between January 1 and July 1 (entries postmarked July 1 but received later are acceptable).

Autumn House Poetry, Fiction, and Nonfiction Contests

Autumn House Press, 5530 Penn Avenue, Pittsburgh, PA 15206. www.autumnhouse.org

Autumn House Press encourages writers, especially new writers, of all backgrounds to apply. It is once again sponsoring their annual contest for fiction, nonfiction, and poetry. Sub-genres such as novels, novellas, short stories, short-shorts, in either fiction or nonfiction, as well as poetry are all welcome to be submitted for consideration.

Length: Poetry collections, 50–80 pages. Fiction and nonfiction, 200–300 pages.

Requirements: Entry fee, $30. Accepts hard copy or online submission through website. Manuscripts will not be returned. Visit the website for complete competition guidelines and submission details. Include SASE for contest results. Contact info@autumnhouse.org with any questions or concerns.

Prizes: Winning entries receive publication, a $1,000 advance, and a $1,500 travel grant. All entries are considered for publication by Autumn House.

Deadline: June 30.

AWP Award Series

Association of Writers and Writing Programs, 5700 Rivertech CT, Suite 225, Riverdale Park, MD 20737-1250. www.awpwriter.org/contests/awp_award_series_overview

The competition is open to all authors writing in English regardless of nationality or residence, and is available to published and unpublished authors alike. AWP sponsors the Award Series, an annual competition for the publication of excellent new book-length works. This competition is specifically an evaluation "of writers, for writers, by writers." Four awards are given out: Grace Paley Prize for Short Fiction, Donald Hall Prize for Poetry, AWP Prize for Creative Nonfiction, and AWP Prize for the Novel. Manuscripts that have been previously published in their entirety, including self-publication, are not eligible.

Length: Poetry, at least 48 pages; short story and creative nonfiction collections, 150–300 pages; novels, at least 60,000 words.

Requirements: Entry fee, $20 for AWP members; $30 for non-members. Upload manuscript to awp.submittable.com/submit as a doc, docx, txt, PDF, or RTF document. No entry fees or manuscripts will be returned.

Prizes: Winners receive awards ranging from $2,500 to $5,500, and publication of their book by the University of Pittsburgh Press, University of Massachusetts Press, University of Georgia Press, or New Issues Press.

Deadline: Entries accepted January 1–February 28. Submission form available at website.

The Black River Chapbook Competition

Black Lawrence Press
www.blacklawrence.com/submissions-and-contests/the-black-river-chapbook-competition/

This contest is open to new, emerging, and established writers. Twice each year, Black Lawrence Press runs the Black River Chapbook Competition for an unpublished chapbook of poems or short fiction. These genre limitations are there to receive and publish the best writing of today.

Length: 16–36 pages.

Requirements: Entry fee, $15. Accepts submissions and fees electronically through Submittable only. Cannot accept submissions via email or postal mail. Simultaneous submissions are allowed. Visit http://help.submittable.com for help with the online submissions system.

Prizes: $500 in cash, book publication, and 10 copies of the book.

Deadline: Spring: April 1–May 31. Fall: September 1–October 31.

The BookLife Prize in Fiction

https://booklife.com/about-us/the-booklife-prize.html

This contest is unique in the fact that all entrants receive a critique of their work. The BookLife Prize is an annual writing competition sponsored by BookLife and Publisher's Weekly. The prize seeks to support independent authors and discover great written works in six categories. The categories in the Fiction Contest are: Romance/Erotica; Mystery/Thriller; Science Fiction/Fantasy/Horror; General Fiction; and Middle-Grade and YA Fiction.

Length: Middle-grade fiction novels must contain 30,000 to 65,000 words. All other submissions must contain 40,000 to 100,000 words.

Requirements: Entry fee, $99. Each entry receives a Critic's Report, a critical assessment of their novel written by a Publisher's Weekly reviewer. Entries are accepted through the website at http://booklife.com/affiliates/pw-prize-single. Files must be in Word, PDF, or RTF format. Novellas, novelettes, short fiction, and collections are ineligible.

Prizes: The winner receives a cash prize of $5,000 and an author profile in Publisher's Weekly.

Deadline: August 31.

Randolph Caldecott Medal

American Library Association, 50 East Huron Street, Chicago, IL 60611.
www.ala.org/awardsgrants/awards/6/apply

Presented by the Association for Library Service to Children, the Caldecott Medal is awarded annually to the artist of the most distinguished American picture book for children published in English in the United States during the preceding year. Winners display excellence of execution primarily in art but also show creative depiction of story, theme, concept, setting, mood, and recognition of the child audience.

Requirements: Must be an American picture book written in English and published in the United States. No entry fee. Submit two copies; one to the Association for Library Service to Children office and one to the award committee chair. Email alscawards@ala.org for address information.

Prizes: The winner is announced at the ALA Midwinter Meeting in January and presented with the bronze medal at an awards banquet the following summer.

Deadline: December 31 of the publication year.

Cascade Writing Contest and Awards

1075 Willow Lake Road N, Keizer, OR 97303. www.oregonchristianwriters.org

The purpose of the contest is to reward excellent writing and to encourage both seasoned and emerging writers as well as to provide a notable achievement for a writer's bio. Open to both published and unpublished writers, this contest awards prizes in a number of categories including young adult book, children's chapter book, memoir, short story, and historical fiction. Visit the website for specific guidelines for each category. Two special awards will also be presented: The Trailblazer Award to a writer who has distinguished him/herself in the field of Christian writing, and Writer of Promise Award for a new author who has shown unusual promise in the field of Christian writing.

Length: Varies for each category.

Requirements: Entry fee: $30 for Oregon Christian Writers members; $40 for non-members ($35 and $45 respectively for hard-copy published book entries). Entry fee must be paid online whether you are submitting your entry electronically or by hard copy. Limit three entries per author. Accepts submissions by email to cascade@oregonchristianwriters.org or by hard copy. Hard copy books should be sent to a P.O. box address that will be provided to you when you enter.

Prizes: Award certificate and pin are presented to winners.

Deadline: March 15.

Karen and Phillip Cushman Late Bloomer Award

http://www.scbwi.org/awards/grants/work-in-progress-grants/karen-and-philip-cushman-late-bloomer-award/

Unpublished authors over the age of fifty are those who are considered for he Karen and Phillip Cushman Late Bloomer Award. One winner will be chosen from the pool of those who have submitted material for the SCBWI Work-In-Progress Grants.

Requirements: Must be a current SCBWI member. Applicants send an additional e-mail with the same Work-in-Progress grant submission they have already submitted to: wipgrant@scbwi.org. Send your Cushman submission with "Cushman" in the subject line and your full name in the body of the email. (You will be sending two emails to the same address with the same attachment but different subject lines).

Prizes: $500 and free tuition to any SCBWI conference anywhere in the world (transportation, hotel, and expenses are not included).

Deadline: March 31.

The Eloquent Quill International Book Award

P.O. Box 3362, Rapid City, SD 57709. www.clcawards.org/Eloquent-Quill.html

Novellas, novels, and chapter books for young adults and children are encouraged to participate in The Eloquent Quill Top Honors Book Award. It was created to recognize distinguished fiction for a youth audience. A highly selective committee will judge the books on their ability to promote character, vision, creativity, and learning, through specific content which possesses the key elements found in well-crafted literature. Self-published books and e-books in ePub or PDF format are eligible. Books may be nominated by authors, publishers, or agents.

Length: No length requirements. All books must possess an ISBN.

Requirements: Entry fee: $45. Send nomination form (on website), entry fee, and 5 copies of the book. Accepts hard copy and electronic entries via form on website. A separate entry form must be completed for each title submitted. Book must have been published within 24 months of the entry deadline.

Prizes: A medal, a signed award certificate with embossed seal, and twenty-five Eloquent Quill Book Award seals for winning book.

Deadline: Early Entry Deadline, January 1. Final Award Application Deadline, April 15.

The Enchanted Page International Book Award

P.O. Box 3362, Rapid City, SD 57709. www.clcawards.org/Enchanted-Page-Book-Award.html

Each year a highly selective judging committee evaluates books for their literary quality and their ability to promote character, vision, creativity, and learning. It awards one distinguished children's story picture book The Enchanted Page International Book Award. Self-published books are eligible; e-books are not. Books may be nominated by authors, publishers, or agents.

Length: No length requirements. All books must possess an ISBN.

Requirements: Entry fee: $45. Send nomination form (on website), entry fee, and 3 copies of the book. Accepts hard copy and electronic entries via form on website. Book must have been published within 24 months of the deadline. A separate entry form must be completed for each title submitted.

Prizes: A medal, a signed certificate with embossed seal, and twenty-five Enchanted Page Book Award seals for winning book.

Deadline: Early Entry Deadline, January 1. Final Award Application Deadline, April 15.

Shubert Fendrich Memorial Playwriting Contest

Pioneer Drama Service, P.O. Box 4267, Englewood, CO 80155.
www.pioneerdrama.com/Playwrights/Contest.asp

This ongoing contest from Pioneer Drama Service is proud to award the annual Shubert Fendrich Memorial Playwriting Contest Award which aims to encourage the development of quality theatrical materials for the educational, community, and children's theatre markets. Playwrights who have not yet been published by Pioneer Drama Service are welcome to enter this contest.

Length: Running time 20 to 90 minutes.

Requirements: No entry fee. Send complete manuscript with 100- to 200-word synopsis, cast list, running time, CD/score for musicals, set designs, proof of production or staged reading, and age of intended audience. A cover letter and/or resume also needs to be included as well as a self-addressed envelope for the return of materials and manuscripts. Accepts hard copy to Submissions Editor (contact information on website) and email submissions of txt, doc or pdf files. See website for further guidelines.

Prizes: Prizes include a publication contract and a $1,000 advance.

Deadline: Ongoing.

Don Freeman Grant-in-Aid

SCBWI, 4727 Wilshire Blvd., Suite 301 Los Angeles, CA 90010.
www.scbwi.org/awards/grants/work-in-progress-grants/don-freeman-illustrator-grants/

The Don Freeman Work-In-Progress Grants are available to all members of the SCBWI, regardless of membership level, who are working on a picture book or their portfolio. Don Freeman was a renowned illustrator and an early supporter of SCBWI. He established this award to enable picture book illustrators to further their understanding, training, and work in the picture book genre.

Length: No length requirements.

Requirements: Published illustrators should supply a book dummy that includes fully illustrated sketches, 2 finished illustrations (1 color and 1 black and white) and the entire picture book text. This book dummy should demonstrate the illustrator's ability to convey the mood of the story, show action and pacing, and reveal characters. Pre-published illustrators can submit either the picture book dummy or 10 completed illustrations (at least 8 in color). Submit one of the above choices as a single PDF file to sarahbaker@scbwi.org; put "Don Freeman Grant" in subject line with either "Published" or "Pre-published." Only these electronic submissions are acceptable. Do not send original artwork.

Prizes: Two grants of $1,000 each are awarded annually. One is given to a published illustrator and one to a pre-published illustrator.

Deadline: Non-members must submit applications to the Society prior to entering the contest. Otherwise, they are not eligible. Application requests must be submitted by June 15 and completed applications should be submitted by February 10. Once the illustrator is either a member or an associate member of SCBWI, they must enter the contest between March 1 and March 31. Submissions received after March 31 will not be accepted.

Genesis Contest

American Christian Fiction Writers. www.acfw.com/genesis

Any Christian author whose work has not been previously published is considered for this award. With ten categories to enter, Genesis provides the opportunity for unbiased feedback on writers' work by published authors and experienced judges, and the chance for finalists to have their work read by Christian publishing house editors and literary agents. Both members and non-members are eligible to participate in this annual contest, under the condition that their work has not been previously published in novella or book-length fiction. Manuscripts in various genres including young adult, speculative, short novel, romance, romantic suspense, novella, historical fiction, contemporary, suspense/thriller, and historical fiction will be considered.

Length: No more than 16 pages.

Requirements: Entry fee, $35 for members; $95 for non-members. Multiple entries are allowed. Enter with the online form only; include a 1-page synopsis followed by the first 15 pages of the manuscript in one entry file. Prologues are acceptable and should be included in the 15-page count. Accepts multiple entries. See guidelines at website for specific category email contacts and other details. No hard copy submissions.

Prizes: Each category will have one first-place winner. The first-place entry in each category will receive a winner's award and a gold Genesis lapel pin. The finalists in each category will receive a certificate and silver Genesis pin.

Deadline: March 15.

Hackney Literary Awards

www.hackneyliteraryawards.org

Sponsored by the family of Cecil Hackney, these awards were established in 1969. This prestigious writing competition recognizes excellence in poetry and fiction with prizes at the national level and for the state of Alabama. They award cash prizes for entries of poetry and short fiction. They also have a special Morris Hackney award for an unpublished novel.

Length: Poetry, to 50 lines. Short story, to 500 words. Novel, length open.

Requirements: Submissions must be original and unpublished. Entry fees: Poetry, $15; Short story, $20; Novel, $30. Payments are accepted online. Multiple entries are accepted. Entries must be submitted with a cover sheet that includes all contact information. PDF, doc, and docx files are accepted. Entries are accepted through the website. Contact info@hackneyliteraryawards.org for more information.

Prizes: The annual competition awards $2,500 in prizes for poetry and short fiction (1st place, $600; 2nd, $400; 3rd, $250). Novel category winner receives $5,000.

Deadline: Short story and poetry submissions due November 30. Unpublished novel submissions due September 30.

Marilyn Hall Awards for Youth Theatre

P.O. Box 148, Beverly Hills, CA 90213. www.beverlyhillstheatreguild.org

This annual competition focuses on youth theatre to discover new theatrical works and to encourage established or emerging writers to create quality works for youth theatre. It presents prizes in two categories: plays for children in grades 6–8 and plays for grades 9–12.

Length: Plays should have a running time of 45–75 minutes.

Requirements: Submissions must be original and unpublished. Each entry must include a signed entry form, available at website. Manuscripts should not contain any information identifying the author. Accepts hard copy submissions only. Visit the website for complete guidelines.

Prizes: First prize, $1,200. Second, $600.

Deadline: February 28.

Aurand Harris Memorial Playwriting Award

The New England Theatre Conference, Inc., Aurand Harris Playwriting Award, 167 Cherry Street, #331, Milford, CT 06460. www.netconline.org

A contest for new full-length plays for young audiences, this award was established in 1997 to honor the late Aurand Harris for his lifetime dedication to all aspects of professional theatre for young audiences. It is open to all playwrights and it accepts original, unpublished entries only. A panel of judges named by the NETC Executive Board administers this award.

Length: Full-length plays.

Requirements: No entry fee. Limit one entry per competition. Entries must include a statement that the play will not have been published or professionally produced as of May 1st in the contest year. Include a list of the play's workshop productions, if any. Send submissions to harris-award@netconline.org. Hard copy submissions are not accepted.

Prizes: A staged reading of the prize-winning scripts will be held along with the Annual Excellence in Theatre Awards ceremony.

Deadline: May 1.

Institute for Writers Writing Contests

The Institute for Writers, www.instituteforwriters.com; www.instituteforwriters.com/contestrules/

Each writing contest from the Institute for Writers provides writers with the opportunity to receive a critique by an expert in the field. Quarterly writing contests on different subjects encourage both new and experienced writers to demonstrate and further improve their skills. All entrants are additionally eligible to attend a webinar where the contest winners will be presented and critiqued. Submissions will be judged on clarity, liveliness, potential in the market, completeness of story, and writer's ability to match normal manuscript format.

Length: Varies for each category.

Requirements: Any original, unpublished piece not accepted by any publisher at the time of submission is eligible. Entry fee, $19. Multiple entries: each entry must be entered separately with its own entry fee. Entries are accepted through the website submission form following payment of the entry fee. See website for complete online submission process details and specific information.

Prizes: Cash awards, publication on the Institute for Writers website, and a personalized critique of the winning entries are awarded to winners.

Deadline: Varies for each contest. Visit the website for complete information.

Leapfrog Press Award

P.O. Box 505, Fredonia, NY 14063. www.leapfrogpress.com/contest.htm

The Leapfrog Press is in search of adult, young adult, and middle-grade novels, novellas, and short story collection for this contest. It looks for an unpublished book with a unique perspective.

Length: Minimum 22,000 words.

Requirements: Entry fee $30. Submissions, queries, and entry fees are accepted through Submittable page on the website. Attach a single Word or PDF file only. The first page should be a formal query letter addressed to the editor, Nathan Carter, followed by opening chapters or story of the manuscript. See website for more details; contact the Leapfrog Press at fictioncontest@leapfrogpress.com with any questions about the Submittable page/process.

Prize: First-prize winner receives a publishing contract with advance, $150, and one or two manuscript critiques. Additional prizes for semi-finalists and honorable mention are listed on website.

Deadline: May 1.

The Little Peeps Award

Chanticleer Book Reviews, 1050 Larrabee Avenue, Suite 104 #334, Bellingham, WA, 98225. https://chantireviews.com/services#!/Little-Peeps-Fiction-Writing-Contests-Chanticleer-Book-Reviews/p/58078150/category=5193080

This award honors the best book written to an audience between the ages of 8–12. Chanticleer Book Reviews is looking for the best books written for early readers featuring stories of all shapes and sizes. In the five categories of story books, chapter books, picture books, activity books, and educational books, the judges evaluate each submissions for professionalism, characterization, uniqueness, writing craft, storyline, intrigue, and more.

Length: No length restrictions.

Requirements: Book must contain an ISBN/ASIN designation. Novels may be manuscripts, self-published, indie published, or traditionally published. The work submitted must be copyrighted after Dec. 31, 2016. Anything copyrighted before this date will not be accepted. See website for more details and to submit your work.

Prize: Grand prize of $1,000 (other cash amounts are given to finalists), prize ribbon, digital badges, and book stickers.

Deadline: September 30.

Maryland Writers' Association Contest

3 Church Circle, #165, Annapolis, MD 21401. www.marylandwriters.org

Encouraging writers to reach their full potential, the Maryland Writers' Association encourages members to submit entries to this annual contest for original fiction or nonfiction with a Maryland theme. This contest will not accept poetry, children's literature, or religious work. Entries are judged on creativity, quality of writing, and fit with the theme.

Length: 500–3,500 words

Requirements: No entry fee. Limit 3 entries per person. Submissions must be publication ready. Contest entries are accepted through the website submission form only.

Prizes: Winners will receive one copy of *30 Ways to Love Maryland* at or around the time of the MWA Conference.

Deadline: July 1–October 31.

Louise Meriwether First Book Prize

www.feministpress.org/louise-meriwether-first-book-prize/

The prize is granted to a manuscript that follows in the tradition of Meriwether's contemporary writing featuring a young Black girl as the protagonist. This prize was founded in 2016 to honor author Louise Meriwether by publishing a debut work by a woman or nonbinary author of color. The prize continues the legacy of telling much-needed stories that shift culture and inspire new writers.

Requirements: All manuscripts should be sent to louisemeriwetherprize@gmail.com with the subject line "First Book Prize" followed by your name and book title. Please send manuscript as a PDF, and also include a cover letter as a separate attachment with author statement, a brief bio, how your work fits with the Feminist Press, your manuscript's word count, and a brief list of writers (up to three) you consider to be part of your writing lineage. The work submitted for consideration may not be under contract elsewhere. Check website for full guidelines.

Prizes: One winner is awarded a $5,000 advance and a contract to publish their book both in print and digitally.

Deadline: June 30.

Mythopoeic Fantasy Award for Children's Literature

David D. Oberhelman, 306 Edmon Low Library, Oklahoma State University, Stillwater, OK 74078. www.mythsoc.org

The Mythopoeic Fantasy Award for Children's Literature was established in 1992 and honors books for young readers to age 13. It honors books in the tradition of *The Hobbit* or *The Chronicles of Narnia*. To qualify, entries must have been written for beginning readers to age 13 and published in the previous year.

Length: No length requirements.

Requirements: Members of the Mythopoeic Society nominate books, and a membership committee selects winners. Authors who are members of the society may not nominate their own titles. For complete contest information email the awards administrator at awards@mythsoc.org.

Prize: A statuette.

Deadline: February 14.

Newbery Award

American Library Association, 50 East Huron Street, Chicago, IL 60611.
http://www.ala.org/alsc/awardsgrants/bookmedia/newberymedal/newberymedal

Awarded annually by the Association for Library Service to Children, a division of the American Library Association, the Newbery Medal was named for eighteenth-century British bookseller John Newbery. It is awarded to the author of the most distinguished contribution to American literature for children published in English during the previous year. It values interpretation of theme, clarity and accuracy, plot development, well-delineated characters and setting, and appropriate style.

Length: No length requirements.

Requirements: No entry fee. All entries must have been published in the United States in the preceding year. Authors must be US citizens or residents. Send 1 copy to the ALSC office and 1 copy to the award committee chair, with a cover letter if you wish. Please e-mail alscawards@ala.org for address information.

Prize: The Newbery Medal is awarded to the winner. Honor books may also be named.

Deadline: December 31.

New Voices Award

Attn New Voices Award, Lee and Low Books, 95 Madison Avenue, Suite #1205, New York, NY 10016. www.leeandlow.com/writers-illustrators/new-voices-award

The New Voices Award is given annually by children's book publisher Lee and Low Books for a children's picture book manuscript by a writer of color or Native/Indigenous writer. Established in 2000, Lee and Low Books honors picture book manuscripts by writers of color that address the needs of children of color with this annual award. Fiction, nonfiction, or poetry submissions need to present stories that can be readily identifiable to readers ages 5–12, and equally important, they must promote mutual understanding.

Length: To 1,500 words.

Requirements: Open to US residents of color who have not published a picture book. No folklore or animal stories. No entry fee. Limit 2 entries per competition. Include cover letter, brief biographical note with cultural and ethnic information, publication history, if any, and manuscript. Accepts hard copy. No simultaneous submissions.

Prizes: $2,000 and a standard publishing contract. An honor grant of $1,000 is also awarded.

Deadline: Submissions accepted between April 1 and August 31.

New Works of Merit Playwriting Competition

www.newworksofmeritplaywritingcontest.com

With a goal of helping playwrights strengthen their script through detailed script analysis, this competition is offered yearly. It looks for scripts that meet at least one of the following criteria: 1) Enhance self-realization; 2) Support peace and social justice; 3) Foster new understanding of minority issues that focus on racial, ethnic, and gender discrimination both in the United States and abroad; 4) Empower youth to build healthy inner foundations; 5) Educate to gain further insight into healthy social/emotional living; 6) Shed new light on religious, spiritual, and cultural differences and issues; 7) Build respect for cultural expression and identity in a world that is experiencing rapid globalization; and 8) Explore the widening gap between the values this country was founded on and the values we present to the world today.

Length: Scripts must be no longer than 2 hours (90 pages).

Requirements: Entry fee, $25. Accepts PayPal payment on website. Transaction ID should be included on the application form. Application form and entry should be sent to the same email. Visit the website for a complete list of guidelines.

Prizes: Reading with Q&A in a professional venue valued at $1,000 plus $300 cash prize.

Deadline: February 1–July 31.

North Street Book Prize

North Street Book Prize, 351 Pleasant Street, PMB 222, Northampton, MA 01060. https://winningwriters.com/our-contests/north-street-book-prize

This award looks for great works by self-published authors. The competition is open to self-published books in the following categories: Mainstream/Literary Fiction, Genre Fiction, Creative Nonfiction and Memoir, Poetry, Children's Picture Book, and Graphic Narrative (novels, memoirs, story collections, etc.).

Requirements: $60 per entry. Include your full name, mailing address, phone number, and email address with your entry. Please also indicate the category for your entry. Accepts hard copy or electronic submission via website. Visit the website for guidelines.

Prizes: Grand Prize winner receives $3,000 and a marketing analysis. One top winner per category receives $1,000. One honorable mention in each category receives $250.

Deadline: Submission window: February 15–June 30.

On-The-Verge Emerging Voice Award

Society of Children's Book Writers and Illustrators, 8271 Beverly Boulevard, Los Angeles, CA 90048. www.scbwi.org/awards/grants/on-the-verge-emerging-voices-grant/

Honoring two writers or illustrators of children's picture books or novels from an ethnic and/or cultural background that is traditionally underrepresented in children's literature in the United States is the purpose of this award established by SCBWI. The grant was created to foster the emergence of diverse voices in children's books. SCBWI reserves the right not to confer this award in any given year. The manuscript must be an original work in English, written for young people, and not under contract.

Length: No length requirements.

Requirements: Send complete manuscript, with 250-word synopsis, 250-word autobiographical statement and career summary, and a 250-word explanation of why your work will bring forward an underrepresented voice. Applicants must be over 18, unpublished, and should not have agent representation. Accepts email entries only to sarahdiamond@scbwi.org (Word attachments; PDF for manuscripts). See website for details.

Prizes: All-expense paid trip to SCBWI Summer Conference in Los Angeles, a press release to publishers, a year of free membership to SCBWI, and an SCBWI mentor for a year.

Deadline: Applications are accepted between September 15 and November 15 only.

Pacific Northwest Writers Association Literary Contests

PNWA Literary Contest, PMB 2717, 1420 NW Gilman Blvd, Ste 2, Issaquah, WA 98027. www.pnwa.org

Created by Pacific Northwest Writers Association, this annual literary contest honors original, unpublished material in English. It recognizes the best works in 12 categories including chapter books, middle-grade books, and young adult.

Length: Varies for each category; see website.

Requirements: Entry fee, $37 for PNWA members; $52 for non-members. Limit one entry per category per competition. See guidelines for specific requirements for each category. Send 3 copies of all manuscript materials and entry form on website. Accepts submissions through the website and mail.

Prizes: First place in each category, $600, the Zola Award, and an opportunity to attend the Agents and Editors Reception at the PNWA summer conference; second place, $250; third place $150. All entries receive two critiques. Finalists (8 in each category) receive special recognition at the conference.

Deadline: March 27.

Katherine Paterson Prize

KPP, Hunger Mountain, Vermont College of Fine Arts, 36 College Street, Montpelier, VT 05602. http://hungermtn.org/contests/katherine-paterson-prize/

The goal of this annual prize sponsored by *Hunger Mountain*, the literary journal of Vermont College of Fine Arts, is to foster the next generation of creative writers and to encourage young people to make their voices heard. It focuses on young adult and children's literature. Original, unpublished manuscripts aimed at young adults and children are eligible for this prize.

Requirements: Entry fee, $20 per submission. One original, unpublished piece up to 10,000 words per submission. Accepts entries both electronically and through the mail. Please see website for electronic submission details.

Prize: First place: $1,000 and publication. Three category winners receive $100 each and online publication.

Deadline: March 1.

PEN/Phyllis Naylor Working Writer Fellowship

PEN America
https://pen.org/literary-award/penphyllis-naylor-working-writer-fellowship-5000/

This fellowship was developed to help writers whose work is of high literary caliber and is designed to assist a writer at a crucial moment in his or her career to complete a book-length work-in-progress. It is offered annually to an author of children's or young adult fiction. The fellowship was made possible by PEN member Phyllis Reynolds Naylor, a prolific author of more than 140 books.

Length: Work-in-progress.

Requirements: Candidates must have published one or more novels for children or young adults that have been warmly received by literary critics, but have not generated sufficient income to support the author. The author's previous titles must have been published in the United States. The submitted work must be fiction. Judges look for entrants whose work has not yet attracted a broad readership. Graphic novels and picture books are not eligible. Writers may nominate themselves or nominations may be made by a fellow writer. Include a 1- to 2-page cover letter describing how you meet the fellowship criteria. Include a project outline and 50–75 pages of manuscript text. Entries are accepted online only.

Prizes: $5,000 fellowship.

Deadline: Entries are accepted April 1–August 15.

Robert J. Pickering Award for Playwriting Excellence

Branch County Community Theatre, 14 S. Hanchett St., Coldwater, MI 49036.
www.branchcct.org/pickering

Full-length unpublished plays and musicals are eligible for this annual award. It was established to honor past member and playwright Bob Pickering and to provide a vehicle for playwrights to see their works produced. Over 30 plays have been produced since 1984.

Length: Scripts must be no longer than 2 hours (90 pages).

Requirements: No entry fee. Plays and musicals must be full-length and unproduced. Send hard copy. SASE. Complete guidelines are available at the website.

Prizes: $200 is awarded to the first place winner; $50 for second-place; $25 for third-place.

Deadline: December 31.

Purple Dragonfly Book Award

Cristy Bertini, ATTN: Dragonfly Book Awards, 1271 Turkey Street, Hardwick, MA 01082.
www.dragonflybookawards.com

Looking for stories that are original, innovative, and creative in both content and design, the Purple Dragonfly Book Awards is an international book competition that was created in 2009 to celebrate the best in children's books. It recognizes and honors accomplished authors in the field of children's literature, but also highlights up-and-coming, newly published authors and younger published writers. With 48 different subject categories, it is looking for stories that inspire, inform, teach, or entertain.

Length: No length restrictions.

Requirements: The entry fee for the Purple Dragonfly Book Awards contest is $65 for one title in one category or $60 for entries completed on or before March 2. All entry fees are per title, per category. Participants may enter one book in one category, one book in multiple categories, or several different books in one or more categories, as long as they pay separate entry fees for each book/category entered, submit a separate entry form for each category, and mail in the appropriate number of book copies. See website for additional information for specific categories. Hard copies are accepted by mail. Electronic books should be sent to cristy@storymonsters.com with "Dragonfly Book Awards" as the subject.

Prize: Grand Prize of $500, 100 foil seals, one hour of marketing consultation, $100 worth of Five Star titles, and publicity. Additional runner-up prizes listed on website.

Deadline: May 1.

The Restless Books Prize For New Immigrant Writing

http://restlessbooks.org/prize-for-new-immigrant-writing

This award looks for extraordinary unpublished submissions from emerging writers of sharp, culture-straddling writing that addresses identity in a global age. Honoring outstanding debut work by a first-generation immigrant, the prize alternates years between fiction and nonfiction.

Length: Fiction manuscripts must be a minimum of 45,000 words. Nonfiction samples must be at least 25,000 words.

Requirements: No entry fee. Limit one entry per competition. Accepts submissions through the website. Candidates are asked to submit a CV and a one-page cover letter as the first pages of their manuscript. See the website for complete competition guidelines.

Prizes: Winner receives a $10,000 cash advance and publication by Restless Books.

Deadline: Submissions are accepted between September 1 and March 31.

San Antonio Writers Guild Annual Contest

P.O. Box 100717, San Antonio, TX 78201-8717.
http://sanantoniowritersguild.org/contest/

Celebrating the best in unpublished works, the San Antonio Writers' Guild's writing contest welcomes nonfiction, poetry, and multiple genre categories in long and short fiction. This contest is open to all writers.

Length: Novel, first chapter or up to first 5,000 words; short story, 4,000 words; flash fiction, 1,000 words; nonfiction memoir/personal essay, 2,500 words; poetry, up to 3 poems, 40 lines maximum per poem.

Requirements: Entry fee, $10 for SAWG members; $20 for nonmembers. Multiple entries are accepted in up to 3 different categories. View complete guidelines and submission information at https://sawritersguild.submittable.com/submit.

Prizes: First place, $100. Second place, $50. Third place, $25.

Deadline: There are presently no open calls for submissions. Check website for updates.

San Francisco Book Festival

JM Northern Media LLC, attn: San Francisco Book Festival, 7095 Hollywood Boulevard, Suite 864, Hollywood, CA 90028-0893. www.sanfranciscobookfestival.com/index.html

The San Francisco Book Festival has no restrictions as to date of publication. It will consider fiction, nonfiction, biography/autobiography, children's books, compilations/anthologies, young adult, how-to, cookbooks, science fiction, business, history, wild card, gay, photography/art, poetry, unpublished, technology, and spiritual/religious works. The grand prize winner is honored at the annual festival.

Length: No length restrictions.

Requirements: Entry fee of $50 per manuscript; multiple submissions are accepted. E-book entries are welcome. Entry forms available on website.

Prize: Grand prize of $1,500 and a flight to the awards ceremony.

Deadline: June 25.

SCBWI Work-in-Progress Grants

Society of Children's Book Writers and Illustrators, 4727 Wilshire Boulevard, Suite 301, Los Angeles, CA 90010. www.scbwi.org/awards/grants/work-in-progress-grants/

The SCBWI Work-In-Progress Grants are open to current members of SCBWI. The grants assist children's book writers, illustrators, and translators in the publication of a specific project currently not under contract. The Work-in-Progress Grants showcase outstanding manuscripts from members of SCBWI. SCBWI reserves the right not to confer this award in any given year. Grants are awarded in the categories of picture book text, chapter book, middle grade, YA fiction, YA nonfiction, and multicultural fiction or nonfiction.

Length: 750-word synopsis and 2,500-word writing sample from the relevant manuscript.

Requirements: No entry fee. Open to members only. Applications accepted online only as PDFs. Send synopsis, first 10 pages of manuscript, and grant category as one PDF document to wigrantp@scbwi.org. Instructions, complete guidelines, and application forms are available at website. For questions, email sarahdiamond@scbwi.org.

Prizes: winners' works will be made available on a secure webpage and presented to a hand-selected group of editors for their consideration. Although this is not a guarantee of publication, having your work presented to acquiring editors with an SCBWI endorsement is a unique opportunity.

Deadline: Application period is March 1 to March 31.

Seven Hills Literary and Penumbra Poetry Contest

2910 Kerry Forest Parkway D-4-357, Tallahassee, FL 32309. www.sevenhillsreview.submittable.com/submit

The Tallahassee Writers Association holds numerous contests annually including one for graphic short story; short story; creative nonfiction; young adult novel excerpt; adult novel excerpt; flash fiction; poetry; and haiku. On alternating years, the TWA also has a competition for children's picture books, ages 4 to 8, and a children's chapter book competition, in addition to contests for adult short stories, creative nonfiction, and flash fiction.

Length: Children's chapter books (ages 6–12) to 2,500 words, excerpt plus short synopsis; children's picture books, 1,000-word maximum; short stories, creative nonfiction, to 3,000 words; flash fiction, to 500 words.

Requirements: Entry fee, $6–15 for TWA members; $8–20 for non-members. Accepts electronic submissions only through Submittable. All entries must be unpublished. For questions, email Donna Meredith at meredithds@comcast.net.

Prizes: First prize, $100; second prize, $75; third prize, $50. Winners are published in *Seven Hills Review* and receive one complimentary copy.

Deadline: August 31.

Kay Snow Writing Contest

Willamette Writers, 2108 Buck Street, West Linn, OR 97068.
www.willamettewriters.org/submit-your-writing/kay-snow-writing-contest

Named in honor of Willamette Writers' founder, Kay Snow, this annual contest has a goal of helping writers reach professional goals in writing through a broad array of categories, and also to encourage student writers. In addition to prizes, winners will be listed on the Willamette Writers website and honored at the Willamette Writers Conference held annually in August. All material submitted must be previously unpublished.

Length: Varies for each category.

Requirements: Entry fee, $10 for WW members; $15 for non-members. Student writers (18 and under), no fee. Submit 2 copies of each entry with registration form and a 3x5 card that includes author name, contact information, book title, and category. Author's name must not appear on manuscript. For questions, email wilwrite@willamettewriters.com.

Prizes: Awards range from $100 to $10 in each category. The Liam Callen award, $500, is presented to the best overall entry.

Deadline: Entries must be postmarked by April 1.

Surrey International Writers' Conference Writing Contest

SiWC Writing Contest, Suite 544, 151-10090 152nd Street, Surrey, BC V3R 8X8 Canada.
https://www.siwc.ca/writing-contest/

Young writers are welcome to enter, but their work will be judged blind among submissions made by adult writers. This annual writing contest is open to unpublished writers 18 and up. Awards are given for poetry, short story, writing for young people, and nonfiction.

Length: Nonfiction and writing for young people, to 1,500 words; short stories, 2,500–5,000 words; poetry, to 100 lines.

Requirements: Entry fee, $15. Multiple entries are accepted. Accepts hard copy and email entries to contest@siwc.ca (no attachments). Author's name should not appear on the manuscript. Include a cover letter with author's name, contact info, word length, and competition category. For questions, email KC Dyer at contest@siwc.ca.

Prizes: First-place winners in each category, $1,000. Honorable mentions, $150. Winning entries are printed and sold as an anthology.

Deadline: Submissions accepted until September 18.

Sydney Taylor Manuscript Competition

Aileen Grossberg, 204 Park Street, Montclair, NJ 07042-2903.
www.jewishlibraries.org/content.php?page=STMA_Rules

The Association of Jewish Libraries is pleased to judge the Sydney Taylor Manuscript Competition and encourages submissions of the highest quality of work in the genre of Jewish children's literature. The Sydney Taylor Manuscript Award for unpublished manuscripts targets ages 8-13. It focuses on the genre of Jewish children's literature. It was established by Sydney Taylor's husband Ralph Taylor to encourage aspiring authors of Jewish children's books. It was first awarded in 1985, and many of the manuscripts have been subsequently published.

Length: 64–200 pages.

Requirements: No entry fee. One entry per competition. Short stories, plays, and poetry are not eligible. Send 6 copies with application and release form found on website, and a cover letter that includes a short personal statement, manuscript summary, and author biography or résumé. Accepts email to stmacajl@aol.com (PDF attachment) or CD (no hard copy). SASE for receipt confirmation only. See website for complete rules. For questions, contact Aileen Grossberg, Competition Coordinator, at 973-744-3836 or by email.

Prize: A cash prize of $1,000 and the opportunity to have the winning manuscript read by an experienced literary agent.

Deadline: September 30.

Times/Chicken House Children's Fiction Competition

2 Palmer Street, Frome, Somerset, BA11 1DS, United Kingdom.
http://chickenhousebooks.com/submissions/

The Times/Chicken House Children's House Children's Fiction Competition looks for original ideas, a fresh voice, a diverse range of entries, and stories that children will love. It accepts novels from unpublished novelists as well as published poets, picture book authors, and short story authors who wish to submit a finished full-length novel for children ages 7–18.

Length: 30,000–80,000 words.

Requirements: £15. Send complete manuscript and cover letter with an explanation of why your novel would appeal to children, brief author bio, 1-page synopsis of the novel, and a chapter-by-chapter plot plan outlining the major events of each chapter. Accepts hard copy and online submissions. For questions, email tina@doublecluck.com.

Prize: Publishing contract with Chicken House with a royalty advance of £10,000, plus representation from a top children's literary agent. The "Chairman's Choice" prize is a publishing contract with a royalty advance of £7,500 plus representation.

Deadline: February 28.

Jackie White Memorial Playwriting Competition

Columbia Entertainment Company, Attn: JWM, PO Box 953, Columbia, MO 65205.
http://www.cectheatre.org/playwriting

The Jackie White Memorial (JWM) contest seeks original or adapted scripts written for young audiences. Named for playwright Jackie Bromstead White, this national-level contest supports the development and production of children's theater plays. This contest is held annually and sponsored by Columbia Entertainment Company. Jackie White herself was a playwright and teacher, inspiring a passion for theater in everyone she knew. Entries should target an audience of children under the age of 15.

Length: Full-length plays.

Requirements: Entry fee, $25. Accepts hard copy and online submissions. Email questions to JWM@cectheatre.org. Multiple submissions are accepted. Entries must include character descriptions and scene synopses.

Prizes: Winner receives a $500 cash prize and a production of their play by CEC.

Deadline: March 31.

Words on Wings Young Adult Book Award

Literary Classics—Awards Dept., 500 East Boulevard #3362, Rapid City, SD 57701
www.clcawards.org/WOW_Young_Adult_Book_Award.html

The Words On Wings (WOW) Young Adult Book Award is bestowed upon those titles which are exceptional in both content and quality. It recognizes distinguished fiction for a young adult audience. This annual award recognizes the best in fiction written for young adults (up to 25 years of age). Books will be judged on their literary quality and how well they promote character, vision, creativity, and learning. Self-published books and e-books are eligible. Books may be nominated by authors, publishers, or agents.

Length: No length requirements. All books must possess an ISBN.

Requirements: Entry fee: $45. Send nomination form (on website), entry fee, and 3 copies of the book. Nominated books must possess an ISBN. Accepts hard copy and electronic entries via form on website.

Prizes: A medal, certificate, and embossed seals for winning book.

Deadline: Early Entry Deadline, May 1. Final Award Application Deadline, August 15.

Yale Drama Series David Charles Horn Prize

Yale Drama Series, P.O. Box 209040, New Haven, CT, 06520-9040.
http://dchornfoundation.org/competition-rules

The Yale Drama Series bestows this award to one original, unpublished play written in English. The competition accepts entries written in English from around the world. Plays that have been professionally produced or published are not eligible.

Length: Full-length plays.

Requirements: No entry fee. Limit one entry per competition. Strongly prefers electronic submissions through the website. Will accept hard copy.

Prizes: Winner receives the David Charles Horn Prize of $10,000, publication of his or her manuscript by Yale University Press, and a staged reading at Lincoln Center's Claire Tow Theater.

Deadline: Entries are accepted between June 1 and August 15.

Agents

Agents

Agents have become a more central part of publishing children's books, especially at major trade publishers. As the industry has shifted in recent years, quite a few respected, long-term children's editors and publishers have joined literary agencies or opened their own.

At some point, almost all book writers consider whether or not to look for an agent. Some successful authors never work with an agent, while others would not be without one to take care of selling, negotiations, and contracts. But a good manuscript will find its home with or without an agent, if you are committed to finding the right publisher for your work.

How to find an agent: To begin, review the listings of children's book agents in the following pages to see which might be likely candidates to represent your work.

Other sources for lists of agents include the standard publishing reference, *Literary Marketplace* (LMP); the Association of Authors' Representatives (www.aar-online.org) member list; the SCBWI Agents Directory (free to members); and the *2021 Guide to Literary Agents* (Writer's Digest Books), which offers valuable information on how to work with agents. Be sure that any agent you contact works with children's writers.

What an agent does: Before taking you on as a client, an agent will review your work editorially. Although agents are willing to take on unpublished writers—they want to find the next great children's writer—an author should aim to impress an agent, just like an editor, by demonstrating commitment to the craft and a professional approach to writing. The primary work of an agent is to contact publishers, market your material, negotiate for rights and licenses, and review financial statements.

How to contact an agent: If the agent has a website, go online for specific contact requirements. If not, send a well-written, professional cover letter describing your work and background, accompanied by an outline or synopsis and sample chapter. Most agents will accept simultaneous submissions, as long as you inform them that you're querying other agents, and perhaps publishers, as well. *Remember to tailor your query to individual agents just as you would to publishers.*

Fees: Be careful about agent fees. Some charge for readings and critiques, even without taking you on as a client. Compare the fees and the commissions to similar agents if you do enter into a contract. A typical rate is 15 percent for domestic sales, 20 percent for foreign.

What you need to know: Once you have an agent interested in representing you, compile a list of questions to ask before agreeing. These might include:

• Why do you like my work?

• What should I expect of you, and you of me?

• What are the terms of the contract, including its duration?

• What is your track record, i.e., how many books have you sold?

• How does communication between us take place, via phone, email, or both?

• What can I do to help sell my work?

• What is required to end the agreement if it doesn't work out?

Adams Literary

7845 Colony Road, C4 #215, Charlotte, NC 28226. www.adamsliterary.com

Agents: Tracey Adams, Josh Adams.

Considering themselves "matchmakers," Adams Literary is committed to excellence. The agency likes to think creatively about problems that may come in the publishing process. It seeks to represent clients and their works that represent diversity in all its forms. It is a place where authors, artists, editors, and publishers come together to create outstanding books for the most important audience: children of all ages. The agency reminds potential authors to address your submission to the appropriate agent, and not to use a generic "Dear Sir" opening. At this time, it is temporarily closed to submissions.

Categories and Submissions: Timeless, character-driven picture books; literary stories for middle-grade and YA; fantasy adventure; high-concept speculative fiction; humor. At this time it is only accepting picture books submissions from author-artists. Submissions are accepted through the website only (doc or PDF files). Response time is 6 weeks.

Contract and Payment: One-page agreement, standard commission, 15% domestic; 25% foreign and film/television.

Aitken Alexander Associates

291 Gray's Inn Rd, Kings Cross, London, WC1X 8QJ, United Kingdom. www.aitkenalexander.co.uk

Agents: Lesley Thorne, Clare Alexander, Lisa Baker, Chris Wellbelove, Emma Paterson, Steph Adam, Gillie Russell.

Representing works from all over the world, Aitken Alexander is one of the leading literary agencies in the United Kingdom. This agency has a reputation for discovering and nurturing new talent.

Categories and Submissions: Middle-grade, YA, adult. Send cover letter, outline or brief synopsis, and first 30 pages in Word format. Email submissions to submissions@aitkenalexander.co.uk. Responds in 6–8 weeks.

Contract and Payment: Commission, 15%.

Betsy Amster Literary Enterprises

607 Foothill Blvd. #1061, La Canada Flintridge, CA 91012. www.amsterlit.com

Agents: Betsy Amster (Adult), Mary Cummings (Children's and YA).

Working with both first-time and established writers, this full-service agency is known for its expert attention to every aspect of the publishing process. Before opening the agency, Betsy Amster spent ten years at Pantheon and Vintage and two years as editorial director of the Globe Pequot Press. Mary Cummings served for fourteen years as education director at the Loft Literary Center in Minneapolis, where she curated an annual Festival of Children's Literature and selected judges for the McKnight Award from top editors in children's publishing.

Categories and Submissions: Adult books: Literary fiction, upscale commercial women's fiction, voice-driven mysteries and thrillers, narrative nonfiction (especially by journalists), travelogues, memoirs (including graphic memoirs), social issues and trends, psychology, self-help, popular culture, women's issues, history and biography, lifestyle, careers, health and medicine, parenting, cooking and nutrition, gardening, and quirky gift books. Children's books: Picture books, middle-grade, graphic novels, and YA. Queries for adult titles should be addressed to b.amster.assistant@gmail.com. For fiction or narrative nonfiction, embed the first three pages of your manuscript in the body of your email. For other kinds of nonfiction, embed the overview of your proposal. Queries for children's and YA titles should be addressed to b.amster.kidsbooks@gmail.com. For picture books, embed the entire text in the body of your email. For novels or literary nonfiction, embed the first three pages. Response time varies.

Contract and Payment: Commission, 15% domestic; 20–25% foreign.

Azantian Literary Agency

azantianliteraryagency.com

Agents: Jennifer Azantanian, Masha Gunic,

Founded in 2014, this agency is especially interested in graphic novels. They are committed to guiding the careers of both new and aspiring authors. The agency represents all genres of fiction, including titles for young adults.

Categories and Submissions: Middle-grade, YA; fiction. Check website for current needs. At press time, agent Masha Gunic was currently seeking middle-grade fiction. Accepts submissions through the website only. Response time varies.

Contract and Payment: Commission, 15% domestic; 25% foreign.

Barone Literary Agency 🔒

http://www.denisegwen.com/BaroneLiteraryAgency/

Agent: Denise Barone.

Journeying with you down the path to publication is the mission of the Barone Literary Agency. It has many years of experience developing a brand for its authors. The agency considers young adult, memoir, fantasy, hi-lo, inspirational fiction, horror, and many other categories. This agency is currently closed to unsolicited submissions. Check the website for updates to this policy.

Categories and Submissions: Query by email to baroneliteraryagency@roadrunner.com or directly through the website. Responds in 4 weeks.

Contract and Payment: Commission, 15% on domestic sales; 20% on foreign sales.

The Bent Agency

19 West 21st Street, #201, New York, NY 10010. www.thebentagency.com

Agents: Jenny Bent, Nicola Barr, Susan Hawk, Molly Ker Hawn, Gemma Cooper, Louise Fury, Victoria Cappello, Heather Flaherty, Beth Phelan, Rachel Horowitz, Sarah Manning, Clare Draper, Amelia Hodgson.

The Bent Agency strives to provide the gold standard of representation and help authors turn dreams into reality, The Bent Agency prides itself on nurturing and discovering authors whom it can help propel to the top of their category. The agency also uses its intimate knowledge of marketing and online expertise to advise clients on how to work with publishers to best market their books. Review each agent's bio prior to submitting material.

Categories and Submissions: Middle-grade, YA; fiction and nonfiction, including mysteries, historical fiction, fantasy, science fiction, realism, humor, and boy books. Story—strong plotting—is key. No poetry, textbooks, sports, or reference. Query with information on your writing background, what the book is about and why you're the one to write it, and the first 10 pages. See website for individual agents' email addresses and submit to one agent at a time. No attachments. Accepts email submissions only. Accepts simultaneous submissions. Responds in 1 month.

Contract and Payment: Standard.

Meredith Bernstein Literary Agency

2095 Broadway, Suite 505, New York, NY 10023. www.meredithbernsteinliteraryagency.com

Agent: Meredith Bernstein.

For more than 30 years Meredith Bernstein has been a literary agent focused on developing a reputation as a place where an author experiences a unique and interactive relationship. The agency welcomes both first-time and established writers in fiction and nonfiction, and has taken many authors in each genre on to best-selling and award-winning careers.

Categories and Submissions: YA fiction, commercial and literary fiction, romance, mystery and thrillers. Bernstein looks for commercial nonfiction in many categories, including parenting, science, travel, women's issues, memoirs, and others. Mail query with SASE or submit online via website. No attachments. Responds in 2–5 weeks.

Contract and Payment: One-page agreement with an agency clause. Commission, 15% domestic; 20% foreign.

Vicky Bijur Literary Agency

27 West 20th Street, Suite 1003, New York, NY 10011. www.vickybijuragency.com

Agents: Vicky Bijur, Alexandra Franklin.

This agency has represented many award-winning titles, as well as many titles that have appeared on the *New York Times* Bestseller List. It was founded in 1988 by Vicky Bijur. The agency is currently open to submissions of literary fiction, women's fiction, coming-of-age novels, literary thrillers, and more.

Categories and Submissions: Send a query letter of no more than 3 paragraphs telling what makes your book stand out. Include your author bio and the first 10 pages of your manuscript. Accepts email submissions to queries@vickybijuragency.com or by hard copy. Responds in 8 weeks.

Contract and Payment: Commission, 15%.

David Black Literary Agency

335 Adams Street, Suite 2707, Brooklyn, NY 11201. www.davidblackagency.com

Agents: David Black, Jenny Herrera, Gary Morris, Susan Raihofer, Sarah Smith, Joy Tuleta, Matt Belford, Deborah Hofmann, Rica Allannic.

This agency advocates for its authors at every stage of publishing. It has earned a reputation throughout the publishing industry for serving the needs of its clients editorially and by attentively taking them through the life of a book, from conception to publication.

Categories and Submissions: Middle-grade, YA. Review the website for each agent's specific interests and submission information. Send 1- to 2-page query letter describing your book with author bio and intended audience. Accepts hard copy only unless specified. Response time is 8 weeks.

Contract and Payment: Standard.

Book Cents Literary Agency

www.bookcentsliteraryagency.com

Agent: Christine Wittholn.

Book Cents Literary Agency seeks to work with clients with fresh and creative voices. Since 2005, this full-service agency not only assists clients in selling their creative work, but also with growing their writing careers. It accepts submissions of women's lit, mainstream mystery, YA, thriller, and romance. At this time, Book Cents is closed to submissions, but has open periods to submit manuscripts. Check its website for open periods to submit material.

Categories and Submissions: Query with first 5 pages of manuscript. Accepts submissions through the website only. Responds only if interested.

Contract and Payment: Commission, 15%.

BookEnds Literary Agency

www.bookendsliterary.com

Agents: Jessica Faust, Kim Lionetti, Jessica Alvarez, Moe Ferrara, Tracy Marchini, Natascha Morris, Rachel Brooks, Naomi Davis, Amanda Jain, James McGowan.

This agency sees itself as "author advocates" with a goal of making author dreams come true. It specializes in representing authors of adult, young adult, and middle-grade fiction and nonfiction. Its agents are lucky to call a number of *New York Times* and *USA Today* bestselling authors clients. As literary agents their goal is bringing the books they love to the public. This agency notes, "Do research every agent you submit to, in order to make the most efficient use of your time and energy in querying—and also to catch our attention."

Categories and Submissions: Middle-grade, YA. Query. No attachments. Accepts email submissions to individual agents. No hard copy submissions accepted. Visit the website for agent contact info and current needs. Response time varies.

Contract and Payment: Commission, 15% domestic; 20–25% foreign.

The Book Group

20 West 20th Street, Suite 601, New York, NY 10011. http://www.thebookgroup.com/

Agents: Julie Barer, Faye Bender, Brettne Bloom, Elisabeth Weed, Dana Murphy, Nicole Cunningham, Hallie Schaeffer, Jamie Carr, Brenda Bowen.

Launched in 2015, The Book Group is a full-service literary agency that seeks to serve as an author's champion throughout their career. They represent a wide range of distinguished authors, including critically acclaimed and best-selling novelists, celebrated writers of children's literature, and award-winning historians, food writers, memoirists, and journalists. This agency takes a hands-on approach at every stage of the publication process. Visit the website for each agent's interests.

Categories and Submissions: No poetry or screenplays. Send query letter with all relevant information, along with 10 sample pages. Email to submissions@thebookgroup.com. No attachments. Include the first and last name of the agent you are querying in the subject line. No paper or phone queries. Response time varies; responds only if interested.

Contract and Payment: Not available.

Brandt & Hochman Literary Agents, Inc.

1501 Broadway, Suite 2310, New York, NY 10036. www.brandthochman.com

Agents: Gail Hochman, Marianne Merola, Bill Contardi, Emily Forland, Emma Patterson, Jody Kahn, Henry Thayer, Carl D. Brandt, Charles Schlessiger.

Representing both classics and new authors, this full-service literary agency has spanned most of the 20th century and continues in this digital age. It aims to give its select list of clients every benefit of its experience and expertise in shaping writing projects, negotiating their contracts, and increasing their visibility throughout the world.

Categories and Submissions: Early readers, middle-grade, YA. Query with a convincing overview of your book (no more than 2 pages). Visit the website for individual agents' interests and submission preferences. Response time varies.

Contract and Payment: Commission, 15% domestic; 20–25% foreign.

Kimberly Brower Literary Agency

110 Wall Street, New York, NY, 10005. www.browerliterary.com

Agents: Kimberly Brower, Jess Dallow, Aimee Ashcraft.

Whether you are a veteran author or just making your debut, this full-service agency welcomes your query. Its agents look to help authors achieve and live their dreams. Check the website for each individual agent's interests.

Categories and Submissions: Send query to individual editor; check website for email addresses. Do not query for projects that are not completed. Include synopsis and first chapter. No attachments. Responds in 6–8 weeks.

Contract and Payment: 15% royalty.

Andrea Brown Literary Agency

1076 Eagle Drive, Salinas, CA 93905. www.andreabrownlit.com

Agents: Andrea Brown, Laura Rennert, Caryn Wiseman, Jennifer Laughran, Kelly Sonnack, Jennifer Rofe, Jamie Weiss Chilton, Jennifer Mattson, Lara Perkins, Kathleen Rushall, Jennifer March Soloway.

Founded in 1981 this agency specializes in children's literature. This mid-size agency invests a great deal of attention into each project, and the agents are hands-on in all aspects of the process. Its agents advise "Do your homework. Know the different categories used to classify fiction and nonfiction and know within which category your work falls."

Categories and Submissions: Digital submissions only. Picture books, chapter books, middle-grade, YA. For picture books, paste complete manuscript. Illustrators should send 2–3 illustration samples and link to online portfolio. Fiction, first 10 pages. For nonfiction, send proposal and sample chapter. For graphic novels, send summary and 2–3 sample page spreads. Include previous publishing experience, if applicable, with all queries. Accepts email only. Put "query" in the subject line. See website for individual agents' areas of expertise and email addresses. No attachments. Responds in 6–8 weeks if interested.

Contract and Payment: Commission, 15% domestic; 25% foreign.

Kimberley Cameron & Associates

1550 Tiburon Blvd. #704, Tiburon, CA 94920. www.kimberleycameron.com

Agents: Kimberley Cameron, Elizabeth Kracht, Amy Cloughley, Mary C. Moore, Lisa Abellera, Dorian Maffei.

Proud to represent many distinguished authors across all genres, this agency feels a tremendous responsibility to its clients. Its agents champion the books they work on and openly collaborate between all of the agents within the agency. This agency is persistent in its pursuit of publication at the most respected publishing houses.

Categories and Submissions: Middle-grade, YA. Accepts queries through the website. Review each agent's interests before sending your query. Responds if interested. Response time varies.

Contract and Payment: Standard contract.

Chalberg & Sussman

115 West 29th Street, 3rd Floor, New York, NY 10001. www.chalbergsussman.com

Agents: Terra Chalberg, Rachel Sussman, Nicole James, Jennifer Grimaldi.

Representing a broad range of fiction and nonfiction authors in the areas of literary and commercial fiction, memoir, narrative nonfiction, lifestyle, humor, and pop culture, this agency is passionate about author advocacy and the business of publishing.

Categories and Submissions: Middle-grade, YA; fiction. Query with first 10 pages of your manuscript in the body of the email. No attachments. Check website for individual agents' specialties and submission information. Response time varies.

Contract and Payment: Standard contract.

The Chudney Agency

72 North State Road, Suite 501, Briar Cliff Manor, NY 10510. www.thechudneyagency.com

Agent: Steven Chudney.

Specializing in books for children and teens, the Chudney Agency is a small, independent agency. It will also consider taking on adult titles, especially if they may be of interest to young adults.

Categories and Submissions: Children's, YA; fiction. At this time it is not seeking fantasy, science fiction, nonfiction, plays, screenplays, or film scripts. Will consider select juvenile nonfiction. Queries only for all novels. For picture books, please email a PDF of the project with some full-color art. Accepts queries by email only. Responds in 2–4 weeks.

Contract and Payment: Offers written contract, binding for one year. Agent receive 15% on domestic sales.

Don Congdon Associates, Inc.

110 Williams Street, Suite 2202, New York, NY 10038. www.doncongdon.com

Agents: Don Congdon, Christina Concepcion, Michael Congdon, Katie Grimm, Katie Kotchman, Maura Kye Casella, Sue Ramer.

This literary agency provides individualized services to their clients. It represents a diverse list of authors with everything from bestsellers to emerging talent. It is committed to developing and representing all aspects of an author's domestic and international literary career.

Categories and Submissions: Middle-grade, YA; fiction and nonfiction; as well as books for adults. Query to appropriate editor with 1-page synopsis and 1 chapter. Accepts hard copy and email submissions to appropriate agent. Emails must include "Query" in the subject line. See website for information on its agents and what they are currently seeking. Query one agent at a time within the agency. Response time varies.

Contract and Payment: Unavailable.

The Corvisiero Literary Agency

275 Madison Avenue, 14th Floor, New York, NY 10016. https://www.corvisieroagency.com

Agents: Marisa Corvisiero, Saritza Hernandez, Cate Hart, Kaitlyn Johnson, Kortney Price, Cortney Radocaj, Rudy Cecera.

The Corvisiero Literary Agency prides itself in providing a sense of community for its authors. It is a boutique agency located in New York City, where authors can partner with professional and experienced representation who will value and guide them toward a successful career in publishing. The agency offers international representation, management, and coaching services to fiction and nonfiction authors in a wide range of genres.

Categories and Submissions: Middle-grade, YA, adult. Accepts queries through the website. Review each agent's interests and choose one agent to submit your work to. For fiction, include a 1- to 2-page synopsis. For nonfiction, include full proposal and one sample chapter. Response time varies.

Contract and Payment: Standard contract.

Curtis Brown, Ltd.

10 Astor Place, New York, NY 10003-6935. www.curtisbrown.com

Agents: Ginger Clark, Katherine Fausset, Holly Frederick, Peter Ginsberg, Elizabeth Harding, Timothy Knowlton, Maureen Walters, Noah Ballard, Kerry D'Agostino, Jonathan Lyons, Steve Salpeter, Sarah Perillo, Sarah Gerton, Laura Blake Peterson, Monika Woods.

Since 1914 this literary agency has represented authors across all genres. Curtis Brown, Ltd. is one of the world's leading literary agencies, representing a wide variety of established and emerging authors. It provides the highest standard of literary representation to its clients.

Categories and Submissions: Picture books, juvenile, middle-grade, YA; fiction and nonfiction. Genres: contemporary, literary, multicultural, mystery, historical, humor, fantasy, adventure. Does not accept stage plays or musicals. Visit the website for individual agents' submission requirements. Response time varies.

Contract and Payment: Written contract. Commission, 15% domestic; 20% foreign.

Laura Dail Literary Agency

350 Seventh Avenue, Suite 2003, New York, NY 10001. www.ldlainc.com

Agents: Laura Dail, Elana Roth Parker, Carrie Pestritto, Samantha Fabien.

The Laura Dail Literary Agency is always excited for new talent. It represents authors of fiction and nonfiction, both commercial and literary, for adults and children. This agency provides thoughtful attention to detail at every stage of a book's life—from editorial to sales and licensing.

Categories and Submissions: Picture books, middle-grade, YA; fiction and nonfiction. LDLA does not represent screenplays, poetry, or illustrated books for adults. Query with synopsis and make them want to read more. Accepts email queries only to queries@ldlainc.com. Include "Query" along with the title and appropriate agent in the subject line of the email. Response time varies.

Contract and Payment: Unavailable.

Liza Dawson Associates

121 West 27th Street, Suite 1201, New York, NY 10001. www.lizadawsonassociates.com

Agents: Liza Dawson, Caitlin Blasdell, Hannah Bowman, Caitie Flum, Havis Dawson, Jonne Fallert, Kayla Lightner, Tom Miller, Rachel Beck.

With offices in New York and Los Angeles, this full-service agency represents books for all ages with a specialty in big commercial fiction and literary fiction. In nonfiction, its agents are drawn to narratives that explore life's complexities. Its agents are former publishers that ensure their material stands out. It represents first-time novelists and those with established careers.

Categories and Submissions: YA. Check the website for each agent's individual interests and submissions guidelines. Query one agent within the agency at a time. Accepts queries by email only. Responds with request for synopsis if interested.

Contract and Payment: Offers written contract.

The Jennifer DeChiara Literary Agency

245 Park Avenue, 39th Floor, New York, NY 10167. www.jdlit.com

Agents: Jennifer DeChiara, Stephen Fraser, Cari Lamba, Marie Lamba, Roseanne Wells, Alexandra Weiss, Alex Barba, Colleen Oefelein, Marlo Berliner, Savannah Brooks, Zabe Ellor, Damien McNicholl.

Named one of the top 25 literary agencies in the country by Reader's Digest, the Jennifer DeChiara Literary Agency represents children's books for all ages, including picture books, middle-grade, and young adult novels, as well as adult fiction and nonfiction. It is open to any and all genres. See each agent's submission guidelines for type of manuscripts they are seeking.

Categories and Submissions: Picture books, middle-grade, YA. Each agent has his or her own guidelines, submission requirements, and contact methods and information. See website for details. Response time varies.

Contract and Payment: Standard contract; 15% commission.

DeFiore and Company

47 East 19th Street, Third Floor, New York, NY 10016. www.defliterary.com

Agents: Brian DeFiore, Meredith Kaffel Simonoff, Laurie Abkermeier, Adam Schear, Rebecca Strauss, Linda Kaplan, Cassie Hanjian, Reiko Davis.

DeFiore and Company is always looking for exciting, fresh, new talent to add to its list of successful authors. It is a mid-sized, dynamic literary agency based in Manhattan. Its staff brings decades of experiences as agents, former editors, publishers, and rights directors at major publishing companies. Covering a broad range of fiction genres and general interest nonfiction books, the company represents dozens of authors and experts, including #1 *New York Times* bestsellers, award-winning fiction writers for adults and children, important nonfiction authors, thinkers and practitioners, and new voices in all areas of writing.

Categories and Submissions: Picture books, middle-grade, YA. Query with brief summary of the book, short description of why you're writing the project, author bio/credentials, and the first 5 pages of the manuscript for fiction. Accepts email to submissions@defliterary.com or to individual agents with "Query" in the subject line. No attachments. See website for agent's email addresses. Accepts hard copy with SASE. Responds in 4 weeks.

Contract and Payment: Unknown.

Joelle Delbourgo Associates

101 Park Street, 3rd floor, Montclair, NJ 07042. www.delbourgo.com

Agents: Joelle Delbourgo, Jacqueline Flynn, Carrie Cantor

This boutique agency seeks quality work with distinct voices and original viewpoints. It represents a broad range of authors writing for the adult market, as well as middle-grade and young adult fiction and nonfiction. For more than 17 years, the agency has negotiated countless contracts with publishers throughout the world. Its agents advise writing a polished query letter. Guidelines for writing a great query are available at the agency's website.

Categories and Submissions: Middle-grade, YA, adult novels. Query to specific agent or to the general email box at submissions@delbourgo.com. Emails must include "Query" in the subject line. Review each agent's specific interests at the website. Accepts simultaneous submissions. Response time varies.

Contract and Payment: Standard contract. Agent receives 15% commission on domestic sales.

Sandra Dijkstra Literary Agency

www.dijkstraagency.com

Agents: Sandra Dijkstra, Elisa Capron, Thao Le, Jill Marr, Jessica Watterson, Jennifer Kim, Suzy Evans.

The Sandra Dijkstra Literary Agency is the West Coast's premier agency for authors. "To find and sell books that make a difference" is the motto of this agency. "To be our clients' best advocates in a mutually supportive and rewarding environment. To make things happen."

Categories and Submissions: Picture books, middle-grade, YA, adult. Review each agent's interests and submit your query to one agent only. Check the website for individual agent's contact information. For fiction, include a 1-page synopsis, brief bio, and the first 10–15 pages of your manuscript. For nonfiction, include overview, author bio, 5–10 takeaways from your book, comparative titles, target audience, marketing plan, chapter outline, and 1–2 sample chapters. Picture books, include a bio with full manuscript pasted into the email. Response time varies.

Contract and Payment: Standard contract.

Donaghy Literary Group

http://www.donaghyliterary.com

Agents: Stacey Donaghy, Valerie Noble, Sue Miller, Amanda Ayers Barnett.

Donaghy Literary Group guides, supports, and promotes its writers to achieve full career potential. This agency provides full-service literary representation to its clients at every stage of their writing career. Specializing in fiction, it seeks middle-grade, young adult, new adult, and adult novels.

Categories and Submissions: Middle-grade, YA, adult. Review each agent's interests and submit your query to one agent only. Submit query through the individual agent's Query Manager Submission Form at the website. Responds in 12 weeks.

Contract and Payment: Standard contract.

Dunham Literary

110 William Street, Suite 2202, New York, NY 10038-3901. www.dunhamlit.com

Agents: Jennie Dunham, Leslei Zampetti.

Since 2000, Dunham Literary has represented quality fiction and nonfiction. It represents writers of children's books and illustrations for all ages and adult literary fiction and nonfiction. It welcomes first-time writers and looks to develop writers' careers, not just books. This agency does not represent individual short stories, chapbooks, novellas, or screenplays.

Categories and Submissions: Picture books, middle-grade, YA. Query by mail or email to query@dunhamlit.com. No attachments. SASE. In one page, describe plot, themes, your credentials, and how you learned of the agency. If interested, an agent will request a manuscript or proposal, biography, synopsis, and market statement. Query letters are read by all agents who might be interested in the project.

Contract and Payment: Exclusive representation; agency clause. Commission, 15% domestic; 20% foreign; 15% dramatic.

Dunow, Carlson, & Lerner Agency

27 West 20th Street, Suite 1107, New York, NY 10011. http://www.dclagency.com/

Agents: Jennifer Carlson, Amy Hughes, Arielle Datz, Henry Dunow, Erin Hosier, Eleanor Jackson, Julia Kenny, Betsy Lerner, Edward Necarlsumer IV, Rachel Vogel, Yishai Seidman, Chris Rogers, Stacia Decker.

Dunow, Carlson & Lerner Agency is open to working with both new and established writers. This agency represents literary and commercial fiction, narrative nonfiction, memoir, popular culture and young adult fiction. In addition to representing publishing rights, the agency works with established networks of co-agents to represent translation rights in all foreign territories as well as film, television, and audio rights.

Categories and Submissions: YA fiction, adult memoir, pop culture. Query with first 10 pages of manuscript. Email queries preferred to mail@dclagency.com. No attachments. Will accept hard copy. Responds if interested.

Contract and Payment: Standard contract.

Dystel, Goderich & Bourret LLC

One Union Square West, Suite 904, New York, NY 10003. www.dystel.com

Agents: Jane Dystel, Miriam Goderich, Michael Bourret, Stacey Glick, Jim McCarthy, Lauren E. Abramo, Jessica Papin, John Rudolph, Michael Hoogland, Ann Leslie Tuttle, Sharon Pelletier, Amy Elizabeth Bishop, Kemi Faderin, Michalea Whatnall.

Dystel, Goderich & Bourret boasts a prestigious client list and well-known reputation. It offers representation for picture books, middle-grade, young adult, and adult authors in both fiction and nonfiction. It prides itself on being a full-service provider and following projects through from inception to publication and beyond. The primary goal of the agency is to offer not just financial and contractual advice to its clients, but also editorial guidance and support. DG&B stresses that it takes unsolicited queries very seriously and has discovered several talented writers in its slush pile.

Categories and Submissions: Picture books, middle-grade, YA, adult. Send cover letter, outline or brief synopsis with word count if possible, and sample chapter. Accepts hard copy and email to specific agent. No attachments. SASE. Submit to only one agent; see website for current needs and email addresses. Accepts simultaneous queries to other agencies. Responds in 6–8 weeks.

Contract and Payment: Commission, 15%.

Einstein Literary Management

27 West 20th Street #1003, New York, NY 10011. www.einsteinliterary.com

Agents: Susanna Einstein, Susan Graham, Shana Kelly.

Working with clients throughout the life of their books, this agency represents a broad range of literary and commercial fiction including middle-grade, YA, commercial fiction, women's fiction, and romance. It also represents nonfiction titles including cookbooks, memoir, and narrative. The agency works with their clients to help to develop ideas, to edit manuscripts, and to negotiate contracts. This agency does not accept poetry or screenplays.

Categories and Submissions: Middle-grade, YA, adult. Query with the first 10 pages of manuscript in the body of the email. Accept email to submissions@einsteinliterary.com. Responds in 6 weeks if interested.

Contract and Payment: Standard contract.

Ethan Ellenberg Literary Agency

155 Suffolk Street #2R, New York, NY 10002. http://ethanellenberg.com

Agents: Ethan Ellenberg, Evan Gregory, Bibi Lewis.

Since its inception the agency has represented several bestselling authors, career novelists, and professional writers. This independent full-service agency has had robust sales all over the world. It is a member of the Association of Authors Representatives, an affiliate member of the Science Fiction and Fantasy Writers of America, and an associate member of the Society of Children's Book Writers and Illustrators, the Romance Writers of America, and the Mystery Writers of America. It represents a broad range of fiction and nonfiction and is actively seeking new clients.

Categories and Submissions: Interested in all kinds of commercial fiction, including thrillers, mysteries, children's, romance, women's fiction, ethnic, science fiction, fantasy, and general fiction. Literary fiction must have a strong narrative. In nonfiction, it's interested in current affairs, history, health, science, psychology, cookbooks, new age, spirituality, pop culture, adventure, true crime, biography and memoir. Does not represent poetry. All submissions must include a query letter. For fiction, a 1- to 2-page synopsis and the first 50 pages of your manuscript. For nonfiction, a proposal. For picture books, the complete manuscript and 4–5 sample illustrations pasted into the body of the email. Illustrators, 4–5 sample images pasted into the body of the email and a link to your online portfolio. Send all information to agent@ethanellenberg.com. Also accepts hard copy. If interested, will respond within 2 weeks.

Contract and Payment: Not available.

Mary Evans, Inc.

242 East Fifth Street, New York, NY 10003. www.maryevansinc.com

Agents: Mary Evans, Leslie Meredith.

This New York literary agency has represented several award-winning and best-selling titles. It works with authors on picture books, middle-grade, and young adult fiction. It also represents a wide range of nonfiction books. It does not accept submissions of stage plays or screenplays.

Categories and Submissions: Picture books, middle-grade, YA; fiction. Review the website for specific agents and their specialties. Query with a brief synopsis and resume. Accepts hard copy or email to info@maryevansinc.com. Email queries must include "Query" in the subject line. Responds in 4–8 weeks.

Contract and Payment: Standard contract.

FinePrint Literary Management

115 West 29th Street, 3rd Floor, New York, NY 10001. www.fineprintlit.com

Agents: Peter Rubie, Lauren Bieker, June Clark, Laura Wood, Bobbie O'Neal.

A strategic agency offering representation and management for new and established writers. This full-service agency represents a wide range of literary and commercial fiction and some nonfiction for adults and children. Their expertise covers traditional and e-book publishing and subsidiary rights.

Categories and Submissions: Middle-grade, YA; fiction and nonfiction. Genres include character-driven picture books, contemporary fiction, historical, fantasy, literary, boy-oriented YA, humor, paranormal, mainstream fiction, books that tackle social issues or taboos, romance. Match the genre to the agent profiles available on the website and submit a query and first 2 chapters for fiction; query, proposal, and sample chapters for nonfiction. Some agents prefer mail, some email. No attachments. See website for details. Response time varies.

Contract and Payment: Standard 1-year contract initially, but the agency strives to represent authors for their careers and through multiple projects. Commission, 15%.

Flannery Literary

1140 Wickfield Ct., Naperville, IL 60563. www.flanneryliterary.com

Agent: Jennifer Flannery.

Flannery Literary is looking for new talent with a fresh voice to help the as-yet-unpublished author find a publishing home. Flannery Literary represents writers of books for children and young adults. The agency's primary goal is, "putting good books in the hands—and hearts—of young readers." The agency looks for strong writing, a unique viewpoint, a memorable story, intriguing characters, and a thought-provoking dilemma that young readers are eager to solve.

Categories and Submissions: Early readers, middle-grade, YA; fiction. Some picture books. Query. Accepts email queries to Jennifer@FlanneryLiterary.com. Responds in 4-6 weeks.

Contract and Payment: Agent receives 15% commission on domestic sales; 20% commission on foreign sales. Offers written contract.

Fletcher & Company

78 Fifth Avenue, 3rd Floor, New York, NY 10011. www.fletcherandco.com

Agents: Christy Fletcher, Melissa Chinchillo, Grainne Fox, Eric Lupfer, Rebecca Gradinger, Lisa Grubka, Sylvie Greenberg Carr, Elizabeth Resnick, Veronica Goldstein, Sarah Fuentes.

Founded in 2003, Fletcher & Company is dedicated to helping a diverse range of writers connect with readers. This full-service literary management and production company works closely with writers and creators of intellectual property to help them connect with readers and audiences across all media. It creates a unique relationship with each of its clients and structures its work around the needs and goals of each particular author.

Categories and Submissions: YA; fiction and nonfiction. Query with brief synopsis, and first 5–10 pages of the manuscript. Accepts email to info@fletcherandco.com. No attachments. Do not query more than one agent at a time. Responds in 4–6 weeks.

Contract and Payment: Standard contract.

Sheldon Fogelman Agency

420 East 72nd Street, New York, NY 10021. www.sheldonfogelmanagency.com

Agents: Sheldon Fogelman, Janine Le, Amy Stern.

This agency prides itself on recognizing the richness and duration of the literature created for the children's market as it passes from generation to generation. It was the first to specialize in children's book authors and illustrators. As a full-service agency, Sheldon Fogelman Agency has the resources and knowledge to assist their clients in all aspects of their creative lives from contract negotiation and rights management to editorial input and long-term career planning.

Categories and Submissions: All genres and types of children's books, from picture books to YA. Send a 1-page letter with a brief synopsis, credentials, and where you learned of the agency; indicate simultaneous submissions. Also send first 3 chapters for novels, or complete manuscript for picture books. Picture book writers may include 2 manuscripts. Accepts hard copy and email to submissions@sheldonfogelmanagency.com (Word or RTF attachments). Submissions can also be sent to individual agents (contact information is available at the website). Prefers exclusive consideration for the work for at least one month. SASE. Responds in 6 weeks.

Contract and Payment: Not available.

Foundry Literary + Media

33 West 17th Street, PH, New York, NY 10011. www.foundrymedia.com

Agents: Peter H. McGuigan, Yfat Reiss Gendell, Chris Park, Kirsten Neuhaus, Jess Regel, Peter Steinberg, Roger Freet, Richie Kern, Adriann Ranta Zurhellen, Tansuri Prasanna.

This full-service agency and media development company's goal is to support authors through every step of the publishing process. It is dedicated to providing the most positive and profitable publishing experience for its clients from the book market to film, tv, merchandise, online media, and beyond. The Foundry team is relentless in finding new and diverse ways for its clients to reach wider audiences throughout the entire publication process.

Categories and Submissions: Picture books through YA, as well as adult commercial and literary fiction and nonfiction. Query with author bio, synopsis, and first 3 chapters for fiction; sample chapters and table of contents for nonfiction. Address one agent; see website for submission method preferences and email addresses. Multiple submissions are not accepted. Responds in 8 weeks if interested.

Contract and Payment: Not available.

Sarah Jane Freymann Literary Agency

59 West 71st Street, Suite 9B, New York, NY 10023. www.sarahjanefreymann.com

Agents: Sarah Jane Freymann, Steve Schwartz, Katherine Sands, Jessica Sinsheimer.

Passionate about books, enthusiastic about new media and excited about projects that introduce new ideas since 1974, the Jane Freymann Literary Agency prides itself on being there for writers and helping its clients from inception through publication. The team of agents have a strong affinity for narrative fiction and represent world-renowned naturalists, award-winning journalists, and memoirists. It also represents a growing number of edgy young adult fiction titles.

Categories and Submissions: YA fiction, literary and commercial fiction for adults, self-help, memoirs, cookbooks. Query with author bio, pitch letter and first 10 pages of manuscript. Strongly prefers email to submissions@sarahjanefreymann.com. No attachments. Will accept hard copy. Responds if interested.

Contract and Payment: Agent receives 15% commission on domestic sales; 20% on foreign sales. Offers written contract.

Rebecca Friedman Literary Agency

110 Wall Street, New York, NY 10005. https://rfliterary.com/

Agents: Rebecca Friedman, Susan Finesman, Abby Schulman, Brandie Coonis.

The Rebecca Friedman Agency represents a wide range of fiction and nonfiction authors. It is always looking for great stories told with strong voices. It is open to working with both new and established authors.

Categories and Submissions: YA fiction and contemporary romance, women's fiction, journalistic nonfiction and memoir. Query with first chapter. Accepts email queries to appropriate editor; check website for individual agents' interests. No attachments. Responds in 6–8 weeks.

Contract and Payment: Standard contract.

Full Circle Literary, LLC

7676 Hazard Center Dr., Suite 500, San Diego, CA 92108. www.fullcircleliterary.com

Agents: Stephanie Von Borstel, Adriana Dominguez, Taylor Martindale Kean, Lilly Ghahremani, Nicole Geiger.

Offering a full circle approach to literary representation, Full Circle Literary is a full-service agency. Its team has diverse experience in book publishing including editorial, marketing, publicity, legal and rights. The agency works with writers and illustrators from development of concepts and proposals for submission to championing a book into the hands of readers.

Categories and Submissions: Picture books, middle-grade, YA; fiction. Adult fiction and nonfiction. Query with first 10 pages for fiction; with 1 sample chapter for nonfiction. Visit the website for each individual agent's specialty. Submit through the website. Responds if interested.

Contract and Payment: Agent receives 15% commission on domestic sales; 20% on foreign sales. Offers written contract.

Fuse Literary

www.fuseliterary.com

Agents: Laurie McLean, Gordon Warnock, Margaret Bail, Connor Goldsmith, Emily Keyes, Carlisle Webber, Michelle Richter.

Fuse Literary represents a wide variety of clients, from bestsellers to debut authors, working with fiction and nonfiction for children and adults worldwide. It does not represent poetry or screenplays.

Categories and Submissions: Middle-grade, YA; all categories. Visit the website to see each individual agent's current interests and submissions requirements. Accepts queries by email only. Do not send full-length manuscripts unless requested. Responds in 4–8 weeks.

Contract and Payment: Commission, 15% domestic; 25% foreign.

Go Literary

www.go-lit.com

Agent: Amaryah Orenstein.

Go Literary strives to establish long-term relationships with its authors to help them build satisfying and enduring careers. This full-service agency aims to give a voice to a broad range of perspectives across the literary spectrum. It is actively seeking fiction and nonfiction that features a strong narrative and that tackles big issues in engaging, accessible ways. This agency takes a particular interest in the editorial process, from concept development through publication and beyond.

Categories and Submissions: Early readers, middle-grade, YA, adult; fiction and nonfiction. Query with synopsis and biographical sketch. Accepts queries by email only to submissions@go-lit.com. Responds in 4-6 weeks.

Contract and Payment: Agent receives standard commission. Offers written contract.

Irene Goodman Literary Agency

27 West 24th Street, Suite 804, New York, NY 10010. www.irenegoodman.com

Agents: Irene Goodman, Miriam Kriss, Barbara Poelle, Kim Perel, Danny Baror, Heather Baror-Shapiro, Victoria Marini. Whitney Ross, Maggie Kane.

The Irene Goodman Literary Agency ignites passionate careers and does it all with joy. It represents commercial and literary fiction and nonfiction for adult, young adult, and middle-grade markets. Its agents accept submissions in categories of young adult and adult fiction, including historical, thrillers, mysteries, and women's titles, and nonfiction with an emphasis on pop culture, memoir, music, social issues, parenting, and lifestyle topics. See the website for agents currently looking for middle-grade and YA fiction. Its website notes, "the quality of writing [of your query] should be as good as the quality of your manuscript."

Categories and Submissions: Middle-grade, YA; fiction and nonfiction. Does not represent picture books. Email query with first 10 pages of manuscript, synopsis (3–5 paragraphs), and author bio in the body of the email to the agent of your choice. See website for interests and contact information for individual agents. Responds in 6–8 weeks, if interested.

Contract and Payment: Simple, 1-page agreement. Standard 15% commission.

Sanford J. Greenburger Associates

55 Fifth Avenue, New York, NY 10003. www.greenburger.com

Agents: Brenda Bowen, Faith Hamlin, Heide Lange, Dan Mandel, Matt Bialer, Rachael Dillon Fried, Stephanie Delman, Ed Maxwell.

Since 1932, Greenburger Associates has found and guided talented authors. It manages its clients' careers professionally, creatively, and financially. Among its current clients are writers of fiction, nonfiction, genre books, and original e-books; authors and artists of children's books; and a small number of poets and essayists. Its agents provide expertise and counsel for first-time and established authors and artists.

Categories and Submissions: Children's books; all genres. Send query letter, first 3 chapters (for fiction) or book proposal (for nonfiction), synopsis, and author bio. If emailing, put letter in body of email and other items as Word attachments. See website for agent listings and interests, email addresses, and specific guidelines; many do not accept hard copy. Responds in 4–6 weeks if interested. No screenplays.

Contract and Payment: Commission, 15% domestic; 20% foreign.

Kathryn Green Literary Agency, LLC ★

157 Columbus Anvenue, Suite 510, New York, NY 10023. www.kathryngreenliteraryagency.com

Agent: Kathryn Green.

This small agency works closely with authors of historical fiction, mysteries, young adult, and middle grade fiction. Kathryn Green is also interested in memoirs, and books on parenting, pop culture, and history. You'll pique her interest with quirky nonfiction. This agency does not represent works of fantasy, science fiction, or picture books.

Categories and Submissions: Middle-grade, YA. Accepts queries. Do not submit manuscripts unless it is requested. Accepts email queries to query@kgreenagency.com. Will accept simultaneous submissions if identified. Responds in 1 month.

Contract and Payment: Standard contract. Commission, 15% domestic; 25% foreign.

Holloway Literary Agency

www.hollowayliteraryagency.com

Agents: Nikki Terpilowski, Rachel Beck.

This full-service agency loves a good story. It has offices in New York, Chicago, Dallas, and Vancouver. Its mission is to help bridge the gaps between books and authors, helping authors to grow their fan base. It represents an eclectic range of fiction and nonfiction in all genres.

Categories and Submissions: YA. Visit the website to see each individual agent's current interests and submissions requirements. Most agents accept email submissions. With submission, include comparative titles, author bio, genre, and word count. If interested, the agent will request to see the first 15 pages of your manuscript. Visit the website for tips for getting this agency's attention. Response time varies.

Contract and Payment: Commission, 15% domestic; 25% foreign.

HSG Agency ★

37 West 28th Street, 8th Floor, New York, NY 10001. www.hsgagency.com

Agents: Carrie Hannigan, Jesseca Salky, Josh Getzler, Soumeya Roberts, Victoria Wells-Arms, Julia Kardon, Rhea Lyons.

A full-service literary agency that through collaborative and client-focused representation manages all aspects of an author's career. This literary agency has a passion for strong young adult material, but also actively seeks children's and middle-grade titles as well as adult fiction. Its agents have represented award-winning authors in many genres.

Categories and Submissions: Carrie (picture books, early readers, middle-grade, YA, and illustrators); Jesseca (adult literary fiction, occasional memoir); Josh (mysteries and thrillers, nonfiction, cozy mysteries); Soumeya (adult literary fiction); Leigh (nonfiction, cook books). For submissions, please check the website, hsgagency.com, as each agent now has a different query policy and time of response. Do not send queries to more than one agent. This agency works closely together and will share material if they think another agent is a better fit for your book. Visit website for agent bios and current needs. Responds in 4–6 weeks.

Contract and Payment: Commission, 15% domestic; 20–25% foreign.

Janklow & Nesbit

285 Madison Avenue, New York, NY 10017. www.janklowandnesbit.com

Agents: Morton Janklow, Lynn Nesbit, Luke Janklow, Anne Sibbald, Bennett Ashley, PJ Mark, Kim Kirby, Emma Parry, Paul Lucas, Richard Morris, Marya Spence, Allison Hunter, Melissa Flashmen, Chris Clemans, Wendy Gu, Richard Morris.

Janklow & Nesbit's approach has always been one of client advocacy combined with meticulous attention to detail. This premier agency is dedicated to the interests of its clients in all aspects of their careers. It has prided itself on offering the care and personal attention associated with a boutique agency and the clout and expertise of a big firm.

Categories and Submissions: Picture books, young readers, middle-grade, YA; fiction and nonfiction. For fiction submissions, include a cover letter, synopsis, and first 10 pages. For nonfiction, include cover letter, outline, and first 10 pages. For picture books, include a cover letter, full outline, and picture book dummy with at least one full-color sample. Accepts hard copy and email submissions to submissions@janklow.com. If you are emailing a submission, include sample pages in the body of the email. Address your submission to an individual agent. Responds if interested.

Contract and Payment: Not available.

Harvey Klinger, Inc.

300 West 55th Street, Suite 11V, New York, NY 10019. www.harveyklinger.com

Agents: Harvey Klinger, David Dunton, Andrea Somberg, Wendy Levinson, Rachel Ridout.

With an eye for spotting talent, this agency represents high-quality writers of adult fiction, nonfiction, young adult, and middle-grade books. The company is always looking for new voices, both published and unpublished, but only takes on a small number of new authors in any given year. Review the website to see each individual agent's interest before sending your query.

Categories and Submissions: Middle-grade, YA; all categories. Queries should be short and to the point. Include a short synopsis, author bio, and the first 5 pages of your manuscript. Do not send full manuscript unless requested. Indicate simultaneous submissions. Agent bios and emails available at website. Do not query more than one agent at this agency at a time. No attachments. Agent email addresses available at the website. Responds in 2–4 weeks, if interested.

Contract and Payment: Simple, to-the-point contract. Commission, 15% domestic; 25% foreign.

KT Literary

9249 South Broadway, #200-543, Highlands Ranch, CO 80129. www.ktliterary.com

Agents: Kate Testerman, Sara Megibow, Renee Nyen, Hannah Fergesen, Hilary Hawell.

This agency believes in the power of new technology to connect authors and readers. It prides itself in creating good books, and providing reading experiences. It leverages a decade of experience in New York publishing to the foothills of the Rocky Mountains, where any major publishing house is just a phone call or email away.

Categories and Submissions: Middle-grade and YA as well as new adult, romance, erotica, science fiction, and fantasy. No picture books at this time. All agents accept email queries to individual emails. Please see website. Send query with first 3 pages of manuscript in the body of the email (include "Query" and the title of the manuscript in the subject line). Responds in 2 weeks.

Contract and Payment: Not available.

Leshne Agency

16 West 23rd Street, New York, NY 10010. www.leshneagency.com

Agents: Lisa Leshne, Sandy Hodgman, Yvette Greenwald, Christine Lee.

The Leshne Agency takes a deeply personal approach by working closely with clients to develop their best ideas for maximum impact and reach, providing hands-on guidance and networking for lasting success. It is a full-service literary and talent management agency representing writers, artists, and entertainers looking to grow their brand across all forms of traditional and digital media.

Categories and Submissions: The Leshne Agency is seeking authors across all genres: narrative, memoir, and prescriptive nonfiction, with a particular interest in sports, wellness, business, political, and parenting topics. Its agents will also look at truly terrific commercial fiction and young adult and middle-grade books. It is not interested in screenplays, scripts, picture books, or poetry. All materials must be submitted through the website via Authors.me. Include a synopsis, table of contents, and at least 10 sample pages. Also provide your author bio, previous publications, and total word count. Response time varies.

Contract and Payment: Not available.

Levine Greenberg Rostan Literary Agency

307 Seventh Avenue, Suite 2407, New York, NY 10001. https://lgrliterary.com/

Agents: Jim Levine, Stephanie Rostan, Melissa Rowland, Victoria Skurnuck, Danielle Svetcov, Kerry Sparks, Monika Verma, Daniel Greenberg, Lindsay Edgecombe, Tim Wojcik, Arielle Eckstut.

Known for trust, transparency, and teamwork, this agency looks to represent people rather than projects. Most of its titles are published by imprints of the major houses, but they also work with many independent presses. It represents books in all categories of fiction and nonfiction.

Categories and Submissions: Middle-grade, YA; fiction and nonfiction. Query with no more than 50 pages of manuscript. Accepts submissions through the website or by email to submit@lgrliterary.com. Include individual agent's name if appropriate. Responds if interested.

Contract and Payment: 15% domestic; 20% foreign. Written contract.

LKG Agency ★

60 RIverside Blvd. #1101, New York, NY 10069. www.lkgagency.com

Agents: Lauren Galit, Caitlen Rubino-Bradway,

This agency specializes in nonfiction, both practical and narrative, as well as middle-grade and YA fiction. It helps ensure authors get the best deal possible in their contract. LKG Agency works with both large and small publishing houses, and prides itself on finding the right fit for each project.

Categories and Submissions: For nonfiction submission, query by email to lkgnonfiction@lkgagency.com. Include table of contents and two sample chapters. For middle-grade and young adult submissions, send query, synopsis, and first three chapters to mgya@lkgagency.com. Responds if interested.

Contract and Payment: Commission, 15% domestic; 20–25% foreign.

Lowenstein Associates

115 East 23rd Street, 4th floor, New York, NY 10010. www.lowensteinassociates.com

Agents: Barbara Lowenstein, Mary South.

Established in 1976, this agency takes a unique approach to handling authors' careers, combining the kind of personal, hands-on attention of a boutique firm with the strong negotiating power of a corporate agency. It represents a variety of authors from *New York Times* bestsellers to Pulitzer Prize nominees. It represents authors of both fiction and nonfiction.

Categories and Submissions: YA fiction and nonfiction, as well as adult titles. Does not accept submissions of westerns, textbooks, and children's picture books. Fiction: query with first 10 pages. Nonfiction: query with table of contents and proposal. Strongly prefers submissions through Authors.me link at the website. Accepts submissions to assistant@bookhaven.com with "Query" in the subject line. No attachments. Responds if interested.

Contract and Payment: 15% domestic; 20% foreign. Written contract.

Maass Literary Agency

1000 Dean Street, Suite 252, Brooklyn, NY 11238. www.maassagency.com

Agents: Donald Maass, Jennifer Jackson, Cameron McClure, Katie Shea Boutillier, Michael Curry, Caitlin McDonald, Paul Stevens, Jennie Goloboy, Kiana Nguyen, Kat Kerr.

This literary agency is a leading agency for fiction writers that is open to working with both new and experienced clients. It is dedicated to developing the careers of professional novelists. This agency does not represent poetry, picture books, or screenplays.

Categories and Submissions: Early readers, middle-grade, YA. Query with synopsis, genre, word count, and first 5 pages of manuscript. Address queries to specific agent. See website for information on each agent's interests and submission requirements. Do not query more than one agent at a time within the agency. Responds if interested.

Contract and Payment: 15% domestic; 20% foreign. Written contract.

Gina MacCoby Literary Agency

P.O. Box 60, Cappaqua, NY 10514. https://www.publishersmarketplace.com/members/GinaMaccoby/

Agent: Gina MacCoby.

Gina MacCoby represents authors of literary and upmarket fiction and narrative nonfiction for children and adults. She is looking for strong mysteries, middle-grade, and young adult fiction as well as biographies, current events, and popular science.

Categories and Submissions: Middle-grade, YA; fiction. Query with synopsis. Accepts email queries to query@maccobylit.com. Responds only if interested.

Contract and Payment: Commission, 15% domestic; 20–25% foreign.

MacGregor & Luedeke Literary ★

P.O. Box 1316, Manzanita, OR 97130. http://macgregorliterary.com

Agents: Chip MacGregor, Amanda Luedeke.

MacGregor & Luedeke have served fiction and nonfiction authors in the general and Christian markets. It assists authors in developing great ideas, expressing them through great writing, and support with a great platform. It encourages authors to think strategically about their books as well as their careers; value long-term friendships with authors, editors, and publishers; strive to remain in step with the changing rhythms of the publishing industry; and long to see lives transformed through the artistry and craft of their writing.

Categories and Submissions: Currently not accepting unsolicited submissions and will not return unsolicited material even with SASE.

Contract and Payment: Not available.

Mansion Street Literary Management

www.mansionstreet.com

Agents: Jean Sagendorph, Michelle Witte.

For over 10 years, this boutique literary agency has worked with exciting new authors. Mansion Street Literary Management guides writers through each stage of publication. At this time, it is closed to picture book submissions.

Categories and Submissions: Early reader, middle-grade, YA; fiction and nonfiction. Query with no more than 10 pages. No attachments. Accepts submissions to specific agents. Visit the website for a list of each agent's current interest and submission requirements. Responds if interested.

Contract and Payment: 15% domestic; 20% foreign. Written contract.

Marsal Lyon Literary Agency LLC

PMB 121, 665 San Rodolfo Dr. 124, Solana Beach, CA 92075.
http://www.marsallyonliteraryagency.com

Agents: Kevan Lyon, Jill Marsal, Deborah Ritchken, Shannon Hassan, Patricia Nelson.

Helping authors achieve their dreams is the goal of Marsal Lyon Literary Agency. It is dedicated to building long-term relationships with its authors and publishing partners, with a goal of helping find homes for books that engage, entertain, and make a difference. Potential authors should have their manuscript in its final version prior to submitting a query.

Categories and Submissions: Midde-grade, YA. No books for younger children. Send query by email to specific agent with "Query" in the subject line. No attachments. Check the website for each agent's areas of interest. Response time varies.

Contract and Payment: Commission, 15% domestic; 20–25% foreign.

Sean McCarthy Literary Agency

www.mccarthylit.com

Agent: Sean McCarthy.

This agency guides authors through all stages of the publishing process. It specializes in children's books from picture books through young adult titles. Established in 2013, the agency emphasizes a comprehensive approach in assisting clients with their careers.

Categories and Submissions: Picture books, early reader, middle-grade, YA. Query with first 3 chapters and a synopsis for novels. Query with complete manuscript for picture books. Text can be in the body of an email or in the form of a Word document. Include an author bio with relevant publishing credits. Accepts email queries to submissions@mccarthylit.com. Responds in 6–8 weeks.

Contract and Payment: Commission, 15% domestic; 20–25% foreign.

Dee Mura Literary

P.O. Box 131, Massapequa Park, NY 11762. www.deemuraliterary.com

Agents: Dee Mura, Kimiko Nakamura, Kaylee Davis.

This agency brings diverse interests and expertise to the table and works as a team to ensure writers get the utmost guidance throughout every step of the publishing process. Both Kimiko Nakamura and Kaylee Davis are interested in YA and new adult fiction. Its agents are looking for hardworking, engaged writers who match their passion and enthusiasm for contributing quality work to the literary world.

Categories and Submissions: Action/adventure, animals, anthropology, archeology, arts and photography, biography, business, chick lit, comedy/humor, contemporary fiction, cooking, conservation and environmental issues, current affairs, entertainment, erotica, ethnic and Jewish, finance, fantasy, gay and lesbian, literary, government, health, historical, home and garden, inspirational, medical, memoirs, middle-grade, military, mind and body, mystery, narrative nonfiction, new adult, New Age, outdoors and nature, paranormal, parenting and families, popular culture, psychology, religion/spirituality, romance, satire, science, science fiction, self-help and motivational, sports, thrillers and espionage, travel, women's lit, young adult. No poetry, no screenplays. Email only with short description, author bio, 1- to 2-page synopsis, and sample writing (25 pages for fiction, an excerpt of the proposal for nonfiction). Accepts emails to query@deemuraliterary.com.

Contract and Payment: Unavailable.

Jean V. Naggar Literary Agency

216 East 75th Street, Suite 1E, New York, NY 10021. www.jvnla.com

Agents: Jean Naggar, Jennifer Weltz, Alice Tasman, Ariana Philips, Alicia Brooks.

The Jean V. Naggar Literary Agency is looking for cutting-edge ideas. It has been in business for more than 40 years. It now represents writers from every genre and has been published in over 50 countries around the world.

Categories and Submissions: See website for agents' individual preferences. Accepts queries through the website. See specific guidelines, but generally, include a brief description of the work, brief biography. Accepts simultaneous submissions if identified.

Contract and Payment: Commission, 15%.

Nelson Literary Agency

1732 Wazee Street, Suite 207, Denver, CO 80202. www.nelsonagency.com

Agents: Kristin Nelson, Joanna MacKenzie, Danielle Burby, Quressa Robinson.

Open to new authors, the Nelson Literary Agency is full-service and hands-on in its representation of adult and children's books and other media. It has represented many *New York Times* and *USA Today* bestsellers.

Categories and Submissions: Middle-grade, YA, adult. Genres include science fiction, fantasy, romance, commercial fiction, women's fiction, and literary fiction with a commercial bent. Submit query through query manager available at website. Do not send synopses, links, or attachments. Responds in 3 weeks.

Contract and Payment: Commission, 15% domestic; 25% foreign; 20% film rights.

New Leaf Literary & Media

110 West 40th Street, Suite 2201, New York, NY 10018. www.newleafliterary.com

Agents: Joanna Volpe, Suzie Townsend, Janet Reid, JL Stermer, Kathleen Ortiz, Jordan Hamessley, Devin Ross.

A passionate agency with a relentless focus on building clients' careers, this agency focuses on the big picture. It offers a one-stop shop with services including international sales, film, television, and branding resources.

Categories and Submissions: Middle-grade, YA. Accepts queries by email only to query@newleafliterary.com. Include "Query" and the agent's name in the subject line. Review each agent's interests prior to submitting material. No attachments. Responds if interested.

Contract and Payment: Standard contract.

Pippin Properties

110 West 40th Street, Suite 1704, New York, NY 10018. www.pippinproperties.com

Agents: Holly M. McGhee, Sara Crowe, Elena Giovinazzo.

Established in 1998, Pippin is always on the lookout for writers who take the challenge of creating books seriously and are willing to give the publishing world nothing less than their very best. It is devoted primarily to picture books, middle-grade fiction, and YA novels, but it does represent adult projects on occasion. It places nearly every project they take on by working closely with the author all the way from the marketing plan to their long-term careers.

Categories and Submissions: Picture books, middle-grade, YA; all genres. Email query letter with first chapter, or complete manuscript for picture books; synopsis of work; author background and/or publishing history; and any other relevant information to individual agent. Review website for information on what each agent is currently seeking. Requests exclusive submissions for one month. Responds in 3 weeks if interested.

Contract and Payment: Not available.

Prospect Agency

551 Valley Road, PMB 377, Upper Montclair, NJ 07043. www.prospectagency.com

Agents: Emily Sylvan Kim, Kristen Carleton, Ann Rose, Rachel Orr.

This agency stands with their authors every step of the way. It values literature that surprises, breaks conventions, transports the readers to new worlds, but never forgets storytelling, strong characters, and a gripping narrative. It represents both adult and children's books and seeks to work with authors and illustrators.

Categories and Submissions: Picture books, juvenile, middle-grade, YA, adult; fiction. Genres: contemporary, literary, urban fantasy, science fiction, mysteries, thrillers, romance, women's fiction. Query with 3 chapters and a brief synopsis, or complete manuscript for picture books. Accepts submissions through the website only (Word, PDF, and HTML formats). No hard copy or email. Accepts simultaneous submissions. Responds in 3 months if interested.

Contract and Payment: At-will agreement. Commission, 15%.

P.S. Literary Agency

2010 Winston Park Drive, 2nd Floor, Oakville, Ontario, L6H 5R7 Canada. www.psliterary.com

Agents: Curtis Russell, Carly Watters, Maria Vicente, Kuerstin Armada, Eric Smith, Maureen Moretti, Kimberley Griffiths, Diana Gallagher.

This agency maintains a small but select client list that receives its undivided attention and focused efforts. It looks to work with clients for the duration of their careers. In addition to contract negotiations, and editorial and marketing guidance, its commitment extends to post-publication in pursuing foreign, audio, digital, TV/film, and serial rights. The team from PSLA stays current and on top of publishing trends by attending national and international industry conferences and traveling to all major publishing hubs to meet and network with top editors.

Categories and Submissions: Picture books, middle-grade, YA. Query with title and category of work with estimated word count and a brief introduction. Include an author bio. Email queries to query@psliterary.com. No hard copy. Response time varies.

Contract and Payment: Standard contract.

Red Fox Literary

129 Morro Avenue, Shell Beach, CA 93449. www.redfoxliterary.com

Agents: Abigail Samoun, Karen Grencik, Jennie Kendrick, Stephanie Fretwell-Hill, Jenna Pocius.

Red Fox Literary was formed in 2011 and specializes in children's books, from picture books through YA titles. It is currently looking for stories about real life and real people, where character development is front and center. At present, it is only accepting submissions from conference attendees and professional references.

Categories and Submissions: Picture books, juvenile, middle-grade, YA; fiction and nonfiction. All genres. Currently only accepting submissions from authors who have presented at conferences which the agents have attended, or by referral.

Contract and Payment: Not available.

Red Sofa Literary

2163 Grand Avenue #2, St. Paul, MN 55105. www.redsofaliterary.com

Agents: Dawn Frederick, Erik Hane, Laura Zats, Amanda Rutter, Stacey Graham, Liz Rahn.

Red Sofa Literary is focused on geek culture over brawn. It is the celebration of quirky, eclectic ideas in the literary community. This boutique agency represents authors all over the world. Potential authors must have their manuscript complete prior to submitting a query to an agent at Red Sofa Literary.

Categories and Submissions: Middle-grade fiction, graphic novels, YA; fiction and nonfiction. Query first before sending entire book or sample. The agency asks that authors have a full book proposal ready upon request at the time of query submission. No email attachments. Will respond in 4–6 weeks.

Contract and Payment: Standard agency contract and commission.

Rodeen Literary Management

3501 North Southport #497, Chicago, IL 60657. www.rodeenliterary.com

Agent: Paul Rodeen.

The agency's mission is to successfully manage the business affairs of the writers it represents so they can concentrate on creating books that children, teenagers, and adults will enjoy. This independent literary agency provides career management for experienced and aspiring authors and illustrators of children's literature.

Categories and Submissions: Actively looking for picture books, early readers, middle-grade fiction and nonfiction, graphic novels, comic books, YA fiction and nonfiction. Send cover letter, contact information, full text for picture books, and up to 50 pages for novels and nonfiction to submissions@rodeenliterary.com. Submissions sent via mail will not be accepted. Accepts simultaneous submissions if identified. Responds if interested.

Contract and Payment: Not available.

Jane Rotrosen Agency

318 East 51st Street, New York, NY 10022. www.janerotrosen.com

Agents: Andrea Cirillo, Kathy Schneider, Meg Ruley, Annelise Robey, Christina Hogrebe, Amy Tannenbaum, Rebecca Scherer, Jessica Errera.

This agency maintains long-term relationships with its clients. It has represented authors of general-interest fiction and nonfiction since 1974. The team represents authors of everything from children's titles to genre fiction and more. It welcomes both new and established writers that want their voices to be heard.

Categories and Submissions: Early readers, middle-grade, YA. Query with concise description of your work, author bio, synopsis, and first 3 chapters in the body of the email. No attachments. Accepts hard copy and email submissions to individual agents. Visit the website for agent contact information and current interests. Do not send queries to more than one agent within the agency. Response time varies.

Contract and Payment: Commission, 15% domestic; 20–25% foreign.

Scovil Galen Ghosh Literary Agency

276 Fifth Avenue, Suite 708, New York, NY 10001. www.sgglit.com

Agents: Russell Galen, Jack Scovil, Danny Baror, Anna Ghosh, Ann Behar.

Boasting an eclectic and diverse list, this agency is open to any kind of book that is "first-rate." At any given moment, this agency could be working on a first sale for an exciting new author, an eight-figure deal for a veteran of the *New York Times* bestseller list, or anything in between. Ann Behar is the juvenile publishing specialist. She looks for strong, distinct voices, vibrant characters, and beautiful writing. The agency is open to both first-time and established authors.

Categories and Submissions: Children's and YA books for all ages. Also represents all genres of adult fiction and nonfiction. Email an "unadorned, unaccompanied" query letter to annbehar@sgglit.com. No attachments. Email submissions are strongly preferred. Regular mail is accepted. No SASE; include email address for response. Check website for contact information for other agents. Response time varies.

Contract and Payment: Not available.

Serendipity Literary

305 Gates Avenue, Brooklyn, NY 11216. www.serendipitylit.com

Agents: Regina Brooks, Charles Kim, Dawn Michelle Hardy, Nadeen Gayle, Allison Janice, Christina Morgan.

Well respected in the literary world, this agency is located in New York. Serendipity Literary prides itself on offering the highest level service and support to its clients. Its specialty is children's and YA publishing. President and lead agent Regina Brooks is very open to first-time authors with talent, and also represents authors of adult fiction and nonfiction. Check the website for other agents' interests.

Categories and Submissions: Picture books to YA; fiction and nonfiction. Currently not accepting picture books, but check website for updates. Use the website form to provide information and upload a submission. It asks for the components of a query letter, including the title, premise, manuscript length, your writing background, long-term writing plans, a 1-page synopsis that details the plot and theme, and the first 50 pages or 3 chapters of your manuscript. The website also offers guidance on nonfiction proposals. No submissions by regular mail. Responds in 4–6 weeks.

Contract and Payment: Commission, 15% domestic; 20% foreign.

The Seymour Agency

475 Miner Street Road, Canton, New York 13617. www.theseymouragency.com

Agents: Mary Sue Seymour, Nicole Resciniti, Julie Gwinn, Elizabeth Poteet, Jennifer Willis, Tina Wainscot, Marisa Cleveland.

The Seymour Agency has a firm belief in exploring every opportunity for its authors. It strives to partner with writers in the ever-changing, and often challenging, publishing landscape. Its agents are currently seeking middle-grade, YA, thrillers, mysteries, inspirational, self-help, and picture books.

Categories and Submissions: Middle-grade, YA; Romance, science fiction, fantasy, mystery, cookbooks, nonfiction. Accepts suspense, action, inspirational fiction, picture books, horror. Email queries only to appropriate agent. Check the website to review each agent's specialty prior to submitting material. No attachments. Response time is 3 weeks, if interested.

Contract and Payment: Commission, 15% domestic; 20–25% foreign.

The Spieler Agency

27 West 20th Street, Suite 302, New York, NY 10011. www.thespieleragency.com

Agents: Joe Spieler, John Thornton, Victoria Shoemaker.

This agency brings personal attention to every phase of the publishing process, from proposal development through marketing and beyond. It has been providing full-service literary representation to fiction and nonfiction authors for more than 30 years.

Categories and Submissions: YA. Query to appropriate agent. Agent bios and emails available at website. Accepts hard copy and email submissions. Do not query more than one agent at this agency at a time. Response time varies.

Contract and Payment: Standard contract.

Stimola Literary Studio

308 Livingston Court, Edgewater, NJ 07020. www.stimolaliterarystudio.com

Agents: Rosemary B. Stimola, Erica Rand Silverman, Allison Remcheck, Adriana Stimola, Peter Ryan.

Eclectic in tastes but not in standards, the Stimola Literary Studio invites unsolicited queries most of the year. Founded in 1997, this boutique agency is devoted to representing authors and author/illustrators of fiction and nonfiction, preschool through young adult, who bring unique and substantive contributions to the industry. Its authors have won many prestigious awards including the Caldecott Honor, Newbery Honor, and *The New York Times* Best-Seller List. It now extends representation into the realms of cookbooks, food, farm to table, and lifestyle books.

Categories and Submissions: Picture books, middle-grade, YA; fiction and nonfiction. Current needs include picture books; middle-grade humor; middle-grade/YA mysteries; YA thrillers, supernatural, and science fiction; multicultural teen fantasy; graphic novels; nonfiction with adult crossover appeal; cookbooks. No Revolutionary or Civil War historical fiction, poetry, or institutional books. Send a 1-page query with synopsis, credentials, and what makes the book distinctive. Use email form on website. Responds only if interested.

Contract and Payment: Commission, 15% domestic, 20% foreign.

Stonesong

270 West 39th Street, #201, New York, NY 10018. http://stonesong.com

Agents: Alison Fargis, Judy Linden, Emmanuelle Morgen, Maria Ribas, Leila Campoli, Alyssa Jennette, Melissa Edwards, Madelyn Burt, Adrienne Rosado, Ellen Scordato.

Stonesong is dynamic and forward-thinking while staying true to its traditional roots. It represents authors of middle-grade and YA fiction and nonfiction, as well as adult authors. Among the specific interests of various agents is children's fiction "that blurs the line between literary and commercial." They also have a custom publishing division and a book production/packaging division.

Categories and Submissions: Middle-grade, YA; fiction and nonfiction. The agency does not accept plays, screenplays, or poetry. Query to a specific agent; review website for each agent's specific interests. Send the first chapter or first 10 pages of your manuscript. Accepts email to submissions@stonesong.com. Responds in 12 weeks, if interested.

Contract and Payment: Not available.

The Strothman Agency

63 East 9th Street, 10X, New York, NY 10003. www.strothmanagency.com

Agents: Wendy Strothman, Lauren E. MacLeod.

Operating out of New York and Nashville, TN, The Strothman Agency offers its clients extensive inside experience and knowledge. It represents middle-grade and YA fiction and nonfiction, as well as many categories of adult books. Lauren MacLeod is interested in contemporary and humorous books, middle-grade, and various YA genres, including thrillers, mysteries, horror, contemporary, romance, and chick lit.

Categories and Submissions: Middle-grade and YA; adult history, science, current affairs, nature/environment, narrative nonfiction, arts, travel, business, memoirs. No commercial fiction, romance, picture books, poetry, or self-help. Send electronic submissions only to strothmanagency@gmail.com. Include a query letter outlining your qualifications and experience, a synopsis of your work, and the genre and word count of your manuscript. For fiction, include 2–10 pages of your manuscript in the body of the email; no attachments. Do not send entire manuscript unless requested. Responds in 4–6 weeks if interested.

Contract and Payment: Commission, 15% domestic; 20% foreign.

Talcott Notch Literary Agency

31 Cherry Street, Suites 100, Milford, CT 06460. www.talcottnotch.net

Agents: Gina Panettieri, Paula Munier, Saba Sulaiman, Tia Mele.

Original thought, original research, and unique concepts set Talcott Notch apart from others. It represents an eclectic mix of authors and projects. Currently looking for middle-grade and YA fiction and nonfiction. No picture books at this time. Its agents advise that potential writers know their market.

Categories and Submissions: Middle-grade and YA; contemporary, fantasy, science fiction, mystery/thriller, paranormal, romance. Query: 1–2 pages telling genre, word count, brief overview of plot and main characters, with first 10 pages of manuscript. Prefers email to specific agents; see website for addresses and interests. Accepts hard copy. SASE. Responds in 4 weeks.

Contract and Payment: Unknown.

Transatlantic Literary Agency 🍁

2 Bloor Street East, Suite 3500, Toronto, Ontario, M4W 1A8 Canada. http://transatlanticagency.com/

Agents: Ana Balmazovic, David Bennett, Elizabeth Bennett, Lynn Bennett, Sandra Bishop, Brenna English-Loeb, Shaun Bradley, Marie Campbell, Jesse Finkelstein, Rob Firing, Fiona Kenshole, Stephanie Sinclair, Amy Tompkins, Timothy Travaglini, Trena White, Andrea Cascardi, Megan Philipp.

With agents spanning the US and Canada, Transatlantic Agency is a vibrant collective of tenacious, independent professionals with diverse backgrounds and specialties. It is a full-service literary agency representing adult trade, children's and young adult authors, and illustrators. This agency curates author's careers and maintains close relationships with editors across the world.

Categories and Submissions: Picture books, middle-grade, graphic novels, YA; fiction and nonfiction. Visit the website for each agent's current interests and submission guidelines. Response time varies.

Contract and Payment: Not available.

Triada US Literary Agency

P.O. Box 561, Sewickley, PA 15143. www.triadaus.com

Agents: Uwe Stender, Laura Crockett, Brent Taylor, Lauren Spieller, Amelia Appel.

Agents at Triada US are always interested in strong works from both new and established authors. It has a wide range of interests from middle-grade and YA to women's fiction, psychological suspense, and mysteries.

Categories and Submissions: Review each agent's interests at the website and email your query directly to the individual agent. Do not query multiple agents at Triada US simultaneously. Responds in 1–2 weeks.

Contract and Payment: Commission, 15%.

Trident Media Group

355 Lexington Avenue, Floor 12, New York, NY 10017. http://www.tridentmediagroup.com/

Agents: Robert Gottlieb, Scott Miller, Don Fehr, Alyssa Eisner Henkin, Ellen Levine, Mark Gottlieb, Erica Spellman-Silverman, Amanda Annis, Claire Roberts, Sarah Phair, Alexander Slater, Alexa Stark.

This prominent literary agency has an eye towards innovation. It continues to rank number one for sales according to publishersmarketplace.com in North America. It represents more than 1,000 best-selling and emerging authors in a range of fiction and nonfiction.

Categories and Submissions: Fiction, nonfiction. Query through the website to one literary agent only. Include a 1-paragraph bio, brief plot synopsis, and contact information. No simultaneous submissions for 30 days.

Contract and Payment: 15% domestic; 20% foreign. Written contract.

Upstart Crow Literary Agency

www.upstartcrowliterary.com

Agents: Danielle Chiotti, Susan Hawk, Alexandra Penfold, Ted Malawer, Michael Stearns.

This agency welcome first-time authors and many focus solely on the juvenile markets. It looks for books that are daring and courageous.

Categories and Submissions: Middle-grade, YA. Query with 20 pages of manuscript to specific agent. Check the website for specific information on each agent. Query and manuscript pages should be within the body of the email. No attachments. Hard copy submissions will be returned. Visit website for agent bios and current interests. Respond in 6–8 weeks.

Contract and Payment: Commission, 15% domestic; 20–25% foreign.

Wernick & Pratt

www.wernickpratt.com

Agents: Marcia Wernick, Linda Pratt, Emily Mitchell.

Focused exclusively on the children's book industry, Wernick & Pratt specializes in children's books of all genres, from picture books through young adult literature and everything in between. The agency is particularly interested in author/illustrators in the picture book genre, humorous chapter books with strong voice, and middle-grade/YA novels that are both literary and commercial.

Categories and Submissions: Interested in all children's book projects, fiction and nonfiction. Not interested in picture books of more than 750 words, work targeting the educational market, or fiction about the American Revolution, Civil War, or World War II. Send query letter with contact information, 1-page synopsis, and author's background and publishing history. Include 3 chapters for novel submissions; 2 manuscripts for picture book submissions. Indicate if submission is exclusive (preferred) or non-exclusive. Submit by email only to submissions@wernickpratt.com and indicate the agent to whom you are submitting. Responds if interested.

Contract and Payment: Not available.

Writers House

21 West 26th Street, New York NY 10010. www.writershouse.com

Agents: Stephen Barr, Amy Berkower, Johanna Castillo, Susan Cohen, Lisa DiMona, Susan Ginsburg, Merrilee Heifetz, Brianne Johnson, Dan Lazar, Simon Lipskar, Steven Malk, Jodi Reamer, Rebecca Sherman, Geri Thoma, Albert Zuckerman, Robin Rue, Susan Golomb, Dan Conaway.

Combining a passion for managing a writer's career with an integrated understanding of how storytelling works, Writers House is one of the largest agencies in the world. Writers House provides an extraordinary amount of individual client attention combined with the benefits of full-service foreign rights, subsidiary rights, and contracts departments. Its agents work in fantasy and science fiction, narrative nonfiction, memoirs, biographies, science, parenting, young adult and juvenile fiction.

Categories and Submissions: Middle-grade, YA. Review each agent's interests and submission requirements prior to submitting material. Do not query more than one agent at this agency at a time. Responds in 3 months.

Contract and Payment: Standard contract.

Podcasts

Podcasts

Podcasts are like Internet radio on demand. They are done in segments and can be listened to right from your computer or any smart device. They aren't limited to audio, either! Some podcasts also include video. Because podcasts are available online, you can listen to them on your own schedule, rather than tuning in to a weekly radio program.

Aspiring writers can learn a lot from podcasts. There are podcasts that focus on the craft of writing for children, as well as podcasts that cover the business of writing and selling your manuscripts. If you're looking for the latest news in the children's book or magazine industry, look no further! There is a podcast for you. We've compiled some of our favorite podcasts that cover writing for children and the children's book or magazine markets.

Books Between

Corrina Allen, Books Between

www.booksbetween.com

Created to help parents, teachers, and librarians connect kids with books they'll love, Books Between is hosted by middle-grade teacher Corrina Allen. Books Between focuses on books for 8- to 12-year-olds. This podcast can be enjoyed by anyone that loves writing for a middle school audience. It gives listeners a deep appreciation of how many good books are out there for this age group.

Past episodes: "Front Desk: A Conversation with Kelly Yang" and "A Conversation with Karina Yan Glaser."

Brain Burps About Books

Katie Davis, Brain Burps About Books

https://podcasts.apple.com/us/podcast/brain-burps-about-books/id385806629

Writer, entrepreneur, illustrator, book marketing expert, and author Katie Davis is the host of this funny and informative show meant to help anyone with an interest in publishing, book marketing, video marketing, general book publishing, and children's literature. Since 2010, there have been regular contributors and reviewers, as well as hundreds of interviews with anyone Katie believes will help her listeners in their quest to succeed in the business.

Past episodes: "Time to Celebrate Picture Book Month" and "How to Get Author School Visits."

The Business of Writing Podcast

Laura Gale and Rachel Mazza

https://www.businessofwritingpodcast.com/episodes/

This podcast focuses on the creative minds of our time as they share how they've used their writing skills to achieve thriving businesses. It aims to kill the myth that writing doesn't pay.

Past episodes: "Dana Kaye: The 3 Part Publicity Plan" and "Justin Goff: Building Wealth as an Author."

The Children's Book Podcast

Matthew Winner, The Children's Book Podcast

www.lgbpodcast.libsyn.com

The Children's Book Podcast features interviews that are insightful and sincere with authors, illustrators, and everyone involved in taking a book from drawing board to bookshelf. It is hosted by Matthew Winner, elementary school librarian and co-founder of All The Wonders.

Past episodes: "Anastasia Higginbotham" and "Michael Genhart."

The Creative Penn ★

Joanna Penn

https://www.thecreativepenn.com/podcasts/

This podcast includes interviews, inspiration, and information on writing and creativity, publishing options, book marketing, and creative entrepreneurship.

Past episodes: "Writing And Selling Short Fiction With Matty Dalrymple" and "Building A Unique Author Brand With Gail Carriger."

Dream Gardens: Talking Up the Children's Books We Love

Jody Lee Mott

http://jleemott.com

This twice monthly interview show is hosted by Jody Lee Mott. It features interviews with teachers, librarians, writers, and other kid lit enthusiasts. Guests discuss their favorite middle grade novels, picture books, and YA titles.

Past episodes: "Dream Gardens: Talking Up the Children's Books We Love."

First Draft

Sarah Enni

https://www.firstdraftpod.com/

This podcast talks to storytellers about how their art informs their lives. Every Tuesday Sarah Enni talks with authors about their unique perspectives on the creative process, and to learn about the professional side of artistic endeavors.

Past episodes: "Julian Winters" and "Trust Your Gut with Liari Tamani."

The Graphic Novel Podcast ★

Mike and Parker Rizzo

https://anchor.fm/graphicnovelpodcast/episodes/Ep42--Taproot---Happy-Pride-Month-eeork3

This podcast focuses on the art of the graphic novel. Join Mike and Parker as they delve into the life of graphic novels, their creators and their stories..

Past episodes: "Maus by Art Spiegelman" and "Check Please! Book 1: Hockey."

Helping Writers Become Authors

K. M. Weiland

https://www.helpingwritersbecomeauthors.com/podcasts/

This podcast focuses on helping writers learn to write, edit, and publish a book. It helps authors produce a book agents will buy and readers will love to read.

Past episodes: "Possible Hooks for Your Opening Chapter" and "The Power of Hopeful Stories in a Stressful Time."

Let's Make Kids' Books

Beau Blackwell, Let's Make Kids' Books

http://letsmakekidsbooks.com/itunes

Let's Make Kids' Books gives you the information, support, and inspiration you need to write, create, publish, and sell your books. Beau Blackwell, author of 4 bestselling self-published picture books, hosts this podcast with a collection of incredible guests from every corner of the publishing world. The publishing world has radically changed in the past few years, and this show helps you take advantage of the latest trends and tips so you can have a successful writing career.

Past episodes: "Why Bother with Free Book Promotions?"

Literaticast

Jennifer Laughran, Literaticat

www.jenniferlaughran.com/literaticast

This podcast focuses on the world of children's book publishing. A literary agent and her friends dish about writing and publishing books for children and young adults. It's about the ins, outs, and the behind-the-scenes dirt of children's publishing.

Past episodes: "Creativity in Crisis with Guest Author Rebecca Stead" and "Marketing Mayhem with Hannah Moushabeck."

The Manuscript Academy ★

Jessica Sinsheimer and Julie Kingsley

https://manuscriptacademy.com/podcasting

The Manuscript Academy provides conversations with agents, editors, and authors. It aims to help you on your writing journey by providing you with knowledge from those already in the business.

Past episodes: "Voice in a Manuscript with Agent Stephanie Winter" and "The First Three Chapters with Simon & Schuster Editor Hannah."

One More Page

Kate Simpson, Liz Ledden, and Nat Amoore

https://podcasts.apple.com/us/podcast/one-more-page/id1317667776?mt=2

One More Page is a podcast full of interviews, book reviews, and industry gossip, and more. It targets both writers and lovers of children's books..

Past episodes: "Episode 48: Serious Business" and "Episode 47: Secret Agent."

Picturebooking Podcast

Nick Patton, Picturebooking

www.picturebooking.libsyn.com

Nick Patton from Picturebooking.com created this podcast to serve those who want to understand what it takes to create these stories. He shares his journey into the world of children's picture books. Follow his path from amateur storyteller to professional author-illustrator and beyond. Join Nick as he meets the people behind some of your favorite picture books. Discover the joys and struggles of living a creative life.

Past episodes: "Ian Lender—The Fabled Life of Aesop" and "Vanessa Roeder—The Box Turtle."

Publisher's Weekly PW KidsCast

Emma Kantor, Publishers Weekly

www.publishersweekly.com/pw/podcasts/

Emily Kantor hosts this podcast from *Publisher's Weekly* that features interviews with children's and YA authors.

Past episodes: "A Conversation with Tracy Deonn" and "A Conversation with Jason Tharp."

Reading and Writing Podcast ★

Jeffr

http://readingandwritingpodcast.com/

This podcast features with authors who share their knowledge. It focuses on not only their books, but their writing habits and how they started writing and got into the business.

Past episodes: "Sarah Pinsker Interview" and "Isla Morley Interview."

Sell More Books Show

Bryan Cohen and H. Claire Taylor

https://sellmorebooksshow.com/

This podcast airs weekly and is focused on helping authors, both new and experienced, sell more books. It focuses on marketing strategies, self publishing news, and the latest tools.

Past episodes: "Bookstores, Email Marketing, and Finding Your 'Why'" and "Meaning, Street Teams, and Amazon Ads."

So You Want to be a Writer

Valerie Khoo and Allison Tait

https://www.writerscentre.com.au/blog/category/podcasts/so-you-want-to-be-a-writer-podcast/

This podcast brings you the latest trends in writing. It engages in author discussions that delve into topics including what not to expect from your agent, avoiding social media burnout, where to find story ideas, and much more.

Past episodes: "Meet E Lockhart, author of 'Again Again'" and "Meet Victoria Mackinlay, author of 'Ribbit Rabbit Robot.'"

Story Studio Podcast

Sterling and Stone

https://www.storystudiopodcast.com/

Exploring ways to tell your story better, Story Studio Podcast discusses ways to know your stories to leave a mark. Whether you want to sell more books, increase profits, or just make a differenc, this podcast will help you get there.

Past episodes: "Making a Living Writing with Rachael Herron" and "The Guys Discuss: When a Story Gets Stuck."

The Writer's Panel ★

Ben Blacker

https://nerdistwriters.libsyn.com/

This podcast engages in conversation with professional writers to discuss the process and business of writing.

Past episodes: "Chappaquiddick" and "Liz Hara Part 2."

Writing Excuses ★

Multiple Hosts

https://writingexcuses.com/

This weekly podcast focuses on twenty minute or shorter segments to help writers hone their skills. Writing Excuses is a fast-paced, educational podcast for writers, by writers.

Past episodes: "Writing For Children, with Shannon and Dean Hale" and "Balancing Plot and Character."

Writing for Children ★

Katie Davis, Institute for Writers

www.instituteforwriters.com/podcast

The Institute of Children's Literature has taught hundreds of thousands of aspiring writers, and the director of ICL is the host of Writing for Children. Do you want to learn how to write for children? The show focuses on the craft of writing for children: how to write a children's book, how to write for children's magazines, how to get paid, and how to get published. There are listener questions, with answers from the experts at the Institute, plus hard-to-find resources and links included in every week's show notes.

Past episodes: "Getting Down and Dirty with Plot" and "Setting as a Character."

The Yarn ★

Travis Jonker and Colby Sharp, School Library Journal

http://blogs.slj.com/theyarn/

A *School Library Journal* production, The Yarn podcast is hosted by Travis Jonker and Colby Sharp. It is a wonderful series of interviews with children's book creators. Travis and Colby invite people like Kate DiCamillo, Mo Willems, and Jon Klassen to chat about how their books were made, the challenges they faced, and what they discovered. The interviews are bite-sized, but impart so much wisdom about the creative process.

Past episodes: "Shannon and Dean Hale: The Origin Story of The Princess in Black" and "Printz Award Winner A.S. King Visits The Yarn."

Index

2021 Market News: New Listings

Category Index

To help you find the appropriate market for your manuscript or query letter, we have compiled a category, subject, and age-range index that lists publishers according to their editorial interests, in addition to the sections of *Book Markets for Children's Writers* for trade, educational, parenting, and religious markets. If you do not find a category that exactly fits your material, try searching a broader term that covers your topic. Categories are listed below.

Action/Adventure
Activities
Animal Fiction
Animals/Pets
Arts
Bilingual
Biography
Board Books
Boys
Chapter Books, Fiction
Chapter Books, Nonfiction
Child Care
College/Careers
Coming-of-Age Fiction
Concept Books
Contemporary Fiction
Crafts/Hobbies
Current Events/ Politics
Drama/Plays
Early Picture Books, Fiction
Early Picture Books, Nonfiction
Early Readers, Fiction
Early Readers, Nonfiction
Education
Fairy Tales
Family/Parenting
Fantasy
Folklore

Games/Puzzles
Geography/Travel
Girls
Graphic Novels
Health/Fitness
Hi/Lo
Historical Fiction
History
Holidays/Seasonal
Horror
How-to
Humor, Fiction
Humor, Nonfiction
Inspirational Fiction
Inspirational Nonfiction
Language Arts
Mathematics
Middle-Grade Fiction
Middle-Grade Nonfiction
Multicultural Fiction
Multicultural Nonfiction
Mystery/Suspense
Mythology
Nature Fiction
Nature/Outdoors
Paranormal Fiction
Picture Books, Fiction
Picture Books, Nonfiction
Poetry
Pop Culture

PreK Fiction
PreK Nonfiction
Realistic Fiction
Real Life/Problem- Solving
Reference
Regional Fiction
Regional Nonfiction
Religious Fiction
Religious Nonfiction
Romance
Science
Science Fiction
Self-Help
Social Issues
Social Studies
Spirituality
Sports Fiction
Sports Nonfiction
Story Picture Books Fiction
Story Picture Books Nonfiction
Technology
Westerns
Young Adult Fiction
Young Adult Nonfiction

Chapter Books, Fiction

College/Careers

Coming-of-Age Fiction

Concept Books

Contemporary Fiction

Early Picture Books, Nonfiction

Early Readers, Fiction

Early Readers, Nonfiction

Fairy Tales

Fantasy

History

Middle-Grade Fiction

Middle-Grade Nonfiction

Multicultural Fiction

Multicultural Nonfiction

Index